AN INDIAN SUMMER OF STEAM

RAILWAY TRAVEL IN THE
UNITED KINGDOM AND ABROAD
1962-2013

By

David Maidment

Sequel to *A Privileged Journey* which covered the same author's
travels between 1940 and 1962.

PEN & SWORD TRANSPORT

Published in 2015 by
Pen & Sword Transport
an imprint of
Pen & Sword Books Ltd
47 Church Street
Barnsley
South Yorkshire
S70 2AS

ISBN 978 1 47382 743 1

Typeset by Milepost
Printed and bound by Replika Press Pvt. Ltd.

All royalties from this book will be donated to the Railway Children charity
(reg. no. 1058991) (www.railwaychildren.org.uk)

Cover photo: 6201 *Princess Elizabeth* at Preston waiting to take over the 70th Anniversary
Train of the 1936 Euston – Glasgow record runs, November 2006: *(David Maidment)*

Back cover: 46238 *City of Carlisle* climbs Shap with a lightweight relief train for Glasgow,
Summer 1964: *(R.C.Riley)*

Second back cover: Preserved German 3-cylinder pacific 03.1010 at Görlitz on regular
passenger express D1854, the 14.47 to Dresden, during the May 1994 *Plandampf* event
between Erfurt, Leipzig, Dresden and the Polish border. *(David Maidment)*

Pen & Sword Books Ltd incorporates the imprints of Pen & Sword
Archaeology, Atlas, Aviation, Battleground, Discovery, Family
History, History, Maritime, Military, Naval, Politics, Railways, Select,
Transport, True Crime, and Fiction, Frontline Books, Leo Cooper,
Praetorian Press, Seaforth Publishing and Wharncliffe.

For a complete list of Pen & Sword titles please contact
PEN & SWORD BOOKS LIMITED
47 Church Street, Barnsley, South Yorkshire, S70 2AS, England
E-mail: enquiries@pen-and-sword.co.uk
Website: www.pen-and-sword.co.uk

Acknowledgements

To those who stimulated and shared my interest in railways, especially the steam engine – my father, Great Uncle George, Aunt Enid, Cedric Utley, John Crowe and Alastair Wood.

Most of the photographs in this book were taken by the author. Every effort has been made to contact persons owning the copyright to any other photographs used in this book, and grateful thanks are given to those who have waived their fees or charged much reduced fees as the royalties of the book are being fully donated to the Railway Children charity (reg. No. 1058991, www.railwaychildren.org.uk), which was founded by the author in 1995. If by misadventure any photographs still under copyright have been missed, please contact the publisher so that matters can be rectified.

Previous Publications: Religious historical fiction
The Child Madonna, Melrose Books, 2009
The Missing Madonna, PublishNation, 2012
The Madonna and her Sons, PublishNation, 2014

Railway fiction
Lives on the Line, Max Books, 2013

Non-fiction
Street Children
The Other Railway Children, PublishNation, 2012
Nobody ever listened to me, PublishNation, 2012

Railway Non-fiction
The Toss of a Coin, PublishNation, 2014
A Privileged Journey, Pen & Sword, 2015
Great Western Eight-Coupled Heavy Freight Locomotives, Pen & Sword, 2015

Contents

Preface

The second volume of my 'railway' autobiography covers the period from 1962 (with one backward look to the previous year), up to the days of writing during my seventy-fifth year. Several chapters describe my last frantic efforts to experience steam traction on Britain's mainline railways before it was too late – when I was privileged to have Divisional, then Regional and finally All-Stations free passes available for my travels. 1962-64 was the period of the last two thirds of my management training on the Western Region; I was based in South Wales during the final six months of 1962 and the first half of 1963, and then in London and the Plymouth Divisions of the Region for the last part of 1963 and early 1964. During this time I had plenty of time to indulge my hobby, taking an increasing number of photographs with, by now, an improved camera – an Ensign Selfix SLR – and taking logs of most trains I travelled behind so that I have a complete record from which to draw the highlights.

And as steam in the UK drew to a close, I began to discover the last remnants of steam on the European continent, and used my annual free continental rail passes to good effect. In *A Privileged Journey* I described my first experiences overseas in the course of my education at London University, which took me to Paris, the Harz Mountains and Munich University, but now I began to explore further, choosing my itineraries carefully to maximize steam haulage. Then, as the curtain fell on steam in France in 1969, and express passenger services in West Germany in 1975, and finally in the former German Democratic Republic (East Germany) in the mid-1980s, it became a matter of trying to replicate the experience as best as I could on the multitude of UK special trains and the uniquely German initiative of the *Plandampf* timetable, when for two or three days, normal public timetabled trains returned temporarily to steam haulage by preserved locomotives. Some of the pleasure then was to watch the expressions of the normal travelling public when confronted by the apparent anachronism of a steam train rushing into their platform.

In later years, when the opportunity for railway safety consultancy came my way, I was able to combine duty with the occasional indulgence of a trip behind a preserved locomotive overseas. In 2002, I forked out for a 'once in a lifetime' tour to the JiTong Railway in Inner Mongolia, while in the UK, some opportunities cropped up for greater involvement in the steam heritage railways, especially with Vintage Trains during the GW 175th anniversary year, having stands at Gala Days and on-train raffles for the Railway Children charity. I usually managed to do a bit of train timing and even experienced the odd footplate run by courtesy of several of the Heritage Railway owners and managers.

As I said in my first volume, but I must repeat it, I owe thanks to a large number of people, and again I'll select a few for special mention. Firstly my parents for encouraging, then tolerating my hobby. My wife, Pat, for permitting it to be such an important part of my life. To my childhood friend Cedric Utley, who accompanied me on my earliest trainspotting trips; Martin Probyn, Conrad Natzio, Philip Balkwill, Jim Evans and other members of the intrepid Charterhouse Railway Society; Alistair Wood who taught me the rudiments of train timing although he was always sceptical of my accuracy and Western Region bias; John Crowe with whom I shared digs in South Wales and who was my companion on many an extramural excursion during my training there; Stan Judd, my 'best man' and fellow refugee in a South Wales valley when appointed to our first jobs and with whom our subsequent careers have been intertwined from time to time; Colin Boocock who encouraged and helped me to write about my experiences; and to all my BR colleagues who encouraged — or at least tolerated my interests – Ray Sims, Shedmaster at Old Oak Common who indulged my enthusiasm, Gerry Orbell who let me develop my ideas in Train Planning, Alan Englert who opened up new opportunities in a wider railway career, Jim O'Brien who took a chance on me and appointed me to the role of Chief Operating Manager of Britain's largest Region and, not least, David Rayner, the Board Member to whom I responded in the last ten years of my career. Then Frank Paterson who encouraged me to reflect on my 'railway life' by getting me to give several long interviews on tape for the National Railway Museum's oral railway history archives. Many others hopefully will find their place in the self-published account of my railway management career, 'The Toss of a Coin'.

All royalties from this book will be donated to the Railway Children charity, which I founded in 1995 with the help of colleagues in the railway industry. A description of how this came about and the work the charity undertakes is included in the last chapter of the book. More information and stories can be found in the book *The Other Railway Children* and on the charity's website: www.railwaychildren.org.uk.

David Maidment
Summer 2015

Chapter 1

Continental free passes

Twelve months after joining British Railways in August 1960 I became eligible for my first continental free pass. I had just one week's leave to take and decided to revisit my 1959 destination of Munich to see if the former Bavarian four cylinder compound Pacifics (class S 3/6, Deutsche Bundesbahn class 18.6) still held sway. So on a cold, drizzly 15 August 1961 I joined the Newhaven boat train with Southern electric loco 20003 and arrived punctually at the port. Remembering my 1956 school trip, I elected to journey to Paris via the Newhaven-Dieppe route and found, as anticipated, the Paris boat train on the quay with an État Pacific (rebuilt by Chapelon with Kylchap exhaust and modified steam passages), 231G 600, at the head of the fourteen vehicle train weighing over 550 tonnes gross.

We crawled along the quayside from Dieppe Maritime to the town station at the regulation walking pace, man with red flag preceding, and after a water stop at Gisors, made a punctilious arrival at St Lazare just a few seconds before time. No great effort was required to maintain the schedule over a speed-restricted and curvaceous main line and my somewhat amateurish attempts at train timing for the first time using kilometre posts gave me no higher speed than a momentary 110kph, with much running in the 90s, in almost total silence from the front end. At this point in my narrative, I have to say that although I quote speeds on the continent in kilometres per hour, since time has not been metricated, I often refer to distances in miles, as the relationship between time and distance is significant for train timers (and I am one). Talking about 'even time' – a mile a minute – somehow loses its impact if one talks about a 96kph run instead! So I ask for your indulgence on my inconsistencies when I am unable to make up my mind whether I am a modern European or a true 'Brit'! (For a speed kilometres/miles per hour conversion , see the table at the beginning of Appendix 2.)

I stayed in a cheap hotel near the Gare de l'Est, unfortunately too near to a cross-roads from which traffic roared away throughout the night and equipped myself with a baguette, some cheese and a huge bunch of green grapes to keep an impecunious voyager satisfied without recourse to the somewhat expensive restaurant car on train 43 — the 8.23am Paris (Est)-Basle. We shall hear more of these grapes later. I saw the

supplementary charge Paris-Strasbourg lightweight rubber-tyred train leave behind former PLM Pacific 231K 43 and a huge train with an SNCF Mountain 4-8-2 built post-war to Chapelon principles, 241P 34, poking out way beyond the platform end, then watched as another former PLM loco, 231G 21, displaced a decade earlier by the Paris-Lyons-Marseilles electrification, backed onto our thirteen coach 535 tonnes gross train.

After a fairly slow start we touched 121kph in the dip beyond Boissy and fell to 75 up the long climb to Verneuil l'Étang before racing down through Longueville at a full and rather naughty 130 – the maximum allowed for steam traction on this route was 120kph. Then we eased considerably as we had by now recovered our 2 minute late start, and we conformed to the SNCF culture of meticulous adherence to the timetable, with speed hovering around a steady 100kph for over 50 kilometres. To my surprise, 231G 21 hooked off at our first stop, Troyes, and another 231G Pacific, number 144 of Belfort depot backed on, its large original PLM tender contrasting with the standard SNCF tender coupled to G 21.

From the Troyes start it was apparent that our new engine and crew were made of enterprising stuff, and a 1 minute late departure had become a minute and a half early arrival at our first stop, Bar-sur-Aube, 55kms and 39 minutes away. We then climbed steadily up to Chaumont, with a minimum of 69kph at Bricon and further efficient progress to Langres saw us to Culmont-Chalindrey and the most memorable part of our journey. Obviously the start from Culmont was steeply downhill and we shot away, clearing Hortes in 7 minutes 47 seconds at well over 120 and hurtled up to 139kph as I scoffed down the tiny green grapes. Charnoy to La Ferté was covered at an average speed of 121kph and the 28km (17½ miles) section to Vitry Vernois was run, start to stop, in 18 minutes 12 seconds at an average speed of 95kph with 535 tonnes behind the tender, gaining 2 minutes on schedule over this short section. The run continued thereafter in exemplary fashion, achieving a 1 minute early arrival at Mulhouse, where 231G 144 gave way to BB 16006 of Strasbourg for the short run to that city (see Appendix 2, Table 1).

Above: The engine change at Mulhouse, where PLM Pacific 231G 144, which had hauled Train 43 from Troyes, departs before electric 16006 took over for the short run to Basle, 16 August 1961. (*Author*)

Opposite page: Former PLM Pacific 231K 43 leaves Paris Gare de l'Est with the morning 'rubber-tyred' stainless steel vehicle train to Strasbourg, 16 August 1961. (*Author*)

The PLM pacific on the author's train, 231G 21 on Train 43, 8.23am Paris-Basle, at the Gare de l'Est before departure, 16 August 1961. The second vehicle behind the parcels van is an SNCF postal vehicle. (*Author*)

Ex-PLM 4-8-4T 242TA 617 at Strasbourg with a local train, made up of pre-war clerestory non-corridor stock, to run to Lauterbourg on the Alsace/German border, 16 August 1961. (*Author*)

After finding my hotel and dumping my suitcase, I returned to the station and had a half-hour run to the German border at Lauterbourg, in an ancient clerestory wooden-seated non-corridor coach behind a former PLM 4-8-4T, 242TA 617, returning behind an unexciting SNCF diesel in the 63XXX series. I then went sightseeing and finished up at the Gothic cathedral where, in the nave, I was gripped by the most painful stomach cramps as the grapes took their toll. I suffered all night and learned a salutary lesson about what not to eat when trying to economise on a long journey.

It was a groggy traveller who greeted the 7.47am express (D-Zug) from Strasbourg to Konstanz, with a somewhat jaundiced eye, although the motive power – another former PLM 4-8-4T, 242 TA 606 – did take me aback somewhat. However, unfortunately, this superb loco only rumbled me across the River Rhine to the Customs stop at Kehl, 10 minutes away, where it was replaced by a 1953 Krauss-Maffei-built diesel hydraulic, V200.033 of Villingen depot, for the run through the Black Forest (Schwarzwald).

At Offenburg, the V200 was detached for another and I waited to see if a following semi-fast (Eilzug) would have steam. However, no such luck; V200.033 now joined our seven coach train and left 10 minutes late through awaiting a connection from Basle. Speed fell on the most acute section to 29kph at Hornberg, although we kept time, then it was easy downhill through the mist and sopping fir trees until by Singen we were only 3 minutes late (V200.033 is one of a couple of V200 diesels that have since been preserved).

I now have some very hazy memories, bedevilled by the fact that I really knew little about German locomotives and perhaps did not realise the value of what I saw. A stopping train to Konstanz was standing in Singen station with 39.134, a former Prussian Railway designed three cylinder 2-8-2, with the original small smoke deflectors and tender (by now most of these class P10s had acquired 'witte' smoke deflectors and the standard large DB tender).

My stopping train (*Personenzug* or P-Zug) to Friedrichshafen, consisting mainly of wooden seated four and six wheelers, was shunted to the platform by the pilot, a Prussian class 94 0-10-0T, and a standard DB 2-10-0, 50.1922 rumbled us along to Radolfzell. Here our '50' disappeared and a small 2-6-2T, 75.419, appeared and coupled up. I really didn't appreciate that we had one of the few remaining first series of Baden Railway tanks – I also saw several of the 75.0 series from the old Württemberg Railway and to my present regret made no attempt to photo or travel behind one.

I abandoned this stopper at Friedrichshafen for something more exotic, I thought, where an Eilzug from Ulm to Lindau exchanged its 03 standard 1930s built light pacific for Bavarian four cylinder compound 18.620. This is what I had come for. Things improved further on arrival at Lindau, for two such pacifics stood side by side ready for the off – 18.629 on D95 for Munich and 18.607 on D75 to Kiel, which it would work only to Friedrichshafen, where the train reversed. Instead of checking in to my hotel, the Hotel Bavaria overlooking the harbour, owned by the friendly Herr Gloggengiesser, I hastily selected the Kiel train and travelled as far as Aulendorf (home depot of many of the little 75.0 2-6-2Ts), which DB Pacific 03.132 had taken over after Friedrichshafen. The return journey to Lindau was enacted by another 03 (108) and a former Prussian mixed traffic P8 4-6-0, (the DB equivalent of a Black 5), 38.3158 of Radolfzell.

Former Prussian Railways P10 3-cylinder 2-8-2 39.134, still with original smoke deflectors and tender, as built, at Singen, with a local for Konstanz made up of a set of post-war six-wheel coaches, 17 August 1961. (*Author*)

11

Now I sought the comforts of the splendid hotel and the following morning discovered that the loco shed was tucked round the corner of the dead-end station, overlooking the Bodensee (Lake Constance). I could sit on the small retaining wall and dangle my toes in the lake and watch various ex-Bavarian pacifics ease out of the roundhouse on to the turntable a few feet away. And the cold drizzly weather had given way to clear blue skies and warm sunshine, and Lindau was home to the entire class of 18.6s and the few 18.4s and 5s remaining (the un-reboilered Bavarian Pacifics), plus putting up a few Kempten P10s that drifted in. If ever I daydream my vision of heaven, my thoughts drift to that dizzy August morning on the lake wall, just after breakfast, as I selected which loco I thought might adorn one of several trains on which I could make my way all through the day to Munich, my final destination.

I went with the first option. 18.613 took a lightweight four coach Eilzug (E689) from the main Lindau station at 8.39am with merry chirrup up the gradients in the Bavarian Alpine foothills, to the summit between Harbatshofen and Oberstaufen at a minimum of 75kph, although it had been delayed a few minutes at Hergatz awaiting a crossing train off temporary single line working, set up for planned engineering work. At Immenstadt, 2-6-2T 64.388 added another seven coaches from the Alpine resort of Oberstdorf to our consist, and we turned a 3 minute deficit into an early arrival in Kempten, only 18 minutes' run away, with a top speed of 120kph, the maximum permitted for these locos. Kempten Allgäu Hauptbahnhof is a dead-end station, and 18.613 was replaced by 18.602 to effect the reversal. Considerable and noisy energy was now displayed to take the 445 tonnes gross train in the low 60s up the grade to the summit at Günzach (Appendix 2, Table 4). Arrival in Kaufbeuren was on time, where I decided to alight (the train was bound for Augsburg) and seek another 18.6.

18.610 stands at Munich Hauptbahnhof [Hbf] with D96, the *Rhone-Isar Express*, 18 August 1961. Thirty of the 1926-30 constructed Reichsbahn Pacifics built to the 1908 Bavarian design, were rebuilt with all-welded boilers in the mid-1950s and were renumbered from 18 509-548 to 18 601–630 in the order in which they were rebuilt. Ten remained in their original form and number until withdrawn. (*Author*)

Former Bavarian 4 cylinder compound Pacifics [class S3/6] rebuilt in the 1950s with all-welded boilers, 18.629 on D95 [Zurich-Munich] and 18.607 on D75 [Lindau-Kiel], which the author took from Lindau Hauptbahnhof [main station] pictured here, as far as Aulendorf on the route to Ulm, 17 August 1961. (*Author*)

The following D-Zug (D91) from Lindau to Munich (it originated in Geneva at 1am) arrived punctually behind 18.615 and ran at 110-115kph until Geltendorf, where the 100kph line restriction commenced. Arrival in Munich Hauptbahnhof was 1 minute early. I had intended to spend the day in the city before starting my return journey, but the 1.48pm *Rhône-Isar* express (D96) stood ready for departure, a nine coach 395 tonnes gross train with 18.610 standing proudly at the head end surrounded by electrics.

I could not resist and was rewarded with my fastest run behind a Bavarian Pacific. 115kph only 10 minutes out of Munich was unusual (and illegal) and thereafter 120kph was attained consistently between the stops at Kaufering, Buchloe and Kaufbeuren. The climb to Günzach was being attacked at a full 80kph before a p-way slack to 45, and I achieved my top speed of 133kph behind one of these locos on the long descent to Kempten – we took the through route via Kempten Hegge instead of going into the main station (Appendix 2, Table 4). I got out at Immenstadt and picked up the following Augsburg-Oberstdorf/Lindau Eilzug with yet another 18.6 (604), which played with its light load weaving around the various temporary crossings and single line working for planned engineering in the descent to Hergatz without coming to a halt. Five 18.6s in one day and the only disappointment was a total absence of the un-rebuilt 18.4/5 series, except for the tender of a dead 18.528 I had spied in the roundhouse at Lindau. Had they all been withdrawn, I wondered, as when I saw them in 1959, they were down to the last seven, all shedded at Augsburg.

After another night overlooking the lake, and a more leisurely morning around the engine-shed on the beach, I reluctantly retraced my steps via the 11.11am Eilzug, Lindau-Basle, as far as Singen, behind another of Radolfzell's P8s, 38.3273, and more V200s through the Black Forest to Kehl, where I experienced another short run over the border to Strasbourg behind PLM 4-8-4 tank, 242TA 83.

I then enjoyed a more peaceful night than on my outward journey, before journeying to Mulhouse. On arrival I found a *train supplementaire* 42A running as relief to Train 42 Basle-Paris. It sported Chapelon 141P 95, an SNCF 2-8-2, at the head end, a class I had not previously experienced. I decided to give it a try and as we left I saw former Est 4-8-2 Mountain 241A 58 backing down onto the main train, which by now had arrived with its electric from Basle. I therefore decided to bail out at Belfort after a steady and somewhat raucous noise from the Mikado and awaited the main train with bated breath. I was not disappointed. 241A 58 arrived on time with an enormous fifteen-coach, 625 tonnes train in tow and proceeded in very sedate fashion out of Belfort, taking over 10 minutes to accelerate this train up the grade to 75kph at Bas Évette. After that we got going and a maximum of 112kph (the 241A class was restricted to 110kph) got us to Lure just half a minute down.

We were delayed for 3 minutes at the Lure station stop, but steadily regained time until we reached Chaumont on the dot. The long climb from Vitry Vernois to Culmont-Chalindrey (down which we had raced with 231G 144) brought us from our top speed of 115kph to a minimum of 60. At Chaumont, 241A 58 uncoupled and disappeared and I waited to see what would back on. To my delight, 241A 63 (both Mountains were based at Chaumont depot) appeared, with an additional coach, making the gross load now sixteen coaches for 675 tonnes. A 4 minute late departure from Chaumont had been converted to a half minute early arrival in Troyes with a top speed of 120kph at La Villeneuve. The non-stop run in from Troyes to Paris, run mostly around 105–110kph, was spoilt by a very long and slow (8kph) p-way speed restriction at Rosny-sous-Bois, approaching the terminus, and signal checks in from Pantin made us a disappointing 2 minutes late (Appendix 2, Table 2).

As if this were not enough, as I alighted from the train at the Gare de l'Est, I spotted one of the 1910 built Est Railway 230K 4-6-0s standing at the head of an outer suburban commuter train. I had seen a couple of these antiquarian-looking machines back in 1956 (although I had never seen any of the exotically streamlined versions converted for the rubber-tyred *rapides*). I hastily purchased a return to Meaux, some 40kms distant, and got myself, plus luggage, onto the train with a few moments to spare. The train was the 7.33pm Train Omnibus Paris (Est) to Château Thierry and the loco, 230K 168 of that latter depot. The load was quite substantial, twelve coaches for 425 tonnes gross and we reached a maximum of 113kph before the first stop at Esbly. Arrival in Meaux was a minute early. In my haste I had not consulted a timetable to check the feasibility of the return journey, so it was with some relief that a Château Thierry-Paris local appeared, another twelve coach train, this time with PLM Pacific 231K 66 at the head end. On time arrival Paris. Easy!

Former Est Mountain 4-8-2, 241A 58, arrives at Belfort with train 42 Basle – Paris, 20 August 1961. At the head of the 15 vehicle train are two parcel vans and an SNCF postal vehicle. (*Author*)

Est 4-6-0 230K 168, with small six-wheel tender, stands at the head of the eleven coach 7.33pm 'Train Omnibus' [stopping train] Paris to Château Thierry at the Gare de l'Est, 20 August 1961. (*Author*)

The only double chimneyed Est Mountain, 241A 7, at Chaumont, taking water, waiting to take over Train 43 [Paris Est-Basle] for the run as far as Mulhouse, 13 July 1962. (*Author*)

Next morning, one week after my departure from London, I boarded the boat train at St Lazare, a modest ten coaches, 420 tonnes gross, behind another Chapelon rebuilt État Pacific 231G 553. Unfortunately it was all too easy with the driver pressing the loco so little that speed on the banks dropped to the low 30s without a whisper of sound emerging from the chimney. I thought it was the absurdly easy schedule, but the driver misjudged it and we actually arrived nearly 3 minutes late at Dieppe Maritime, his coal efficiency reward being offset by his lost punctuality bonus.

After this quiet and 'gentle' journey, we experienced the Channel at its worst (a force ten gale and the navy out from Portsmouth on patrol – the only time I've seen sailors being seasick) and a consequent late departure from Newhaven behind BR third rail electric E5010, which then lost its path and arrived in Victoria 43 minutes late – the only train on my week's tour that arrived at destination more than 3 minutes late!

I so enthused over my 1961 continental free pass experience that I persuaded a former student colleague, a keen and more professional train timer, Alistair Wood, to join me in 1962, even though he had to pay! We became more ambitious and planned a fortnight's round tour of Germany, taking in part of my 1961 route. Starting on 12 July 1962, the Victoria-Dover boat train was an EMU, but we had decided to try the Calais-Paris route instead of Newhaven-Dieppe, as Alistair persuaded me that the steam section from Calais to Amiens would require more premium locomotive performance – and after my previous experience, the shorter sea route had its attractions. So we found the 7.25pm Calais Maritime-Paris Gare du Nord boat train headed by Chapelon pacific, 231E 38, as far as Amiens, with eleven coaches, 515tonnes gross. We took the climb to Caffiers easily at a minimum of 43kph and ran efficiently across the Somme flats at a steady 112-115kph to arrive in Amiens 1 minute early.

I had motivated Alistair to repeat my 1961 Paris-Mulhouse trips on Trains 43 (eastwards) and 42 (return) and found a significant motive power change. A group of Chapelon 241P 4-8-2s had been drafted to Noisy-le-Sec (the freight depot had taken over the steam allocation of La Villette) and 241P 21 had replaced the previous year's 231G 21 which we passed stored dead in a siding en route to Troyes. The huge Mountain with its 120kph maximum speed made mincemeat of the schedule and averaged 109kph from Émerainville to Romilly-sur-Seine, over 100kms, and spent the last 40kms dawdling at 100kph and still arrived in Troyes nearly 6 minutes early. After a long wait at Troyes, with no change of locomotive this time, and despite a permanent way check to 30kph at La Villeneuve, we were 4 minutes early into Bar-sur-Aube and 9 minutes early into Chaumont! (Appendix 2, Table 1)

I didn't know what to expect from Chaumont and was gratified to find our new loco was not only a Chaumont-based 241A, but the only double-chimneyed specimen, 241A 7. The thirteen-coach, 510 tonnes train was conveyed with meticulous French punctuality at all points with speed steady around its maximum 110kph for large sections of the journey. We achieved an identical time to 231G 144 for the 95kph start to stop downhill section from Culmont-Chalindrey to Vitry Vernois, but this was achieved by dint of an even faster start. However, every time we reached 110kph, the brakes were applied to keep us to our stipulated maximum. A punctual arrival at Belfort was changed by slow station work in detaching four coaches to a 3 minute late departure and arrival at Mulhouse (Appendix 2, Table 1). Our return journey over this route two weeks later mirrored this journey with 241A 18 performing very competently to Chaumont and 241P 26 whisking the fourteen coach train in similar fashion to the 241P on the outward journey until we drifted over the last 30kms in the low 80s to avoid too embarrassingly early an arrival (Appendix 2, Table 2).

Est Mountain 241A18 at the head of Train 42 Basle-Paris [Est] at Mulhouse, 22 July 1962. (*Author*)

17

Knowing the Black Forest line was completely dieselised, Alistair and I chose the little-known route from Basle to Lake Constance (Bodensee) via Schaffhausen in Switzerland, rejoining the other route at Singen. The 8.56am Basle-Lindau Eilzug (E732) was only a four coach formation and was hauled throughout by P8, 38 1794 of Radolfzell. We did suffer a 10 minute delay at Waldshut, waiting to cross a DMU off the single line, but we had regained time by Friedrichshafen, where I spotted the Kiel-Lindau D76 standing on the adjacent platform waiting a new loco for the final leg. When I saw one of the last Bavarian Pacifics in original form backing onto the six-car train, we disembarked quickly from our Eilzug and enjoyed 18 508's snippet 19-minute run at a steady 100kph round the lake shore.

18 508 was the last of the Bavarian State Railways Maffei Pacifics, built in 1924 to the 1908 design – it was exhibited at the Railway Technical Exhibition in Berlin that year, painted royal blue with brass boiler rings, cylinder covers and chimney cap (GWR style). The later series 18 509–548 was built by the newly formed Reichsbahn from 1926-30, as the DR had not yet developed the 03 standard pacific with lighter axleload, and thirty of these were converted in the mid-1950s to series 18/6 by provision of an all welded boiler and other detail design changes. I found later that 18 481, 508 and 528 lasted until August, October and November 1962 respectively and that 18 478 was already in Lindau depot purchased by Herr Lory and ready for restoration, now gloriously achieved with its original Bavarian State Railway number 3673 (it has been painted since restoration both in the State green livery and more recently in the royal blue livery that 18 508 exhibited in 1924). 18 508 was therefore virtually at the end of its thirty-eight year career and such was its propensity in these last days for filling the cab with steam, that it was nicknamed by drivers as the 'Saunalok'!

I managed to hold Alistair in Bavaria for three days while we sampled the last summer of the 18/6s on all the services to Kempten and Munich (the V200s had taken over the D-Züge by the end of the year). I was unaware that several of my favourites from my 1959 university visit and my 1961 trip had already been withdrawn in 1961 and early 1962 (including 18 604, 606, 610, 618, 621, 624 and 626) – in fact twelve of the thirty strong class had been withdrawn in the previous twelve months. We went to Immenstadt and by branch train to Oberstdorf (a class 86 2-8-2T), hiked in the mountains, and had a series of 18/6 runs (602, 605, 614 and 622 – the latter was the class last survivor, being withdrawn in September 1965 and scrapped in November 1966) as well as one of the P10 survivors (39 122) in the Alpine section from Lindau to Immenstadt. We eventually tore ourselves away and took the 9.33am Lindau-Munich (D91 12.33 am from Geneva) on 17 July with 18 614 throughout. The six-coach lightweight train was an easy task for the Pacific and we were on time or early throughout with nothing over 105kph, although hill climbing was energetic (Appendix 2, Table 5).

From Munich, I remembered my 1959 journey to Würzburg on the *Tirol Express* behind an 01 Pacific and a P8, but by this time the line had been electrified as far as Treuchtlingen and we had an early Bavarian electric, E16 06. At the locomotive changeover point I'd hoped for an 01 again, but was disappointed to see V200 008,

The 1924 built last Bavarian State Railways Pacific, 18.508, runs to shed at Lindau after arrival with D76 from Kiel, which it has worked round the shore of the 'Bodensee' [Lake Constance] from Friedrichshafen, 14 July 1962. (*Author*)

18.605, one of the thirty former 1926-30 constructed Reichsbahn Pacifics to the 1908 Bavarian design, rebuilt in the mid-1950s with an all-welded boiler, backs onto the evening D-Zug [express] for Munich at Lindau, 15 July 1962. (*Author*)

also since preserved, which gave a very ordinary run to Würzburg. This city was full of V200s – we had hoped for steam on the main south-north artery, but nothing came, so we made our way to Fulda. We studied the train formation displays on the platform, which conveniently (and accurately) showed a little V200 or 01.10 (a DB pacific) outline at the appropriate end and noted that the heavy overnight trains were mainly steam hauled but the daytime trains were nearly all diesels. We watched a P8 depart cut inside a V200 and were tempted, but waited for a train destined for East Germany at Bebra, which was diagrammed, according to our platform board, for steam. The train duly arrived behind 01 1082, a three-cylinder oil burning Pacific, which made a lot of noise on a modest load (340 tonnes) but was constantly delayed by electrification work. It handed over the train to an East German rebuild of the DB standard 01 Pacific, an 01.5, at Bebra 7 minutes late.

Another diesel section from Bebra to Göttingen, was enlivened by being banked by 2-10-0 50 1883 at one stage, and we dismounted in the hope of a steam train off the Frankfurt route, which joined us here. The 8.03am Basle-Hamburg (D73) turned up with a filthy and rather sluggish standard DB two cylinder coal-burning 4-6-2, 01 064, which was unable to recover from a 15 minute delay waiting a connection at Kreiensen, taking us to Hanover and a welcome overnight sleep.

Next morning we went to the main station on spec, to see what was on offer for continuing our journey to Hamburg. A fourteen-coach, 630 tonne train (the

From train D91, 9.33am Lindau-Munich, [12.33am from Geneva] near Oberstauffen in the foothills of the Bavarian Alps, hauled by rebuilt Bavarian pacific 18.614, 17 July 1962 (*Author*)

A South – North D-Zug from Frankfurt-am-Main to Hamburg departs Würzburg behind a double-headed V200 1953 built diesel hydraulic and ex-Prussian P8 4-6-0 38.3344, 17 July 1962. (*Author*)

Schweiz Express) rolled in double-headed by 01 043 and 01 111, of later Hof fame, and produced between them a very jolly affair, roaring through the flat countryside at a steady 120-125kph and would have converted a 9 minute late start into an on time arrival but for a 2 minute signal stand outside Hamburg main station (Hauptbahnhof). We spent the day travelling to Kiel and back, but this was a bit of an anticlimax when our travel-stained 03 was suddenly piloted at the last moment by a V100 centre-cab diesel. After a bit of sightseeing, we found our return journey was with the same 03 062 but now minus the V100.

We had been looking forward to the next day on the *Rollbahn* – the entirely steam worked mainline from Hamburg to Cologne, with most trains changing from one 01.10 to another at Osnabrück. This was the last significant main line in Germany that was all steam worked – I exclude the Hof-Bamberg, Hamburg-Westerland and Rheine-Norddeich lines as these were not at the heart of the DB network like the Hamburg-Cologne route which, with Cologne-Frankfurt-Nuremburg-Munich along the Rhine and Main rivers, must have been DB's equivalents of the 'Premier Line'. The 300 mile route was almost entirely in the hands of the very capable three cylinder oil-burning 01.10s (later classified as 012s) which were reputed to be ready for the road only 45 minutes after lighting up and were as versatile as the V200s, which eventually replaced them. I'd had night runs over this route in the winter of 1960 when I attended the wedding of one of my college friends in Plön, near Lübeck, and I remember being impressed with the outward running behind oil-burning 01 1075 and 01 1059 respectively, but the return journey was a different matter. The first leg was with a very overloaded 03 078, which dropped 30 minutes on schedule to Osnabrück and coal-burning 01 1078 (later class 011) did no more than hold scheduled timings thereafter.

DB standard post-war 2-6-2 23.023 on arrival at Frankfurt-am-Main with D384 from Cologne, 20 July 1962. (*Author*)

I had a sneaking hope for one of the post-war semi-streamlined class 10s of which there were only two – later I found out that they were employed almost exclusively on the Frankfurt-Kassel-Hanover route. Our train was D94, the 8.26am Hamburg-Cologne and the twelve-coach, 445 tonnes train was headed by ex-works 01 1079. I had had the one recent run behind 01 1082 from Fulda, but I was not expecting the continuous roar that these engines emitted at speed – a steady 120kph for most of the journey. Although we were ahead of schedule at Bremen, we were delayed on departure by 10 minutes and the roar increased to a crescendo as we finally topped 130kph at Barnstorf, just before the Diepholz stop. At Osnabrück, we exchanged our 01.10 for another, 01 1068, and proceeded to whittle away the deficit as we charged through the Ruhr, arriving at Cologne just a quarter of a minute late, despite a 1 minute signal stop at Cologne Deutzerfeld (Appendix 2, Table 6).

Before we retired to our hotel, we took a trip to Aachen and back and had a truly phenomenal run behind one of the ugly, all-welded boiler 03.10s, which were all based at Hagen. The thirteen-coach, 550 tonnes Cologne-Ostend boat train had 03 1013 and gained 4 minutes of a late start on the 51-minute run, climbing to Grosskönigsdorf at 88kph, achieving 120 at Sindorf and accelerating to 110 after the Düren 80kph slowing, then a series of permanent-way slowings before Aachen. I had got used to the din of an oil-burning 01.10. It was nothing to the noise produced by this coal-burning three-cylinder light pacific; it gave the impression of being driven flat out. Of course, it was making way at Aachen for a Belgian diesel, so it did not matter that most of the fire had disappeared up the chimney! (Appendix 2, Table 6).

The last few days of our holiday were spent ambling round the German countryside south of Cologne. Alistair was keen for a run behind one of the DB standard class 23 2-6-2s and we selected D384 Cologne-Giessen-Frankfurt as a likely candidate. To our surprise, the nine-coach packed train had a P10 2-8-2, 39 232, which performed very sluggishly – we were crammed into the vestibule end immediately behind the tender although our view was very limited anyway as the rain streamed down and the windows misted over. We had dropped 5 minutes by Au (anyone know of a shorter station name?) and our 10 minute late arrival in Siegen was extended to 20 minutes awaiting a connection. However, 39 232 gave way to the desired 23 023 at Giessen, which regained nine of the lost minutes to Frankfurt.

We wandered from Frankfurt to Aschaffenburg and Crailsheim behind a freight electric (E40), a class 50 and a P8, which included backing out of Miltenburg in a similar operation to that encountered in days of yore at Templecombe. In fact my notebook expressed great similarities of our journey to a run over the Somerset & Dorset. We encountered a reboilered 01 4-6-2 on a Crailsheim-Stuttgart four-coach D232 and more P8s through pretty countryside to Rottweil, Tüttlingen and Singen before returning the way we had come with yet another P8 (38 3797) through to Basle and so back to Paris.

And our last impression – the immaculate 231K 46 backing on to our 550 tonnes train at Amiens and accelerating us noiselessly up to 120kph by Hangest and averaging that same speed across the Somme Valley and depositing us, once more on the dot of time, at Calais Maritime. The begoggled engineer grinned from his coal-dusted face as we passed his engine at Calais and pride in 'his' polished and adorned *machine titulaire* was obvious. (Appendix 2, Table 3)

Three-cylinder all-welded boiler post-war rebuild of a Reichsbahn streamlined 03.10 Pacific, 03.1013, at Cologne, where it has taken over from electric traction, on the evening boat train to Ostend, 19 July 1962. (*Author*)

Chapter 2

A free pass in West Wales

On 4 June 1962, I caught the 7.55am from Paddington to Swansea to report to the District Operating Superintendent, Jack Brennan, on arrival at 12.30pm. About 50 per cent of the South Wales expresses were 'Hymek' hauled by this time, especially the Cardiff and Landore turns, as both depots were now builders' sites and their engines had been dispersed to Cardiff East Dock, Neath and Llanelli. However, the Old Oak turns remained steam for a few more weeks and I determined to take advantage of them. 5067 *St Fagan's Castle* of Reading (81D) headed the eight coaches, 276-300 tons, and promptly lost 10 minutes to Slough, running round 'Warship' D804 stuck on the fast line which had failed at Iver on the 7.45 Paddington-Bristol. After a special stop at Didcot to pick up passengers waiting for the failed service, we left Swindon 14 minutes late, but with a minimum of 53mph at Badminton and speed in the mid-70s afterwards, we reached Cardiff 4 minutes late only and Swansea on time. A week later, I had double-chimney Castle, 5060 *Earl of Berkeley* of Old Oak Common (81A), on the same train and it ran punctually throughout, with 75mph before the Slough stop, 70-72 up the Vale of the White Horse, 84 at Brinkworth and a minimum of 62 at Badminton. After that, an early arrival was guaranteed unless signals intervened, but we got a clear road.

The interview with Jack Brennan was eccentric to put it mildly. Having greeted me and told me gruffly that I was not to expect to be able to turn up at midday every Monday morning, he fell asleep in the middle of a question. I was completely thrown, did not know whether to wake him up, creep out or sit it out. He suddenly woke, shook himself and finished the question. I later found out that he had contracted sleeping sickness in the jungle during the war and my experience was common – but no-one had thought to warn me!

I spent the next week at Margam Yard in the Hump Tower Control Panel, in one of the most glorious June weeks ever – one night shift was so light that the sun had hardly disappeared before dawn was already breaking. There was an evening local back from Port Talbot station (we had to use a transit van for shuttles from the yard to the station) I caught that week, which was hauled by 0-6-2T 6680 of Duffryn Yard, a train obviously intended mainly for steelworkers from the Steel Company of

Wales Port Talbot plant. The next evening, I spent the first of many travelling out from Swansea High Street on the West Wales portion of a London express to Llanelli or Carmarthen. There was a steep climb out of Swansea to Cockett tunnel (2 miles of 1 in 52), then a straight downhill stretch at 1 in 50 to Llanelli. The onward run to Carmarthen was flat along the estuary wall past Kidwelly.

I joined the 1.55pm Paddington on a glorious sunny evening with 5013 *Abergavenny Castle* of Neath, with eight coaches, 276-290 tons. That was the maximum load unbanked for the short steep climb to Cockett. With heavier loads a pilot would be attached in front of the Castle or Hall and a brief stop made at the summit to detach, which was usually accomplished in less than a couple of minutes. 5013 cleared Cockett in 9min 28sec at 21mph and touched 78 at Gowerton before a 30mph p-way slack at Loughor. We stopped at Pembrey, Kidwelly and Ferryside after Llanelli, so nothing over 61mph before a punctual Carmarthen arrival was made. My regular return run from Llanelli or Carmarthen was made on the 6.50pm Neyland sleeping car train, a twelve-coach train of 398-420 tons, rostered for a Carmarthen (87G) Castle just as far as Swansea. This load meant that a banker was required from Gowerton at the foot of a 3 mile, 1 in 50 climb to Cockett and 9408 of Llanelli (87F) was on the job most often. 5039 *Rhuddlan Castle* was the locomotive used most frequently that summer (the other Carmarthen Castles, 4081, 5027, 5030, 5054 and 5098 appeared infrequently) and on 5 June it quickly accelerated to 68mph before a dead stand for signals at Kidwelly. 9408 duly buffered up (but was not coupled) at Gowerton and banked us vigorously to the summit taking 6min 23sec from a standing start to clear the summit at 27mph. At the end of a fascinating first week in South Wales, I managed to find a steam hauled Friday relief train from Cardiff headed by 5075 *Wellington* of Cardiff East Dock (88A), but the load was light, eight coaches, 256-280 tons, and did not tax the loco or crew. Without exceeding 68mph anywhere, we sailed into Paddington a good 7 minutes early.

I risked Jack Brennan's wrath the following Monday, as I was told that the following week would be the last rostered for steam before the Hymeks took over and got 5060 as indicated earlier in this chapter. In view of the weather the previous week I had brought beachwear, swimming trunks and summer shirts in my hand luggage and it poured with rain for the rest of the summer. I was in lodgings with a Mrs Beynon, a good 10 minute walk along the main Walter Road towards Sketty and I got soaked so many times that, by week three, I had invested in my first umbrella. The digs were again bed and breakfast only and a fellow trainee, John Crowe, and I ventured out most evenings as we had no wish to be regaled by Mrs Beynon's extreme right wing views. She opined that Winston Churchill was a 'pinky' – my colleague was a young Conservative and was tempted to argue – but I made the mistake of admitting voting Liberal, which was totally off her political spectrum and I needed to make myself scarce! On the few dry evenings, John and I would go down to a little pitch and putt golf course between the Mumbles Road and the Swansea Victoria Central Wales line dividing the course from Swansea Bay, but most evenings we made our way to High Street station and caught the 1.55 or 3.55pm Paddington on its West Wales leg.

After a brief stint at Margam the second Monday afternoon to confirm my week's itinerary and shift pattern, I returned to Swansea on the 11.55 Paddington, behind spotless double-chimney 4080 *Powderham Castle* (88A) and eleven coaches, 382-410 tons, which regained 5 minutes of lost time just between Neath and Swansea with a glorious echoing exhaust from the damp rock cutting reverberating as we forged up the 1 in 88 to Skewen at 34mph. John and I changed, found a meal and took a short excursion to Llanelli on the 3.55 Paddington with 5030 *Shirburn Castle* (87G) on eleven coaches (358-400 tons) so we were piloted by 9431 (87D) to Cockett, sustaining 22mph on the bank and reaching 74 on the descent to Llanelli. 5039 again performed on the short return trip, banked by 9408 once more and cleared the summit at 22mph, not quite so noisily as on the previous occasion. Pleased with this, we repeated the excursion the next evening, 13 June, and got 5030 once more, with pannier tank 3641 (87D), making identical times to the second as the previous evening, with 23mph at Cockett and 75 on the descent. 5027 *Farleigh Castle* made its one foray onto the Up Sleeper and banker 9441 (87D) pushed us up the bank to Cockett at 23mph.

By the next Monday, a Hymek had replaced the London based Castle, so the first excitement was a quick trip to Llanelli on the 1.55 Paddington with 4081 *Warwick Castle* (87G) looking very smart, still garnished with Landore's decorations. The load was light, 6 coaches, 204-215 tons, and 4081 charged up the bank unaided at 31mph and touched 77 down the other side stopping at Llanelli in 16min 43sec for the 12 miles. 5039 and 9408 were back on the Neyland sleeper and shaved over a minute off their previous best time to Swansea, sustaining 28mph on the steepest part of the climb. On the following day, as part of my authorised training, I explored the colliery

Churchward 2-8-0T 5216 stands at Duffryn Yard, 9.7.50. The author's first experience of the Welsh Valleys was a trip behind this locomotive from Margam past Duffryn Yard to Maesteg North's Colliery in June 1962. (*R.K.Blencowe Collection*)

5246 at North's Colliery, Cwmdu, Maesteg with a coal train from the Colliery to Margam via Duffryn Yard, circa 1962. (*MLS Collection*)

workings fanning out from Margam up the Maesteg Valley to North's Colliery at Cwmdu, in the brakevan behind a train of unfitted mineral wagons, hauled by Churchward 2-8-0T 5216 (87B). Our load of thirty-nine mineral wagons was reduced to twenty-five at Duffryn Yard as no banker was available, and we held a minimum of 17mph up the 1 in 41 to Bryn Tunnel just short of Maesteg. We returned to Margam with nineteen loaded coal wagons, 460 tons gross, having taken four and a half hours for the 40 mile round trip excluding time at Cwmdu dropping off the empties and collecting our loaded train.

On the 20 June I was back to Carmarthen again on the 1.55 Paddington, with double chimney Castle 4093 *Dunster Castle* (87A). The load was eight coaches, 275-290 tons, and a good climb to Cockett – 25mph minimum – was followed by a full 85 down the bank and running in the mid-60s between stops on to Carmarthen. It was 5039 and 9408 again on the Neyland, minimum 27mph up Cockett bank. Friday journeys via London were now inevitably Hymeks – they were hard put to maintain Castle timings with heavy loads and you could feel the snatch in the train as they changed gear, which cannot have been good for them.

The next week, I needed to return to Swansea on the Sunday evening and I chose the 4.55pm Paddington, diverted via the Vale of Glamorgan because of planned engineering work on the main Cardiff-Bridgend route. This was still a steam turn and 7033 *Hartlebury Castle* (81A) fulfilled the turn with ease, the eight-coach train being totally inadequate for the returning weekend crowds as we were packed in like sardines. It was dark and raining steadily by the time we reached the Vale of Glamorgan and I did not time the train. More runs with 4081 on the 3.55 Paddington and 5039/9408 on the sleeper followed and I stayed the following weekend to watch some of the engineering work with the District Signalling Inspector. Somehow, I squeezed in a

27

run on the Sunday morning from Carmarthen with 5078 *Beaufort* (87A) on the 9.35 Pembroke Dock-Paddington, eight coaches, 246-255 tons, as far as Swansea and I got a rare clean climb of Cockett from the West without needing to stop for a banker. 5078 ran at 72 across the Kidwelly Flats and attacked the climb passing Gowerton at 64mph, falling to 26 at the summit.

I had now, I thought, run out of steam options for my journeys to and from London, until it occurred to me that by changing out of my Hymek hauled train at Cardiff, I could go home via a Cardiff-Portsmouth service and pick up the last Exeter-Waterloo express to my Woking home.

I tried this three times during the summer months and found the 4.25pm Cardiff was booked for a Hall – 6950 *Kingsthorpe Hall* (88A) performed in June, 5939 *Tangley Hall* (86B) in September and 6954 *Lotherton Hall* (82B) in October. The overall time from Cardiff to Salisbury was just 10 minutes short of 3 hours, with twelve scheduled stops. The hardest work was climbing from the Severn Tunnel to a stop at Pilning, then recovering up the grade to Patchway and then later climbing from Westbury up onto Salisbury Plain, past the signalbox where I played as a 5-year-old child during our escape from East Molesey during the war to the relative peace of the village of Upton Scudamore in Wiltshire. Both 5939 and 6954 worked hard uphill with their nine-coach 325 ton loads (reduced to seven coaches after Westbury), falling to 41-42mph before the Pilning stop and accelerating afterwards to 28-29 through the Patchway single bore tunnel. 5939 left Westbury 3 minutes late

The author discovered a variation on his route home to Woking once the Swansea-Paddington trains were fully dieselised – via Salisbury and an up West of England train like this 2.30pm Exeter with 35007 *Aberdeen Commonwealth* entering Seaton Junction station, 1 June 1961. (*MLS Collection*)

4213, a Llanelli based 2-8-0T from the first 1912 batch, taken around 1958-9. The author spent a morning on the footplate of this engine on Margam-Ogmore Vale coal trip workings, when it was a Tondu engine in June 1962. (*R.K.Blencowe Collection*)

after station overtime detaching the two vehicles, and touched 74mph before the Wishford slowing between Warminster and Salisbury. 6954 was more restrained until it was stopped for 18 minutes outside Salisbury (reason unexplained). The Salisbury-Woking section was always an Exmouth Junction Merchant Navy, most frequently 35025 *Brocklebank Line*.

Much of July was spent on a 1,000 mile round trip using my free continental pass facilities as recounted in the last chapter. Normal life was resumed on the last day of July, with 4081 on the 3.55 Paddington to Llanelli and former Laira double-chimneyed 5098 *Clifford Castle*, banked by 9408 on the 6.50pm Neyland return. Little new there! Another exploratory trip up the valleys, this time the Ogmore Vale, on the footplate of 2-8-0T 4213, and other brakevan sorties behind 92233 in the Margam area and 4232 from Swansea East Dock followed. I had to go to London for a training interview with the Assistant General Manager, Lance Ibbotson, and duly got a drubbing as I admitted I had not yet visited the site of the Landore Diesel Depot, which, in truth, was no more than a field of mud.

Duly chastened, I returned to South Wales on the 11.35am relief train as far as Bridgend. Double chimney 5097 *Sarum Castle* (88A) was the motive power, on ten coaches, 322-345 tons, and we ran non-stop to Newport in 149 minutes, 138 net, for the 133 miles with speed in the upper 60s as far as Swindon, 76 at Little Somerford, a minimum of 56 at Badminton and no more than 71 on the run down to the Severn Tunnel. I alighted at Bridgend, because the steam hauled 9.30am Manchester-Swansea was not far behind and duly ran in with Llanelli's 4099 *Kilgerran Castle*. P-way and signal checks turned our 9 minute late departure into a 15 minute late arrival in Swansea.

I took a Saturday off in early August to venture farther north, now my training did not require me to work Saturday mornings, and joined the 10.10am King's Cross-Edinburgh with Grantham A3, 60048 *Doncaster*, and a heavy twelve-coach, 450 ton gross load. 54mph minimum at Potters Bar and 66 at Knebworth was good and was followed by 82 at Biggleswade, 66 at Leys and 85 at Connington giving us an excellent 75 minute run to passing Peterborough. Signal checks at Greatford Box and Little Bytham (tardy crossing gate operation?) spoiled the climb to Stoke summit, but we accelerated back up to 53 and stopped in Grantham in 111 minutes. I was interested to see Thompson A2/3 pacific 60500 *Edward Thompson* take over, but its running was undistinguished and we took 107 minutes non-stop for the 83 miles on to York, with a 4 minute stand for signals at Newark as the only real excuse. 73mph after Retford was the highest speed. I returned from York on the thirteen coach 10.10am Edinburgh with King's Cross A3, 60039 *Sandwich,* which ran steadily and unspectacularly to Grantham in 101 minutes with speed in the high 60s most of the way (a mirror-image of 60500's run). I transferred to the 9.40am Glasgow-King's Cross there and got 60033 *Seagull* (again – my fourth long-distance run behind this superb engine) on a thirteen-coach, 460 ton load which distinguished itself with 90mph down Stoke bank, and after the Peterborough stop, 30min 33 sec start to stop, cleared Abbots Ripton at 55, 81 at Huntingdon, 73 at Sandy, then a 3 minute signal stand at Arlesey clearly following a slower service, presumably off the Cambridge line, to the terminus, in 87 minutes from Peterborough. I did not note our punctuality, but given the slack Summer Saturday timings, I guess we were on time. On another occasion, I did a similar trip with Alistair Wood and intended only to go to Peterborough with the 1.00pm *Heart of Midlothian* and 60063 *Isinglass,* which ran punctually, going well uphill, but was unusually restrained on the racing downhill section with nothing over 75, but still got to Peteborough in 80 minutes, as scheduled. There we watched the engine change and Alistair got excited (for him) when A1 60137 *Redgauntlet* backed on, as he was now an academic at Stirling University, specialising in Sir Walter Scott's novels. He persuaded me against my better judgement to buy a further ticket to York – at least cheaper for me than him – and, bearing out my worst fears and to Alistair's disappointment, we managed a very pedestrian run, almost identical to that of 60500, with only 48mph minimum at Stoke and nothing over 70 all the way, reaching York in 130 minutes (112 miles) from Peterborogh, non-stop with only a couple of p-way checks. Alistair persuaded me to return to Grantham on the Up *Heart of Midlothian* with Deltic D9010 and we finished up with 60122 *Curlew* again – another engine that kept turning up on trains I caught – on the last Up Hull.

On another weekend I was tempted by 5011 *Tintagel Castle* (81A) on the 9.15am Paddington-Hereford which went splendidly, though punched quite hard as it was only a month away from withdrawal, on a very manageable nine-coach, 330 ton load as far as Worcester, where five coaches were detached, and hustled the remaining four coaches to Hereford, connecting with the Brush Type 4 (Class 47) hauled North & West express to Shrewsbury. There I waited for a Scot-hauled train, the 11.5am Swansea-Manchester, onto Crewe – 46135 *The East Lancashire Regiment* –

which dropped 2 minutes unchecked on schedule, and was both surprised and really satisfied to find red 46208 *Princess Helena Victoria* appearing on the 4.15pm Liverpool relief to the *Red Rose* – reminiscent of my trip some eight years previously with 46205.

That August I took a weekend break in Scotland – 73036 from Swansea to Shrewsbury on the Central Wales line, 46167 *The Hertfordshire Regiment* on to Crewe, where I stayed up watching the night mail and newspaper train activity. In the morning I tried to wake myself with a snippet to Wigan on the 9.20am Crewe-Blackpool, to ensure some steam in case the 9.25am Crewe-Perth on which I intended to travel north was diesel-hauled. 45593 *Kolhapur* was as sluggish as I felt, but I was cheered up by the sight of 46141 *The North Staffordshire Regiment* (5A) running in on the 9.25 Crewe with ten coaches, albeit 16 minutes late already. 74 before Euxton Junction regained nine minutes (!) through a 19 minute run to Preston and a cut in the long scheduled halt there enabled us to leave only a minute late, but then we began to drop time steadily, with no more than 71mph before the Lancaster stop. Now 3 minutes late, signals at Hest Bank made us six late at Carnforth, and station overtime there made us 8 minutes late at Oxenholme. From the standing start we got our 315 gross ton load up to a sustained 45mph on Grayrigg, which was better, before a stop at Tebay. Leaving there still eight late at the foot of the climb to Shap, we just held schedule, accelerating to 35 at first, but then falling away to 27mph at the summit. We left Penrith 9 minutes late, but 77mph at Southwaite and generous recovery time saw us into Carlisle only 4 minutes down.

Now came one of the main objectives of my trip. I had been told that this train was diagrammed to one of Kingmoor's three Princess Royal Pacifics – 46200, 46201 and 46203. I watched with bated breath as a high-sided green tender backed round the corner and saw with relief that it was 46201 *Princess Elizabeth*. The engine change was effected smartly and we left on schedule. We took it steadily to Lockerbie and Beattock station where we were still on time, but I was surprised that a Pacific with such a comparatively light load took a banker, Fairburn 2-6-4T 42239 of Beattock. Perhaps it was because we were stopping at Beattock in any case. We left on time and the two engines held a steady 33mph nearly all the way to the summit, where 42239 dropped off, and we continued with a maximum of 76 at Lamington, arriving at Carstairs over 5 minutes early. We held schedule all the way to Stirling without too much trouble and with 33mph after Dunblane and 76 after the Gleneagles stop would have been in on time, but for a signal stand at Hilton Junction which made us 2 minutes late in.

I returned to Glasgow Buchanan Street with a late running Inverness-Glasgow train behind Black 5, 45443 of Eastfield and walked down to Glasgow Central in the hope of steam on the 10pm to Euston. I was pleased to find it hauled by Polmadie Scot 46107 *Argyll & Sutherland Highlander*, whose train was made up to a massive fifteen-coach, 530 gross ton load at Carstairs. At least this time the Scot showed what it could do and the recently ex-works locomotive did well with this load to reach 64 before Lamington, clear Beattock summit at 26mph, and sustain speeds in the low 70s most of the way to Carlisle where we arrived on time. The three Princess Royals lost their diagrammed turn in the Winter Timetable and were promptly withdrawn, although of course two – 46201 and 46203, live on.

I watched the night working, nearly dropping with exhaustion, with Alistair Wood, who persuaded me to join him on a Crewe-Carlisle-Glasgow relief with Black 5 45243, instead of waiting for an anticipated Pacific 46249 *City of Sheffield*, which Alistair said was on too light a train to be worth timing. The other key weekend objective was a Corkerhill Britannia on the 8.45am SO Glasgow St Enoch-St Pancras to Leeds, but it was a rundown Jubilee, 45673 *Keppel,* which appeared, piloted to Kilmarnock by Dumfries depot's 45171. It soon became obvious that all was far from well at the front end, and at Kilmarnock choice expletives from *Keppel's* crew were enough to retain the pilot to the Black 5's home depot. At Dumfries, a furious argument broke out, with the local shed foreman reclaiming his steed. In the end, the Holbeck crew only agreed to go forward if a new engine was obtained at Carlisle, and *Keppel* was flailed up to some sort of respectable speed, albeit with an ear-splitting din, on this understanding.

At Carlisle the Jubilee, whose brick arch had now collapsed, slunk off to Upperby, whilst a Clan stood on the middle road, waiting to take its place. My companion, who had had experiences of Clan pacifics before, groaned and feared the worst, but I was curious, as this class was new to me. 72005 *Clan Macgregor* was a total revelation. The train romped away, regaining time in handfuls and my colleague train timer sat open mouthed as we stormed Ais Gill at well over 40mph and ran hell for leather down the other side in the high seventies. My abiding memory is of standing in the corridor taking in the vista of waterfalls and streams pouring down the fell sides, as the whole run was conducted in pouring rain, and watching the locomotive wheels whirling as we swept round the numerous curves on the descent, chime whistle echoing over the storm swept hills. Finally I wended my weary way home to London on the *White Rose* behind the A1 destined to be the last survivor of the class, 60145 *St Mungo,* which slipped and slithered its way out of Leeds and had difficulty in keeping its feet all the way to London, in time for a brief sleep at the home of my parents in Woking before returning to South Wales the next day.

The last down South Wales express still booked for steam was the 2.55pm from Paddington to Swansea, a train I found difficult to find an adequate excuse to experience from London. However, on 24 October, I did manage to join this train at Paddington and was rewarded with a splendid run behind Llanelli's 5037 *Monmouth Castle*, albeit with only eight coaches, 272/290 tons. Two dead stands for signals before Southall were hardly auspicious, but recovery to 75 by Taplow showed the driver didn't intend to hang around. We left Reading 13 minutes late, touched 80 at Didcot but three signal checks between there and Swindon meant we took 41min 46sec for the 41 miles (36 minutes net). Leaving Swindon 10 minutes late, we topped Badminton at 63, touched 83 at Winterbourne, 81 in the middle of Severn Tunnel and, despite checks from East Usk into Newport, arrived triumphantly on time in 58min 17sec (56 minutes net). After that it was easy, the only effort achieving a minimum of 44 at Stormy Sidings after the Bridgend stop. Arrival in Swansea was 1 minute early.

Our Swansea evenings progressed through August, September and October as before. I made evening – and half day – forays into West Wales, many behind the nimble Churchward 63XX moguls (6326, 6349, 7312, 7318 and 7319 most frequently) in the company of my fellow lodger, John Crowe, and spent a pleasant afternoon exploring the Whitland-Cardigan branch, our two-coach 45XX-hauled branch train meandering past mossy-banked streams and threading ancient oak

Churchward mogul 5353 of Carmarthen shed on a stopping train for Aberystwyth at Carmarthen, 25 June 1955. (*GW Trust Collection*)

7319, a frequent performer in West Wales in the early 1960s, previously a Newport Ebbw Junction engine, at an unknown Southern Region location in the late 1950s. (*GW Trust Collection*)

Large Collett Prairie 4131 at Carmarthen having arrived with the Pembroke Dock portion of the Up Pembroke Coast Express, 25 June 1955. (*GW Trust Collection*)

Churchward 'Small Prairie' 4569 of Whitland threads an ancient oakwood near Llandissilio on the Whitland – Cardigan branch, August 1962. (*Author*)

The evening Cardigan-Whitland branch train hauled by Churchward Small Prairie 4557 passes post-war built pannier tank 1648 westbound at Llanglydwen station, August 1962. (*Author*)

woods. We sought in vain the site of the real Cardigan Castle during a brief sojourn in the County town, although we came across the longest funeral foot-procession I'd ever encountered – male only and all garbed in ceremonial black. They take such events seriously there!

I was now based in the District Office itself and undertaking a variety of duties both in and outside the office, including some small projects. This meant hours were variable and so occasionally I'd have a midday trip to Carmarthen, as on 15 August with 5905 *Knowsley Hall* of Fishguard (87J) on the West Wales portion of the 8.55am Paddington, which climbed Cockett with its six coaches, 204/220 tons, at a steady 23mph and touched 73 on the descent. A lively affair was Churchward mogul 7306 (87G) on 26 September, when it replaced the usual Castle on the 1.55pm Paddington. With eight coaches it needed the assistance of 9431 (87D) to Cockett, but it achieved identical times to Castle-hauled trains with similar loads. An unusual combination on the 1.55pm Paddington occurred in early November, when 7826 *Longworth Manor* of 87G replaced the usual Castle and was piloted to Cockett by 0-6-2T 6602 (87D) instead of the usual pannier tank. The eight-coach load weighed 272/285 tons and the Manor and tank combination sustained 30mph on the climb, my fastest, and 72 down the bank. In September I had another couple of runs to Llanelli and back, out with 5098 *Clifford Castle* (87G) on the 3.55pm Paddington, assisted to Cockett by 8431 and 8794 respectively, and returning on the 6.50pm Neyland sleeper, with 5054 *Earl of Ducie*, newly transferred to Carmarthen. Banker from Gowerton to Cockett was the ever faithful 9408.

During my management training in the Swansea District Office in the autumn of 1962, I spent a few days with the train crew inspectors. One of their roles was to examine new drivers, and I was invited to join a day's duty in passing out a Llanelli fireman. We were to start with a freight to Margam, before taking over a Manchester-Swansea express at Port Talbot. We found our loco in the roundhouse at 87F, a Churchward 2-8-0T, 4279, but lost our trainee, who failed to show up. The Inspector decided to continue with me in tow instead, and we made our solid and somewhat pedestrian way, bunker first, to the Hump Reception Sidings with a heavy and unfitted load of coal. Since there was no need to test the trainee on the passenger train – I later saw a resplendent 5054 *Earl of Ducie* sweep past us – we ran down to the Knuckle Yard and picked up fifty empty cattle trucks for Fishguard, which we would run back as far as Llanelli and complete our turn for the day.

Once 5054 was clear of us, we followed her out and took the Swansea Avoiding Line for a direct run to our destination. As we got into our stride, the train now being fully braked, I relaxed and enjoyed the passing scenery as we got well into the 50s, with the old engine bucketing along cheerfully and in good voice. I peered along the running plate and watched, mesmerized, as the front end of the plate above the cylinders seemed to be having a separate life to the rest of the engine. I stared and sure enough, the plate above the buffer beam was jigging rhythmically up and down as we also shook and rattled to a different tune. Perhaps I would not have enjoyed my outing so much had I realised that the maintenance staff would later find a total fracture of the front end of the plate, which was apparently only held in position by the two struts from the saddle under the smokebox door to the top of the bufferbeam!

I also made several evening excursions with John Crowe to the remote railway that ran from Neath Riverside to Brecon, a railway that ran through coal mining areas to Onllwyn, then took to the hills. There was an evening branch train that we could catch after a day's 'learning' which gave us just time for a pint in Brecon before catching the same pannier tank and 'B' set back to Neath. We were invariably the only

6741 and 6714 doublehead a coal train from Ystradgynlais Colliery to Swansea East Dock past Pontardawe station, December 1962. (*Author*)

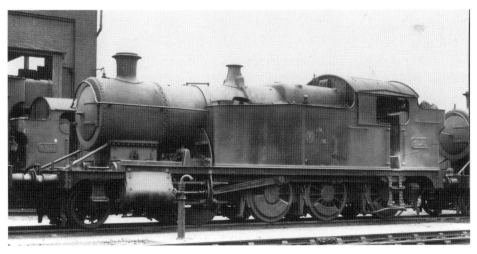

4279, built in 1920, at Newport Ebbw Junction, 24 March 1938. On the author's footplate run from Margam to Llanelli in the autumn of 1962, the running plate fractured at the step in front of the cylinders and was only held in place by the struts from the smokebox saddle. (*J.M.Bentley Collection*)

The early evening train from Neath Riverside to Brecon climbs into the Black Mountains near Dan-yr-Ogof behind one of the regular 57XX pannier tanks, September 1962. (*Author*)

passengers in both directions and it was not surprising when the line – along with the other railway connections to Brecon – was a victim of pre-Beeching cuts. John and I attended the melancholy last day and saw the last train entering Brecon, the final train requiring several coaches and two panniers, a far cry from the lonely grandeur of our solitary trips.

In December, I was summoned before the District Manager to be told that he wished me to act as Stationmaster at Pontardawe in the Swansea Valley, covering a five week gap before a new man was appointed. This outpost was on the freight route between Swansea East Dock and Ystradgynlais and involved the management of one colliery and a pit props yard, and a parcels sub-depot to Swansea itself. The office was Dickensian and I had just five staff, three of whom were Welsh speaking and had no English. I amused myself by joining the signalman to watch the 67XX hauled freights passing in the station (a crossing loop on the single line) and accompanying our daily shunt to the pit prop sidings to place empties and remove the loaded wagons, usually with 6754.

I managed a couple more steam runs on the main line to Paddington before moving on to four weeks of Work Study training at the centre at Paddington, near Ranelagh Bridge, in the New Year, returning to the Cardiff Divisional Office for further training in mid-February. I had travelled one Monday morning on the 'Rattler', the Redhill-Guildford-Reading South route, behind a Southern 'U' mogul, to pick up the 7.55am Paddington from Reading. I caught the 7.45am Paddington to Bristol at first for some variety – it was a D8XX Warship – and alighted at Swindon to join the 7.55. Time dragged on and I began to hope that perhaps something untoward had occurred to the Hymek. Sure enough, it eventually appeared, over an hour late, with tender first 6991 *Acton Burnell Hall* of Southall, which had been commandeered from an Up freight at Wantage Road, hauling an expired Hymek, D7039. The pair were replaced by a very down-at-heel looking Grange, 6835 *Eastham Grange* (82B), which managed to recover 5 minutes of the 73-minute late start from Swindon, albeit the load was light, seven coaches, 246/270 tons. 72mph was the top speed descending past Pilning to the Severn Tunnel and there were indications west of Cardiff that steaming was troublesome although we kept rolling at a reasonable speed.

I returned home for Christmas on 22 December and was extremely surprised to find the eleven-coach, 388/420 tons *Capitals United Express* (11.10am Milford Haven to Paddington) standing at Swansea High Street with 5037 *Monmouth Castle* (87F) – again – at the head end instead of the booked Hymek. The run to Cardiff was first class with a minimum of 37mph on the bank to Skewen – better than the normal Hymek performance – 32mph at Stormy Sidings summit and 46 on Llanharan bank before the colliery subsidence slack. All looked set fair at Cardiff for a good run to London, when there was a sudden explosion of steam between the tender and first coach as a steam heating pipe burst. They couldn't find a replacement pipe quickly, so a poor decision was made and 5037 was exchanged for the Cardiff standby pilot, another Castle, 5096 *Bridgwater Castle* (88A), which was in nothing like 5037's excellent condition. We left 5 minutes late, which had grown to 10 minutes when we stopped at Severn Tunnel Junction to attach Large Prairie 4156 (86E) to pilot us through the tunnel and all the way to Badminton. The vigorous assistance of the tank engine enabled us to make a very respectable climb out of the tunnel, with 32mph at Patchway, but we could only sustain 45-48 on the gentle climb to Badminton, where 4156 was detached. With nothing over 67 down through Little Somerford, we were 24 minutes late into Swindon where I gave up timing.

Summary of runs between Swansea and Llanelli:

Loco	Date	Train/Load	Time to Cockett/ to Llanelli	Speed Cockett/ Gowerton	
5013 *Abergavenny Castle*	5.6.62	1.55 Pdn/ 8 chs	9.28 21.11 (18 net)	21	78
5030 *Shirburn Castle*/9431	12.6.62	3.55 Pdn/11 chs	8.15 19.20*	22	74
5030 *Shirburn Castle*/3641	13.6.62	3.55 Pdn/11 chs	8.15 19.20*	24	75
4081 *Warwick Castle*	18.6.62	1.55 Pdn/ 6 chs	7.32 16.43	31	77
4093 *Dunster Castle*	20.6.62	1.55 Pdn/ 8 chs	8.15 16.47	25	85
4081 *Warwick Castle*	29.6.62	3.55 Pdn/ 6 chs	9.00 18.36	22	65
5030 *Shirburn Castle*	1.7.62	12.55 Pdn/ 6 chs	8.00 17.03	24	71
4081 *Warwick Castle*	31.7.62	3.55 Pdn/ 6 chs	8.26 19.15 (18 net)	24	72
5905 *Knowsley Hall*	15.8.62	8.55 Pdn/ 6 chs	8.37 18.05	23	73
5078 *Beaufort*	16.8.62	1.55 Pdn/ 8 chs	8.54 21.20 (18.5net)	20	73
5087 *Tintern Abbey*	8.62	1.55 Pdn/ 8 chs	10.00 19.31	19	74
5098 *Clifford Castle*/8794	17.9.62	3.55 Pdn/10 chs	8.37 22.07*	23	73
5098 *Clifford Castle*/8431	19.9.62	3.55 Pdn/10 chs	8.24 22.05*	25	70
7306 / 9431	26.9.62	1.55 Pdn/ 8 chs	7.19 19.20*	28	74
7826 *Longworth Manor*/ 6602	8.11.62	1.55 Pdn/ 8 chs	7.02 19.55*	30	72

(Note* stop at Cockett to detach pilot)

Summary of runs between Llanelli and Swansea:

Loco	Date	Train/Load	Banker	Time	Speed /Cockett
5039 *Rhuddlan Castle*	5.6.62	6.50 Ney/ 12 chs	9408	25.59	27
5039 *Rhuddlan Castle*	12.6.62	6.50 Ney/ 12 chs	9408	27.01	22
5027 *Farleigh Castle*	13.6.62	6.50 Ney/ 12 chs	9441	25.22	23
5039 *Rhuddlan Castle*	18.6.62	6.50 Ney/ 12 chs	9408	24.04	28
5039 *Rhuddlan Castle*	20.6.62	6.50 Ney/ 12 chs	9408	24.53	27
5039 *Rhuddlan Castle*	30.6.62	6.50 Ney/ 10 chs	9408	25.32	22
5078 *Beaufort*	1.7.62	9.35 P.Dk/ 8 chs	-	20.37	26
5039 *Rhuddlan Castle*	1.7.62	6.50 Ney/ 12 chs	8794	27.09	24
5098 *Clifford Castle*	31.7.62	6.50 Ney/ 12 chs	9408	24.44	23
4081 *Warwick Castle*	31.7.62	10.50 MH/ 6 chs	-	21.18	20
5054 *Earl of Ducie*	17.9.62	6.50 Ney/ 11 chs	9408	25.34	24
5054 *Earl of Ducie*	19.9.62	6.50 Ney/ 11 chs	9408	27.48	21

Chapter 3

And in the Border Country

Over Christmas in 1962 and the beginning of January 1963 it snowed. All the Western Region Traffic Apprentices were closeted for four weeks at the Work Study School near Royal Oak station, where they subjected the two lecturers, used to compliant recruits intending to become Work Study practitioners, to a verbal mauling – to such an extent that no future set of trainees was ever allowed to inflict their criticisms through attending such a course again. After four weeks of hell, the authorities despatched the trainees to test their skills in real activity on the ground, and I found myself with three others in a foot of snow, stop-watching maintenance activities in Laira Diesel Depot. The shed was meant to be steam-free, but every morning a dozen steam locos could be observed queuing at the ashpits and coaling plant, rescuing the service from the frozen and damaged diesels. Most were visitors from sheds like Bristol St Philips Marsh, but two Castles were still stored in the shed (7022 *Hereford Castle* and 4087 *Cardigan Castle*). Before February was out, they were both restored to traffic for the rest of the winter – 4087 was then transferred to St Philips Marsh to cover for the withdrawal of diesels from the North & West between Bristol and Shrewsbury and 7022 remained at Laira as 'standby' to cover diesel failures.

After the second freezing week, I returned home (before resuming training in South Wales) on the 4pm Plymouth-Manchester, the North & West Postal, as far as Exeter, where I took the SR route to Woking. Instead of the rostered Type 47, the train engine was 1021 *County of Montgomery* (82B) and the pilot to Newton Abbot was 2,700hp diesel hydraulic, D1008 *Western Harrier*, super power for the nine coach train (303/335 tons). Despite signals to walking pace all the way to Laira Junction and a minute dead stand at Tavistock Junction, the pair roared up Hemerdon bank, initially accelerating to 50mph, then dropping back gradually to 31mph. A p-way slack to 15mph was inconveniently at the foot of the climb to Dainton, but again the pair charged to 53 before dropping back at the summit to 36mph. The 52-minute schedule was only exceeded by two minutes (about 48 minutes net).

From March to September 1963, I was attached to the Cardiff Divisional Office in Marland House, opposite Cardiff General Station. Once more with fellow Traffic

Apprentice, John Crowe, I lodged at 14, Dispenser Street, by the River Taff, right opposite Cardiff Arms Park. It was only a 5 minute walk to the office and I missed the daily commute on the many days when I was doomed to 'sit next to Nellie' as we used to call it; we were given files to read or told to watch what the clerk was doing instead of a more active role. Breakfast was fairly early as the other lodgers were mainly commercial travellers who wanted to get out on the road, so John and I frequently invented our own commuter trip to Newport and back to Cardiff!

There was an 8.20am Cardiff-Pontypool Road which either connected with or joined up with a train from the Bristol direction to make a through train for Manchester. The loco from Cardiff was usually a Pontypool Road (86G) engine, which did not go beyond that depot, the Bristol engine, presumably a diesel, taking over. I never timed any of these trips – the loco was normally a Hall or Grange, of which there were numerous examples at 86G, most of which were new to me as that depot had few passenger turns. I just went for the ride and accumulated new locos, normally returning on a cross-country Swindon built DMU which operated on the Bristol-Cardiff service. Occasionally, if for some reason a 9am start at Marland House was unnecessary, we would wait for something more interesting for the return from Newport, or, if released early, we might catch an early evening departure to Newport and wait for a steam return. I noted four Counties – 1005, 1006, 1011 (several times) and 1020 – on this return jaunt, 1005 and 1006 on consecutive days – a couple of Hereford (85C) Halls – 4907 and 5970 – and four Shrewsbury (89A) Jubilees – 45572, 45577, 45651 and 45660 – all of which appeared on this short run.

Jubilee, 45577 *Bengal,* acts as station pilot at Shrewsbury station, March 1963. This was one of four Jubilees allocated to Shrewsbury at that time, which worked frequently to Pontypool Road and Cardiff. (*Author*)

4087 *Cardigan Castle* in store at Laira, January 1963. 4087 was rebuilt with new front end frames in 1954, and was equipped with a 4-row superheater boiler and valveless mechanical lubricator, the oil reservoir beside the smokebox, in 1956, and finally, double chimney in February 1958. It was taken out of store in February 1963 and reallocated to St Philip's Marsh in March 1963 for express passenger work between Bristol and Shrewsbury and was withdrawn in October 1963, being broken up at Sharpness. (*Author*)

The 4pm Plymouth – Manchester Mail Train waiting to depart Plymouth North Road, with D1008 *Western Harrier* piloting 1021 *County of Montgomery* over the South Devon banks to Newton Abbot, February 1963. (*Author*)

However, the most regular jaunt, as I said previously, was on the 8.20 Cardiff. It was always interesting to go to the front end of platform 2 at around 8.10-15, to see what had turned out – it was hardly ever the same engine two days running, unlike many of my previous WR commuting runs. In all, I noted runs behind twenty-two Halls, eleven Granges and five Castles, the latter towards the end when suddenly the turn reverted to a Cardiff East Dock loco and Castles 5029, 5043, 5073, 5081 and 5092 appeared several times each. The Halls behind which we did these 'unnecessary' commuter runs were 4919, 4936, 4955, 4956, 4958, 4964, 4988, 4990, 5922, 5934, 5948, 5954, 5984, 6901, 6908, 6912, 6918, 6932, 6936, 6946, 6947, and 6957. There were no Modified Halls allocated to Pontypool Road at that time – or if there were, they never graced that train. The Granges were 6810, 6820, 6826, 6836, 6847, 6850, 6852, 6859, 6867, 6872 and 6876.

More adventurous trips during the latter part of that winter were confined to weekends, or rather Friday evenings or Saturdays, when the odd trip to and from Reading or Peterborough might be squeezed in. We also had an occasional sortie across to the Vale of Neath – perhaps from Pontypool Road over Crumlin Viaduct to Aberdare or, once or twice, through to Neath and back along the main line. The motive power was normally a pannier tank, both 87XX and 94XX varieties, or a 56/66XX 0-6-2T, although Prairie Tank 4169 of Neath was a frequent performer and the rare smaller-wheeled 81XX, 8102, turned up once. On one occasion, Aberdare's 6361 appeared but this was normally confined to freight work.

These longer sorties were in the evening after trips out to Pontypool Road on trains like the 4.40pm Cardiff-Liverpool, which usually had a Cardiff East Dock Castle or Hall, until around the end of March 1963, when something very interesting happened. We'd been steam hauled on the Cardiff-Liverpool to Hereford and were contemplating a routine return behind a Brush Type 4, when it was announced as being very late. It eventually turned up behind 6935 *Browsholme Hall* (Cardiff East Dock - 88A), which was clearly out of steam and was promptly exchanged for the Hereford standby, 5993 *Kirby Hall*. We assumed that the earlier engine itself was a replacement for a diesel failure, but rumour spread that the turn we observed had become one of several North & West expresses that had reverted to steam traction after months of diesel haulage. We watched and saw that the 2pm and 4pm from Plymouth to the North West were both suddenly Castle or County hauled and obviously the return workings were also, one of which was clearly the night train – the 12.45am from Manchester to Plymouth. John and I therefore became more ambitious and began extending our evening runs beyond Pontypool Road to Hereford, and on a couple of occasions through to Shrewsbury and back by the night train.

Further enquiries elicited the news that 4093 had been transferred from South Wales to Bristol St Philips Marsh and had been joined by 4087 from Laira, as well as a couple of extra Counties, to augment engines like 5050, 5071 and 5085 which were already domiciled there. On 2 April John and I made our first deliberate effort to experience the new situation. We connected at Pontypool Road with the 4pm Plymouth-Crewe Postal, which ran in 4 minutes late, with the anticipated St Philips Marsh newly acquired 4093 *Dunster Castle*. The load was eight coaches, 248/260 tons, and the main feature of the run was an energetic and efficient climb of the 1 in 82/95 6 mile bank from Abergavenny to Llanvihangel summit, just below the Sugar Loaf mountain. The steepest part of the climb (1 in 82) was surmounted at 30mph and the summit at 34. Elsewhere we took it very easily. Top speed at Tram Inn was 61mph and the time for the thirty-four switchback and speed restricted miles was just under 51 minutes (47 net).

0-6-2T 5642 takes water at Aberdare on one of the evening jaunts over the 'Heads of the Valley' route enjoyed by John Crowe and the author, March, 1963. (*Author*)

The 4pm Plymouth – Manchester climbs past Abergavenny on Llanvihangel Bank, the Sugar Loaf Mountain ahead, behind 4093 *Dunster Castle*, 2 April 1963. (*Author*)

Three days later I travelled from Bristol to Shrewsbury throughout on the 2pm from Plymouth, which had 1021 *County of Montgomery* (82B) on four coaches and four vans, 257/280 tons, with a fifth coach being added at Pontypool Road, making the gross tonnage 320 tons. Although the train arrived at Pontypool Road early, the shunting made us 3 minutes late away and we dropped 2 minutes further on the 42-minute schedule, with Llanvihangel climbed at 30-33mph and a top speed of 67 mph at Tram Inn. The 2pm Plymouth, being a much lighter train, had a very tight 42-minute booking for the thirty-four difficult miles, compared with 46 minutes for the mail train.

A fortnight later, 19 April, I did a double evening trip to Hereford, initially behind 5092 *Tresco Abbey* (88A) on the 4.40pm Cardiff-Liverpool, six coaches, 208/215 tons. This train stopped at Abergavenny Monmouth Road, at the foot of the steepest part of the climb to Llanvihangel, but we recovered easily enough, accelerating to 32 mph at the summit and running into Hereford nearly 3 minutes early, 45½ minutes for the combined two sections, about 40 minutes net if non-stop. Back to Pontypool Road on a diesel hauled service and then I awaited the 4pm Plymouth, which arrived over half an hour late, with Old Oak Castle, 5014 *Goodrich Castle*, on eight coaches, 248/265 tons. With 29-31mph on the climb and 64 at Tram Inn, 5014 completed the journey in 43 minutes. I then decided to carry on to Shrewsbury and was treated to a very valiant effort from an obviously run-down machine. The 51 miles were completed in exactly the hour (59 minutes net) with a minimum of 50mph at Onibury and 47-48 sustained most of the way to Church Stretton just falling away to 42 at the top. 78mph was then reached round the curves to Dorrington. I stayed overnight in Shrewsbury and came south on the 9.30am Manchester-Swansea, with one of Shrewsbury's Jubilees, 45699 *Galatea*. The load was a very light five coaches, 172/180 tons, although I noted that the engine was working (roaring) hard to Church Stretton at a modest 38mph on the 1 in 90/100. However we were able to take it easily after that and our 64 minute run improved on the schedule by 4 minutes.

A picture comes to mind; R.J.Doran's prize-winning photo in an early 1950s *Trains Illustrated*. I was at a boarding school and I used to await with great expectation the monthly magazine to arrive at the little school shop. This photo was full-page size and captured my imagination completely. It was a snow scene, with a Castle, 5089 *Westminster Abbey*, backlit by the winter sun, nearing the summit of Llanvihangel Bank with a heavy northbound North & West express. At the time I had no idea where Llanvihangel was, but this picture and the exotic name conjured up magic for me and the route is still my favourite and later became a focus for my half days when I was a stationmaster in the Monmouthshire Valleys, whether travelling by train or climbing the Sugar Loaf.

Back to the 23 April 1963, St George's Day, and I set out from Cardiff on the 4.40pm behind a Castle – I can't remember which, but I suspect either 5029 *Nunney Castle* or 5081 *Lockheed Hudson,* both of which were frequent performers on that train through to Shrewsbury. I was aiming for the connection at Pontypool Road with the 2pm Plymouth-Manchester express, one of the two northbound West of

Llanvihangel station with 5089 *Westminster Abbey* climbing the bank in the first prize-winning photo of the *Trains Illustrated* 1953 Photographic Competition. (*R J Doran*)

England-Manchester expresses now diagrammed for steam between Bristol Temple Meads and Shrewsbury. I was looking forward to another Castle or County from the St Philip's Marsh allocation, in particular being keen to get my favourite Castle, 4087, which I knew had been transferred from Laira to Bristol for these services in March.

Imagine the scene; I'm standing at the south end of Pontypool Road station, still an imposing and busy station surrounded by green fields and hills bathed in the early evening spring sunshine, waiting with bated breath to see what will turn up on the 2 o'clock. Should I have stuck to the 4.40pm Cardiff and gone through to Hereford and returned with a diesel to pick up the 4pm Plymouth, an alternative option? I'm used to the revised trains often being a few minutes late, but I've scarcely taken up my position before a Castle appears at an unaccustomed rapid rate between the portals of the overbridge beyond the end of the platform at the summit of the climb from Cwmbran through Llantarnam. And I know immediately that it's 4087 *Cardigan Castle* – I'd know it anywhere. It's as I saw it in January stored at Laira, front numberplate missing, silver painted smokebox hinges, the smokebox mounted mechanical lubricator reservoir very visible, Hawksworth flush-sided tender.

It's a light load, only five coaches, 185 tons gross, but the driver of 4087, although not flogging the engine, is reasonably energetic and we streak out of Pontypool Road down the hill, then brake hard for a 40mph p-way slack at Little Mill. We race up to 64, the brakes go on again for the 50mph permanent restriction at Penpergwm just at the foot of the climb to Llanvihangel, which steepens to 1 in 82/95 after Abergavenny. I'm in the best of moods and as we swing round towards Abergavenny, speed even accelerating slightly after the slowing, I slip into the corridor and gaze out of the window at Blorenge, the hill opposite, and the 1,750ft cone of the Sugar Loaf mountain straight ahead, glowing in the low sun of this April evening. It's a sight that gladdens my heart at the best of times, but this evening, enjoying a run behind my favourite locomotive, all seems right with the world. Abergavenny station passes in a flash and we're on the steepest part of the bank, but the galloping 4087 takes it in its stride, a pleasant steady exhaust as we drop to 41mph then actually accelerate on the 1 in 95, reaching 46 at the summit. I lean out of the window taking it all in, the white exhaust is clearing the coaches and I can feel the warmth of the sun on my face despite the draught from the speeding train.

Now we roll round the curves crossing and recrossing the dappled River Honddu that is joined by the River Monnow after Pandy. The train winds down the river valley, the tree-lined rippling stream ever beside us, first one side, then the other, and the fresh green leaves catch the sunlight, as we freewheel, the driver allowing speed to reach 68mph before reaching for the brake and the 60mph permanent Pontrilas restriction. Over the gradually rising gradients, ranging from 1 in 200 to 1 in 400, the driver opens the regulator again and 4087 accelerates its train to 74mph at Tram Inn, where most trains seem to continue to drift in the low 60s. Unfortunately we're too soon for Hereford and after slowing to 40 at Red Hill Junction, even accelerating again to 60 afterwards, we are brought to a crawl, then a stand at Rotherwas Junction and take 43 minutes 46 seconds to Hereford against the 42 minute schedule, instead of arriving 4 minutes early, which we had threatened to do. I alight at Hereford and go forward to admire the engine and am tempted to go on to Shrewsbury, but I have not bought a ticket and I need to get back, so I enjoy just staring at it in the sun and watching it depart efficiently, surefooted, and on time towards Barrs Court Junction where it curves out of sight … What a memory!

I later commissioned David Charlesworth to paint a water colour picture of 4087 climbing to Llanvihangel from the same vantage point as the Doran photo, but this time in the snow, as this was to be used for a couple of years as a Christmas card of the Railway Children charity.

On the 26 April, I had a run, which outshone all the others, with, of all things, a Shrewsbury based Hall, 6922 *Burton Hall* on six coaches, 208/215 tons. It was on the 4.40pm from Cardiff to Liverpool and I sat up as we set off from Cardiff at an unprecedented rate touching 79mph at Marshfield of all places – this was too much for the Newport signalman who made us stand for a minute outside the Gaer Tunnel. Then we roared up through Cwmbran at a steady 56-52mph, 7 miles of 1 in 106/1 in 95, arriving at Pontypool Road an impossible 9 minutes early. We rocketed round the Penpergwm 50mph curve at 62, braking from 70 at the last moment, before screeching to a halt at Abergavenny, 10 miles in 10min 40sec start to stop. We reached 46 from a standing start at Abergavenny approaching Llanvihangel summit and at last took it easily down the other side, arriving nearly 8 minutes early in Hereford. I have never been so fast from Hereford to Shrewsbury – for my log, see Appendix 1, Table 5. Admittedly it was a light train, but we did it in 58min 45sec with a p-way slowing to walking pace at Ludlow, and dead stands for signals (unsurprisingly) at both Sutton Bridge Junction and Coleham, by Shrewsbury engine shed. And we were still over 9 minutes early in (exactly 50 minutes net – a better than even net time run over this difficult route). Why the driver pushed his engine so hard, I'll never know – perhaps it was his last run before retiring or last steam run before moving to the diesel link. The engine was in excellent condition – ex-works only the month previously – and sounded a treat. Highlights of the Hereford-Shrewsbury section were 62 minimum at Dinmore, 2 miles of 1 in 100, 74 at Woofferton, 62 at Onibury, a couple of miles at 1 in 112, and 57 sustained on the 7 mile climb to Church Stretton, the majority of the climb being also 1 in 112.

After that run it was going to be an anti-climax. I should have returned to Hereford to try the 4pm Plymouth but I went for a meal and greeted 4087, also arriving early on that service at Shrewsbury. I thought it was booked to return on the 12.45am Manchester-Plymouth through to Bristol and I joined it anticipating a run worth timing as 4087 was obviously in good condition and form. I was therefore

6922 *Burton Hall* runs back to shed after its early arrival at Shrewsbury on the 4.40pm Cardiff-Liverpool, 26 April 1963. (*Author*)

desperately disappointed to see a Hall, 4993 *Dalton Hall* (82B), backing on, albeit with a pilot to Church Stretton in 1014 *County of Glamorgan* of Shrewsbury (89A). Someone told me that the depot kept back 4087 for a daytime southbound service to cover one of its own turns, as the night train had an easy schedule, but 4993 laboured after 1014 was released and was late into Bristol, although being very weary, I didn't note by how much. I'm sure now that it was the 2pm Plymouth engine, diagrammed to return south on the night train and the 4pm Plymouth loco took a midday or early afternoon Manchester service the following day.

I had two more goes at the 4pm Plymouth after that on 29 April and 9 May, both with eight coaches, but both were anti-climaxes. 1024 *County of Pembroke* (82B) took a full 49 minutes from Pontypool Road to Hereford unchecked, dropping 3 minutes, with speed falling to 24 at Llanvihangel and only a momentary 62, drifting away to 54 at Tram Inn. 7022 *Hereford Castle* (83D) seemed a better proposition on the second run, but the driver took it even easier, allowing the speed to drop to 22mph on Llanvihangel Bank without appearing to open the regulator more than the first port. Unfortunately, the North & West reverted to diesel haulage in the Summer Timetable and the St Philips Marsh Castles and Counties finished their days on a few Summer Saturday reliefs and diesel standby duties.

Then in June I was drafted to Fishguard Harbour for a month's project planning the car ferry roll on-roll off deck arrangements. This meant that I was unable to ascertain whether the diesels really did return reliably – I returned to Cardiff and got 5050 *Earl of St Germans* (82B) on 6 June, which dropped 3 minutes on the sharp 2pm Plymouth schedule with six coaches, falling to 28 at Llanvihangel and for some unknown reason drifting to 42 at St Devereux; perhaps I missed a 40mph track restriction, but on a couple of later occasions when I checked, both previous steam workings were Class 47 hauled. Apart from a dramatic crossing of the Irish Sea in a Force 8 gale on the St David, the proposed car ferry, to attend a meeting with CIE officials in Wexford, the main excitement was commuting between Fishguard and civilisation, with connections at Clarbeston Road, and always with the same pannier tank, 9602 of Goodwick.

After that it was farewell to the Cardiff Division, until I returned in April 1964 to be appointed to my first permanent post, Stationmaster, Aberbeeg.

Chapter 4

Summer 1963

My training was becoming office based – six months in the Cardiff Divisional Office during the spring and summer and then four months in the Western Region Headquarters offices at Paddington, alongside platform 1. I was now aware that steam was beginning to disappear fast and, one by one, routes were succumbing to diesel traction. Most of the Western Region had already gone. London to Swansea had been dieselised by the end of the previous summer timetable, as had the Wolverhampton route, the Kings were no more and a major cull of Castles had occurred at the end of September 1962. The North & West had resumed full dieselization in June '63 and Castles were now reduced to Summer Saturday reliefs, trains on the Chester line north of Wolverhampton and the Gloucester, Worcester and Hereford areas.

The Midland main line was the territory of the Peaks (Class 45s and 46s), and all the most important West Coast main line trains were in the hands of the English Electric Type 4s (Class 40s). The Deltics had arrived in force and the East Coast route south of Peterborough would be banned to steam after mid-June. I was still footloose – it would be another two years before I began to pay serious attention and time to a particular girl – so it was the opportunity to use my free and privilege tickets to the full and experience as much steam as I could before it all disappeared. I was still in lodgings in Cardiff and had stored up plenty of leave I was due, so – often in company of John Crowe or Alistair Wood – I set about an orgy of travel throughout the length and breadth of the UK.

The previous autumn had seen an influx of Royal Scots, pensioned off from the West Coast Main Line, transferred to run lightweight Great Central semi-fasts from Marylebone to Nottingham and back. They were pretty rundown and most had already had their regimental names removed for safekeeping. They were said to be rough-riding, but occasionally one would have a surprising burst of speed if an enterprising driver felt in the mood, or there was a late departure to recoup. Typically, 46112 *Sherwood Forrester* (that was) appeared on the 5.20pm Nottingham when I joined it at Woodford Halse on 3 November, after a circuitous route from Woking via Basingstoke, on the northbound 'Pines Express' with 34105 *Swanage* to Oxford

(2 minutes early at Oxford without exceeding 58mph!). Then, 5063 *Earl Baldwin* on to Banbury which just about made 61 at Heyford before a 15mph p-way slack at Fritwell, and finally , 7900 *St Peter's Hall* back to Oxford with the eleven-coach York-Bournemouth which recovered all 3 minutes of a late start and touched 70mph at Kidlington. I then took a four coach local back to Banbury with 6827 *Llanfrechfa Grange* of Stourbridge Shed and finally got across to Woodford Halse. 46112 had a paltry load of six nearly empty coaches, 215 tons gross, and kept time touching 73 before the Brackley stop, climbing from Aylesbury to Wendover at 50mph – throwing a lot of fire according to my notes. After a p-way slack to 20mph at Great Missenden we accelerated to pass Amersham at 66mph, but then we got behind a London Transport train and it was stop and start all the way to Neasden.

46101, 46143, 46156 and 46169 all appeared around then and, although looking woebegone, usually gave a few lively snippets between the frequent stops when few passengers got in and even less got out. 46122 *Royal Ulster Rifleman* (still with nameplates) gave me a real hell-raising journey on one trip north on the 2.38pm Marylebone when it rocketed round the curves and reached a full 86mph through Wendover before the Aylesbury stop, throwing coal and sparks in all directions. Heaven knows what had got into the driver that day. We tore through Neasden with our six coaches at 68 and reached our first stop at Harrow-on-the-Hill 4 minutes early! The climb to Amersham was interrupted by two p-way slacks, but after our frantic descent we were still early into Aylesbury. 83 before Brackley, 79 at Culworth and a final 80 on the outskirts of Leicester meant we were early at all stops and 5 minutes early into Leicester. Perhaps the driver was celebrating getting a Scot that was actually in good condition and which must have ridden tolerably well. I'm afraid 46101 on the return 5.15pm Nottingham was an anti-climax. The reign of the Scots on the Marylebone route was short-lived. Their condition was bad and the load was well within the capability of Stanier's Black 5s, and engines like 45222, 45234, 45334 and 45408 were soon the staple fare.

As relief from my main line running, I was given a new task in May, which enabled me to sample freight running in the South Wales valleys. Jack Brennan, now the Divisional Operating Officer at Cardiff, asked me to design and produce graphs for use by Controllers to plan and record the movement of the coal mining trip engines and I persuaded myself (and Jack Brennan) that I needed a few brakevan trips to check I'd got it right. So I spent the best part of a month riding up the Rhondda, Tredegar and Western Valleys behind Churchward 2-8-0 and 2-8-2 tanks (4294, 5200, 7221 among others and throw in the odd 9F), did an Alexandra Dock Junction-Llanwern ore train both ways with 4283 at one end and 5244 at the other and even convinced myself that runs on the main line from Margam-Severn Tunnel, and Newport to Hereford behind Collett 2-8-0s 3801, 3812, 3818 and 3839 were essential. Jack Brennan liked the end result but did mutter that he thought I'd taken an unnecessarily long time! In addition I was now able to finish early enough on a Friday afternoon to catch the 4.25pm to Salisbury regularly and I note I had 4933, 4991, 4992 (twice), 4993 (three times), and 6944 *Fledborough Hall* (four times).

In May, I'd had another training interview with Lance Ibbotson. I was prepared this time. I'd been advised to take the initiative and not let him bully me, so I launched into an account of the project I'd been set by Jack Brennan. Ibbotson, a former North Eastern man, was delighted and said that I must see the way Control staff worked with graphs in the Durham coalfield, so I was despatched at his command to spend a week in Middlesbrough and Tees Yard amid Q6s and J27s. At the end of the week, I decided to explore Scotland as I was over halfway there, so I boarded a Friday evening relief train (1.45pm from King's Cross) to Edinburgh from Darlington, headed by that over-endowed named V2, 60809 *The Snapper, The East Yorkshire Regiment, The Duke of York's Own*. After a noisy but slow run to Newcastle, it was replaced by a Gateshead A1, 60150 *Willbrook,* which performed efficiently enough, despite a special stop for water at Drem, to arrive more or less on time in Waverley.

My real reason for going north, however, was that the following day was 1 June and I had a ticket for the rail tour from Glasgow Queen Street to Mallaig, advertised behind the preserved D34, *Glen Douglas*. Early morning at Queen Street and 62469 masquerading as North British 256 was there piloting J37 64632. We set off with gusto in the mid-50s through the north Clyde suburbs and the day dawned clear as we rounded the sides of the Gareloch and Loch Lomond. As we forged further north, we experienced a rarity, a day of total cloudless sunshine, accompanied by absolute clarity so that mountain peaks could be seen from miles away. The exhilaration lasted for a while, and then, somewhere around Gorton, we ground to a halt while people were seen to be examining the bearings of the J37. The 0-6-0 was detached with a hot box and the Glen struggled on to the open moorland at Corrour when we stopped again, this time for over 2 hours. Apparently the Glen's brick arch had collapsed and we were allowed to disembark and sunbathe and eat our sandwiches on the heatherclad Rannoch Moor, while a Type 2 D61XX was summoned from Fort William to help us complete that leg of the journey.

Now nearly 3 hours late, we dragged ourselves into Fort William in the middle of the afternoon and two further J37s backed down, 64592 and 64636. When we eventually arrived at Mallaig, still in brilliant sunshine, at teatime, it was found that 64592 had also developed a hot box and only 64636 of all our specially prepared engines was still fit. To our disappointment, but inevitably, D5351 was found to take us all the way back to Glasgow – the long summer evening, enabling us to appreciate the staggering scenery being the only consolation. Arrival at Queen Street was well after midnight; I couldn't find a hotel that was open at a price I could afford so I eventually tucked up on the cushions of stock standing in Glasgow Central, ready for the first southbound Sunday train, D2XX hauled.

The previous autumn, I'd resumed my occasional trips to Peterborough and back as the end of steam out of King's Cross was drawing ever nearer. I didn't really have much time to spare, but when I had a quick look at the end of platform 8, I couldn't resist 60021 *Wild Swan* at the head of the 4.05pm to Newcastle. I had a good run in 73 minutes net for the 76 miles, with a top speed of 88mph at Arlesey. We arrived 2 minutes early at Peterborough, and as soon as I had crossed to the Up platform, lo and behold, another A4 was wending its way in, with the *West Riding* from Leeds,

Two J37s, 64592 and 64636 doublehead the *Jacobite* special train on the Fort William-Mallaig section at Arisaig, 1 June 1963. (*Author*)

next stop King's Cross. 60022 *Mallard*; I couldn't believe it! Two new Top Shed A4s in the last year before nemesis! 60022 had an eleven-coach load, 405 tons gross, leaving Peterborough just a minute late. We showed our intention by accelerating across the Yaxley marshy area to 68 at Holme, falling to 56 at Leys summit and passing Huntingdon at 80mph. After slowing to 70 for the Offord curve, we were up to 80 again by Biggleswade and then it was all plain sailing, coasting down into King's Cross in 78 minutes from Peterborough, nearly 4 minutes early. The last day for steam at the Southern end of the ECML was to be 15 June 1963. I'd have to try one more time.

However, I'd been in Scotland the previous week with Alistair Wood, experiencing for the first time the accelerated Glasgow-Aberdeen services, the 3-hour schedules worked by Gresley pacifics newly transferred to Glasgow St Rollox and Aberdeen Ferryhill. 60094 *Colorado* had been my first and very successful shot at this, returning to Stirling with a Ferryhill V2 that I saw a lot of over the next couple of years – 60955.

My intention had been to pick up the evening 3 hour *St Mungo* and I was disappointed to see the train running in with Caprotti Standard 5, 73152, instead of the A4 that had worked the balancing morning service from Aberdeen (60011). I need not have worried. The noise from that locomotive as we held a steady 82mph between Perth and Forfar was staggering and we kept the difficult schedule with our substitute engine (Appendix 1, Table 10). The 7.10am *Bon Accord* from Aberdeen the next morning, 14 June, was powered by 60009 *Union of South Africa*, which I took as far as Stirling before returning to Perth on a Dundee train behind 60090 *Grand Parade*, changing there to a semi-fast behind Black 5 44960 of Perth through to Aberdeen, eventually returning with A2/3 60524 *Herringbone* on the Postal. For more logs on the 3-hour Glasgow-Aberdeen trains, see Appendix 1, Table10.

Kingmoor Duchess 46244 *King George VI* at Perth on the 8.15pm Stirling-Kensington Olympia sleeper, 20 June 1963. (*Author*)

to keep my head in as blocks of coal tumbled from the overfilled tender which was jagging around as we tore round curves at a somewhat liberal interpretation of speed restrictions.

After Preston, life became even more spectacular as we flattened Grayrigg, made a dramatic dash through the Lune gorge, soaking most of the train from the overflow from Dillicar troughs, and assaulted Shap, never falling below 60mph. Not content with this, the driver kept steam on after the summit and only eased when tearing through Southwaite at 94mph, still hurling coal, spray and smoke over the diminutive train. When we arrived at Carlisle, having recovered all but 1 minute, all became clear as the driver and fireman leapt from the footplate and raced across the track to the main Up platform where a London express was being whistled away. The guard told me that if the crew had missed it, they'd have had a 2-hour wait. And I thought they were just enjoying themselves! (See Appendix 1, Table 7). We changed our Pacific for 73121 at Carlisle and proceeded northwards in a more demure fashion, reaching Glasgow Central on time.

Next morning, I turned up in anticipation of a Pacific on the 8.25am to Aberdeen, only to find Type 2 diesel D6123, which had been experimentally re-engined and was on trial on the 3-hour service. Hiding my disappointment, I let it go and found the rostered St Rollox A4, 60027 *Merlin,* allocated to the 9.15 to Dundee instead. Despite a heavier load of ten coaches after Stirling, compared with the normal seven on the Aberdeen train, we virtually matched the faster schedule from Stirling up through Dunblane (minimum of 47mph) and arrived in Dundee on time. I continued to Aberdeen on a D3XX hauled express from Edinburgh Waverley and took lunch in the restaurant car next to an African gentleman whom I later discovered was the Prime Minister of Uganda, Milton Obote – he became President in 1966 until he was deposed by Idi Amin. I was in time to catch the Postal, the 3.30pm Aberdeen, which

46235 *City of Birmingham* passes Stirling with a fish train for London, August 1963. (*Author*)

had a different Ferryhill V2 for once, 60970, which dropped 5 minutes unchecked to Perth on a very tight schedule. I returned from Carlisle to Euston on the sleeper and got 46235 again.

I had one last journey north before the end of the summer timetable and my Paddington HQ training began. I started from Euston on the heavy relief sleeper, the 6.40pm Euston-Inverness, which had 46150 *The Life Guardsman* of Longsight on thirteen coaches, 515 tons gross. We staggered up Camden bank, fell from 45 through Willesden to 32mph at Harrow and stopped at Watford to top up the water supply. 43mph at Tring was followed by speed wavering between 45 and 60 all the way to Rugby – 142 minutes for the 82 miles – and expired there with a hot box of all things! The replacement was Rugby Black 5, 44862, which fared no better and that was eventually itself replaced, well after midnight, by Britannia 70051 *Firth of Forth* at Crewe, which at last demonstrated some respectable energy and speed. I awoke after Carlisle to find rebuilt Patriot 45535 *Sir Herbert Walker KCB* now in charge with the sun already well up.

I was able to pick up the seven-coach 8.25 Glasgow *Grampian* from Perth with St Rollox A3 60090 *Grand Parade*, which did the 32 miles to Forfar in just over 31 minutes, with 81 at Alyth Junction. Station overtime at Forfar made us 5 minutes later away, but 80 at Glasterlaw, 63 minimum at Kinnaber Junction, 59 minimum on the 1 in 105 to Laurencekirk and 65 on the 5 miles of 1 in 170/141 to Drumlithie got us on time by Stonehaven, and, with a recovery margin approaching Aberdeen, we arrived 3 minutes early. The 12.30 Saturdays Only Aberdeen to Edinburgh Waverley had Norman McKillop's (alias 'Toram Begs') famous A3 60100 *Spearmint* of St Margaret's which ran punctually to Dundee. All this activity north of the border whetted my appetite for more, and I went back to enjoy the Glasgow-Aberdeen trains for two more years as other routes tumbled to the diesels and all the LM pacifics were withdrawn and somewhat inadequately replaced by the homing Britannias massing at Kingmoor and Crewe.

During all this gallivanting around the north I had not forgotten my native Western Region, though good steam runs were becoming harder to find. I discovered that the heavy 9.45am Paddington to Weston-Super-Mare on a summer Saturday was normally an Old Oak Castle turn, and on 20 July I had 7029 *Clun Castle* and four weeks later it was 7010 *Avondale Castle*. 7029 had fourteen coaches, 530 tons gross, and sustained 65-70 on the level to Swindon, and touched 76 at Dauntsey, 77 at Box and arrived at Bristol just 2 minutes late, after signals all the way in from St Anne's Park. 7010 with one coach less, but still 500 tons gross, did even better, with 72 at Iver, 85 at Dauntsey and arrived at Bristol a minute early. On the first excursion, I travelled on to Hereford with 7034 *Ince Castle* which was in very poor condition and needed a banker from Abergavenny to Llanvihangel, amply provided by 2-8-2T, 7206. On the second outing I took a Grange, 6829 *Burmington Grange* (86G), from Bristol on an Ilfracombe-Manchester Exchange train of twelve coaches, 430 tons gross, which left Temple Meads 4 minutes late, fell to 20 on Filton Bank, was held at the portal on the east side of the Severn Tunnel for 15 long minutes, then touched 65 in the tunnel and emerged at 33mph at the top of the climb and sustained 36 on the steep bank through Llantarnam Junction to Pontypool Road which was excellent, but we were 23 minutes late by then.

I alighted to see what else was going north and the next train was a badly overloaded Black 5, 45403 of Chester, on thirteen coaches, 455 tons gross with the 8am Newquay-Manchester. It left Pontypool Road 21 minutes late and slogged up the 1 in 82/1 in 95 from Abergavenny below the Sugar Loaf mountain at a painful 15mph on the steepest bit, recovering to 18 at the summit and then ran downhill freely at 70, reaching Hereford in 47 minutes and gaining 8 minutes on the easy Saturday schedule. I alighted again at Hereford to try my luck once more and this time got an ex-works Scot, 46152 *The King's Dragoon Guardsman* of Holyhead, on the 10.45am Kingswear-Manchester, with a lighter ten-coach load, 335 tons gross. The driver took it pretty easily and without any excitement, just one p-way slack and a 3 minute wait outside Shrewsbury waiting a platform; we took just over 73 minutes for the 51 miles, picking up just a minute and a half of our 10 minute late start.

I had stretched my time chasing steam to the limit that summer. It was now time to buckle down and do some work. Until, of course, I found that Paddington-Worcester trains were still steam that autumn, running under my nose from platform 1 at Paddington.

Chapter 5

Living on the Southern

the last years of steam, 1963-1967

The end of 1962 had seen the demise of the last Maunsell passenger locomotives. The two last Nelsons (*Lord Anson* and *Lord Collingwood*) went at the end of the summer timetable, along with N15s *Sir Gareth* and *Sir Brian*, although 30770 *Sir Prianius* lingered on until the end of the year. Fifteen Schools were still active in December, but suddenly became victims of the accountant's edict and all were withdrawn at the end of the financial year, notified in January 1963. And so we were left with the BR Standard 4s and 5s and Bulleid Pacifics, most rebuilt, but with a diminishing number of un-rebuilt light Pacifics – already 34011, 34035, 34043, 34049, 34055, 34067, 34068, 34069, 34074 and 34110 had gone by the end of 1963. These included the one Bulleid Pacific that 'escaped' from my clutches (34035), a couple of regulars from my university commuting days (Salisbury's 34049 and 34055) and 34067 *Tangmere*, now miraculously restored and behind which I celebrated a birthday during the seventy-fifth Golden Arrow Anniversary tour. The 'Merchant Navies' had long since been rebuilt and I'd now had runs behind all of them, amassing over 400 runs, mainly in their new conventional form.

Waterloo had changed too. The M7s were long gone, initially replaced by WR pannier tanks, led experimentally by 9770, and followed after the successful trial by a batch of the 46XX series. Then BR standard tanks displaced from duties by closures and DMUs began to infiltrate the Waterloo-Clapham ECS duties, the type 4 2-6-4Ts and particularly the 820XX type 3s from the Exeter area.

The variety had suddenly disappeared on my journeys home from far-flung Western territories. After my first year as a Western Region Traffic Apprentice, I was sent to undergo training in the Swansea District and Cardiff Division and most of my free time was spent exploring West Wales and the Valleys, still alive with a host of GW engines, large and small. If I returned home via London, a Maunsell S15 from Feltham depot might occasionally grace a Basingstoke local, especially on a Summer Saturday – most lasted until 1964 and 30838 and 30839 survived until the Autumn of 1965. Even half a dozen Urie S15s lasted into 1964. Mostly I caught a Friday teatime departure from Cardiff, with a Canton Hall as far as Salisbury, connecting with the last Up Exeter as far as Woking. This was invariably a 72A Merchant Navy.

35011 *General Steam Navigation* just ex-works after rebuilding leaves Woking with the 3.54pm Clapham Junction – West of England milk empties, July 1959. (*Author*)

Standard 3 2-6-2T 82018 displaced from the East Devon branch services waits for its next ECS duty while 34089 *602 Squadron* backs out of Waterloo station, 1966. (*Author*)

However, during my 1963 frenetic dashing around the British Isles endeavouring to sample main line steam runs before it was too late, I had, on the whole avoided the Southern Region, partly because I still used it to get to London from my home and partly because there seemed to be prospects of steam remaining longer there than on the other regions. Some interesting rumours were being flung about; that Stanier Duchesses would come to replace the Bulleids on the Bournemouth route, though apparently the curves in Northam Tunnel outside Southampton put paid to that idea, and that some of the Hawksworth Modified Halls would replace the King Arthurs and light pacifics at Salisbury on the Salisbury-Waterloo semi-fasts (even the 70XX series Castles got a mention) on account of their assumed better acceleration and sure-footedness on stopping services, though if this was serious, the curves at Clapham Junction and the width across cylinders of the GW 4-6-0s made that impracticable. And how the innate conservatism of drivers would have viewed that after their Bulleids was another unknown, although I suspect it would not have gone down well. There were some ex-GW drivers, of course, at both Basingstoke and Salisbury who might have relished this; one Basingstoke driver certainly told me that he'd like to try a Hall on the 5.09pm Waterloo!

However, Alistair Wood, whose home territory was the Stirling-Perth main line, persuaded me to join him on a trip on the *Atlantic Coast Express* before the WR got their hands on it and Warships replaced the Merchant Navies. So on 10 June 1963, I joined him at Waterloo to see 35029 *Ellerman Lines* (70A) – now sectioned in the NRM at York – backing on to thirteen coaches, 435 tons tare, 465 gross, sticking out beyond the signal at the end of platform 10. There was a 20mph p-way restriction through the Clapham Junction platforms but after that we got going well, with 74mph by Hampton Court Junction, 64 minimum at MP 31, 75 at Fleet, 86 at Andover Junction, arriving at Salisbury in 15 seconds under the scheduled 80 minutes. We were overtime at Salisbury taking water and left 4 minutes late, but 66 minimum at Semley with this load was good, followed by a p-way check to 24mph, then maxima of 83 at Gillingham, 87 before Templecombe, 88 at Sherborne and 86 at Seaton Junction before the climb to Honiton were excellent. We climbed Honiton bank at a minimum of 39mph, recovering to 41 at the entrance to the summit tunnel and were only 1 minute late at Sidmouth Junction, where we detached two coaches. Overtime doing this and signal checks in from Exmouth Junction, despite 88 at Broad Clyst, made our arrival in Exeter a disappointing 5 minutes late. Alistair and I went through to Padstow behind 34020 *Seaton* (72A) and a gradually diminishing train – six coaches to Oakhampton, three onto Halwill Junction, and finally just two coaches to Padstow.

We stayed in the seaside town overnight and somehow got ourselves to Ilfracombe the next morning via the Torrington branch, about which I can remember little except the gorgeous array of purple Rhododendrons in the surrounding woods. 34072 *257 Squadron* (72A) ran the 8.10am Salisbury under easy steam from Barnstaple Junction round to Ilfracombe – 17½mph at Mortehoe summit with four coaches was too easy! The 2.20pm Ilfracombe to Waterloo was a five coach train behind 34011 *Tavistock* (72A) shortly before its withdrawal, which struggled to 14½mph on

35029 *Ellerman Lines* of Nine Elms climbing Honiton Bank with the 11am Waterloo *Atlantic Coast Express*, on 12 June 1964, roughly a year after the author travelled on this train behind the same locomotive. (*MLS Collection*)

the initial 1 in 36, then recovered to 27 at the summit at Mortehoe and ran easily enough to arrive at Exeter Central without needing a banker from St David's – 18mph on the grade there. Leaving Exeter at 4.30pm on time, now eleven coaches, 385 tons gross, behind rebuilt Battle of Britain 34071 *601 Squadron* (70A), we fell to 28 on the eastbound climb to Honiton tunnel, coasted down the other side and, with just a 30mph p-way slack at Axminster, dropped 6 minutes to the Yeovil Junction stop, with nothing over 72mph. We dropped another minute on to Templecombe, were 4 minutes overtime waiting a connection, fell to 40 at Semley and only 72 at Dinton, thus 9 minutes late into Salisbury. We were a further 5 minutes overtime there, but then began to regain time on an absurdly easy schedule, until we arrived at Woking just 5 minutes late, where I alighted. But it had been a pretty dismal performance throughout, only the last leg from Basingstoke to Woking receiving any vigour, when we covered the 24 miles in 23 minutes, 20 seconds start to stop with a maximum of 76mph at Fleet.

Six months later with the transfer of the Salisbury-Exeter and North Devon lines to the Western Region imminent, I decided to try the 'ACE' again, this time on my own. 35020 *Bibby Line* (70A) had twelve coaches, 455 tons gross, and we took 82½ minutes to Salisbury with one severe p-way slowing to 15mph at Walton-on-Thames. Running was steady rather than brilliant, although we did dash down Porton bank at 87mph, leaving it to the last minute to brake for the Salisbury tunnel and curve, but we'd left it too late for a punctual arrival. The new driver took things too easily and leaving Salisbury 5 minutes late – more station overtime – we dropped 8 minutes on schedule to Sidmouth Junction with just one p-way slack at Axminster, although the climb to Honiton at 36mph was belatedly energetic. We took the full train through, so regained 4 minutes at Sidmouth Junction and were 10 minutes late into Exeter Central. I returned on the 4.30pm Exeter the same day, this time with rebuilt light pacific 34108 *Wincanton* (72A), with a full load of thirteen coaches, 475 tons gross, which performed very creditably to Yeovil Junction with 38 minimum at Honiton and 82 at Seaton Junction, 80 at Crewkerne, arriving at Yeovil Junction in 53 minutes from Exeter, a minute early. Then I fell asleep!

A month later, just before Christmas, I was tempted to run down to Bournemouth on the 10.30am Waterloo, as a colleague I'd met a few times in my travels had a footplate pass for a local newspaper article he was writing. 35014 *Nederland Line* (70A) was the motive power for twelve coaches, 450 tons gross, but the run was a disappointment to both of us, as the Merchant Navy, unusually, was shy for steam and with a p-way slack to 25mph at West Byfleet and signals to walking pace at Winchester, we dropped 10 minutes to Southampton, where my colleague alighted. We lost another couple of minutes to Bournemouth and I hoped for a better run for the journalist on the return with 35012 *United States Lines* (70A) as he was joining at Southampton. It was not to be; the Southern was having an off day. Many have the impression that the last few years of Southern steam on the Bournemouth line were a riot of extraordinary performances. I regret this was not so. They had their share of failures and struggles as the condition of the locomotives deteriorated, the London depots found it hard to retain expert steam fitting staff and BR management had its eyes on the new traction and accelerated schedules elsewhere rather than lines in the throes of being electrified.

In March 1964 I was due to finish my training with a spell as an acting relief stationmaster and I was appointed for six weeks to Gillingham station in Dorset. Although this chapter is about steam on the Southern Region and the Salisbury-Exeter line had been transferred to the Western Region in January 1964, frankly there was little at that stage to indicate the new ownership. After my day turn of duty was over, I often took the opportunity to ride the evening Salisbury-Exeter expresses, sometimes just to Yeovil and back, sometimes through to Exeter, and always had brisk and sometimes exhilarating performances. Often there was time to be made up from heavy delays experienced the London side of Salisbury – for instance, on 5 March, 35025 on the 325 tonnes 6 o'clock from Waterloo regained 8 minutes of a 23 minute late start just between Axminster and Exeter with a minimum of 42½mph on Honiton bank and 87mph at Broad Clyst. 35003 *Royal Mail*, with eight coaches on the 7 o'clock Waterloo regained 10 minutes from Salisbury to Exeter, starting 30 minutes late, touching 90mph at Gillingham and Sherborne and sustaining 49mph on Honiton bank. 35009 *Shaw Savill* with the same load left Salisbury 8 minutes late and arrived at Exeter 3 minutes early with a minimum of 69 at Semley, 88 at Gillingham, 89 at Sherborne and 45 on Honiton bank.

I travelled back to Gillingham one evening from a day off, going from Woking to London to join the 7 o'clock Waterloo, which I took through to Yeovil Junction. Our loco was, unusually, an un-rebuilt light Pacific, 34086 *219 Squadron*, with a heavy load of eleven coaches, 410 tonnes gross. Despite signal checks at Wimbledon, Esher, and Woking and a complete dead stand at Weybridge and a p-way slowing to 25mph at Hook, we were only one and a half minutes late into Yeovil. Highlights were acceleration from the Woking check (55mph) to 67½mph at milepost 31 summit, 85 on the level at Fleet, 69mph at Worting Junction after the Hook pws and a full 90mph at Hurstbourne (Appendix 1, Table 1).

Later, in 1964, when I was undertaking my first permanent job with on call responsibility (Stationmaster Aberbeeg), I found I could not get away early for my alternate weekends off, so I had a few runs on the Saturday morning 9.10am Llanelli-Cardiff-Dorchester-Brockenhurst seasonal train from Newport, with a Llanelli (87F) Grange to Westbury, a Weymouth Standard 5 to Dorchester Junction (banked on each occasion by 'U' 31802 to Evershot) and a West Country on to Brockenhurst. On one of these trips the last leg was hauled by the sole Giesl ejector-fitted Bulleid, 34064 *Fighter Command*, which performed in a very lively fashion, with 77mph at Moreton, 60 minimum up to Worgret Junction and acceleration of the ten-coach, 345 tonne gross train to 42mph up Parkstone Bank to Branksome before the Bournemouth stop. Our arrival, for a Summer Saturday Cross-Country train, was surprisingly on time. I had a couple of other journeys between Woking and Waterloo behind 34064 in this condition and it was a strong engine, with the added advantage that the Giesl ejector seemed to lift the exhaust more effectively than the usual exhaust and smoke deflector arrangements.

In 1965 I moved on to Bridgend on the Cardiff-Swansea main line and, in a larger organisation, found it a little easier to get home with time to spare for runs to London or Basingstoke and occasionally further afield to Southampton or Bournemouth. By this time, the WR management had turned their attention to the West of England main line they had inherited and Warships had taken over from the Bulleids. WR General Manager, Lance Ibbotson, was busy cooking up the singling schemes that would create so many problems west of Salisbury in following years. The pacifics in good order were redistributed to Nine Elms, Bournemouth and Weymouth sheds and my West of England favourites like 35003, 35008 and 35013 started appearing regularly on the Bournemouth route. During 1965 and the early part of 1966 the engines seemed better maintained and performance was good, if nothing exceptional. In the late Summer of 1964 I'd acquired a taste for trips on the Bournemouth Belle and two up runs behind 35022 *Holland Amerika Line* (a former 72A engine then at Nine Elms) and 35016 *Elders Fyffes* are shown in Appendix 1, Table 2, along with a later 1967 run, just before class 47s took over for a few months, with a filthy 34098 *Templecombe* which was driven flat out to achieve 88mph on the level at Fleet and arrive 7 minutes early into Waterloo. Both the Merchant Navy runs were punctual and very competent, with climbs to Roundwood with 515 tonnes gross in the mid-50s and speed sustained in the mid-80s from Basingstoke – 35016 just topping 90mph at Brookwood.

The un-rebuilt Pacifics were by now disappearing fast and the remaining ones in reasonable condition became the target for my occasional trips to and from London – 34002, 34006, 34019, 34023, 34041, 34057 and 34102 in particular. They were sometimes to be found on my former commuter trains – the 6.45am Salisbury and the 6.04am Southampton Terminus – and I recorded runs with 34002 on the Salisbury and 34102 on the Southampton, both ruined by constant signal checks. However, 34019 *Bideford* and 34041 *Wilton* on the eleven-coach Southampton train both showed it could still be done and I have shown their logs in Appendix 1, Table 3, along with a snippet from a total surprise, 77014 of Guildford on the 06.39am Basingstoke, which

35022 *Holland-America Line* at Beaulieu Road with the Up *Bournemouth Belle* on 25 July 1964, exactly two weeks before the author logged the same locomotive on this train [see Appendix 1, Table 2]. (*MLS Collection*)

I recorded for curiosity's sake. The run behind *Bideford* was memorable for another reason – it was the last Up train through Clapham before the signalbox straddling the line on a gantry on the Waterloo side of the station collapsed causing total chaos for a few days.

Whilst wandering in the West Country in March 1966 – I can't remember quite why I was there – I came across the LCGB rail tour on the S&D at Evercreech Junction behind double-headed 34006 and 34057 and scrounged a lift to Bath Green Park, although an unscheduled photographic stop at Chilcompton made us 11 minutes late at our destination. 34006 *Bude*, with its unique double length smoke deflectors (34004 and 34005 were similarly equipped before rebuilding) turned up the following day at Woking as I was returning to South Wales and I have added its run with the twelve-coach Bournemouth train, which ran via the Portsmouth direct line this Sunday, to my runs in Table 3.

A few weeks before, I had enjoyed a splendid run with 34057 *Biggin Hill* up from Bournemouth after going down on the 10.30 Waterloo, and an excellent run with 35007 *Aberdeen Commonwealth*. Although 34057's train was only seven coaches, 69mph at Roundwood summit after a standing start from Winchester was exceptional and 82mph after the Woking stop near Walton was also good.

We now come to the last year of steam working when the remaining locomotives were beginning to look bedraggled, filthy and were increasingly minus nameplates, but in contrast, performance grew more spectacular as enthusiastic crews had their last runs on steam traction and some decided to bow out with flags flying.

It did not always work of course, because some of the locos were very rundown and poor steaming or rough riding could spoil the driver's intentions. 34004 and 34093 were said to be very rough and I had a couple of poor steaming runs with 35014, although my previous experience of this loco – with the one exception mentioned earlier – had been good. There are plenty of reports that 100mph was reached by a number of locos in those last few weeks, but although I put in an

34006 *Bude*, one of the dozen remaining unrebuilt light Pacifics in the last year of Southern steam, at Bournemouth Central, 1967. 34006 [with 34004 and 34005, both subsequently rebuilt] had double-length smoke deflectors. (*Author*)

35007 *Aberdeen Commonwealth* slips furiously on starting the 2.34pm Bournemouth Central – Waterloo at Bournemouth, June 1967. (*Author*)

35013 *Blue Funnel*, minus front smokebox numberplate and nameplates as so many Southern locomotives in the last months of steam, on arrival at Weymouth with the 10.30am Waterloo, June 1967. (*Author*)

intensive spell of logging at the time, one 97 and two 95s were the best I managed to record. Driver Hendicott's last steam run on 23 June 1967 was a typical last fling – he had a rundown rebuilt Battle of Britain, 34060 *25 Squadron* of Eastleigh depot, with a light seven-coach, 250 ton load on the evening 6.15pm Weymouth – Waterloo. After stops at Southampton Airport, Eastleigh, Winchester and a p-way slack to 15mph before Wallers Ash, he let fly and we stormed over Roundwood summit at an astonishing 79mph! After the Basingstoke stop, he went for it again and roared through Fleet sparks soaring to the firmament at 95mph. The 24 miles from Basingstoke to Woking were accomplished in 22 minutes inclusive of a p-way slack to 60mph at MP 31 and a signal check to 30mph on the approach to Woking Junction.

35008 *Orient Line* was one of the Merchant Navies in the best condition at the end and performed some of the 'last rites'. I had a couple of superb runs with it on Bournemouth expresses. The highlight of a run on the 8.30am Waterloo-Weymouth on 5 July 1967 was taking eleven coaches, 400 tonnes gross, over the rise to MP 31 at a full 72mph, although signals ruined the run from Basingstoke onwards. I'd had 35008 a few days before (2 July) on the twelve-coach, 425 ton 11.17 Weymouth-Waterloo from Bournemouth which converted an 11 minute late departure from there into a 2 minute late arrival in Southampton with a fall in speed from 71mph to only 65 up Hinton Admiral bank and running in the high 70s through the New Forest. Again, from Southampton onwards we were plagued by signal checks, but showed bursts of power between these – 0* - 55 Winchester-Wallers Ash, 0* - 46 Micheldever-Roundwood, 10* - 85 Basingsoke-Hook, 15* - 82 Brookwood-Weybridge. Despite six heavy signal checks, one dead stand and two p-way slacks to 15mph, our arrival at Waterloo was only 6 minutes late.

I have left my two *tours de force* until last. On 9 June 1967, 35013 *Blue Funnel* had eleven coaches on the 11.17 Weymouth, 400 tons, and left Bournemouth 4 minutes late but still arrived on time at Southampton Central. After a fairly normal climb to Roundwood, interrupted by an awkward p-way slack at Winchester Junction and a signal check approaching Worting Junction, Driver Saunders of Nine Elms piled on the speed, culminating with 93 at Winchfield and 97mph at Fleet. After another p-way slack at Brookwood, the high speed was resumed with the upper 80s around Weybridge building up to 90mph at Esher and a full 92mph as we screamed through the Up Fast platform at Surbiton scaring dogs and little children alike. Despite a signal stand at Raynes Park, we arrived 5 minutes early in a net time of 76 minutes from Southampton.

The other run, back in February, was even more unexpected. The 2.34pm from Bournemouth had a filthy rebuilt West Country 34044 *Woolacombe* at the head of eleven coaches, 400 tonnes gross, but was driven by Driver Hooper of Nine Elms with Inspector Smith on the footplate acting as second fireman! I can only assume it was driven flat out. We sustained 66mph on Hinton Admiral Bank but a signal stand at Totton made us 8 minutes late away from Southampton. We then recovered from a 15mph slack at Winchester Junction to clear Roundwood summit at 68mph and continued in great style, unwinded, to achieve 95mph on the level at Fleet and ran into Waterloo nearly 2 minutes early in seventy-two and a half minutes net for the 79 miles. Both logs are given in Appendix 1, Table 4.

I had an evening run to Southampton and back on the last Friday, 7 July, my farewell, but it was a bit of an anti-climax. The 5.23pm (FO) Waterloo-Bournemouth had the very run-down 34093 *Saunton* to haul its twelve-coach, 420 ton train and it was so uninspiring, taking 84 minutes to get to the Winchester stop, with just one signal check outside the station, that I gave up timing it after that. I returned on the 5.30pm Weymouth-Waterloo from Southampton, which sported a better-groomed 34013 *Okehampton* and this performed very respectably, with its eleven-coach 400 ton train, with 56mph at Roundwood, 83 at Fleet and 86 at Byfleet and sailed into Waterloo unchecked, 11 minutes early!

Living on the Southern now meant a choice between VEP units or D800s on the West of Englands. I was by now Divisional Train Planning Officer at Cardiff, which filled my time more than adequately. I was courting a girl in Ealing, which meant frequent day trips to Paddington behind Western D10XX diesel hydraulics and I turned my interest to the last years of main line steam in France, the German Federal Republic and finally the German Democratic Republic, although these excursions became less frequent as I gained both family and increasing work responsibilities. Occasionally I allowed myself the luxury of a bit of nostalgia – 30777 and 30850 on the Settle and Carlisle in the early 1980s and a footplate run on 35028 between Banbury and Marylebone in 1985 (see Chapter 15) when, as Chief Operating Manager, LMR, I could claim to be undertaking my annual audit of the safety of steam specials! And finally, in May 2004, the Golden Arrow seventy-fifth Anniversary with 34067 *Tangmere*, although I have to admit the draw was really the sewing-machine running of the PLM SNCF Pacific 231K 8 between Calais and Paris!

Chapter 6

Special trains, 1963-1968

After the elimination of steam traction from British Rail's metals in 1968, I began to explore the remaining outposts of steam in Europe's railways and – after the successful trial of 6000 on the North & West at the behest of Peter Prior of Bulmer's – to join some of the many enthusiast specials that developed during the 1970s and became firm fixtures from the 1980s onwards. However, whilst most of my energies had been spent exploring BR steam traction on scheduled services up to 1968, I had participated in a few specials from 1959 onwards, most of the early ones being arranged by the Ian Allan organisation.

The first one I participated in was back in May 1959 on a special train named *The Potteries Express*, which I described in *A Privileged Journey*. One more Ian Allan special, *The Severn and Wessex Express*, followed in 1960, and then there was a gap until the *Jacobite*, which I described in a previous chapter. Then in May 1964, I took part in the celebrated swansong of the Castles, when Gerry Fiennes authorised an attempt on the 100mph barrier on the Paddington-Plymouth-Bristol-Paddington triangle. The facts of this excursion are well known, with 4079 having to come off at Westbury as the firebars melted just as we were hitting the upper 90s in the descent from Lavington; the replacement, 6999 *Capel Dewi Hall,* distinguishing itself across Athelney marshes by reaching the upper 80s, before 7025 relieved it at Taunton; 7029 *Clun Castle* established its reputation with the record breaking leg from Plymouth to Bristol; and 5054 *Earl of Ducie* having a go on the Bristolian leg, achieving a 95 minute run to the capital without quite making the magic 'ton'. It was an emotional roller coaster of a day, with the exhilaration of the early part of the run behind the venerable *Pendennis Castle* being dashed by the emergency stop at Westbury, amazement at the Hall's exploit and the sheer thrill of listening to 7029's machinegun exhaust as we raced across the Somerset flats through Bridgwater.

It is well known that a number of Castles were put through their paces on the 9.15am Paddington-Worcester and Hereford, to see what speed they could achieve down Honeybourne Bank under the eye of an inspector, in order to select the locos for the specials. On the 26 October 1963 I was on this train and 7032 *Denbigh Castle*, with an inspector and passenger on the footplate, achieved 102mph at Littleton &

Badsey (Appendix 1, Table 9). Whether this was part of the test, I'm not sure – it seems a little early for that. However, 7032 was the standby engine for the special at Bristol Bath Road.

Later in the year, I took part in one of the increasing number of specials organised by various amateur railway societies as steam was declining rapidly. These were always cliff-hangers, as the routes and number of different locomotives involved were ambitious, resulting in a more than average number of loco failures or problems and much significant late running. On the 28 November 1964, a Warwickshire Railway Society special started from Birmingham New Street behind Britannia 70052 *Firth of Tay,* a last minute replacement for the booked 70050, and it failed at Carnforth with injector problems. We'd already dropped 10 minutes by taking water at Wolverhampton, which suggested that the engine had had insufficient preparation and a lacklustre run thereafter on an absurdly easy schedule had restored us to time, before a halt at Garstang to try to get our injectors working. Arrival at Carnforth was 19 minutes late before our total failure. Kingmoor Black 5 45018 took over as the emergency replacement and was worked flat out with its 400 ton load, leaving 40 minutes late, topping Grayrigg at 30mph before being brought to a dead stand by signals in the Lune Gorge and then falling from 52 through Tebay to an earsplitting 21mph at Shap Summit, by which time our lateness was nearly the full hour. We were pushed downhill, reaching 82mph at Calthwaite.

Our return was via the Settle & Carlisle, departing 70 minutes late behind Kingmoor Royal Scot 46160 *Queen Victoria's Rifleman* and we managed to recover 20 minutes of lost time by dint of a very easy schedule and a clear run into Leeds unchecked. The last section was a disaster. The engine change to 45647 *Sturdee* was done efficiently and we left 50 minutes late but after Huddersfield we ran into heavy snow and the Jubilee really struggled, falling to 21mph on the climb to Diggle and dropping time consistently. We arrived, now 70 minutes late again, at Wilmslow, only to find Single Line Working had already been introduced for the Saturday night engineering work to commence and with continuing loco problems, we were 94 minutes late into Crewe, where I bailed out.

In 1965, I enjoyed two outings in which the now celebrated 7029 *Clun Castle* took the main part. On 6 February it headed the *Western Venturer* from Paddington to Gloucester via Bristol Dr Day's Junction. The outward journey was uneventful with top speeds in the mid-70s, arriving at Gloucester 8 minutes late after two p-way slowings on the final section. An ex-works Grange, 6848 *Toddington Grange* took us forward to Birmingham Snow Hill. Delay in changing the engine and a slow start with the 375 ton load as 6848 still seemed very stiff and had trouble in clearing water from the cylinders until opened out on the Henley-in-Arden bank, made us nearly 40 minutes late at Stratford-on-Avon, but the vigour on the last section made us just half an hour late at Snow Hill. More loss of time as 7820 *Dinmore Manor* was tardy in being attached and we waited the road, leaving now 47 minutes late. Time recovery began at once and 7820 held 14mph on the 1 in 52/58 past Dudley after a slowing to 15mph at the foot of the bank, and, with speed in the low 60s past Kidderminster, arrived just 28 minutes late at Worcester Shrub Hill, where 7029 resumed control. Unfortunately, a local DMU was given precedence in front of us, leading to a dead stand at the foot of Chipping Camden bank, and running in the upper 70s after Oxford was spoiled by signals and p-way slacks from Hayes onwards and the tour termination was still three quarters of an hour late.

On the 27 March 1965, 7029 made a tour round a good part of the country. *The Lickey & Midlands Rail Tour* started from Paddington with nine coaches, 330 tons gross, and arrived at Worcester 5 minutes early with 78mph on the level at Maidenhead, and 85 down Honeybourne bank. The Old Oak driver was replaced there by a Worcester man, who made hay with the Midland route schedule, leaving 1 minute late and gaining 7 minutes just to the foot of the Lickey. Banked by D6938, the pair raced up the Lickey Incline at 28mph and passed Barnet Green 15 minutes early! We were too soon for Saltley and tarried there for over 10 minutes, but as we tore through Tamworth High Level at 80mph we were back to fifteen minutes early, which had grown to 20 minutes by Derby. Another 10-minute wait at Spondon Junction reduced this but we were still 4 minutes early into Nottingham. After a suitable time for 7029 to be serviced, we left Nottingham at four o'clock but were delayed heavily between Trent Junction and Loughborough by floods. We soon dealt with this, the 10 minute loss of time being recovered by Leicester and a fierce acceleration from there plus 78 past Kibsworth meant we were on time at Market Harborough, before taking the Northampton line where we arrived 10 minutes early. We then touched 74 on the West Coast mainline before a p-way slack to 15mph over Castlethorpe troughs, which entailed a special stop at Bletchley to take water. Unfortunately, this caused a 13-minute late departure, which lost our path at Ashendon Junction where we had to wait for 8 minutes and then got behind a Marylebone service stopping at Princes Risborough. 82 through Denham could not prevent us being a disappointing half-hour late into Paddington after running so early all day.

I had two further excursions at the back end of 1965, with 4079 to Exeter and back but the load was only eight coaches and did not stretch the locomotive and a much more ambitious trip from Birmingham to Edinburgh and back in a day in December. This was another Warwickshire Railway Society special, 1X20, named *The Waverley,* which Peak D37 took to Duddeston Road (already 10 minutes late) where it swapped with Black 5, 45134. The load was a very manageable nine coaches for 325 tons gross and we made our way via the Midland route to Leeds, with timekeeping oscillating from 7 minutes late at Derby to sixteen late on arrival at Leeds after dead stands at Holbeck and Leeds City Junction. Jubilee 45697 *Achilles* backed on with an additional coach, making the load 365 tons gross on departure and we began to lose time steadily all the way to Carlisle. We lost 8 minutes between Hellifield and Blea Moor, sustaining a laboured 26mph most of the way from Settle to Ribblehead, and with nothing over a momentary 69 on the descent, arrived at Carlisle 50 minutes late. We had been promised the last working A3, 60052 *Prince Palatine*, over the Waverley route, but it had been withdrawn the previous week and A2 60528 *Tudor Minstrel* of Dundee substituted. This didn't do much better and with a 5mph signal check at the foot of the climb to Whitrope we lost 9 minutes on this stretch with a steady 22-24mph accompanied by a syncopated roar. Another 3-minute stand outside Hawick made us 73 minutes late there and a better 47mph minimum at Fallahill meant we only dropped another 5 minutes to Edinburgh.

We continued on our way southwards behind A4 60034 *Lord Faringdon,* now at Ferryhill, and just held schedule (still 70 minutes late), taking 141 minutes for the 124 miles with just one p-way slack at Annitsford, which was disappointing. The Darlington-York racing stretch did not tempt our driver – 77 at Tollerton was our highest speed and with checks at Thirsk and outside York station, we were now 86 minutes late. A York V2, 60886, took over, leaving 91 minutes late, and we ground to a halt at Burton Salmon in pitch darkness, to be warned of a derailment ahead. We plodded on with numerous mining subsidence slacks to Rotherham, where we overshot the station and had to set back, losing us more precious minutes. We continued on, with the usual loud V2 noises, still losing time and I gave up and bailed out at Derby now virtually 2 hours late. Such ambitious outings in the dying days of steam were not, I'm afraid, unique and the enthusiasts who braved them were usually resigned to missing their late night connections home.

1966 saw a couple of Southern Region snippets, when I gate-crashed an S&D final excursion double-headed by two un-rebuilt Bulleid pacifics (34006 *Bude* and 34057 *Biggin Hill*) for the Evercreech-Bath section over Masbury summit and a Waterloo-Salisbury-Yeovil and back from Bournemouth tour for which V2 60919 had been brought south all the way from Aberdeen only for it to fail on shed at Nine Elms and be substituted by 34002 *Salisbury.* However, in September, glutton for punishment that I was, I risked another fiasco by joining a two day tour, *The Granite City* from London to Aberdeen and back, run by the South & West Railway Society. The load was just eight coaches for 300 tons, light compared with most tours after the finish of scheduled steam. The special started from Euston behind AL6 electric E3136 and at Crewe it was replaced by Jubilee 45593 *Kolhapur.* Departure was 6 minutes late and arrival at Preston was, contrary to my previous experience with Jubilees, 8 minutes early! 80mph just after Weaver Junction, 53 minimum at Boars Head and 82 at Balshaw Lane were the highlights; the run was completed in 51 minutes 47 seconds. 70032 *Tennyson* took over at Preston, departed on time and reached Carlisle 4 minutes early, with 46 minimum on Grayrigg and 37 on Shap. Maximum speeds were 77mph at Bolton-le-Sands and again at Plumpton. A Dundee V2, 60836, took over the special at Carlisle for a run over the Waverley route and kept time to Hawick by dint of leaving 3 minutes early, but 22mph on the steepest part of the climb to Whitrope summit, past Riccarton Junction, was not brilliant. Although we arrived on time at Hawick, we left, for a reason I cannot now remember, 8 minutes late and arrived unchecked into Edinburgh 6 minutes behind schedule. My notes say 60836 was worked very hard, often 'all out', with this comparatively light load. The last leg of our northbound journey was powered by A2 60532 *Blue Peter.* Departure was ten minutes late, and we recovered six minutes of this on the run to Perth despite, as my notes say, being worked very easily. However, after Perth it was a different story and *Blue Peter* was clearly in trouble for steam and I ceased timing. I failed to record the arrival time in Aberdeen, but for the first time on this trip we were substantially late – my recollection, possibly faulty, is around half an hour.

60836 at Hawick on the two-day steam special, 1X75 'The Waverley' from London to Aberdeen, 3 September 1966. (*Author*)

60836 on 1X75 *The Waverley* climbing to Whitrope summit, 3 September 1966. (*Author*)

After a comfortable night in an Aberdeen hotel, we set off on the Sunday morning behind one of Ferryhill's last two remaining A4s, 60024 *Kingfisher*, on its final official run before withdrawal. For an A4, *Kingfisher* always seemed to me to have a particularly harsh exhaust, but we ran well enough when Sunday engineering works allowed. We had single line working before Stonehaven, but with 47 minimum at Carmont and 87 at Craigo, we were 2 minutes early into Montrose. More single-line-working before Dundee made us 5 minutes late there and two further bouts of the same made us 12 minutes late into Edinburgh. Our total running time from Aberdeen was 3½ hours, but the net time was 6 minutes under 3 hours. I had a last experience at Edinburgh of being on a train when A4s were exchanged, Ferryhill's other working A4, 60019 *Bittern,* now being attached for the run to York. I will quote my notes: '60019 was in excellent condition, ran very quietly and with a beautiful beat. Initial acceleration from checks was superb, and performance on the level was outstanding, especially Darlington to York. The conclusion of the run was spoilt by a hot box detector being activated at Alne and it transpired that the left-hand bogie axlebox of 60019 was becoming overheated, but the engine was able to continue to York with no difficulty.' As a result of this we were 16 minutes late having been on time throughout earlier. The highlights were 77 before Drem; 44 minimum on Cockburnspath bank; 75-78 after a special planned water stop at Alnmouth; 85 just before Darlington; 85 at Thirsk and 90 sustained for 4 minutes between Pilmoor and Alne, where the hot box detector halted our flight. Brush Type 4 D1511 regained just five of the lost minutes to King's Cross, where we arrived 10 minutes late. The spreading of the tour over two days at least allowed more realistic schedules and although timekeeping was not perfect, especially on the last legs of both steam sections, there were no worries about being stranded.

A month later I joined a day excursion with 4472 *Flying Scotsman* from King's Cross to York and back, but the most interesting bit was the use of Merchant Navy 35026 *Lamport & Holt Line* for the York-Newcastle section. 4472 behaved perfectly on the down run and the ER crew sized up the Southern Region engine to their satisfaction and arrived punctually in Newcastle. They let fly on the return trip after Darlington and whisked the nine-coach, 325 ton train up to 90mph by Thirsk and held it to Pilmoor, this time escaping the attention of the hot box detector. Darlington (passed at 25mph) to York took 38 minutes 17 seconds for the 44 miles. 4472 with the additional weight of its second tender excelled itself on the return to King's Cross, with 86mph at Moss before Doncaster; 88 at Carlton; 64 minimum at Peascliffe Tunnel and 93 at Little

35026 *Lamport & Holt Line* of Nine Elms spent a month in the north on enthusiast specials, in October/November 1966. It powered a special between York and Newcastle and return on which the author travelled on 22 October 1966, and here it is shown being prepared at Stockport Edgeley, 19 November 1966. (*MLS Collection*)

Bytham, arriving 4 minutes early at Peterborough. Then followed 80 at Huntingdon; 81 at Arlesey; 73 minimum at Stevenage and 80 at Welwyn, arriving 2 minutes early at King's Cross. This was by far the best run I ever had with a single-chimneyed A3. It was also the first steam run south of Peterborough for over two years.

In 1967, BR steam was drawing to its close. On certain routes, booking for enthusiasts' specials was the only way to get steam. I'll rush quickly over another Jubilee disastrous performance in February when 45562 *Alberta* – said to be a good engine – lost three quarters of an hour going to Carlisle from Leeds via the Diggle route, almost stalling on the climb, then via Manchester Victoria, Preston and Shap. Shap was surmounted – if that's the right word – at 17mph with our nine-coach train and clearly the Jubilee was struggling to maintain steam all the way. After an effort to right things at Carlisle, we set off on our return journey 76 minutes late via Hexham and Newcastle, stopped on the main line between Thirsk and Tollerton to raise steam and arrived at Leeds City a staggering 159 minutes late. What more can I say? At least we had a diversion at Carlisle while the Jubilee was being serviced, as 'Flying Pig' 43106 took us to Beattock and back, touching 84mph at Gretna Junction on the way back – far more than *Alberta* managed on the whole trip!

4 March 1967 saw the end of through WR services from Paddington to Chester and this was celebrated with two specials, with steam traction between Didcot and Birkenhead in both directions, with 4079 and 7029 respectively to and from Chester. Both performed with distinction. I travelled with 4079 *Pendennis Castle* on eleven coaches, 410 tons gross. 42 minimum at Hatton with this load was good, but signal checks and p-way slacks made us 17 minutes late into Wolverhampton and time recovered afterwards was thwarted regularly by more signal stands, so that arrival in Chester was still 17 minutes late. 73035 took us to Birkenhead and back, and when 4079 resumed the return journey, we left 12 minutes late, picked up 2 minutes by a vigorous climb of Gresford Bank (29 minimum) and continued on our way gradually recouping the lost time until our arrival back at Didcot was eventually a minute early. 82mph at Shifnal was our fastest speed but the best performance was mainly in hard acceleration from slacks and checks and uphill work. Apparently 7029 performed well also, although several people were of the opinion that 4079 had the edge.

In September of that year, 7029 *Clun Castle* began a series of excursions onto 'enemy territory'. It was sent to the Eastern Region and conducted a number of route clearance tests before being allowed to power an eight-coach special, 276/290 tons, from King's Cross to Leeds on Sunday 17 September. It encountered the usual Sunday engineering slacks, including slow line running before Potters Bar, but in between the slacks and signal stands it touched 78 at Hatfield; 78 at Langley; 80 at Arlesey and 82 at Connington. A long wait at Peterborough, while 7029 went to New England depot to be watered, led to a 25 minute late departure, then a dead stand for a minute at Essendine (crossing gates not opened in time?) was followed by acceleration to 52mph at Stoke summit; 84 at Claypole; 69 minimum at Dukeries Junction and 83 before Retford and a series of signal stands outside Doncaster, making us 38 minutes late there. A vigorous run on to Leeds recovered a quarter of an hour. The coaches were late being berthed at Leeds for the return run, causing a

Ivatt mogul 43106 at Carlisle after its 84mph dash through Gretna Junction on the 2.50pm Beattock-Carlisle special, before handing the enthusiasts' special back to *Alberta*, 25 February 1967. (*Author*)

26 minute late departure, but we ran vigorously to Peterborough in order to connect with the last service Hull-King's Cross train for those that needed to get back to London for onward connections. 84mph at Crow Park; 76 after the Newark slowing falling only to 72 at Peascliffe Tunnel and then a steady 77-82 all the way down Stoke bank saw us into Peterborough only 13 minutes late despite a 2-minute stand outside the station. Water was taken again at New England, this time quickly, and we departed only 2 minutes late, but had to recover from the long stand when clinker had formed. However, the fireman soon turned things round and we dashed for King's Cross with a minimum of 65 at Knebworth and 77 afterwards through Welwyn, arriving after more checks 11 minutes late.

Two weeks later 7029 was the motive power for a rail tour from King's Cross to Carlisle via Leeds and the Settle and Carlisle. 7029 backed onto the ten-coach 338/360 ton load at Peterborough and set off steadily with 56 at Stoke summit and 74 before Newark, reached on time. Efficient running in the mid-70s saw us arrive early at Doncaster and then we threaded our way slowly over a series of colliery slacks, being routed via Hemsworth, Normanton and Woodlesford to Engine Shed Junction where we changed crews. Leaving 11 minutes late, we stopped and took water at Skipton then tackled the climb to Ribblehead and Blea Moor in the teeth of a strong South West gale, which blew our exhaust horizontally to the east across the barren landscape. We fell momentarily from the low 30s to 27 just before Ribblehead, but recovered to 32 across Batty Moss Viaduct and held that speed to the summit, recovering 4 minutes lost by a p-way slowing just after Skipton. 83mph on the descent through Griseburn was unusual and we would have recovered more time, but Carlisle was not ready for us and we stood for a couple of minutes outside the station arriving 11 minutes late.

The return to Peterborough with 4498 *Sir Nigel Gresley* was an anti-climax. Two stops before Appleby to try to release brakes (possibly because of problems with 7029's 25 inches of vacuum replaced by 21 inches from 4498, which no-one bothered to check at Carlisle) made us 18 minutes late at Appleby, where we stood while fitters dealt with the brake problem. The 35mph minimum at Ais Gill was followed by continuous signal checks after Settle, a stopping DMU having been allowed to precede us, and arrival at Skipton was 26 minutes late. This had increased to 37 minutes when we stopped at Engine Shed Junction for the crew change. We tried after Doncaster – my notes say 'working hard, sparks being thrown high but performance seems to be lacking its usual edge'. A lot of fire was coming from the ashpan and the crew took the opportunity to examine the engine during a stop for a signal failure at Werrington Junction. We were almost a full hour late at Peterborough, where 4498 was replaced by a Brush Type 47 for the run to King's Cross.

A month later, 7029 was let loose on the West Coast Main Line. On 14 October, 9F 92091 departed Liverpool Exchange with the featherweight seven-coach, 214/235-ton rail tour to Carlisle. We ran easily enough, gaining time on an undemanding schedule, arriving 8 minutes early at Appley Bridge, leaving Wigan Wallgate on time and, routed via Blackrod, reached Preston 2 minutes early. We touched 64mph on the last stretch past Farrington, the only time 60mph was exceeded from Liverpool. 7029 then took over and played with the train. After a long 20mph p-way slack before Bay Horse we roared through Lancaster reaching 78mph at Hest Bank, passed Oxenholme 2 minutes early doing 54mph, held the upper 40s on Grayrigg Bank, another p-way slack to 40mph at Dillicar, then assaulted Shap clearing the summit at 47mph, now 10 minutes early. Despite crawling at 2mph through floods at Shap station and a dead stand for signals at Eden Valley Junction, we were still 10 minutes early into Carlisle. On the return run we ran to the Appleby photographic stop on schedule, where we took water and received attention to dragging coach brakes. Leaving Appleby nearly 18 minutes late, we roared over Ais Gill at 48mph, having already recovered 7 minutes of lost time, passed Ribblehead on time and arrived at Hellifield where 7029 came off 10 minutes early once more and 92091 took us back to Liverpool, still early. This was the first rail tour I'd ever travelled on that had been early at every scheduled stopping point!

During the last few weeks of steam and the flurry of specials in the North West, I went on a number, typical of which was a run on 18 May 1968. The train started from Birmingham behind AC electric (class 85) E3058. At Stockport, Black 5 44949 and Standard 5 73069 took over for a circuitous run via Copy Pit and Rose Grove to Preston. Diesel D7515 took us to Blackpool and back, whereupon 70013 *Oliver Cromwell* took us from Preston to Morecambe via Hellifield and the pair of Black 5s took us back to Stockport. Timekeeping was typical – half an hour lost on the first leg, mainly because of various signal checks, lost time grown to an hour before 70013 took over at Preston, the Britannia just holding schedule. Then a further half hour lost by the pair of Fives on the return run, finishing over 90 minutes late. A few engines appeared several times on specials around this period, 73069 several times, although its Caprotti sister, 73134, appeared at least once for a run from Manchester Victoria over Diggle.

Then there was the infamous fifteen-guinea special on the last day. But that was a lot of money in 1968 and I let it go.

Chapter 7

Trainee stationmaster, Gillingham (Dorset)

Let us go back to 1964. For the last six months of my 'Traffic Apprenticeship' I was due to act in a supernumerary capacity as Assistant to Station Managers, Yard Masters and Goods Agents and I made my way from London Western Region Headquarters to the Plymouth Division to carry out this part of my training. But first, I essayed a further trip north to experience again the Glasgow-Aberdeen 3-hour services, travelling up overnight – diesel-hauled this time, so I got some sleep! I arose at some unearthly hour at Perth, sighting Britannia 70035 *Rudyard Kipling* of Kingmoor on the 6.25am Perth-Edinburgh eleven-coach train, then suffered a most dreary climb to Glenfarg summit, the Britannia staggering from 10 to 16mph and falling again to 10 at the summit dropping 16 minutes to Kinross Junction. I abandoned the train at Dunfermline Lower and got back to Perth in time to pick up St Margaret's V2 60816 on the 8.25am Glasgow *Grampian Express*. With just six coaches, the V2 made a reasonable fist of it, leaving Perth late but recovering a little on the last leg, arriving 4 minutes late into Aberdeen, with 80mph on the level sustained between Alyth Junction and Forfar and a very noisy climb out of Stonehaven onto the cliffs above Cove Bay. Back with the familiar Ferryhill V2 60955 on the 1.30pm, with just six coaches and two vans, was easy and we ran into Perth a minute early without exceeding 73mph. I went back to Aberdeen behind former King's Cross A4 60010 *Dominion of Canada* on the 5.30pm Glasgow *St Mungo*, which recovered 9 minutes of a 15 minute late start, with 82 between Perth and Forfar and 80 at Fordoun and again in the descent to Stonehaven, with an unusual 78 above the cliffs and the grey North Sea before Portlethen.

Next morning, muffled against what seemed to be two inches of frost, I tiptoed out of my lodgings (I had paid the night before!) to find Ferryhill 60010 again on the seven-coach 7.10am Aberdeen-Glasgow and scraped the ice off the inside of the window. 83mph above Muchalls warmed me up and we had a copy-book run to Perth where we arrived a minute early. I braved the cold for a further day and enjoyed a couple of runs behind another new A4 for me, St Margaret's 60012 *Commonwealth of Australia,* which ran to the standard, but was over 10 minutes late on both occasions when I joined it, and a new V2 as well, 60919, which ran well with a heavier, ten-coach load on the 1.30pm Aberdeen, running the 32 mile Forfar-Perth stretch in exactly 32 minutes, with a top speed of 80mph over the Tay Viaduct (the other one) just before Stanley Junction. We were also a minute early into Perth.

Returning to a somewhat milder Devon January, I acted as Assistant Stationmaster Plymouth North Road but then the arctic conditions returned and in a freezing February I tried to make myself useful at Taunton Yard and Coal Concentration Depot. I was lodged for two weeks in a B&B with total absence of heating in my room, so after my rather unnecessary work – there didn't seem an awful lot to do – I spent most of my evenings on trains to Bristol or Barnstaple, just to keep warm. I couldn't see anything as it was pitch dark. The Taunton-Barnstaple branch was run entirely by the Churchward moguls of the 43XX class and I grew familiar with 5336, 6326, 6345, 6372, 7303 and 7337. I broke the monotony by going home one weekend via Plymouth and managed to get a steam/diesel combination over the South Devon banks – 6990 *Witherslack Hall* piloting D806 – before going back to Woking on the 4.30pm Exeter Central behind 35019 *French Line CGT*. The last weeks of February and early March were spent uselessly as Assistant Goods Agent, Exeter St David's – useless because the local Trade Union barons wouldn't allow management trainees on the goods deck and the local management wouldn't stand up to them!

In March 1964, I was at last due to finish my training with a spell as an acting relief stationmaster and I was appointed for six weeks to Gillingham station in Dorset. Having spent three years seeing modernisation at first hand throughout the Western Region – traction, signalling, depots, marshalling yards and management methodology (it was the time of Stanley Raymond's sweeping 'de-great westernisation') I found in Gillingham that I was in a time warp untouched by the modern world. I spent the months of March and April 1964 there, with control also of Semley and on arrival, I was rung by someone in the Plymouth Divisional office to ask me to assume command of Tisbury and Dinton as well, as the relief stationmaster there was wanted somewhere more important urgently. I shared on call with the neighbouring stationmaster at Templecombe.

The Salisbury-Exeter main line had been transferred to the Western Region in January 1964, but I have to say that nothing had yet changed from SR days during my sojourn there – indeed, I don't believe anything had changed for twenty years or more! Perhaps this is not quite true, as a few Standard 4 4-6-0s (75000/1/3/6) had infiltrated the Yeovil-Salisbury locals although the majority of trains serving my stations were three-coach locals hauled by the inevitable Exmouth Junction un-rebuilt West Country or Battle of Britain pacifics.

My main problem was that I had no transport – no stationmasters were allocated cars in those days – and as there was no road parallel to the old Southern mainline between my stations, there was no public transport other than the Salisbury-Exeter or Yeovil stopping services running at approximately two hourly intervals. My duties involved supervision of staff at all four locations and the visiting of signalboxes and crossing keepers in my stretch of line, so I spent a fair amount of my time travelling on a local to one station and walking through the spring flower bedecked cuttings and embankments to my next port of call. And it really was a gorgeous spring. The primroses were enormous! I visited Templecombe in the spring of 2010 and noticed with pleasure from the train that between Dinton and Gillingham the primroses were still there and were just as huge as I'd remembered them.

There were other antiquated practices. The only way I could pay the crossing

Unrebuilt 'Battle of Britain' 34065 *Hurricane* of Exmouth Junction [one of the few unrebuilt light Pacifics with a poor reputation for steaming] on the 3.05pm Salisbury – Exeter stopping train, near Axminster, 1 June 1961. (*MLS Collection*)

Unrebuilt 'West Country' 34015 *Exmouth* of Exmouth Junction shed at Templecombe on an up stopping service from Exeter to Salisbury, June, 1964. (*MLS Collection*)

Unrebuilt West Country 34002 *Salisbury* of Exmouth Junction climbs from Gillingham to Semley with the 10.30am Exeter-Waterloo, 29 August 1964. (*David Clark/Rodney Lissenden Collection*)

34093 *Saunton* of Nine Elms nears the summit at Semley with an afternoon Waterloo-Exeter restaurant car express, 29 August 1964. (*David Clark/Rodney Lissenden Collection*)

Unrebuilt 'Battle of Britain' 34072 *257 Squadron* on the up pick-up goods at Seaton Junction, 15 August 1963. (*MLS Collection*)

keepers on the main line was to commandeer the engine of the local pick-up goods and hang out of the cab delivering the monthly pay packets like the exchange of a single line token! The practice elsewhere of obtaining signatures did not apparently apply here. I carried out this manoeuvre once during my stint there – the engine was a rebuilt West Country, 34048 *Crediton,* with half a dozen short wheelbase freight wagons trailing behind on this occasion.

The main event of the day at Gillingham was the stopping of an early morning express around 8.30 (it must have been the 7.30am Exeter) to take our commuters to Salisbury or even London. The train was heavily loaded – I recollect thirteen coaches but my memory may be exaggerating – and was always hauled by a Merchant Navy (35013 was the most common) and for some reason I never fathomed in my eight week sojourn, often pulled up twice as it hung way out of the short station platform. This was quite a rigmarole with a Bulleid, especially when it tried to pull away the second time as the engine was now over the dip and on the 1 in 80 climb to Semley, and what a palaver the Pacific used to make of this manoeuvre, slipping and sliding, scattering cinders into adjoining cottage gardens and blackening the washing hanging on their lines. The role of the stationmaster was to act as station announcer, in charge of a battery operated loudhailer, although all the regulars must have known 'Salisbury, Andover, Basingstoke, Woking and Waterloo' off by heart.

The return evening service was the 6pm Waterloo, although by the time of its arrival I was off duty enjoying a hearty meal at my lodgings overlooking the station. One evening, however, I was called out to Templecombe. I was nervous – this was my first 'emergency' – and on arrival at the joint station, my confidence was not boosted by the discovery that the Somerset & Dorset signalling system was a total mystery to me. However, the problem was on the LSWR mainline. The 6pm Waterloo had disappeared in section between Gillingham and Templecombe and the last connecting trains for Bath and Bournemouth were waiting impatiently with their meagre number of passengers, both Standard 4 2-6-4 tanks blowing off steam furiously. The express was an hour overdue by now, and we were just about to set off on foot to see if it had met with an accident in Buckhorn Weston tunnel, when the problem solved itself and the train appeared on the horizon. The locomotive, unusually an un-rebuilt Battle of Britain, 34063, rather than a Merchant Navy, had slipped itself to a standstill on the approach to the tunnel and had taken coaxing by the fireman hand feeding the rails with sand to get it going again.

Above: Salisbury's unrebuilt 'Battle of Britain' 34054 *Lord Beaverbrook* nears Buckhorn Weston Tunnel with the 1pm Waterloo – Exeter, 15 August 1964. 34054 would have worked the 6.45am Salisbury-Waterloo that morning [the regular train to college of the author between 1957 and 1960] and would return to Salisbury that night on a freight from Exeter. (*R.C.Riley*)

Left: Rebuilt West Country 34096 *Trevone* leaves Buckhorn Weston Tunnel and begins the descent to Gillingham with an up Exeter-Waterloo express, 15 August 1964. (*R.C.Riley*)

34096 *Trevone* on an Exeter-Waterloo express passes Standard 4 2-6-0 76007 on a down Salisbury – Yeovil Junction local train, 15 August 1964. 76007 was one of the regular locomotives that hauled the afternoon school train from Gillingham to Salisbury. (*R.C.Riley*)

For me, the operation, which epitomised the rural culture of the line, was the late afternoon school train from Gillingham to Salisbury. We had a grammar school in the town which served children from a wide area and every school weekday, the empty stock – four coaches – would arrive behind a tender first Standard 4 2-6-0 from Salisbury depot, run round on the down side of the station yard and draw back into the up platform. The train would fill up with exuberant children, boys in the first two coaches and girls into the rear two, and the corridor gangway between them was locked (we were spoil sports in those days!). At Semley we gravitated a loaded milk tank from the dairy private siding onto the back of the train for its connection at Salisbury to the main West of England-Clapham milk train. We never had an incident as far as I'm aware in the gravitational movement, but I wouldn't like to propose such an operational ploy to the Health & Safety Inspectorate these days! At each station en route, the station time varied from 6 to 15 minutes to enable the lone porter and train guard to load mountains of watercress punnets, no 'Brutes' or pallets here. The cress was grown locally in disused wartime underground storage bunkers. I often travelled on the train to assist because, at the peak times, we could lose time even on this schedule. We would finish soaked through with sweat and water from the produce. All this activity was carried out under the bantering gaze of the schoolkids hanging out of the windows and cheering on the porter and guard as they flung the sodden punnets into the brakevan. You won't be surprised to learn that the 760XX Standard 2-6-0 took its allowed 79 minutes to do the 22 miles to Salisbury (average 16.7mph) – was this the slowest scheduled train on BR at the time? It was certainly an opportunity for the children to do their homework, but I never noticed any such activity on my patch.

Exmouth Junction's 34107 *Blandford Forum* at Salisbury with the daily Brighton – Plymouth through train, 1 September 1964. (*MLS Collection*)

The milk tank traffic got me into hot water during my brief stay at Gillingham. One of the porters told me that the dairy management was tarmacking an area round the loading point to allow the rail traffic to be replaced by a road tanker and during the first grand tour of his new domain by the WR General Manager, the affable but astute Gerry Fiennes, I mentioned this intelligence to him. He clearly took action because a couple of days later I received an anonymous phone call from someone – presumably in the Plymouth Divisional Marketing office – threatening my future career if I corroborated my statement to the GM. Clearly someone had been taken to task for not discovering this themselves. This was the only time in my railway career that I received such pressure and I am glad to say I stuck to my guns. In fact, we lost the milk traffic to road shortly afterwards.

Despite seeming to be from another age, there were aspects of the operation that were totally admirable. I remember the reliability with which the Brighton-Plymouth and Plymouth-Brighton through services used to pass each other at speed through Gillingham station with a regularity that was uncanny. I remember the sheer excitement of the down *Atlantic Coast Express* thundering through our little station, whistle howling, at the foot of Semley bank hitting the dip under the road bridge where the gradient changed abruptly, and seeing the pacific appear to bounce several times vertically in reaction. My most vivid memory of this is the extreme speed of 35016 on one occasion. I was so startled that I assessed its speed by the rail joint noise as its train passed over and got a reading of around 96mph!

At the end of April, my three-year training scheme came to an end and I was told to report to the Divisional Manager at Cardiff for appointment to a permanent job. However, a couple of months later, I had another encounter with Gerry Fiennes. It was customary for Traffic Apprentices to be interviewed by the General Manager at the end of their training, and although my session had been postponed, I found myself and my fellow trainee, Stan Judd, summoned to Paddington in June. My interview was at midday with Stan to follow half an hour later. When I was sent into the sanctum, I was greeted by the General Manager with the words, 'Do you like cricket?' When I affirmed this, Gerry Fiennes said, 'Oh, good!' and took a transistor

Rebuilt Merchant Navy 35026 *Lamport & Holt Line* passes through Semley station with a morning Waterloo – Exeter and North Devon Express, 29 August 1964. (*David Clark/Rodney Lissenden Collection*)

radio from his top drawer and we listened to the Lords Test Match for 20 minutes. In between overs he plied me with very acute questions, then we were interrupted by a newcomer, introduced to me as his sister-in-law back from a Harrods shopping spree. After a 10 minute pleasant three-way conversation she left and he admitted that he was terrified of women like her who sat on school governing boards and ran half a dozen charities! We then checked the lunchtime score before Gerry Fiennes realized he had another interview to conduct and I was ushered out to allow poor Stan to enter who must have wondered what on earth was going on.

There is a postscript to this period of my career. In the summer of 2009, I saw an advertisement in the railway press about a proposed celebration of the 150th anniversary of the opening of the railway at Gillingham. I got in touch with the organiser and found myself invited, as a former railwayman employed there, to partake in a march from the town centre to the station along with the town band and other dignitaries. On arrival at the station, I was asked, with the mayor, to unveil the blue plaque on the station building commemorating the digging of the first sod with a silver shovel that still exists. After the ceremony I was introduced to a middle-aged lady and her husband whom I'd known forty-five years previously. She was then the very shy granddaughter of the couple with whom I lodged and I'd developed a rapport with the auburn haired four-year-old involving surreptitious hide and seek games and reading her bedtime story. Afterwards I had a stall for the charity Railway Children in the old goods yard alongside the other stalls and displays by the local townsfolk and their children. I recognised the pathway from my digs to the station and the station building and signalbox were familiar, but everything else had changed – in particular the 159 series diesel units bore little resemblance to the thundering restaurant car expresses and the wastefully overpowered stopping services of yesteryear.

Chapter 8

Stationmaster, Aberbeeg

After completing the BR management training scheme at the end of April 1964, my colleague, Stan Judd, and I appeared before the Cardiff Divisional Manager, Bob Hilton, who informed us that he intended to appoint us to two stations in the Monmouthshire Western Valley, pending the replacement of the yard managers, shedmasters and stationmasters by a Western Valley Area Manager some ten months hence. The two vacancies, for some months covered by relief stationmasters, were at Ebbw Vale and Aberbeeg. Bob Hilton drew a half crown from his pocket, tossed it, Stan called correctly and chose Ebbw Vale, because he'd heard of it. I became Stationmaster Aberbeeg, the Operating job, by default. This choice coloured the rest of my BR career, leading ultimately to four years as Chief Operating Manager of the London Midland Region in the mid-80s and my last years before retirement as Head of Safety Policy for BR and Railtrack.

We were a shock to the system. Two Londoners, in their mid-twenties, dropped into a Welsh Valley previously used to a succession of Welshmen in their sixties. Doubts were openly expressed as to whether we would cope. The only digs we found and shared were at the Hanbury Arms Hotel, abutting the Webb Brewery in the vee junction of the valley overlooking the small yard, junction signalbox and station at Aberbeeg. Any attempt at sleep was abandoned until after midnight when the last raft of coal empties for the early morning trip to Marine Colliery was safely berthed in two portions in the little yard, until the clanging of buffers ceased and we were convinced they were not 'off the road' again!

Initially I was very nervous, such confidence as I had being rapidly undermined by the relief stationmaster who stayed on supposedly to help me and the two clerical staff – and my urgent desire to get away and honour my ticket on the May 9 Paddington-Plymouth Castle swansong. I managed to persuade the former stationmaster to cover my on call that weekend – I think he thought I'd not come back – and forgot about my troubles in the excitement of the performances of 4079, 6999, 7025, 7029 and 5054.

The passenger service had been withdrawn a year or so previously and the track layout around Aberbeeg rationalized and the stations left to rot. My office was in the

The view of Aberbeeg Junction signalbox, station and Hanbury Hotel, taken from the Llanhilleth Road, June 1964. (*Author*)

middle of the vee-shaped station between the branches to Ebbw Vale to the West and Abertillery and Brynmawr to the East. The office was dingy, lit by gas mantles, with two buckets strategically placed on the floor to catch the drips from the incessant rain through the leaky roof. The telephone was archaic, hung on the wall, until one evening a spectacular lightning strike surged through the power lines and it exploded into a myriad fragments. Filing appeared to be by carbon copied memos speared onto a forbidding looking spike on the desk.

My pessimistic encounter with the office environment and systems was countered by the way I was welcomed by the seventy operating staff outside. Charlie Sargeant, Secretary of our LDC was a signalman in the Junction (Middle) Box, Charlie Shepherd, his burly shift-mate, and Relief Signalman Terry Parsons, the Trade Union organiser, were superb and shared their problems and ideas in a constructive and enthusiastic way. I was encouraged to instigate a number of changes to improve the working and their lot, a win-win situation which bolstered my credibility with both the staff and the Divisional Office. I started to spend long periods tramping around my territory, getting lifts from our local pannier tanks and occasional new 1750hp English Electric diesels (later class 37) which were infiltrating from their Newport Ebbw Junction home.

My southern border started under the impressive Crumlin Viaduct and included the derelict station at Llanhilleth and the colliery, which were under the watchful eye of Charlie Corfield, my Inspector there. Charlie supervised the workings there so efficiently that I soon learned to leave things in his capable hands. Llanhilleth station

2-8-0T 5264 approaches Aberbeeg Junction with a full load of coal from Six Bells Colliery on the Abertillery/Brynmawr branch, circa 1963. (*ColourRail*)

Two 94XX Hawksworth pannier tanks await their banking turns to Ebbw Vale at Aberbeeg South, 7 November 1963. (*R.O.Tuck/Rail Archive Stephenson*)

1913 built 2-8-0T 4227 with a train of coal empties and a few wagons of pit props from Rogerstone to Aberbeeg Yard, between Llanhilleth and Aberbeeg, seen from the junction of the road to Llanhilleth village and the main A467 from Newport to Abertillery and Brynmawr, 5 May 1964. (*ColourRail*)

was a mess, the only resident being a large and vicious ram, which later was the inspiration for a *Thomas the Tank Engine* video. Our railway had permanent trespassing sheep – there was no point in stopping trains to warn of animals on the line. This ram appeared to have the old waiting room at the station as its residence and one day Charlie went in to shoo it away, when he slipped on loose floorboards disturbed by vandals, and being a large and heavy man, unfortunately fell through and broke a leg. This accident gave rise to a Court case for compensation, when BR's lawyers tried to argue against my advice that he shouldn't have entered the room, whilst I maintained he had a perfect right, and indeed duty, to protect our property from marauding animals. I don't think my evidence was very popular with our lawyer and I'm glad to say Charlie got his compensation.

The main activity centred on Aberbeeg yard and engine shed. At that time, there were still six working collieries in the area and the provision of empties to the colliery sidings was made by the Aberbeeg trip engines, by May 1964 predominantly Class 37s although we still had two Churchward 2-8-0 tanks, 5214 and 5218, to cover our 8am 'anywhere' turn, used to mop up variations in coal production, and stand by for diesel failures. The loaded coal trains made their way down the valley to Rogerstone Yard, still under the iron grip of a Welsh yardmaster, who viewed our goings-on with considerable suspicion. Our engines and Aberbeeg men would return with empties from Rogerstone, or even East Usk if they managed to slip past the Rogerstone border controls, and bring them up to our yard for breaking down into manageable loads on the fierce gradients to Marine or Six Bells Collieries. We had a fleet of pannier tanks – the preserved 9682 was one of them – including three 94XX (9493-5) for banking the heavy coal and ore trains up the 5 miles to Ebbw Vale steel works, and for shunting the yard between turns. One of my first managerial actions was to replace our 350hp diesel shunter, which spent most of the day idling, by a steam banker awaiting its next turn, a move so obvious that the staff had no argument

Two of our Aberbeeg pannier tanks, 8778 and 3647, shunting Aberbeeg Yard just before the influx of the class 37s in 1963. (*ColourRail*)

about the loss of a turn and the Divisional Office rejoiced, because they'd been trying to persuade my predecessor to give it up for years. I was therefore uniquely congratulated in the post 'Stanley Raymond' era for replacing diesel with steam traction – for a few months anyway!

Stan and I shared on call duties for the Western Valley from Crumlin northwards in the days before mobile phones and bleepers, which meant we were tied to the valley for a week at a time, one or other of us escaping alternate weekends on the 'Jones' bus (never the Western Welsh option) and the main line to London at Newport. Minor derailments were common – the 37s were a nasty shock to the local S&T lineman, whose maintenance of signals and points had to cope with constant colliery subsidence. It was apparently very common for a steam engine to mount the guard rails at points and either drop back on again or be swiftly rerailed with ramps from the yard without bothering the Newport breakdown gang. The diesels had a habit of splitting the points and derailing a bogie and we only tried driving it back on with ramps once. The damage to the under bogie traction motors was not well received.

I had a propensity to invite call outs for some reason – indeed during our stay, Stan was only called out three times, while I had sixteen emergency calls. Within days of my arrival, a diesel and the Guinness tanks from the brewery were on their side fouling three of the four lines approaching Aberbeeg Junction – shades of *Whisky Galore* – and I had to open up single line working over a complex junction layout with red-padlocked points, now out of use, littering the remaining single line open. Charlie Sargeant saw me nervously looking at the mess and said, 'Follow me, boss, stick this red armband on as pilotman, and do what I say.' We never looked back.

During one night of torrential rain, I was called out to an earth slip opposite Marine Colliery on the Ebbw Vale section. Not only the bank, but a large mature tree had slid down the cutting and was now in the middle of the line from Ebbw Vale, with, behind it, a large 2-8-2 tank, 7249, and a full load of fifty vanfits of steel tinplate. We opened up single line working and then had to get the tinplate train to reverse its load to the crossover at Marine Colliery about a mile to the rear. We were way over the load for a 72XX and there was no engine north of us to assist, so we had to try. I shall never forget the crashing and very deliberate exhaust and the rocking motion of the engine as it propelled its heavy train in slow motion without the trace of a slip through the stormy night.

Our constant 'emergencies' had their humorous side. Stan and I could occasionally venture out together provided our inspectors knew where we were and we were not too far from reach. Adjacent to Llanhilleth station was a little cricket ground and we had both joined the club and played an occasional match. I can remember vividly one sunny afternoon being at the crease and had just snicked my first runs through the slips when a thunderous voice came from the Llanhilleth Middle Box loudhailer 'Mr Maidment, you're needed, they're off the road at Ebbw Vale.' The scorecard read 'Maidment, derailed … 4.' Turning up at Waunllwyd Sidings in cricket whites was apparently another first!

I managed to get away from the valley with difficulty. Every other weekend I got home while Stan covered my 'on call', but in the other week I just had a half day and usually escaped only as far as the Abergavenny area where I was fond of climbing the Sugar Loaf – steam had now gone for good on the North & West. One afternoon I did make it as far as the Gloucester-Chalford push-pull service, taking a Brush Type 4 to Hereford, then 6381 on the branch across to Gloucester Horton Road where I joined the auto-train with 0-4-2T 1445. They must have been short of auto-trailers or 14XX, for, to my surprise, my return trip was with 2-6-2T 4100 and a GW 'B' set.

In the summer, with the longer evenings, I ventured further north as part of a week's leave from my daily valley routine to Shrewsbury, as the Wolverhampton-Chester portions of the Paddington expresses were still steam, although mostly powered by Black 5s since another Regional boundary shift had allocated that area to the London Midland Region. On 1 July I took 44835 northbound and had a fast snippet southbound with 45353 of Chester, with eight coaches, 28mph minimum on Gresford Bank, and the 18 miles from Gobowen to Shrewsbury, mainly downhill, completed start to stop in 20 minutes 47 seconds with a top speed of 77mph before Baschurch, arriving 5 minutes early. At the end of the month I spent a weekend of my leave in the area, before another visit to Scotland, starting from London behind a EE Type 4, then E3032 from Nuneaton, which touched 106mph at Betley Road, to Crewe, only to find that if I'd waited I could have had 46237 *City of Bristol* all the way from Euston on a relief to North Wales. The Stanier pacific came off at Crewe and I embarked behind 44917 as far as Chester, from where I changed to 45403 to Shrewsbury in order to make a run right through to Portmadoc. 7819 *Hinton Manor* gave a good run on the 11.10am Paddington with five coaches, recovering a significant amount of the 20 minutes lost time handed over by the D10XX until disaster struck at Caersws where a token failure caused a 55 minute delay. Afterwards, the Manor roared up Talerddig Bank and accelerated very hard from each token exchange point with a top speed of 62mph only a couple of minutes from Machynlleth. Luckily I had decided to stay overnight in Portmadoc so I had no tight connections to make.

Next morning, 7811 *Dunley Manor* brought me back with the Up *Cambrian Coast Express* as far as Barmouth, where I changed for a run over the Bala route. The LM influence in motive power was indicated there by 75006 heading the 10.20am Barmouth-Birkenhead, but it was only a three coach train of little value for timing so I just enjoyed the scenery. I alighted at Ruabon, where another quick sortie found 45353 again on the southbound run to Shrewsbury and a Hall, 6922 *Burton Hall,* still showing the GW flag on the 12.10pm Paddington, which arrived in Chester 2 minutes early after an energetic performance. There was still time to pick up the 3.30pm Holyhead-Manchester Exchange behind BR Standard Caprotti 5, 73127, with an eight coach load, although progress was pedestrian rather than stimulating. I failed to record the lateness.

The next day I made my way north behind a diesel on the 9.25am Crewe, in the hope that the Scottish Region element of the journey would still be steam, even though Carlisle's Princess Royal pacifics were long gone. I was in luck as 70007 *Coeur de Lion* backed onto the nine coaches, 315 tons gross. The first part of the journey was hampered by two 40mph p-way slacks at Rockcliffe and Kirtlebridge and we didn't really get going until after Lockerbie, just reaching 73mph before the climb to Beattock began. We fell to $27\frac{1}{2}$mph at Greskine Box, but then accelerated gradually, topping the summit at 31mph. 77mph at Symington then got us to Carstairs on time. The further we went, the better we got and our start after Stirling with our nine-coach train was not that much different from the A4s with seven coaches, with 45 mph at the summit at Kinbuck and 81 on the descent through Auchterarder after the Gleneagles stop.

The purpose was to pick up the Ferryhill A4 on the 5.30pm Glasgow Buchanan Street at Perth and 60009 *Union of South Africa* bowled in on time only to be hurriedly detached having dropped its firebars and fire on the ascent of Dunblane Bank. 44703 was substituted but was a hasty and not very adequate replacement, pinched from the stopping train waiting to follow the *Grampian* and I soon gave up timing and stared out of the window instead. The following morning on a bright summer's day, rather more inviting than my last stay in Aberdeen, I turned up curious to see what Ferryhill A4 would have replaced No.9, and found 60004 *William Whitelaw* which lost 2 minutes to Stonehaven, slipping badly on the morning dew, but then held schedule to Forfar and regained the lost time with a sprint across the last stretch to Perth, 32 miles in 29 minutes, start to stop, with a sustained 76-78mph all the way. Apparently, though, this was too much, for our new A4 then suffered a hot box on the tender, which had flames licking up the offending bearing, and was replaced by a Perth Black 5, 44722, which I took to Stirling before returning once more to Stonehaven via 73152 on a Dundee train and an EE Type 4 on an Edinburgh-Aberdeen express. I was just in time to get the 1.30pm Aberdeen, which sported A4 60006 *Sir Ralph*

Wedgwood instead of the usual V2 or A2 and kept time to Stirling despite a special stop at Alyth Junction to set down a large party. I waited for the 8.15pm Perth-Euston in the hope that a Kingmoor Duchess might still grace that train, but it was nearly the end for them, and 70011 *Hotspur* took me to Stirling and a Black 5 onto Glasgow where I stayed overnight.

I was up early for a B1 (how my views of these engines changed – ten years previously I'd wait for anything other than a B1). 61262 (62B) powered the 7.15am Glasgow-Dundee, an eight-coach train on which the B1 performed adequately, and I assumed I travelled on by diesel traction on the East Coast as my next recorded note is finding 60027 *Merlin* on the 1.30pm Aberdeen instead of the usual V2, which performed more than adequately. I was expecting a Black 5 or St Rollox replacement engine instead of 60004 on the 5.30pm Glasgow *St Mungo* and was surprised when someone had discovered another Ferryhill A4, 60034 *Lord Faringdon,* which was no slouch, with 85mph down Auchterarder bank at Dunning; 79-80 on the Alyth Junction-Forfar section then 84 at Bridge of Dun, arriving 2 minutes early at Stonehaven, where I alighted once more, just in time to catch the 7.45pm FO Aberdeen-York, which arrived behind 60019 *Bittern,* a former rare Gateshead A4 which I saw a lot of over the next couple of years. This enabled me to connect with a Black 5-hauled 11.45pm FO Edinburgh-Birmingham overnight train, which upgraded to one of the remaining Carlisle Duchesses 46237 *City of Bristol* for the run southbound. As we left Carlisle we seemed to be throwing an awful lot of sparks from the ashpan and once again found that the firebars were collapsing and the fire was dropping over the fourfoot. We stopped to report our problem and then drew into a loop somewhere near Clifton & Lowther to await help.

I feared rescue from a Black 5 at best or even a diesel, but was surprised and gratified to find our 'knight in armour' was another Stanier pacific, 46250 *City of Lichfield*, also of Carlisle Upperby. Initially I timed the train, and after early slipping, we gradually accelerated our ten coaches to 46mph at Shap summit and ran in a restrained fashion thereafter with a maximum of 73, but speed mainly in the high 60s until, after Carnforth, sleep took over. I awoke bleary eyed in the dawn as we entered Crewe, 46250 still at the front end where it would remain until its arrival in Birmingham New Street. I kept going in a fit of madness and staggered out at Wolverhampton High Level and stumbled downstairs to the former Great Western station to find the 8am Wolverhampton-Ilfracombe holiday express. This sported a former Stafford Road Castle, 5063 *Earl Baldwin,* now based at Oxley under LM ownership, with a heavy and well filled train of twelve coaches, 440 tons gross. We stopped at Wednesbury and West Bromwich to load yet more on board and set off with energy once on the Stratford-on-Avon route to Cheltenham and Bristol. We attained 75mph before the Stratford stop, then progressed in a more careful way to Broadway and Toddington with a final 67 before the Cheltenham Malvern Road stop. I decided to get out and see what the following relief *Cornishman* for Plymouth would bring. The answer was a Black 5, 44765, one of the few equipped with a double blastpipe and chimney. Running with ten coaches, 365 tons gross, was smart until we were stopped on the outskirts of Bristol for 11 minutes, waiting a platform.

I now looked round for something to turn up and, somewhat to my surprise, a Sheffield B1 61394, formerly a King's Cross regular on the Cambridge buffet trains, appeared on the 12.45pm Bristol-Sheffield eight-coach train. We stormed out of Temple Meads, accelerating to 27mph on Fishponds Bank, and then proceeded more normally in the high 60s to Gloucester, Worcester and Birmingham New Street, being pushed up Lickey Bank by WR pannier tank, 8401. I then meandered to Rugby to see if I could find a last steam turn before going back to Woking to catch up on sleep and a good bath before appearing in my somewhat out of place stationmaster's garb in an industrial Welsh valley once more. I was in luck. The 10.53am Workington-Euston rolled into Rugby behind 70010 *Owen Glendower,* now allocated to Willesden. We left Rugby 6 minutes late and it was obvious from the word go that the driver did not intend to hang around. 66½mph at Roade with our eleven-coach, 400 ton train was fine, as was 63 minimum at Tring, followed by a glorious sweep through Harrow and Wembley at 80mph plus, arriving, as there were no electrification slacks now, a full 16 minutes early.

A couple of weeks later I escaped on my half-day for a quick trip from Shrewsbury to Chester and back with a Standard 5 on the 12.10pm Paddington (73026) and a Black 5 (45044 of Chester) on the 4.30pm Birkenhead. I then settled down to running my patch, playing cricket and tennis with my Ebbw Vale colleague and fellow lodger, Stan, in hailing distance of a signalbox – one of us was always on call – before Scotland lured me for another long weekend in early August. I travelled overnight behind diesel traction and was pleased to see 60007 *Sir Nigel Gresley* on the 7.10am Aberdeen which I took from Perth to Stirling, then, finding the 8.25 Glasgow was diesel, I took the St Rollox A4 60031 *Golden Plover* on the 9.15 Glasgow through to Dundee. Another sortie by EE Type 4 up the East Coast to Montrose and Stonehaven brought me to the 1.30pm Aberdeen with 60034 *Lord Faringdon,* which hurried me westwards to Gleneagles where I alighted to see what was on the 9.25 Crewe, expecting a Britannia – not a St Margaret's V2, 60931, which in fact appeared. I was subsequently told that the V2 had replaced a failed Clan at Carstairs.

News from the informant also suggested that it might be worth taking 73145 on the 6.15pm Glasgow-Dundee in order to pick up the 7.45pm FO Aberdeen-York, for which rare former Gateshead A4 60023 *Golden Eagle* had been requested. Sure enough, the Ferryhill running foreman had obliged and we all rejoiced, although an A4 on just seven coaches on the restriction strewn line from Dundee to Edinburgh Waverley didn't really get a chance to show off. I'm told that my fellow enthusiast and I continued together on an Edinburgh-Birmingham train behind 45126, although I have no note or recollection of this; sleep must have finally caught up.

My purpose was to go north again, this time via the G&SW route, returning to Wales via the West Coast and the North & West. The 9.05pm FO St Pancras-Glasgow St Enoch looked a likely candidate for steam, but I was a little surprised when a Leeds based A1, 60154 *Bon Accord,* rather than a Jubilee appeared off the Settle & Carlisle. The load was a lightweight eight coaches, 265 tons and the A1 should have played with it. We left 7 minutes late, were 2 minutes overtime at

Dumfries and with much slipping by the locomotive leaving there and two p-way slacks at Carronbridge and Hurlford, we were twelve late into Kilmarnock. We laboured thereafter and ground to a halt at Lugton, short of steam, with the brakes leaking on. We restarted fairly quickly, then the same happened again just short of Pollokshaws where – once again – it was found that 60154 had dropped its firebars. It was beginning to be an epidemic! Only ample recovery time on the last leg kept our lost time down to 18 minutes.

The 9.56am relief from Glasgow Central to Euston via the G&SW produced a Black 5, 44972 of Hurlford, again with just an eight-coach load and it made heavy weather of it. We fell to 14mph on the 1 in 70 past Neilston and took 45 minutes to run the 24 miles to Kilmarnock, were cautioned past Bowhouse Box and did rather better recovering to 32mph on the 1 in 100 to Mauchline. A couple of signal checks approaching Carlisle didn't help, although running after Kilmarnock had been satisfactory. I was not inclined to go further south with it, however, and waited at Carlisle until the 10.35am Glasgow Central to Blackpool appeared, with recently out-shopped Kingmoor Britannia, 70006 *Robert Burns*. A nicely manageable ten coaches, 345 tons gross was the load and we left 6 minutes late and promptly stood for 2 minutes at Wreay, waiting the line ahead. Another check at Penrith; 43 minimum at Shap; 77 on the descent and general running in the low 70s and late 60s saw us 10 minutes late into Preston, after which I abandoned any further effort to get steam and nodded off, remembering to change at Crewe. After all this hectic travelling around the north of England and Scotland, it was time to devote some time to my responsibilities in Wales.

The Aberbeeg Shedmaster retired in the autumn of 1964 about two months before the depot was due to close when full dieselisation would be completed. As there was little point in filling the post for such a short time, I was asked to take over the reins there for this interim period and had one brief moment of glory when I managed to persuade the diagramming people in Cardiff to let our Aberbeeg men learn the road and go through to Gloucester with a Mondays Only tinplate train with one of our two 52XXs. I don't think the route learning costs amounted to anything – the men were so keen, I think they learned the road in their own time! So I vividly remember bowling down the valley in the cab of 5214 on our inaugural run and whistling rudely at Rogerstone Yard as we escaped into the big wide world outside the Valley. I bailed out at Newport but rumour has it that some of the signalmen on the Newport-Gloucester line had never seen an old 52XX in such a hurry.

The 37s reigned almost supreme – an occasional Churchward 2-8-0 tank or 9F would foray up to Ebbw Vale from Alexandra Dock to the end of our time there. Our trusted panniers were replaced by Paxman Class 14s, D95XX, we must have had some of the first, and dreadful they were. Their attempts at banking heavy trains to Ebbw Vale were farcical. Around Marine Colliery, halfway up the 1 in 50, the engine would often overheat and trip out, and the class 37 train locomotive would be left to haul the dead D9501 or one of its sisters all the way to the top. I have to say this for the 37s – they were man enough to do this without falling down, so I began to wonder whether they really needed a banker at all.

Above: Collett 1924 built 2-8-0T 5238 hauls a load of iron ore for Ebbw Vale steelworks past Aberbeeg Junction, banked by a 2-8-2T, 7218, circa 1963. (*ColourRail*)

Right: The hopper train for Waunllwyd is banked away from Aberbeeg up the 1 in 50 by 2-8-2T 7229, June 1964. (*Author*)

Churchward 2-8-0T 4273 lifts a hopper train of iron ore out of Aberbeeg for Waunllwyd Sidings at Ebbw Vale, June 1964. (*Author*)

One consequence of the switch from steam to diesel was the sudden shortage of coal at all the signalboxes on the patch. We had to start actually ordering domestic coal and the Aberbeeg Junction signalmen asked for a coal store, as they could no longer replenish themselves from the bunkers of pannier tanks. I ordered a breeze-block coalhouse from the District Engineer at Newport and got a quote of £465. I remember being horrified as there was a terraced miner's cottage in the road just below the signalbox going for £325 and I offered to buy that instead. I don't think my irony was appreciated, but we did get our coalhouse.

Just before I completed my turn of duty at Aberbeeg – I was made redundant on the introduction of Area Management and was moved to Bridgend as Assistant Area Manager – I was host, with a member of the local press, to witness the last steam turn from Aberbeeg depot. It was a Saturday lunchtime turn, a set of coal empties from Marine Colliery at Cwm, to be stabled in our yard. The pressman set up his tripod and 9494 duly appeared round the curve from the Ebbw Vale branch with its string of 16 ton mineral wagons. It had just reached the underbridge at the end of the platform when the pannier tank derailed all wheels and continued to run towards us hitting the paving slabs at the edge of the platform and throwing them like frisbees across the deserted station. The noise was incredible and I backed away quickly out of the line of fire, only to see the reporter haring out of the station. He never did get a photo! Miraculously, all the wagons stayed on the line and we were faced with a pannier tank at the signal protecting the junction sitting upright in the fourfoot. Saturday at midday when Newport County was playing at home was not the best time to call out the Ebbw Junction breakdown crew, so our foreman got a set of ramps from the yard and with much creaking and splintering of wood, we drove 9494 back onto the rails. And the local press missed their story!

I often look back at the ten months spent at Aberbeeg as the time I learned most about human nature – not just in the railway activities, but also from the experiences in the Hanbury Arms Hotel, now no more. However, that would need a whole new book to describe … A lifelong friendship with Stan Judd was bonded there and we helped each other escape from our Welsh confines for a few brief hours each week. The Western Valley not only provided such valuable experience and a rich encounter with some marvellous and generous characters, but it shaped both Stan's and my railway careers for years to come, in that Stan became a 'Marketing Man' and I became an Operator. With hindsight, I wonder that I managed so much time roaming round Scotland, sacrificing time when I could have been at home in Woking rather than chasing exotic steam. However, I was still unmarried – indeed, no serious girlfriend yet, a situation to be remedied shortly – so I spent my leave days experiencing the last summer of significant mainline steam (except on the Southern).

Chapter 9

Area Manager, Bridgend

I arrived at Bridgend as Assistant Area Manager in the winter of 1965 and had to find lodgings. I was recommended a semi-detached house about half a mile from the station in North Street with a widow and her teenage son and installed myself, noting that my main heating was an old 'Valour' oil stove. There was also no sign of a telephone and as I would be on call every other week I advised my landlady that I might get called out any time of day or night, which would mean being knocked up by a taxi driver sent by the station inspector. 'That won't be often, will it?' my landlady asked hopefully and I reassured her as best I could, remembering my reputation as a 'Jonah' at Aberbeeg, having been called out sixteen times in ten months compared with Stan's three times! Sure enough, I was called out every evening or night that first week to some minor derailment. I discovered later that the Area Manager and I had replaced eight stationmasters who liked the overtime to supplement their on call allowance, and therefore encouraged their staff to call them however minor the incident. As management staff, neither Eric Warr, my boss, nor I would receive any additional payment.

On the first Friday evening we did have an accident which warranted my attention. Our '08' shunter in Bridgend West Yard managed to derail and turn over and we had to summon the Canton breakdown crane. We toiled all night and I arrived back at my digs just before six absolutely exhausted. I had thrown off my clothes and flung myself into bed and had fallen into a deep sleep, when, at just twenty past six, I heard hammering on my bedroom door. It took me a long time to make sense of the noise but in the end I realised that I was being called out again and that a taxi was waiting for me. It took me straight to Tondu loco shed where they had managed to derail a pair of wheels of a wagon of loco coal inside the shed limit and clear of the running lines. It only needed a pair of ramps and a pannier tank to give it a shove, and as I stared stupefied in the steady drizzle at my feet, I realised that in my brain fog I had put on one brown shoe and one black. The inspector looked at my misery and said, 'I think you'd better go home, guvnor, you'll not be much help to us here.' From then on we made it clear that we expected the supervisory staff to deal with minor incidents that did not affect running lines and managed to reduce call outs to a more reasonable level, although there were plenty of derailments in the Welsh Valleys in the early years of dieselization.

Eric Warr was the former Shedmaster of Southall, an extrovert Londoner with a very practical and, at times, unorthodox way of dealing with problems. On one occasion, we had an incident with the ground frame that controlled the entrance to Bridgend West Yard from the Up Main Line. It had failed with the points set to the yard causing a stoppage on the main line. Eric took me down with him and I watched as he dismantled the ground frame mechanism and clipped the points to allow trains to start running again. 'Don't let me ever see you doing that!' he said, 'I know what I'm doing; it's against the rules but I'm taking responsibility. You can only do that sort of thing when you've a lot more experience under your belt.'

One week that winter it rained – as only it can in Wales – and at 4am there was a loud knocking on the door, which woke the whole household. The taxi driver said, 'They say it's serious, you'd better come quick!' With some foreboding I arrived at the station, the night pitch black, the wind howling and rain lashing on the station roof and platform. There were coaches standing on the Up Main, luckily, as I discovered shortly afterwards, empty stock as the Fishguard Boat Train had been cancelled because of storms in the Irish Sea. I fetched my Bardic lamp from my office and ventured out into the eerie darkness and came across a sight I shall never forget. My way was blocked by mangled wreckage some three vehicles high filling the cutting just where the Vale of Glamorgan line parted from the main line to Cardiff. Underneath the angular jagged metal of coaches and wagons I could just see the rear of a Class 47 burrowing under the snout of a class 37 that had clearly met it head on. There was obviously nothing I could do to rescue the train crews before the fire brigade arrived with cutting gear and within minutes the darkness and silence had been transformed as fire engines, police and ambulances converged on the station. As dawn broke I could see the scale of the disaster – the cutting was filled to the brim with twelve coaches, fifty-two wagons, and three diesel engines, for the coal train had been double-headed by two class 37s. The torrential rain had loosened rock from the cutting just east of the station and this had spilled onto the track in the storm and darkness and had derailed the empty stock, which had been travelling at around 60mph. The loco had been derailed and unfortunately had slewed foul of the Down Main and had met the double-headed coal train travelling at around 35mph head on. As the class 47 was on the trackbed, the front 37 rode over it crushing the cab, killing the second man immediately and severely injuring the driver, injuries from which he subsequently died. The crew of the freight train was lucky and survived with comparatively minor injuries.

The line clearance in appalling weather, cutting strengthening and track renewal – including the whole double junction – took nearly two weeks, during which time trains to West Wales were diverted via Pontypool Road and the Vale of Neath. However, the rain continued and lines became flooded and at one stage the only way we got the down Fishguard Boat Train through was to send it, with its Western diesel hydraulic, via Treherbert through the tunnel to Cymmer Afan, then down the Llynfi Valley through Maesteg and Tondu to Pyle and back onto the main line. Cliff Rose,

Divisional Movements Manager, was in my office when the decision was taken. He had no idea whether the diesel was cleared for this route – it had never been tested – but he took a chance and it crept down the valley successfully as we all held our breath. This was a time of great stress for all concerned – I spent most of the period on 12 hour nights and by the end was so shattered that the Assistant Divisional Manager, Jack Page, seriously wondered if I was up to the job. I survived and my lack of good fortune continued, and I seemed to get more than my share of mishaps. As a painful reminder of the accident, the mutilated corpse of D1671 *Thor* stood for several weeks in my goods yard right beside my office, shrouded in tarpaulins to screen it from the sight of passengers as they passed.

I also got more than my fair share of Sunday engineering work to supervise. Many were the winter nights spent putting in single line working between Bridgend and Stormy Sidings – a very apt name – or near the Cardiff end of my patch, between Llantrisant (now more correctly called Pontyclun) and my border at St Fagan's. For some reason the track formation under the main line in the River Ely valley was 'fragile' and we had a number of plain line derailments there, culminating in a spectacular incident when the empty gunpowder van forming part of the brake force behind the locomotive jumped plain line when travelling at around 45mph and the train of coke behind it reared up on end and deposited several hundred tons into the river just after Miskin. A local coal merchant was granted the franchise of emptying the river and track of the coke and I shudder to think how many householders received a motley collection of ballast with their fuel! This was one of a series of derailments involving plain line, when all the ingredients were near to their limit – speed, track voiding and uneven wagon loading or stiff springs. After several such derailments and analysis of each by the Derby derailment research team, it was decided to restrict the large number of short wheelbase freight wagons to 35mph.

It was during one of my engineering possessions in yet another steady downpour that we actually caught a fish – and a decent size one at that – from between the sleepers in the main line where the Llanharan Colliery workings had caused subsidence and a 40mph permanent restriction was in force. It was around this time that I enjoyed one of my last steam footplate runs in BR service. Tondu depot had closed although men remained stationed there and our Churchward 2-8-0 tanks at Llantrisant for the iron ore trains to Llanwern had been replaced by the new 37s. However, the engineering Sunday turns would sometimes produce a steam engine, and I enjoyed one Sunday managing affairs from the footplate of 0-6-2 tank 5691.

I had hoarded some leave to spend in the summer and determined to go north to Scotland again before the A4s were completely supplanted on the Glasgow-Aberdeen route. On 14 July 1965, I made my way to Crewe and found at least one short steam interlude with 70012 *John of Gaunt* on the 9.31pm Crewe-Blackpool as far as Preston. We only had eight coaches and we left on time, but that did not deter the Preston driver from wanting to get home to bed, and we roared out past Crewe Coal Yard spitting fire, screaming through Hartford at 84mph, 12 miles in 12 minutes 43 seconds, and then reaching 81 again at Moore after a 30mph p-way slack at Acton

Bridge. Even with this we were 3 minutes early into Warrington. We accelerated to 57 on the 1 in 132/1 in 156 up to Golborne but signals into Preston made us three late there. I continued northbound by night to Carlisle and then dallied until the 9.25am Crewe arrived, and the diesel was replaced not by the hoped-for Britannia pacific but a rundown Kingmore Black 5, 44670, to haul our nine-coach, 310 ton train to Perth. The start was inauspicious with a p-way restriction to 40mph at Kirtlebridge and a dead stand for signals at Wamphray, so that Beattock station was passed at only 47mph, but the engine was flogged, dropping to 24 at Greskine Box, then opened out further to sustain 28mph on the upper part of the bank. Our rough-riding steed was then allowed to run at 75mph both before and after Carstairs, and the further we went, the harder the engine seemed to work. Clearly, despite the external condition of the engine, steaming was not a problem. Just to make matters more difficult, three vehicles were added at Stirling, now making the load twelve for 390 tons, and the Black 5 was worked in seemingly full forward gear to surmount the climb through Dunblane to Kinbuck at 35mph, and after the Gleneagles stop, ran downhill to Perth at a steady (well, on the footplate, not so steady) 75mph. The driver and fireman well deserved congratulations on arriving at Perth a minute early!

I was thus in ample time to pick up the 5.30pm Glasgow-Aberdeen which ran into Perth behind 60019 *Bittern*. The A4 made the task seem easy. The load was only six coaches for 225 tons gross, and although we left 4 minutes late, sustained running in the mid-70s got us to Forfar in 31 minutes and we continued in excellent fashion reaching Aberdeen exactly on time. Next morning 60019 was again the Ferryhill motive power for the 3-hour Glasgow service return diagram and I joined the same 6 coaches and had an efficient run to Stirling where we arrived 2½ minutes early, without appearing to break sweat. The noisiest part of the journey was the 7 mile 1 in 100 climb on the last section to Gleneagles, started at 70mph and finished at 52. I picked up the 9.15 Glasgow-Dundee at Stirling with 73146 and relaxed on the diesel hauled Edinburgh-Aberdeen connection, in order to join the 1.30pm Aberdeen *Grampian* at Stonehaven. 60024 *Kingfisher* was just ex-works, but something didn't seem quite right and it had to be punched hard to keep time, although the load was only eight coaches. Despite the noise – the exhaust from this A4 always seemed harsher than that of its sisters – it seemed sluggish and the driver suggested that the valves needed resetting.

Then it was back from Stirling to Perth on the 5.30pm Glasgow behind 60019 again, with a Friday load of nine coaches, 330 tons. The A4 climbed to Kinbuck at an excellent 46mph and touched 82 through Dunning, regaining 2 minutes of the late start. I got out at Perth intending to return to Carlisle on the 8.15pm sleeper to Euston and found to my surprise Kingmoor's 72008 *Clan Macleod*. We left Perth with seven coaches, made up to eleven at Stirling and another couple at Carstairs making our load thirteen coaches, 475 tons gross. Although virtually on time into Carstairs, the shunting made us 8 minutes late away, but the Clan did well with its very heavy load, surmounting Beattock at 33½mph and touching 79 at Murthat. Unfortunately, two severe p-way checks at Castlemilk and Kirtlebridge caused us to lose 6 minutes on schedule and we were just over 13 minutes late into Carlisle, where the Clan was relieved by 70036 *Boadicea*.

I was not yet ready to return south, however, and I planned to get the 9.05pm FO St Pancras-Glasgow St Enoch and cross to Edinburgh to pick up the 9.50am SO Edinburgh-Carlisle-Leeds via the Waverley route which I'd seen with a St Margaret's V2 before. Holbeck's 45675 *Hardy* duly arrived on the train off the Settle and Carlisle more or less on time, and I got into the ten-coach 315 ton train and waited … and waited. My anxiety mounted as the minutes ticked by and the prospect of crossing to Edinburgh to catch the Waverley route train retreated. Apparently we were awaiting a guard and finally departed 75 minutes late on a very wet and stormy morning. The Jubilee was worked hard, climbing the 1 in 200 through Auldgirth to Closeburn at 48mph and reaching the summit at Carronbridge at 42, but we were still losing time, with a couple more p-way slacks at Kirkonnel and New Cumnock and a dead stand for 3 minutes at Mauchline, so I decided to bail out at Kilmarnock and caught a Peak-hauled express back to Carlisle, arriving just in time to see what I'd missed on the 9.50 Edinburgh which rolled in behind the last remaining Royal Scot, 46115, now of course preserved. I was devastated.

To rub it in, the Scot was replaced at Carlisle by a Kingmoor Black 5, 45295 on a light seven-coach train and it was not until I was experiencing an energetic climb to Mallerstang and Ais Gill at a creditable 48-50mph that I cheered up. I went right through to Leeds City and can't complain – the '5' did all that was asked of it and we arrived on time. I crossed to Leeds Central expecting to slumber behind a Deltic or Brush Type 4 all the way to King's Cross, only to find the next express to London standing with A1 60145 *St Mungo* out beyond the end of the platform. But I was too tired and could not force myself to time it. Every time I attempted to count the rail joints against my second hand, I dropped off before the time span was complete. I just remember that the A1 was particularly bad at keeping its feet in the wet conditions and that we were late. Back home then to recuperate and prepare myself for return to South Wales.

Just a fortnight later I was tempted to have another much shorter go – it was as though I was now addicted. Up the North & West after work on the Friday evening and I picked up the 7.20pm FO Euston-Perth, which left Crewe 5 minutes late with 70032 *Tennyson* on eleven coaches, 405 tons gross. We added an extra three coaches at Wigan giving a gross load of 515 tons – this shunting manoeuvre lost us a full quarter of an hour. We heaved this load up the 1 in 104 to Boars Head at 26½mph and by Standish we were doing 39, only falling to 38 on the last mile of 1 in 119. 75 mph through Farington got a minute back, then at Preston someone discovered that our buffet car had developed a hot box and the vehicle had to be removed from the middle of the train. There was ample time in the schedule, however, and the station staff did exceedingly well to get us away just 24 minutes late. But we were now out of our path and a p-way check at Brock and a signal check to walking pace at Lancaster made us 28 minutes late into Carnforth, where we were stopped for Fairburn 2-6-4T 42210 to be attached to us as pilot through to Shap summit. This meant we were now forty-two late, although the pair of locomotives did well, clearing Grayrigg at 46mph, passing Tebay at 71 and only falling to 36 at the summit before shutting off steam to detach the pilot. 78mph before Penrith was too much for whatever was in front of us and we were forced to stand for 2 minutes at Eden Valley Junction before an 80 near Southwaite. But we were 50 minutes late into Carlisle. It was now late and I slept through to Perth and caught an early morning train back to Edinburgh.

For some unfathomable reason (now) I caught the 11.30am local from Princes Street back to Carstairs with an odd combination of Fairburn tank 42058 and Clayton diesel D8562 and from there joined a Dundee-Blackpool train with Black 5, 45475 of Perth. This performed quite happily with its 10 coach load, leaving Carstairs 11 minutes late but arriving in Carlisle on time, with 42mph minimum on the southbound climb to Beattock, and the low 70s afterwards. I was looking forward to a Britannia pacific southwards as had happened two weeks before but the Black 5 was replaced by another, 44896, a Leeds engine, which, despite my disappointment, was more than adequate for timekeeping. 36 at Shap summit and 81 on the descent got us into Oxenholme on time and 78 at Milnthorpe and steady running in the 60s after that made us over 3 minutes early into Preston.

Life proceeded normally, that is with more than my fair share of call outs and night work supervising weekend engineering work. I'd added frequent trips to London, as I was now courting a girl I'd met on holiday in the summer and she'd started college and lived in a students' hostel in Ealing. My steam trips now diminished in number, partly because of these distracting pursuits and partly as, during the winter especially, main line steam other than on the Bournemouth line, was becoming hard to find. The Western Region was now steam free, so, apart from my home patch at Woking, attempts to find steam involved long overnight journeys up the West Coast to Scotland and my work was causing me to value my sleep rather more highly.

I occasionally had a little fling on the Great Central, but that was now reduced to four coach semi-fast services with Black 5s. I did turn out for the last day of steam there, 19 February 1966, before the Beeching axe, finding 45222 on the 4.38pm Marylebone which chirruped happily with its toy train, with 37 minimum at Amersham and 75 through Great Missenden. I alighted at Woodford Halse to connect with the last Up service, the 5.15pm Nottingham – six coaches on the last day with 44985 – but we only got as far as Culworth Junction, just 4 minutes into our journey, before injector problems forced the driver to seek a new engine whilst still within hailing reach of Woodford depot. 45211 rescued us and we carried on our way now 36 minutes late, an undistinguished anti-climax. A 2 minute dead stand outside Marylebone was the last straw and we finished over 40 minutes late. Another last rite I visited at the end of that winter was a farewell to the Somerset & Dorset on 5 March, making my way to Bath Green Park and taking a local to Evercreech Junction with an 8F, 48760, on a three-coach stopping train. There I discovered and talked my way onto an LCGB special with a pair of un-rebuilt Bulleid pacifics, 34006 *Bude* and 34057 *Biggin Hill,* although I might have savoured the atmosphere better had I stuck to the S&D locals, regretfully mostly BR Standard 4 tanks rather than LMS 2P 4-4-0s now.

In the middle of my spell at Bridgend I was summoned to attend BR's Middle Management Course – six weeks at the former LMR Training School in Derby. A couple of dozen budding senior managers were bombarded with outrageous ideas

– thinking the unthinkable was doubtless the remit the lecturers had been urged to deliver to shake us out of any complacency we may have had. My abiding memory of the course, however, was the 48 hours we spent in groups on a specific project. My team, which included (deliberately) no engineers, was sent to Crewe Works to devise ways of reducing the downtime of Class 47s in the Works by at least 24 hours. Our confidence what not boosted by the news that our project presentation would be assessed by the Board's Chief Mechanical & Electrical Engineer, R.C.Bond, no less. We were further dismayed to discover that one of our number, an architect by trade, had wasted a whole day minutely recording the activities of a group of fitters on a large blue locomotive which turned out not to be a Class 47 but A4 Pacific 4498 *Sir Nigel Gresley*, and one of us went to Crewe station that evening and bought him an Ian Allan ABC to try to teach him the difference between a steam and diesel engine! In the end we did produce some suggestions and Mr Bond was very kind to us – whether Crewe Works management ever implemented any of our ideas was never fed back to us.

After eighteen months or so, Eric Warr was promoted to the Divisional Office in Marland House, Cardiff and I took over as Area Manager. My problems in the valleys above Tondu continued unabated. A loaded train of coal – eighteen unfitted wagons – ran away from Abergwynfi colliery with its Paxman D95XX (class 14), despite twelve of the wagons having brakes pinned down, and derailed at the trap points protecting the Treherbert-Cymmer Afan single line, damming a stream in the process which then flooded the track. Before the wheels stopped spinning, doors of the miners' cottages on the hillside above the line opened and dozens of small children descended on the train stripping it of anything removable and filling their buckets with coal dust (destined for Margam Steel Works) even though they were all entitled to free coal from the mine. A few weeks later another D95XX was propelling four empty wagons up the 1 in 27/36 to Glyncorrwg Colliery when it buffered up to another wagon left foul over the entrance to the colliery siding. These five wagons overpowered our weak tool and the train ran back down the gradient accelerating rapidly, the locomotive brakes inadequate to slow the runaway. The train crew decided discretion was the better part of valour and jumped before the train reached the catch points protecting the junction at Cymmer and the D95XX made a spectacular somersault at an estimated 35mph and lay in the ditch between track and cutting bank.

Our most horrendous and indeed, miraculous, runaway was in the Garw Valley. A class 37 had hauled fifty-two empty mineral wagons up the 1 in 50 and stopped at the ground frame controlling the entrance to the Garw colliery. The guard walked forward to operate the frame and called the train forward. The train started with a bit of a jerk and the coupling between the first and second wagons snapped and fifty-one wagons and brake van set off down the hill with the guard in hot and vain pursuit. It was a hopeless quest and the entire train of unbraked wagons quickly accelerated to a frightening speed. It smashed through crossing gates just missing a bus and I received a phone call from the signalman at Brynmenyn Junction at the foot of the bank and about a mile from Tondu, saying 'Listen to this guvnor!' and

Churchward 2-8-0T 4243 hauls a train of coal for Margam from Ogmore Vale Central Washery through the 5mph restricted four-way reverse curve junction at Tondu, through which 51 empty mineral wagons and guard-less guard's van careered at an estimated 60mph without a disaster, 1 June 1962. (*B.W.L.Brooksbank/Initial Photographics Collection*)

Cymmer Afan station with the single-power unit 550XX ['Bubble-car'] used on the Llynfi Valley service to Bridgend. Here it has just arrived with an unadvertised miners' train from Duffryn Rhondda Colliery. In the far distance a Class 14 Paxman diesel can be seen about to tackle the gradient to Glyncorrwg Colliery, 29 September 1966. (*Robert Darlaston*)

in my office I was treated to the roaring sound of the runaway train then estimated at 70mph! At the inquiry the signalman was criticised for not turning the raft of wagons through the trap points into the river in order to protect Tondu Junction, depot and village, but the signalman claimed that he was unsure whether the guard was still on board and did not want to condemn him to certain death. By Tondu, after a mile on the level, speed had reduced to about 60mph, but the four-way junction ahead had double reverse curves and a speed restriction of 5mph. Staff had already cleared the terraced cottages in the line of fire and later described how the train seemed to scream round the curves on two wheels. How it did not spread itself all over the junction no-one knows, but it sped off up the gradient to Pyle and Margam with two quick-witted shunters in pursuit in their old banger. They correctly surmised where the train would have slowed sufficiently to pin down enough brakes to stop the train rolling back to Tondu and having another go at demolishing the junction. When it was eventually stopped and the train examined, thirty-seven of the wagons out of the fifty-two vehicles were found to have hot axle boxes.

Another source of vexation, although not nearly so serious, was the constant theft of the tiny oil lamps, which lit the wooden platforms at Maesteg – the line served by a 'Bubble Car' (single-power car DMU of 550XX series) shuttling between Bridgend and Cymmer Afan. We were worried that someone would slip or fall from one of the platforms in the darkness and kept replacing the lamps only to find they would disappear again within days. Eventually we discovered that these lamps were highly prized by local entrepreneurs for hatching out baby chicks!

Gerry Fiennes was General Manager until 1966 and he was getting increasingly dissatisfied with what he considered to be the lack of sufficient horsepower on WR expresses – certainly compared with the Deltics on the East Coast. He therefore

A pannier tank with a raft of loaded coal wagons from Abergwynfi Colliery at the spot where the D95XX derailed and dammed the stream in 1966, 5 August 1959. (*Robert Darlaston*)

directed that a pair of 37s in multiple were to be tried out on the South Wales-London expresses with the prototype XP64 stock and I rode on the 8.20am Swansea to a London meeting one day in May with a pair of Newport Godfrey Road engines, D6877 and D6892. The acceleration from scratch was phenomenal and we sustained 100mph on level track (see log in Appendix 1, Table 11) but after a couple of weeks, the experiment was called off as the heavy freight locos were unsuited to continuous high speed and began to develop serious traction problems.

That spring of 1966 I spent much of my time back in Woking, when not courting, taking the familiar Bulleid Pacifics down to Southampton and Bournemouth as recounted in Chapter 5, until my summer leave was due. In August I had committed myself to taking my girlfriend down to Swanage to a holiday with my family, but before that, I had one last midweek break on the Glasgow-Aberdeen just before steam finished there. There was no steam to get there now, so it was a diesel overnight sleeper, but on the 6 July I was at Buchanan Street in time to catch the 8.25am *Grampian* with one of the remaining two active A4s, 60024 *Kingfisher*. This A4 was now back on top form, and handled its six-coach, 215 ton gross train with ease, arriving at Stirling on time; climbing to Kinbuck at 46mph; 74½ on the still rising gradient to Blackford and 80 down the bank to arrive Perth 2 minutes early. After Perth it became much livelier, with speed rising on the level to 86mph, the 32 miles start to stop to Forfar being covered in just under 30 minutes. We continued on our merry way speed varying between 75 and 85mph and arrived triumphantly 5 minutes early in Aberdeen.

A2 60532 *Blue Peter* was on the 1.30pm Aberdeen and climbed strongly with its 245 ton load above the cliffs passing Cove Bay at 56, and climbing out of Stonehaven to Carmont at a similar speed. *Blue Peter* was not as fast as the A4s on the Forfar-Perth stretch but we cruised in the mid-70s and arrived at Stirling on time. Back to Perth where I picked up *Kingfisher* on the returning 3-hour Aberdeen; 78mph at Dunning; 52 on the 1 in 100 to Gleneagles; 80 afterwards, and just before time into Glasgow. Next morning it was *Kingfisher* again on the 8.25 and it was almost a carbon-copy trip to Forfar, with 49 at Kinbuck; 82 at Auchterarder; 83 at Forgandenny and 83-85 from Alyth Junction to the outskirts of Forfar. The driver took it more easily after that but we were still a minute early into Aberdeen. *Blue Peter* was on the 1.30pm again and posted very similar times to the previous day and was punctual into Perth.

I alighted to get a good meal, for I had something new in mind for the evening that would preclude getting much to eat later. *Kingfisher* duly appeared on the 5.15pm Aberdeen and was again punctual into Glasgow, where I made my way across to St Enoch for a semi-fast on the G&SWR with a Corkerhill decorated Jubilee, 45718 *Dreadnought*. Then it was to Ayr, for my intention was to catch the Stranraer Boat Train each way between Ayr and Carlisle, with booked Kingmoor Britannias. The *Northern Irishman*, as the Boat Train was named, arrived in the late evening at Ayr with 70016 *Ariel* on ten coaches, 330 tons gross. We left 5 minutes late and accelerated up the 1 in 100 from Annbank Junction to 35mph, 55/47mph through Auchinleck to the summit at Polquhap Siding and then easy in the high 60s down to Dumfries. 72 maximum across the levels after Annan, but a signal check at Gretna Junction made us 3 minutes late into Carlisle.

The northbound *Northern Irishman,* 8.40pm from Euston, had Kingmoor's 70038 *Robin Hood* on eleven coaches, 355 tons gross, from Carlisle, setting off into the night 12 minutes late. 73 at Powfoot and 62½ minimum at Ruthwell on the 1 in 200 got us to Dumfries efficiently enough, but 70038 spent 8 minutes taking water there (perhaps there was no water in the Floriston troughs) and we left 20 minutes late. We now heard the staccato exhaust of a hard-working Britannia echoing around the dark hills and 67mph, only falling to 58 on the 1 in 150 to Carronbridge, was excellent. We were restrained downhill with nothing over 68, and had regained 7 minutes to Ayr, arriving 13 minutes late. Bleary eyed, I now made my way back to Glasgow, found some breakfast at Central and walked up the hill to Buchanan Street and there was *Kingfisher* yet again. Another splendid run, two early into Stirling, 48½ at Kinbuck; 76 at Blackford; 82 at Forgandenny and into Perth 3 minutes early. The running in the last month of the 3-hour Glasgow-Aberdeen was as good as it had ever been with 60019 and 60024 sharing the work very consistently.

It was now time to return home and I hoped some Friday afternoon extras might produce steam on the West Coast. I returned to Glasgow with a Black 5 and found the 2pm FO Glasgow Central-Liverpool & Manchester with a very clean 70003 *John Bunyan* (but minus nameplates). We had just eight coaches to Carstairs, but made up to eleven there, 395 tons gross. We worked hard to Beattock summit, passed at 47mph, and braked whenever speed drifted up to 75 on the descent. From Beattock station to Carlisle we ran in the 68-72 speed range, with two p-way slacks at Kirtlebridge and Gretna Junction. We left Carlisle 3 minutes late, took water at Penrith, then roared away, 46 minimum at Shap summit, and a flamboyant 84 through Tebay, chime whistle blaring. After the Oxenholme stop, we touched 81 at Milnthorpe, then ground to a halt at Carnforth with much hammering and cursing in the cab – the injectors were playing up again. The driver was forced to let 70003 go and exchange it with a filthy and rundown sister, 70011 *Hotspur* – no sign of a nameplate on this one either. We struggled to Lancaster, with much black smoke and nothing over 60, and bided our time while the fireman stoked furiously until we ran alongside the M6 near Garstang. Then the driver roused *Hotspur,* determined to put on a show for the motorway and we flogged up to 83 with much noise and filthy smoke – we must have been quite a sight from the cars we overtook, the driver drawing attention to our progress, as if it were needed – with frequent use of the chime. As soon as the M6 curved away, the driver shut off steam and a pall of brown smoke smothered the whole train. We were late, of course, after our enforced engine change, but it had been great fun.

Increasingly now, I had to rely on the bevy of 'end of steam' specials and the dying swansong on the Bournemouth line. And then on 7 July 1967, I had my last runs behind scheduled steam. It was a filthy, rundown 34093 *Saunton* on the 5.23pm FO Waterloo-Bournemouth, as far as Southampton – surely this wasn't to be my last memory – then, thank heavens, a tolerably clean 34013 *Okehampton* on my last British Rail steam train. We broke no records, but we did get an 83 at Fleet and 86½ at West Weybridge, arriving in Waterloo 11½ minutes early – a fitting end but hardly typical of my recorded 4,646 runs behind BR steam between 1944 and 1967. After that it was specials, France and Germany – and, in 2002, even China, but I'll leave that until later.

Near the end of my time at Bridgend, I was alarmed to hear that I was to be host for a full day's saloon tour by the new General Manager, my bugbear, Lance Ibbotson. I had to report to the saloon arriving in Bridgend West Yard at 8am and present myself for breakfast. I was so nervous that I was physically sick just before climbing into the vehicle and I doubt I did justice to the eggs and bacon served up. At least there were no kippers. This time I'd done my homework well and having been in the area for nearly four years, I was able to answer all the GM's questions or bluff successfully. A couple of years later, my successor had a similar tour, which he told me was going pretty poorly until they got to Llantrisant Yard. The General Manager had been scathing about the need for Llantrisant at all and its few wagons from the Ministry of Defence Depot and colliery above Mwyndy Junction. My colleague was fearing another diatribe when the saloon arrived back in the yard, expecting to find it empty. However, the place was a hive of activity, dumbfounding Lance Ibbotson, with two iron ore trains and a coal train awaiting the road. After the General Manager, somewhat appeased, had gone on his way, Ken Shingleton asked Bill Heard, the Area Inspector, how come the yard had been so busy. 'Ah, we've been holding them here since lunchtime. We thought you deserved a show for the General Manager!' Llantrisant depot survived a few more months.

Not all memorable activity took place on the railway. As in Aberbeeg, social history was being lived out. I was in 'chapel country'. In the 18,000 population town of Maesteg there were said to be thirty-two different chapels (I didn't count them) – doubling up because there was an English and Welsh language version of each denomination. In the Ogmore Vale, there were two Methodist chapels a hundred yards from each other, but rivalries were such that they wouldn't merge. One chapel was apparently praying for children for their Sunday School – they had potential teachers. The other had so many children they were praying for teachers. That condition continued without either prayer being answered! When one was in financial trouble, the other chapel, which was well endowed, paid their bills to save them having to join up. Down in Bridgend, I was prevailed upon to act as an 'auxiliary preacher' although I felt my calling was to youth work rather than taking Sunday services. When the quarterly 'plan' came out I discovered that I was allocated to take the services at the chapels at the heads of the valleys only because I had my railway car and I could drop the other preachers off as we passed the chapels as we went up the valley. Then I knew why I was 'called to preach'! If you looked at Welsh Sunday bus timetables you could understand why I was in such demand.

In the end, my performance before the General Manager paid off, or perhaps someone from a valley chapel said they'd had enough of me – I was probably too radical/liberal in my beliefs for traditional Welsh chapel Methodism – and I found myself promoted to be Train Planning Officer at the Divisional Office in Cardiff. At least my on call duties would be less frequent, I could get home more often or conduct my long distance courting with greater ease with my girlfriend (who later became my wife). I now became a commuter from Bridgend to the Divisional Headquarters in Marland House opposite Cardiff General Station.

Chapter 10

Cardiff Divisional Office

Initially I went to Cardiff to cover the absence of the Terminals Manager for three months, a man who seemed terrified every time he received a summons from Bob Hilton, the Divisional Manager. Hilton was a manager of the old school, autocratic but decisive and forceful, embracing the new 'management thinking' that was de rigueur under Richard Beeching. He was only interested in solutions, not problems, and expected his managers to get on and do things – as long as they were 'on message'. This was fine as long as his management instincts were right – and they usually were – but occasionally things would go badly awry when he pushed something and his managers were too timid or fearful to argue. I was not particularly happy as Terminals Manager, finding myself required to confront a very militant set of Trade Union representatives covering the terminal and freight staff – Sectional Council D. As often as not I had the unhappy role of negotiating closures of depots or stations, and it was with some relief that I was transferred to the Operations side, where I had more support in the powerful and gifted Cliff Rose, who became a Board Member at an early age and died of cancer tragically young.

After another temporary period as an Operating Assistant, the Train Planning Officer's job became vacant and I was appointed on a permanent basis. The main line services between Severn Tunnel Junction and Swansea, Carmarthen and Fishguard were timed and diagrammed by the Western Region HQ staff in Paddington, but I was responsible for the passenger services in the Cardiff Valleys and all the internal South Wales freight services. After a few months, my job was amalgamated with that of the Trains Office Superintendent who was responsible for the Cardiff Control Office, so I found myself having to implement my own plan and correct any of its shortcomings on a daily, even hour by hour, basis.

By and large, the Cardiff Valley passenger service needed little action unless the whole timetable was to be recast and I found that I spent many hours each week negotiating requirements with the Coal Board Transport Officers in Cardiff and Neath. There were large flows of coal moved internally to the steelworks at Margam and Llanwern and also for export via Newport, Barry and Swansea Docks. I would agree longer distance coal flows with the NCB and then negotiate paths with the

Regional Office – my first achievement of note was to run a coal train to Newcastle, albeit a specialist train of anthracite that was only mined in West Wales. On a daily basis we received forecasts of tonnages available at the pitheads and my job was to ensure a sufficient provision of empty wagons to clear the tonnage and not, in the worst case, to hold up the mine production, as the coal could not be loaded. We had a number of locomotives designated to cope with the daily variations under 'Control Orders' and these would be diagrammed by roneo notice to depots only the afternoon before implementation.

It soon became apparent to me that we were having to improvise far too much on a daily basis and every weekend we were running a special expensive programme to tackle backlogs to avoid NCB criticism and penalty payments. Under the slash and burn principle that had been in operation since the Beeching/Raymond era, many yards and depots had closed and spare resources of track, trains and men severely restricted, but it had been done piecemeal without any overall strategy. By now we had a new Divisional Movements Manager, Gerry Orbell, who joined us from the Eastern Region and Cliff Rose had been elevated to Assistant Divisional Manager. We were having crises nearly every day, exemplified by the congestion in yards like East Usk, Alexandra Dock Junction and Radyr, which were often so full that we could only move a train towards them if Control simultaneously took a train from them for somewhere else. It was all very wasteful, made worse by the fact that the longer distance diesel engine diagrams were so complex that, once we were out of the plan, chaos reigned. We had the stray ends of Tinsley or Toton engines booked for trips from Margam to Severn Tunnel Junction and similar, engines that were rarely traceable and never in the right place when you wanted them. There was also a Divisional initiative to develop block coal train working from the pits through to destination, being planned by John Hodge supporting the HQ project manager, T.C.Baynton-Hughes, which would significantly lighten the workload of the marshalling yards at the foot of the valleys, which became known as the 'Blocplan' and gave opportunity for further significant rationalization. Gerry and I decided that something drastic and radical needed to be done and the concept of the South Wales Freight Strategy was born.

We decided to involve senior Operations staff from Paddington Headquarters as we wanted to analyse and review all freight working in South Wales, including flows of traffic into and out of the Principality. This was a brave move on behalf of my manager as some senior officers, including the Divisional Manager himself, were paranoid about any potential interference from HQ in their affairs and we had to keep their involvement under wraps. We built a Divisional team including train planners and productivity staff from Management Services and the HQ team with Ray Fox, Train Planning Officer; Vic Gregory, Freight Officer; Dennis Mann the Diagramming Officer and others led by the Regional Operating Manager himself, Leslie Lloyd. I – under direction from HQ – arranged overnight stays at seaside hotels in Barry and on the Gower for the team to have a meal together and spend a couple of hours preparing the agenda and key issues for the next day's discussions. We were joined during the two day session by Baynton-Hughes and John Hodge to

116

integrate the Blocplan with the overall yard and freight train strategy. These evening sessions invariably started with sport of some sort – bowls, croquet, a golf driving range on one occasion – at which we all made sure Leslie Lloyd, an ardent competitor, won. After dinner and the real work, around 11pm, we would adjourn over pints to a fearsome game of 'Liar Dice', which again Leslie would win and Baynton invariably lose as I don't think he ever fathomed the rules. At around 1am, most would retire to bed, while I had to drive round the Vale of Glamorgan back to my home – now a former summer-rented seaside cottage balanced on the cliff top above the sands of Southerndown Bay, near the dismantled Dunraven Castle (dismantled apparently in days of yore so that the owner could avoid paying tax on it!).

Next day, we would assemble at some secret place out of the sight of spies from the Divisional Office and bring together the evidence and analysis we had been gathering in our South Wales team. We reviewed the role of every marshalling yard, got Management Services with local management to draw up consistent siding allocations in the light of the Blocplan proposals, which took a lot of coal tonnage out of the yards, and simplified the engine and crew diagrams. When we were sufficiently advanced in our thinking, I was delegated to spend time with every local trade union representative group (LDCs), explaining our proposals and seeking staff ideas and input. The only proviso was that I was accompanied by a senior Trade Union official from Sectional Council to see fair play and ensure no local group put forward biased proposals that would unduly benefit their depot at the expense of others – a highly contentious issue. All LDCs except one – Margam – agreed to meet me on this basis and we benefited enormously from the staff input, coming up with finalised plans that local staff believed were practicable and were 'owned' by them. The upshot was when we held the final consultation meeting with 150 LDC representatives and Sectional Council staff from all over South Wales in the city's Temple of Peace (usually given a very ironic cheer when large controversial meetings were held there), it lasted just under an hour and a half. I spent the first 45 minutes going through the proposals, explaining the staff ideas we had accepted and included in the strategy and which ones we had had to reject and why. Instead of a longwinded and protracted argument from staff representatives that was usual, one LDC member after another stood up to confirm their agreement and express their satisfaction with the way this huge and potentially controversial plan had been developed and consulted on. Only Margam, who had held out against co-operation, found any argument with the plans and other LDCs soon made it clear to them that they had turned down the opportunity to influence things, which was their loss and got little sympathy.

What the plan did was to rationalise the piecemeal changes that had taken place over the previous years, make the freight flows work with reduced yard and locomotive resources, meet the NCB's justified criticisms and reduce the overall cost considerably without any substantial staff redundancies. As an example of the changes we made, we designated Severn Tunnel Junction to be the starting place for wagon-load traffic to England, with increased frequency of trains round the clock for English destinations, instead of spreading them over Margam and Severn Tunnel. We diagrammed two 2,700hp diesel hydraulics to do nothing but round trips from

Margam to Severn Tunnel and back, reducing the shunting need at Margam and giving the wagons a faster and more frequent service from Severn Tunnel Yard. For the network of high speed steel freight services to the Midlands and North East, we concentrated on A.D.Junction, with East Usk becoming our main collection and dispersal point for coal empties in the Newport and Cardiff Valleys. When the plan was implemented with the vast changes, we all expected teething problems. They did not happen – why not? Because the local staff made sure it worked; it was their plan as much as ours. I'm astonished that this method of staff consultation was never picked up and copied by other Divisions and Regions.

In 1971, I was appointed as Planning Officer in the Parcels Business at the BRB headquarters at 222, Marylebone Road to undertake a special project – to look at strategic options for the business. I had a team drawn from each Region and we explored various business scenarios, from divesting ourselves of much of the business to heavy investment in mechanised concentration centres. The future of the mail order business from the north Manchester area – Oldham and Bolton in particular – were central to any proposal and the decision by the major mail order companies to invest in their own road transport pre-empted the publication of our findings and aborted the investment we had intended to recommend. This was a frustrating period, albeit useful in learning the ways of the Board systems and procedures.

Partly, I suspect, as a result of the impressive Critical Path Analysis diagram that I concocted for the project, I came to the attention of Alan Englert, the Board's Productivity Manager, and was appointed in 1974 to replace Geoff Goldstone, Management Services Manager of the Western Region when he went to the Board to develop the application of IT to BR's vast administration. Thus began eight years in the productivity business, an advisory role which took me eventually all over the BR system at both Regional and subsequently Board level, before appointment in September 1982 as Chief Operating Manager of the London Midland Region, a surprise to many, including myself, who had never worked on the LM before and had been out of direct Operational work for over ten years.

Meanwhile, with the cessation of steam operations in the UK in 1968 and the ban on steam specials using preserved locomotives that lasted three years, I turned my attention, when business and family responsibilities allowed, to the remaining steam in the continent of Europe.

Chapter 11

The Indian Summer of French steam

After spending two summers in 1961 and 1962 experiencing steam on the continent (chapter 1) other priorities kept me in this country for several years – the three year BR management training scheme on the Western Region, the realization that steam was rapidly drawing to a close here and courtship. However, my interest in steam on the continent was resurrected in 1968 and I spent a number of happy hours studying SNCF locomotive diagrams on the *Bourbonnais* (Paris-Clermont Ferrand), which a friend had sent me, whilst listening in my South Wales bedsit to *Eleanor Rigby*, *Lady Madonna* and other Beatles hits on my transistor radio and developing a taste for twentieth-century Russian classical music.

So, in late July 1968, just in time to get back for steam's last rites in the UK, I set off for Calais and ten intensive days on the Calais-Amiens, Le Mans-Nantes and Bourbonnais routes. Continental free passes by then consisted of a number of coupons, each of which was valid for 48 hours travel, so I was not restricted to sticking to a specified route to an ultimate destination, but could go wherever fancy took me. My first priority was to check out that my planning was robust and I made for the Le Mans-Nantes route initially before travelling to Vierzon via Angers and Tours, to pick up the Bourbonnais. Having spent a couple of days there, I returned to Paris and the Amiens-Calais route before doing the tour all over again, throwing in a Summer Saturday on the Paris-Granville line for good measure.

Ex-PLM pacific 231G 81 was a reassuring sight at the head of the *Flèche d'Or* at Calais Maritime and it ran its 450 tonnes train effortlessly through the Somme flats at a steady 105-110kph, after a maximum of 125 descending from Caffiers. Arrival in Amiens was a meticulous 1 minute early. No change there then! A BB16000 electric took me punctually on to Paris and I adjourned for an early night before joining Train 953 next morning – 10.05am Paris Montparnasse-Les Sables d'Olonne/Pornic on the Atlantic Coast. The huge fifteen-coach, 650 tonnes gross train was headed by the 1937 built État 2D2 electric 5403 and we stopped at Versailles and Chartres before arriving punctually in Le Mans. I suspect the locomotive was restricted to 120kph although we slightly exceeded this in a couple of places.

At Le Mans, the electric cut off and I was relieved to see the huge outline of the post war Mountain 4-8-2 built to Chapelon principles, 241P 5, waiting to back down. The heavy train was no hindrance to this powerful locomotive and we'd achieved 100kph within 5 miles and 110 by eight. We fell to 85kph before kilometre post (km) 255 after 4 kilometres of 1 in 200 before Sablé, then held our maximum 120kph (or slightly over) for miles over undulating gradients of 1 in 200 and absorbed a p-way slowing to 20kph at Ecouflant before arriving in Angers bang on time in 61 minutes 27 seconds (57½ minutes net) for the 97 kilometres (60.6 miles). The next section along the Loire valley to Nantes was taken at a very steady 120kph for the first 30 kilometres and then drifted noiselessly to around 110kph for the remaining distance to Nantes, where we arrived 2 minutes early (52 minutes 37 seconds for the 88 kilometres (55 miles – comfortably inside 'a mile a minute'). A week later, I repeated the journey and 241P 12 had an enormous load of eighteen coaches (800 tonnes gross), which it treated with contemptuous ease. We only fell to 95kph on the 1 in 200 to km 255 and without the previous week's p-way slack, we were nearly 3 minutes early into Angers despite a crawl up to the water column which extended our start-stop time to 59 minutes 37 seconds. We ran the entire Angers-Nantes section at 115kph as if the loco had been set onto auto-drive and our arrival was again 2 minutes early into Nantes (Appendix 2, Table 7)

In the meantime, I stayed for a couple of nights in Nantes and took an early *rapide* from Nantes to Le Mans behind an SNCF Co-Co diesel 68065 which actually barely matched the times of the 241 Ps with a lighter load (550 tonnes) and lost 5 minutes

241P 12 waiting to back down onto the eighteen coach 'Train 953' at Le Mans, 28 July 1968. (*Author*)

SNCF 4-8-2 'Mountain' 241P 5 on arrival at Nantes with the fifteen coach 'Train 953' 10.03am Paris to Les Sables d'Olonne & Pornic, which it had worked from Le Mans, 20 July 1968. (*Author*)

on the schedule with one p-way slack. I joined Train 953 again, where I found 241P 16 waiting for the fifteen coach Paris train. The climb to km 255 was even faster (100kph) and the time to Angers was identical to the previous day with 241 P 5, with the same p-way slack. This time I alighted at Angers, as I had worked out that I could fit in a couple of steam-hauled Angers-Le Mans runs, sandwiching a diesel hauled (720XX) return to Angers. 241P 32 was on Train 954, 1.53pm Nantes-Paris, thirteen coaches, 590 tonnes gross (the reciprocal of the Paris-Sables d'Olonne train) and ran the 60 miles in 64 minutes dead including the 20kph pws and a signal check to 20kph outside Le Mans station.

The second steam hauled run was a magnificent effort on the heavy Sunday 6pm Le Croisic-Paris (Train 762) – a seventeen-coach, 680 tonnes gross train hauled by 241P 33. Despite the pws at Écouflant only 8 minutes out of Le Mans and another signal check to 25kph outside Le Mans, we ran the 60.6 miles, mainly against the grade, in 60 minutes 48 seconds (56 minutes net). We accelerated very hard from the p-way check with a glorious throaty roar and worked up to 120kph on rising grades, only falling to 112kph at the km 255 summit (4 kilometres of 1 in 167 up in this direction). After that it was back to 120 again all the way to Le Mans with a maximum of 125kph at Voivres (Appendix 2, Table 7). 241P 32 and 33 had originally been Lille engines until electrification, when they had transferred to Rennes for the Le Mans-Quimper route. Since that electrification, the 241 Ps had regrouped at Le Mans along with the other 241 Ps, which had gone straight from the PLM route to Rennes.

241P 32 enters Angers station with 'Train 954', 1.53pm Nantes – Paris Montparnasse, which it will work as far as Le Mans before handing over to electric traction for the run to Paris, 21 July 1968. (*Author*)

141R 1177 on arrival at Clermont Ferrand with Train 1111 from Paris to Nimes, which it worked from Vierzon as substitute for a failed 67XXX diesel locomotive which had replaced the booked Nevers 241Ps in May 1968, 22 July 1968. (*Author*)

Next day, I travelled cross-country via Tours to Vierzon on the Paris-Bourges-Nevers route. Until a year or so before, I would have been hauled by a Tours 231G pacific but their day was over. However, I was looking forward to a Nevers 241P on Train 1111, 9.03am Paris (Austerlitz)-Nîmes, as far as Clermont Ferrand. I was very disappointed to find the waiting locomotive to take over from the electric was not a 241P but an *Americain*, oil burning 141R 1177 of Vierzon depot. In my chagrin, I had not appreciated how lucky I was, as this diagram had been taken over by Bo-Bo 67XXX diesels from May 1968, and today the diesel had failed! The train was a heavy fifteen coaches, 575 tonnes gross, and the 141R had to be pushed very hard to keep time, as it was restricted to 100kph. It managed to keep reasonable time with occasional flashes of 110kph between stops at Bourges, Saincaize, St.Pierre le Moutier, Moulins, Varennes and St Germain des Fossés to Vichy, where three coaches were left, making the load twelve for 450 tonnes gross. From Vichy the main feature is the steep 1 in 91 climb to Randan tunnel through wooded hillsides and 141R 1177 sustained a very creditable 78kph – comparable to 241P runs later with similar loads. Consequently we were only 1 minute late into Clermont Ferrand, my destination.

Before retiring to bed in my station hotel room, I ventured onto the platform to view the arrival of Train 1109 (6.57pm Paris Gare de Lyon-Clermont Ferrand) and the overnight train to Paris (Train 1116, 4.35pm ex Marseilles), both of which according to the diagrams I'd had, were booked for 241Ps of Nevers depot. However, after my experience on Train 1111, I was getting nervous and it was very reassuring to see 241P 24 arrive punctually from the north and watch 241P 23 back onto the sleepers. The Bourbonnais was the last main line out of Paris booked for weekday steam for the majority of its route – the first 68 kilometres being electrically hauled to Morêt les Sablons, where a Nevers 241P would take over for the 186km to Nevers, to be replaced by a second 241P for the further 166km on to Clermont Ferrand. The 241Ps were working two daily return services between Clermont and Morêt – morning and night departures from Clermont and lunchtime and evening departures from Morêt, all changing locos at Nevers, for which only 4 minutes were allowed. The service during my two days was handled by four regular locos, 241P 3, 8, 23 and 24, although 241P 22 made one appearance on the night sleeper, as did one 141R. Both 241P 3 and 241 P23 were withdrawn a month later in August, although there was no hint of any problems in their performances.

It was with some confidence therefore that I turned out for the 8.35am to Paris, Train 1110, and found 241P 24 already at the head of a ten-coach rake, weighing 411 tonnes (440 tonnes gross). We were doing 124kph by Gerzat, passed in 6 minutes from the start and, after the first stop at Riom, accelerated to 125 before the climb to Randan tunnel commenced, falling to 97kph only at the summit. After Vichy, 125kph was sustained on level track and on the final leg to Nevers we just touched 130kph, arriving 2 minutes early. 241P 23 now added a further three coaches, making the gross load 590 tonnes and we continued on our merry way with speeds oscillating between 112 and 125 all the way before a 2 minute early arrival in Morêt les Sablons (Appendix 2, Table 8).

123

A raft of De Caso 2-8-2 141TC tank engines heading suburban trains to Beauvais and Creil, alongside an SNCF 160XX BB electric on a wagon-lits train of empty stock after arrival from Lille and the Belgian border at Paris Gare du Nord, July 1968 (*Author*)

After an afternoon spent sampling 141 TC 2-8-2Ts from the Gare du Nord to Persan Beaumont and back, I returned to Clermont on the 6.57pm Paris (Lyon) – Train 1109. We had post war 2D2 electric 9112, built for the PLM electrification, to Moret and then 241P 23 with 241P 24 again on the second leg. The train formation was the same, thirteen coaches to Nevers and ten thereafter, and the performance very similar, with Randan summit being stormed at 100kph with Randan station beyond the summit being passed in 12 minutes 12 seconds from the Vichy start. I knew the sleeper from Clermont could not be 241P 23, as we had left it at Nevers, but I was disappointed to get 141R 1214 instead of another Nevers based 241P. However the coal burning large diameter chimneyed *Americain* did us proud with its fifteen-coach train, including several sleeping cars, weighing 650 tonnes gross and I timed the climb to Randan at a minimum of 87kph, with sparks literally raining down on the rear coaches before sleep took over (Appendix 2, Table 8). I roused myself at Nevers to see the engine change and found the inevitable 241P 23 once again, so I went back to sleep.

Going straight to the Gare du Nord for a couple of days based at Amiens, I found a BB 16000 on the 8.10am boat train to Calais Maritime. Ex PLM Pacific 231K 27 took over the fifteen coach 640 tonnes gross train at Amiens and ran the 122km to Boulogne Ville in 78 minutes net, a loss of a couple of minutes attributable to a pws to 76kph at Dreuil les Amiens. We took it a little too easily, crawling up the incline (1 in 167) past Boulogne Tintelleries at only 22kph, and

124

falling to 37kph on the 9 kilometres of 1 in 125 to the summit at Caffiers so that, despite a hurried descent just touching 130kph, we were just over 3 minutes late into Calais Ville. I treated myself to a formidable lunch (a rare luxury on this intensive trip) and had a pleasant afternoon interlude to Étaples and back on semi-fasts with 141Rs – 357 of Boulogne outwards, a standard coal burning loco and 141R 1294 on the return, another Boulogne loco, but with large diameter exhaust and Boxpok wheels.

231K 27 turned up again on the 7.19pm Calais Maritime boat train, piloted as far as Boulogne by large exhaust 141R 1201 on the sixteen-coach, 690 tonne gross train. The PLM Pacifics were normally given a pilot over Caffiers with any tare load over 620 tonnes. However, the existence of the 141R meant we were limited to 100kph and time had to be kept by vigorous uphill work. Also, we had a 23 minute late departure caused by the incoming channel ferry. The 141R certainly did its stuff and we roared up the 12 kilometres of 1 in 125 to Caffiers summit at a full 85kph and gained 3 minutes on the schedule, before detaching the pilot at Boulogne Ville. 231K 27 then displayed considerably more vigour than in the morning and ran from Étaples to Abbéville averaging 118kph, before suffering a severe signal check at Hangest which cost us our net gain of 8 minutes on schedule (Appendix 2, Table 3).

Ex PLM Pacific 231K 27 at Amiens, where it has taken over the 8.10am Paris-Calais Maritime Boat Train from a BB 160XX electric locomotive, July 1968. (*Author*)

After a night's sleep, I tried the 8.10am Paris again, picking it up at Amiens along with 231K 16. The load was even heavier – sixteen coaches, 700 tonnes gross – but the elderly pacific kept time easily, running the 122km (76.4 miles) start to stop in 78 minutes 17 seconds actual (77 minutes net) with a top speed of 125kph near Abbéville. I returned quickly to Amiens to pick up the 11.58 Paris *Flèche d'Or* – 231K 27 once again, with a lighter ten-coach train of 440 tonnes gross. This created little problem and by dint of a faster start out of Amiens, got to Boulogne in exactly 'even time' – 76 minutes 22 seconds for the 76.4 miles (Appendix 2, Table 3). I alighted at Boulogne in order to get back to Paris in time to catch the evening *rapide* on the Bourbonnais. Two boat trains connected with the ferry, which docked at Calais around 1pm – the 2.14pm Train 82 *Flèche d'Or* and the 2.27pm Train 84, both diagrammed for Calais PLM pacifics. I photographed 231G 81 sweeping through Boulogne with the first and caught Train 84 which turned up behind 141R 994. This managed to keep time despite the schedule requiring 120kph running, because of the hill climbing and acceleration of the 141R on a relatively light train (11 coaches for 470 tonnes gross). The 141R kept to its 100kph maximum meticulously throughout.

Back again at Morêt les Sablons it was like old times, with 241P 24 performing the honours at the Paris end of the journey. This was a particularly lively double act with 241P 24 working hard on the thirteen coach 590 tonnes train, although I noted an unusual amount of slipping in starting from the intermediate stops. A 3 minute early arrival at Nevers allowed ample time for the exchange with 241P 8 and

Ex PLM Pacific 231K 16 waiting to back onto the 8.10am Paris-Calais Boat Train at Amiens, July 1968. (*Author*)

SNCF 'Mountain 4-8-2 241P 8, built to Chapelon principles, stands at Clermont Ferrand before departure with Train 1110, 8.35am to Paris, July 1968. (*Author*)

the removal of three vehicles from the rear; I noted early arrivals at every station en route to Clermont Ferrand, which was reached 4 minutes early. Next morning, 241P 8 was on Train 1110 as booked and climbed to Randan with its ten-coach, 450 tonnes train at 95kph and thereafter touched 125-128kph between each stop. At Nevers, a new Mountain, 241P 3, backed three coaches onto the packed train (now 620 tonnes) and we ran at speeds varying only between 110 and 120kph over a seesaw route with ruling gradient changes of mainly 1 in 167. After Montargis we sped through the forest on the level at a steady 120kph, arriving slightly early at Morêt, where a BoBo 92xx electric took over for the final short sprint to the Gare de Lyon. It was back to Clermont in the evening, with 241P 3 and 241P 8 once again. I was tempted at Morêt, as there was a Fridays only relief and 241P 7 was standing in the bay awaiting the arrival from Paris, but it only went as far as Nevers and was a comparatively light train so I stuck with 241P 3. Although the train was well on time at Vichy, I decided to alight to get food and watch the night activity instead of making a quick turnaround to the sleeper at Clermont Ferrand. I was rewarded with 241P 22 on the sleeper (and 241P 3 again from Nevers to Moret).

It was a bleary-eyed traveller who glimpsed steam outside Montparnasse and decided to spend a day on the line to Granville instead of further identical runs to Clermont with 241P 3, 8, 24 et al. I realised it was a peak Summer Saturday and the 8am SO Paris-Granville was booked for a 141P, an SNCF compound 4 cylinder Mikado designed to Chapelon principles, from Argentan depot. Grubby 141P 228 backed on to the twelve-coach, 445 tonnes gross load and made pedestrian and smoky progress to Dreux, 82km (51 miles) in exactly 1 hour. After Dreux the engine cheered up as the dull grey sky cleared to a brilliant blue and we attacked the undulating gradients of 1 in 100, 1 in 125 and 1 in 200 at 88, 100 and 105kph respectively. This was gaining us time in handfuls and despite no speed higher than 110kph, we ran the 116km (72 miles) to Argentan in 72 minutes 33 seconds including a p-way slack to 60kph at l'Aigle (Appendix 2, Table 7). To my surprise, 141P 228 cut off at Argentan and another much sprucer member of the class, 141P 108, took us forward. We made some quite sharp start to stop times as we got nearer the coast – 33 minutes to Flers (28.5 miles); 21 minutes to Vire (18 miles) and 31 minutes onto Folligny (26.5 miles), where we dropped four coaches for Pontorson. Arrival in Granville was on time to the second.

A glorious sunny day enabled me to get some suntan to cover up previously acquired grime, but I could find no steam return working – BoBo 67xxx diesels everywhere – so I got myself a bag of ripe peaches, noted with resignation 67111 which slammed into our coaches throwing everyone off their feet, before noticing a most beautiful girl nursing a huge tabby cat in the opposite seat grinning at me, whereupon I decided to enjoy the scenery all the way to Paris! I even wrote a poem about the journey when I was back in Paris, which earned me £50 second prize in the Crewe & Nantwich Writers' Group annual competition in 2010!

Chapelon's standard SNCF improvement of the PLM 141E and 141F 2-8-2s, Argentan's 141P 108 on arrival at Granville with the 8am train from Paris Montparnasse, which it took over from sister 141P 228 at Argentan, 27 July 1968. (*Author*)

Etat pacific 231D 511 running into St Nazaire with the Sunday 'Train 762', 6pm Le Croisic to Nantes and Paris, which was booked at a 'mile-a-minute' start-to-stop over the 39 miles to Nantes, 28 July 1968. (*Author*)

I couldn't resist a last fling on the Le Mans-Nantes run, so I stayed near Montparnasse overnight and found another État 2D2 electric on the 10.05am Paris-Sables d'Olonne, giving way to 241P 12 to haul our eighteen packed coaches – a run I described earlier. I was told that Nantes depot still had two or three État pacifics – including 231D 648 and 231G 558, the latter being subsequently preserved – and that they used these on some of the seasonal trains for the short runs from Nantes to the coast. I had expected one on Train 953 after the 241P came off, but a couple of 66000 diesels took over. I did have a run behind the last of its class, 141R 1340, on a semi-fast to La Roche sur Yon, returning behind one of the early 650XX diesels.

There was a Sundays only *expresse* (Train 762) from Le Croisic to Paris which was rumoured to be diagrammed for a pacific, so I travelled in hope out to St Nazaire and was greeted by 231D 511 on its nine-coach train (395 tonnes gross). Acceleration was decidedly brisk and the noise from a French compound unusually staccato, as our 231D (the Ds were single chimney – the Gs had the Kylchap exhaust) had got up to 120kph inside 10 minutes from off. After slowing to 75kph at Saveney, we roared away again to 125kph and ran into Nantes in 39 minutes flat (37 net) for the 64 near level kms (40 miles) – a net average of 104kph (65mph) start to stop (Appendix 2, Table 7). The schedule for this train was a very exacting 38 minutes (63mph average). 241P 5 added eight coaches to the consist, which now weighed 700 tonnes gross and ran the 88km (55 miles) to Angers in 53 minutes 37 seconds without exceeding 120kph – two consecutive mile a minute runs for a Sunday evening train – not bad!

Like a moth drawn to the flame, I could not resist one last return to Nantes, so I alighted at Angers and caught a diesel hauled (3,800hp 72002) *rapide* back. This whisked the 590 tonnes train to Nantes in just over 46 minutes and ran at a steady 140kph. There was a night relief train for Paris (*train supplementaire* 12.11am from Nantes), which I hoped would be steam, and 241P 32 duly backed on to the eleven-coach, 500 tonnes train. However, the night services were either restricted in speed or ran to a very easy schedule, and after the usual fast acceleration to 100kph, we ran under very easy steam and after noting a minute early arrival in Angers, I gave in to sleep.

The excessively early arrival in Paris at least gave me no qualms about making the morning boat train for Calais, and at Amiens I was delighted to see a 'new' PLM pacific, 231K 30, backing on to our sixteen-coach 685 tonnes train. The usual steady and noiseless run followed with speed hovering between 110-120kph through northern France and we reached Boulogne Ville in 78 minutes 10 seconds (77 minutes net) for the 123km (77 miles). Since we were one coach overload for the climb to Caffiers, 141R 991 was attached as pilot, and the 4 minute late start caused in making the attachment was recovered completely by Calais Maritime, with a minimum of 72kph at the summit.

I had been so impressed by this Indian Summer of SNCF steam, that I made a brief return in November of 1968 and a final weekend in August 1969 just before the final demise of main line steam there – and my wedding in September!.

241P 8 at Moret les Sablons after arrival with Train 1110, November 1968. (*Author*)

241P 24 in the snow at Clermont Ferrand before departure with train 1110, 8.35am to Paris, November 1968. 241P24 will be replaced by 241P 8 for the run north of Nevers. *(Author)*

My experiences were very similar, so I will not repeat my journeys in detail but a few vivid impressions remain with me. In November, the Bourbonnais line was already bathed in a covering of snow and the morning and evening Paris-Clermont Ferrand *rapides* were monopolized by 241P 24 south of Nevers and 241P 8 at the Paris end.

Both locos performed with exemplary vigour and punctuality, but I remember one run in particular. 241P 8 was hauling the twelve-coach, 550 tonnes Train 1110 on 17 November and, after leaving Cosne, there was a long 15kph p-way slack over single line working. Once clear, 241P 8 was opened out and the exhaust echoed back like machine gun fire as we accelerated the heavy train from 15 to 110kph in under 3 minutes and to a full 125kph in 7 minutes before we eased. From Gien we ran into a heavy snowstorm and it was exhilarating to tear through the near white-out at 120kph. After Montargis, with the huge snowflakes still falling, we raised the echoes from the lineside forest and I watched fascinated as the exhaust mingled with the snow swirling among the trees as we charged towards Paris, already back on schedule. This was my final run with steam on the Bourbonnais. That run with 241P 8 remains etched in my memory as one of my favourites of all time (Appendix 2, Table 8).

In August 1969 I returned very briefly to the last remaining 241P outpost at Le

131

Mans and had a couple of runs with the 10.05am Paris-Les Sables d'Olonne, one of the last diagrammed steam turns. Although both 241P 11 and 241P 33 the following day were now pretty filthy and days away from final withdrawal, their mechanical condition was excellent and the running was virtually indistinguishable from the previous year. Indeed, 241P 11 actually achieved the fastest times (but unchecked) covering the 60.6 miles to Angers in 59 minutes 25 seconds start to stop and the 55 miles onward to Nantes in 51 minutes 59 seconds with speed rock solid at the maximum 120kph permitted. The swansong however, just like 241P 8 on the Bourbonnais, was my last on the route. 241P 16 was on Train 10762 (relief to Train 762), but left 13 minutes late after uncharacteristic poor operating. With just a twelve-coach train weighing 475 tonnes gross (a light load for these machines) we set about time recovery with a vengeance. Three minutes had been regained by Angers, but then we covered the 97km (60.6 miles) to Le Mans in 54 minutes 54 seconds, an average of over 105kph (66mph). There was an inspector on the footplate, so the 120kph maximum speed was observed to the letter. 241P 16 handed over its train to the electric only 5 minutes late, 8 minutes having been regained on mile a minute schedules, just days before dieselisation was completed (Appendix 2, Table 7).

I will recall events in Calais on my November trip. After my snowy runs on the Bourbonnais, Amiens-Calais was cold and raw. 231K 16, 231K 27 and 231G 81 were all still around, with the odd 141R, but no sign of the other three remaining Calais based pacifics, 231K 8, 22 and 82, which coincidentally have all been saved from the cutter's torch. On my last evening, I was at Calais Ville, ready to return to Amiens before catching the boat train in the morning. I was waiting for the 7.19pm Maritime boat train and my spirits rose despite the cold wait on the bleak station when a polished 231K 8 ran light engine tender first from the depot towards the Maritime station. But when the Paris boat train ran in, it was 231K 27 (again!). I realised then that there was also an 8pm departure connecting from the ferry to Lille and points east and that 231K 8 was to work that service. For years 231K 8 stayed in my mind as 'the one that got away' and when its preservation was announced I determined that I'd get a run behind it one day. The opportunity finally arrived in May 2004, nearly thirty-six years later, when 231K 8 powered the Golden Arrow seventy-fifth Anniversary special between Calais and Paris in both directions.

231K 8 stands at Calais Ville with the *Golden Arrow (Flèche d'Or)* anniversary train to Paris, May 2004. *(Author)*

231K 8 stands at the Gare du Nord in Paris with the return *Golden Arrow* anniversary train to Calais Ville, May 2004. (Author)

Chapter 12

012s to Friesland

Ex-Prussian 0-10-0T 094.150-0 [formerly DB 94.1150] with the Loco Club of Great Britain Special Train at Emden, 29 April 1972. (*Author*)

After squeezing in a last swansong visit to disappearing SNCF steam in 1969, I got married in the September of that year. For a couple of years I had other priorities, but early in 1972 I saw an advertisement that had my wanderlust simmering again. My colleague of university days had been regaling me about high performance by Deutsche Bundesbahn (DB) 012 three cylinder oil-burning Pacifics on the Hamburg-Westerland route, but I'd left it too late and the Rheine-Emden-Norddeich line in northern Germany close to the Dutch border had become the last sojourn of these impressive machines. The Locomotive Club of Great Britain had proposed a novel rail tour, which included a cruise from Harwich to Emden, using the ship as overnight hotel, with special trains and photo opportunities in the Friesland and Ruhr areas.

Our vessel was met at Emden harbour by former Prussian Railways 0-10-0T 94.150-0 (ex 94.1150) which trundled us on a drenchingly wet afternoon – typical for the area as I was to discover over the following three years – to the wayside station of Ihrhove to allow us to take shots of a couple of 012s on Eilzüge and oil-burning three cylinder 2-10-0 043s on the ore hopper trains. After a masochistic damp and freezing couple of hours, an oil-burning 2-8-2 with all welded boiler, 042.241-0, took us noisily to Oldenburg where a class 50 2-10-0 with Kabin-tender, 052.529-5, took us for a tour around the desolate, windswept Friesland coastal region through Wilhelmshafen and a freight only branch back to Emden – flat fields, Friesian cows, grey skies and grey sea.

Two cylinder oil-burning 2-8-2 with all welded boiler 042.241-0 with the LCGB Special Train at Oldenburg, 29 April 1972. (*Author*)

Three cylinder oil-burning 2-10-0 'Jumbo' 043.100 – with an iron ore hopper train at Ihrhove, one station south of Emden on the mainline to Rheine and Münster, during the LCGB photo stop in pouring rain, 29 April 1972. (*Author*)

Standard DB 2-10-0 052.529-5 [50.2529] at Sande on the freight line on the Friesland North Sea coast on the LCGB Special Train, 29 April 1972. (*Author*)

Three cylinder oil-burning Pacific 012.092-3 [01.1092] at Rheine after taking over from the 011 on the LCGB Special for the next leg to Münster and Hagen, 30 April 1972. (*Author*)

Ex-Prussian Railways 0-8-0 055.455-0 [55.4455] halts for a photo stop with the LCGB Special en route to Wuppertal in the Ruhr, 30 April 1972. (*Author*)

The last surviving DB three cylinder coal-burning Pacific, 011.062-7 [01.1062], at Emden with the LCGB Special, 30 April 1972. (*Author*)

Next day, the last day of April 1972, the last remaining 011 (coal-burning) three cylinder DB pacific, 011.062-7, backed on to our eleven-coach special at Emden Hauptbahnhof (main station) and took us steadily in the 100-110kph range to our first stop, Lingen, where a couple of dining cars were added, making our load thirteen coaches, 510 tonnes tare, and we made a quick tour of the locomotive repair works due to close a week later. At Rheine, ex-works oil-burner 012.092-3 replaced the 011 and we had a very noisy run through Münster and Hamm to Hagen, where the special drifted onto various secondary lines behind another 050 2-10-0, an ex-Prussian G8 0-8-0 55.4455, and finally through the Ruhr to the Dutch border with coal burning three cylinder 2-10-0 Jumbo, 044.687-2.

This snippet merely whetted my appetite for more, and I obtained a 'leave pass' from my wife for a longer visit in July the following year. I stayed at the north German town of Rheine throughout the visit, having travelled via Harwich-Hook of Holland and the Hengelo-Bentheim border points. I spent four days on the Rheine-Emden-Norddeich section. D and E trains were hauled exclusively by one of the remaining thirteen oil-burning 012 three cylinder pacifics, de-streamlined after the war, rebuilt in the early 1950s with new all-welded boilers and converted to oil firing in the late 50s, early 60s. Initially they dominated the Cologne-Bremen-Hamburg and Frankfurt-Kassel-Hanover-Hamburg main lines, but after dieselization with the V200 hydraulics, the 012s cascaded to the Westerland and Rheine areas. The few stopping services were mainly in the hands of the 042 2-8-2s and the heavy freights, 043s and a few coal burning 044s.

After the overnight sea and train journey, I alighted at Rheine to join my first steam-hauled D-Zug, D735 08.25 Cologne-Norddeich, onto which 012.063-4 backed to replace an E10 electric. This first run was not typical, in that the Pacific was not pushed hard and managed to drop 7 minutes on the 84 minute non-stop schedule to Emden (88 miles) although the net time after a couple of signal checks and a signal failure at Papenburg was the scheduled 84 minutes exactly. After that, the next four days were spent savouring virtually continuous thrashing and roaring three cylinder

Oil-burning Pacific 012.063-4 [01.1063] departing Rheine with an Eilzug for Emden, July 1973 (*Author*)

beat, as the oil-burners could be flogged without detriment to a labouring fireman. 012.081-6 was waiting at Norddeich Mole (jetty) with D1334, 13.35 Norddeich-Cologne ten-coach, 335 tonnes train which ran smartly between the stopping stations of Emden, Leer, Papenburg, Meppen and Lingen, maintaining near 60mph start to stop times over 15-20 mile distances. Papenburg-Meppen, 46km (29 miles) was covered in 29min 9sec with a top speed of 120kph at Hemsen just before the Meppen stop.

D714 Munich-Norddeich (4.55pm Rheine) was the star train of the week, its seven-coach, 260 tonnes train being booked at mile a minute start to stop speeds over much of its steam hauled section: Rheine-Lingen 19.4 miles in 18 minutes; Lingen-Meppen 13.1 miles in 13 minutes; Meppen-Papenburg 28.75 miles in 28 minutes; Papenburg-Leer 10.6 miles in 11 minutes; and Leer-Emden 16.25 miles in 17 minutes. My first run with 012.055-0 managed to regain 3 minutes of a 4 minute late start even on this schedule, with electric starts and a steady roar between stops, with 130kph at Leschede; 128 at Geeste; 126 at Lathen; 128 at Ihrhove and 127 at Petkum (maxima between each stop). The following day 012.068-3, which was in very poor condition, lost 5 minutes on the demanding schedule despite being driven hard, but 012.081-6 on the next day duplicated 012.055's effort including another 130kph maximum (Appendix 2, Table 9).

A train also of considerable interest to train loggers was the evening D730 sleeper Norddeich-Munich, another seven-coach flyer booked non-stop from Leer to Lingen, 52.5 miles, in just 50 minutes. 012.104-6 did it in 47 minutes exactly (44½ net) and 012.101-2 in 48 minutes (45½ net) both with 130kph maxima. 012.077-4 did an incredible double, with the ten-coach, 320 tonnes D1335 from Rheine to Leer first stop, 71.9 miles in 65min 46sec (net 62 minutes) with speed between 120 and 130kph throughout except for a long p-way slack to 30kph at Papenburg. It returned later that day on D730 after a mile-a-minute run over the 16.5 miles from

138

Emden to Leer, running the 52.5 miles on to Lingen in 46 minutes 29 seconds (44½ net) including a solid fifteen continuous minutes at 130kph (Appendix 2, Table 9).

By the fourth day of my visit I'd collected runs behind all thirteen of the 012s, the final ones being 012.061-8 on the Emden Aussenhafen (Outer Harbour)-Munich D-Zug, which was hauled tender first from the harbour station to the Hauptbahnhof, where it ran round its train, and 012.080-8, which I picked up on D1334 from Norddeich Mole on my last afternoon. I believe the 1973 summer was the zenith of 012 performance on that route – the speed limit had been lifted from 110 to 120kph during 1972 and the evidence of my 1973 runs is that the crews were pushing this to the limit and more. By 1974, one or two key trains had been dieselized, like D714, except at weekends. I've left until last on this visit a stupendous run with 012.075-8 on D1337 (8.41am Munster-Norddeich) which left Rheine 18 minutes late with ten coaches, 397 tonnes tare, and got to Leer, 71.9 miles in 60½ minutes net (64 minutes actual) with sustained running at 135kph between Meppen and Papenburg and an ear-splitting racket enough to waken the dead (Appendix 2, Table 9).

My notes to nearly all these fast runs relate bad weather, rain and strong cross winds, especially over the open heathland north of Papenburg. Whatever the weather at Rheine – even clear blue sky – it inevitably deteriorated later in the journey and the lowering skies and squally lashing rain created plenty of atmosphere and what must have often been trying conditions on the footplate. On a couple of runs, the side winds and the continuous flogging seemed finally to beat the boiler over this exposed section – 012.082-4 which must have been overdue for overhaul was the culprit a couple of times. However, all the 012s were in action – a remarkable availability during their last years of existence.

Another oil-burner, 012.075-8 [01.1075] waits at Rheine to take over late running D1337 from an electric locomotive at Rheine, 23 July 1973. In recovering 6 minutes to Emden on a fast schedule, it touched 136kph [84mph], the author's highest speed with steam on the DB. (*Author*)

I was so exhilarated by this experience that I determined to return the following year and July 1974 saw me again on the *Holland-Skandinavien Express* which deposited me in Rheine in time for D735 and 012.055-0 on the nonstop mile a minute run to Emden. The 88 miles were covered in exactly the scheduled 85 minutes with 364 tonnes tare, including threading a dramatic rainstorm at Lathen. I had several runs behind this loco on this trip and my notes all remark on its outrageous syncopated three-cylinder exhaust. I had taken a tape-recorder this time, and a recording of 012.055 leaving Emden across the wastes to Leer with the afternoon Eilzug to Münster is most dramatic as the syncopated roar goes on and on getting louder and louder as the engine is pushed to overcome its sluggish acceleration. A cold wind was sweeping across the heathland as we set out from Emden, and the locomotive was way off-beat, so that it sounded like a drunken V2 as it attempted to accelerate a not too onerous load over this flat track through a flat landscape. We got up to about 45mph, making a fearful staccato racket, and then every few minutes the crescendo increased as the driver made a further vain attempt to get the train up to a respectable speed. Black smoke was pouring across the countryside to the east almost as fast as the clouds were scudding by, and the rhythmic schizophrenic beat, with one exhaust beat almost missing and another accentuated to explosive effect, drowned out all other sounds. Suddenly a mournful howl of the stricken pacific's whistle broke though, as if in desperation. My last recollection, as I descended at Papenburg to await a north bound train, was – as the level crossing barriers went clattering up – to hear 012.055's emphatic exhaust disappearing into the far distance, on and on, carried in the gusty wind and swirling round, getting softer and then louder again, still 5 minutes later a faint echo as I huddled from the first raindrops of the next approaching squall.

Oil-burning Pacific 012.055-0 [01.1055] passing Emden loco shed with the departing Eilzug for Rheine and Münster, 13 July 1974. (*Author*)

012.066-7 [01.1066] waiting to take over D1731 Münster-Norddeich at Rheine, 13 July 1974. (*Author*)

The star locomotives in 1974 were 012.066-7, newly overhauled and 012.081-6 obviously after a light overhaul. The beat of 012.081 was a joy to behold and a further recording I treasure is of the evening D730 sleeper, leaving Leer behind 012.081 accelerating with a sure-footed even staccato beat, reaching 100kph in less than 3 minutes. It was doing 120kph in 5 minutes and completed the 52.5 miles in 45min 51sec including a p-way slowing to 60kph at Papenburg (44min net), an average of 71.6mph (Cheltenham Flyer schedule). This was achieved with no higher speed than 125kph (78mph). My notes say that the engine 'purred' (Appendix 2, Table 9).

The noisiest tour de force – apart from 012.055's histrionics – was 012.100-4 (the preserved 01.1100) on the Sundays only 7.07am Rheine-Norddeich. This was an incredible train, scheduled for five coaches only, at furious start to stop times. I have no idea of its purpose – on the day I caught it (14 July 1974) we had eight coaches, 293 tonnes virtually empty. The noise from the engine was so deafening that

012.066-7 taking water at Emden on D1334 to Rheine and Cologne, July 1974. (*Author*)

The now preserved and restored 012.100-4 [01.1100] accelerates past Papenburg station with a morning Rheine-Norddeich D-Zug, July 1974. (*Author*)

I retreated after a while from the front to the third coach in order to stop distortion on the recorder as the din was just too much. We left 4 minutes late and were stopped dead at Salzbergen for 2 minutes before the first stop. Salzbergen-Lingen (14 miles) we did in 14½ minutes, dropped a minute to Meppen (13 miles in 14 minutes), did the 29 miles on to Papenburg in 35 minutes with three stops at Haren, Lathen and Aschendorf! We managed to drop nearly 3 minutes from Papenburg to Leer (10.6 miles in 12min 23sec). How many other 60mph start to stop runs existed for steam trains for this distance (10.6 miles in 10 minutes)? And it was entirely level - no help from gravity. The last section from Leer to Emden was just too much and either the crew or the boiler gave up and we lost a further four minutes arriving at Emden 13 minutes late. I got out at Emden. The engine took water in a howling freezing gale, lashing with rain, and eventually woofled off sounding as though its spirit had been broken. But what was the point of all this noise and fury? A train for foreign railway enthusiasts only? (Appendix 2, Table 9)

One quirk of these locomotives was the regular sand-blasting that crews gave the oil-burners at speed leaving a pall of black smoke hanging over the countryside. A run up on the last Eilzug to Rheine with 012.081 on 6 coaches (221 tonnes) was typical – the 88 miles were covered in an actual running time of 98 minutes including nine stops! 120kph was reached between virtually every stop – sometimes within a run of only 7 minutes in total. After a signal stand for 2 minutes after Lingen waiting to enter a single line over a river bridge, 012.081 accelerated to a full 130kph (80mph) at Leschede in exactly 4 minutes from the standing start. My notes comment on the sand-blasting leaving the cloud of pitch black smoke obscuring the dramatic orange sunset.

The final rites were due in January 1975, when the 012s would be replaced entirely by the small class 216 diesels (Hymek-like) although the steam freight ore services would run a few months more. I could not resist one final effort, believing that I would have little opportunity to sample steam in Eastern Europe, India or China, because of both my full time railway duties and a young family at home. I left the UK on 20 May on the *Hook Continental* and arrived at Rheine behind a 216 diesel in time for D735 which was still diagrammed to an 012. 012.066-7 was now one of the most regular locos and performed on this first run with total efficiency as if the end was not yet in sight. This D-Zug was now scheduled to stop at the main intermediate stations rather than being nonstop to Emden as in previous years, but we ran from Rheine to Lingen, 19.4 miles in 19min 32sec, Lingen-Meppen 13.1 miles in 13min 19sec, Meppen-Papenburg 28.75 miles in 28min 25sec, Papenburg-Leer 10.6 miles in 11min 20sec and Leer-Emden 16.25 miles in 18min 35sec arriving nearly 2 minutes early with a 260 tonnes tare load. 012.055, restored to health, almost duplicated the times the next day and achieved a top speed of 131kph.

For some reason the fast D714 had reverted to steam haulage on weekdays as well as weekends and I caught it each day of my three day visit. 012.061 on 21 January and 012.066 on the next day maintained the timings, apart from a rather slow approach to a couple of stations, the best intermediate time being the 28.75 miles from Meppen to Papenburg in 27min 2sec with 012.066 in (again) pouring rain and gale. My favourite, 012.081, performed with distinction on the last day and the driver took on a fast car leaving on a parallel road after Meppen and won, with electrifying acceleration. It actually regained time on this schedule after a late start from Rheine and covered the Meppen-Papenburg section in 26 minutes at an average of 66mph (Appendix 2, Table 9).

An iron ore hopper train double headed by two oil-burning 'Jumbo' three cylinder 2-10-0s, 043.636-0 leading, at Rheine, July 1974. (*Author*)

On 23 January I was able to walk around Bw Rheine (the loco depot) and as well as a few remaining 012s in steam – 012.061 and 012.081 on shed with a number of 042 2-8-2s – there were a number of derelict condemned engines making a sorry sight in the gloom. Some had obviously been withdrawn for some time and had parts stripped for spares, including the last coal burning three cylinder pacific, 011.062, and two 012s, 071 and 084, whilst 012.082 was intact, with only numberplates removed, but recently condemned.

My last northbound journey was on E3114 (Brunswick-Norddeich) behind 012.081 from Leer to Norddeich, arriving a minute early, where I transferred to the last Eilzug, E2730, from Norddeich Mole to Rheine. 012.055-0 did the honours and it would be fitting to say my last 012 on normal public service disappeared into the sunset. However, it was a winter evening and even more apt to say that we exited to the sounds of wind and rain lashing against the *silberlinge* coaches whilst the three cylinder syncopated roar from the pacific reverberated across the blasted heath. As we stood at Papenburg station, we passed 012.063 on a northbound Eilzug, and in the silence, heard it accelerate out of the station, its exhaust echoing around, sometimes being lost in the swirling wind, then chattering again in the distance as the level crossing gates rose and a tractor burbled into motion before silence was restored. The last steam passenger turns of the Deutsche Bundesbahn were nearly over …

Three cylinder oil-burning Pacific 012.081-6 [01.1081] arrives at Meppen with the 'mile-a-minute' D-Zug, D714 4.55pm Rheine-Norddeich, January 1975. (*Author*)

Chapter 13

Last Rites in Europe

East Germany 1979

The 1970s were much occupied by my growing family and promotion to management posts at the British Rail Headquarters at 222, Marylebone Road and the Western Region General Management team at Paddington. Whilst my activities may be of interest to some – my autobiography of my railway professional career is entitled *The Toss of a Coin* – my railway enthusiast activities were restricted to the occasional UK steam special (see chapter 17) and my forays overseas and the time has come to share with you my first expedition behind the Iron Curtain.

Since the demise of steam in West Germany, friends had been trying to persuade me to visit the German Democratic Republic and its railway, the Deutsche Reichsbahn (DR), bringing back tales of a resurgence of high performance steam expresses, especially with 01 two-cylinder coal-burning Pacifics on the Berlin-Dresden main line. A mixture of the complexities of arranging visas and hotels in a communist country and a general lack of time because of professional and family duties, coupled with an inability to plan in sufficient time, meant that by the time I got round to it, I was too late for the plum choice as the Dresden D and F trains were dieselized while I was still deliberating. However, I was assured there were still rich experiences to be had – three cylinder 03 oil-burning Pacifics on the Berlin-Stralsund main line in the north, the two cylinder coal-burning versions on some secondary services on the Leipzig route and the modernized 01.5s further south on the Halle/Leipzig routes to Saalfeld.

So the winter of 1978-9 had me busy constructing itineraries and completing the formalities, just as news filtered through of heavy snows and chaos on the DR. I was on tenterhooks until the last moment as the rumours circulating were expressing not only considerable disruption, but also the temporary withdrawal of some of the main steam services that I was intending to visit, especially north of Berlin. However, I realised that if I called things off at this stage, I would be unlikely to face all the problems of replanning the visit, so I decided to risk it and hope for the best.

Anyway, I set out, admittedly with some nervous apprehension, in April 1979, via the Dover-Ostend ferry and Cologne, intending to cross the East German border at Oebisfelde. For some unknown reason I changed my mind en route, and caught a direct train to Berlin via Helmstedt and Brandenburg. My anxiety to be in time to see the *Meridian* D270, with through coaches from Budapest and Prague to Stockholm, starting its steam leg from Berlin Ostbahnhof to Sassnitz, had got the better of me. I suppose I wanted to know as soon as possible if this northern section was still disrupted and whether I could afford to spend time there, or whether I had to make my way south as soon as possible and try to renegotiate hotels and travel plans with the GDR immigration authorities. And so in the early hours of 19 April 1979, I found myself on D241 *Ost-West Express* approaching the border and – to me – the unknown.

We left Helmstedt on time very early in the morning behind a DR class 132 mainline diesel, threatening to arrive exceedingly early at the capital city, until thick black oily smoke began to pour from our locomotive near Brandenburg and we covered 10 kilometres at about 30kph. We ground to a halt at a small station called Gross Kreutz and duly meditated there for over an hour while we were overtaken by a succession of trains including a 2-10-0 (class 52.8) hauled freight. Eventually we were rescued by another 132 diesel, which despite my rising anxiety, duly got me to Berlin in time for a quick passage through the Friedrichstrasse checkpoint – a brief look at my papers, camera and total lack of interest in my tape-recorder – and I was at the Ostbahnhof by 8.30am, which was more than the *Meridian* was. Having glimpsed the back of the oil-burning tender of an 03.00 poised ready for when it would arrive and rejoicing over the 'bulled up' 03.0010 which arrived on the dot of 8.52 with the southbound boat train from Sweden and Sassnitz, I retired with confidence to buy a return ticket to Neustrelitz on the route to Stralsund via Neubrandenburg which was this train's booked route – the first of many minor disasters which were subsequently transformed into something beyond my expectations.

The *Meridian* duly appeared some 30 minutes late and a very clean 03.0046-7 backed on – the only time during my stay that I was to see this locomotive. Although

Three cylinder oil-burning Pacific 03.0046-7 at Berlin Ostbahnhof with D270 *Meridian* from Prague to Sassnitz, which this steam locomotive would take from Berlin to Stralsund, 19 April 1979. (*Author*)

I did not know the route, I was conscious that something was not going according to plan almost from the word go, and it was no real surprise when Bernau and a large female ticket collector arrived together. The formidable lady waggled her finger at me, told me that she had announced the train's diversion via the Pasewalk route five times – I must have been gazing fondly at the 03 or buying my incorrect ticket at the time – and was trying to calculate how I could get to Neustrelitz when I threw her by calmly asking for a ticket to Stralsund, saying I'd go to Neustrelitz tomorrow. She gave up when later in the journey I decided to go to Bergen and avoided my compartment. The diversion of D270, and its equivalent southbound service D316, via Pasewalk started on this very day and would go on to the end of the Winter timetable so that a complete blockade could take place between Demmin and Grimmen in the far north to repair the ravages of the winter snows. I don't even know if these services north of Berlin were running at all before this date.

My connoisseur of DR steam who'd inveigled me into taking this trip later told me of his jealousy that I had experienced a 'mile-a-minute' on my very first DR steam run – and on an international heavily laden train to boot. 03.0046 set off, now only 9 minutes late, having cut the excessively long 45 minute Berlin station stop by 20 minutes, with a load of eleven heavy DR and MAV pale blue coaches, 439 tonnes tare, and an estimated 475 tonnes gross. After the half hour run to the first stop, we ran the 68.15 miles from Bernau to Pasewalk in 68min 03sec, with 112kph at Biesenthal, 95 Eberswalde, a full 120 at Herzsprung, and after a 90kph slowing through Angermunde, another 120 at Wilmersdorf before a p-way slack to 20kph at Prenzlau. After that we had a final rip-roaring fling to 126kph before another p-way slowing to 45kph at Nechlin and pulling to a halt by the water column, where we stood and waited time for 21 minutes!

Then we accelerated again with a full throated and very satisfying thunderous exhaust, covering the 70 miles to Stralsund Rügendamm in 77min 35sec including a dead stand for signals outside Stralsund and a 30kph signal check at Ducherow. Speed over the flat heathland was held at a steady 115-120kph and arrival at the Rügendamm station via this diversionary route was 2 minutes early (Appendix 2, Table 10). 03.0046 cut off here and was replaced by another oil-burner, 03.0090-5, for the short run to Bergen, where I alighted, and Sassnitz, where through coaches of the train would be shunted onto the Swedish train ferry.

I returned to Stralsund Hauptbahnhof in a double-decker coach set hauled by a 110 Bo-Bo diesel and just made connection with D717, the 2.57pm Stralsund-Leipzig which was standing ready to go, with ex-works oil-burning two cylinder pacific 01.0530-4 blowing off steam furiously and twelve lightweight standard DR coaches, 383 tonnes tare, 410 gross. I had been led to expect no fireworks in the early stages of this run, and I was astonished, despite a hasty on-time departure, to experience a vigorous acceleration, which carried on until 125kph was reached at Mesekenhagen! The 19.4 miles to the first stop, Greifswald were covered in 21min 30sec start to stop and the 11.25 miles on to Zussow took just 13 minutes exactly with a top speed of 110kph. The next 10.6 miles to Anklam took 12min 10sec with another 110 maximum, then we roared off again to pass Borckenfriede in 12 minutes at 120kph and ran after a slowing to 96, in the 100 – 110kph range until we stopped at Pasewalk, the 01.5's home depot, in 28min 08sec for the 26.25 miles (Appendix 2, Table 12). We took water and changed crews and continued in a competent but less spectacular fashion with speeds between stops around 115kph, early at all stations until a signal check on the final section made us a disappointing 2 minutes late at Berlin Lichtenberg.

I then watched coal-burner 01.1511-3 slithering out of the carriage sidings with the stock of the *Gydania* for Danzig in Poland, but had to leave it to cope with the bureaucracy at the Alexanderplatz, having had an unexpectedly full day in Stralsund. The police could not be prevailed upon to enter more than *Stadt* (City) Berlin, *Bezirk* (District) Gera and *Bezirk* Magdeburg on my visa, despite my customs entry card being endorsed for day trips to Stralsund, Neubrandenburg and Wittenberg. I gathered that if I was prepared to acquire a hotel booking at Stralsund, they might rethink, but I left this ploy for use in an emergency and risked it and had no difficulty whatsoever. Indeed, later my visa was checked by police at Probstzella (*Bezirk* Suhl) and Wernigerode (*Bezirk* Halberstadt) and, despite my trepidation, I was handed back my papers with a smile and greeting. Two things helped – firstly, I could speak German and secondly, the issue of the visa in London which seemed to make a good impression.

Next day I was up at five o'clock to catch the 5.42am S-Bahn to Lichtenberg – having saluted the guards pacing up and down by the May Day plinth outside the Berolina Hotel, in case anyone wanted to deface Lenin's portrait – and onto the already crowded platform to see with sinking heart the 132s pulling out of the carriage sidings with what I feared was the 6.10am to Stralsund amongst others. Oh ye of little faith! At 6.05 a billowing of white smoke from the direction of Lichtenberg depot heralded its arrival behind 03.0077-2, with twelve coaches, 372/390 tonnes. We left

Three cylinder oil-burning Pacific 03.0077-2 at Stralsund station with a D-Zug for Berlin, circa 1978. (*Alistair Wood*)

on time, got to Oranienburg (right route this time) in half an hour with a top speed of about 110kph – I couldn't find any kilometre posts on the Ring – and had to wait time for 6 minutes. The 31.2 miles to Fürstenburg took 34min 13sec including two severe p-way slacks and a top speed of 116kph at Altlüdersdorf. The next 13 miles to Neustrelitz took 16min 33sec and despite another p-way slowing, we were still 2 minutes early in.

A punctual run to Neubrandenburg ensued despite yet another p-way slack. I enjoyed this section from a scenic point of view with its rolling hills, attractive trees, castles and small towns. The further north we went, the more frequent became the checks and we suffered four slacks to Demmin – two p-way, and two signal checks, including a dead stand at Gültz to pass a local. The reason for this bad operating became obvious at Demmin where we arrived 6 minutes late, for we terminated abruptly and all the passengers trooped meekly out to waiting buses for Grimmen and heaven knows what transport from there to Stralsund. I decided to play safe, having spied 03.0090-5 waiting in the goods shed the right way round, doubting if anyone would hold a connection at Stralsund for someone going back the way they had come!

I now had 2 hours to kill in a strange and (apparently) forbidden town, so I set about furtively exploring this small administrative centre, which was much decorated with party slogans and flags ready for May Day. There was a distinct shortage of paint or whitewash on the houses, which gave a rather grey sombre effect. However, it was sunny and there were tradesmen with horses and carts and even a donkey cart, one of those gateway arches over the road of which north Mecklenburg seems fond (much battered by oversized lorries by the look of it), a nice stretch of waterway petering out into marshes, a decrepit rusty siding running alongside into a small wharf with a couple of huge modern bulk grain wagons being loaded from a silo and lots of people fishing this Saturday morning who clearly recognised me as a stranger – I must say I felt a little conspicuous in this closed community. The time soon went and beginning to feel a little footsore, I wandered back to the station and became the sole occupant of D613, now simmering in the station with the same twelve coaches and 03.0090. The buses eventually turned up at 11.20, some 15 minutes after booked departure time, and we got away with a packed train – the buses must have been bulging – at 11.32, 25 minutes late.

We made a gentle start, more p-way checks and a dead stand for two minutes to cross another train off a single line, a 5kph bridge slack, making us 35 minutes late into Neubrandenburg. Here my heart sank as a 130 or 131 diesel backed on as pilot and we roared out with the 03 a somewhat sulky passenger, then coasting at around 90kph before a 7-minute stop outside Neustrelitz. The farce continued as the diesel was cut off (I can only assume the single line was so congested that this was the only hope of getting the diesel back to base) and we were 4 minutes overtime, partly because the driver of the diesel insisted on unloading a barrowful of fresh vegetables from the rear cab as he was relieved, and it disappeared ahead of us into the unknown.

03.0090 now set off for real, 43 minutes late and after yet another p-way slack outside the station to 15kph, with a maximum of 112kph after Düsterforde, we got to Fürstenberg in 16 minutes 16 seconds. Belatedly we then got a clear road and went crisply up to Drögen at 78, touched 118 at Dannenwalde, and after a permanent speed restriction to 100 at Gransee, sustained a steady 120kph all the way to Oranienburg, almost achieving even time for the 31.2 miles (32min 09sec). I alighted and watched D613 on its way, still 43 minutes late.

One benefit of this appalling timekeeping was that I only had 40 minutes to wait at this dirty ramshackle station – I couldn't find any food anywhere and the weather had deteriorated, there being a decidedly cold draught wherever one stood. I was hoping for 03.0010 on D814 – this had been the loco I had seen on the diagram the first day – but punctually at 2.33pm it rounded the corner behind a loco that I was to see a lot of over the next week, 03.0085-5. The engine was clean and in good condition and was hauling eleven coaches, 351/375 tonnes, reduced from Neubrandenburg to eight coaches, 258/275 tonnes. The 35 minute booking to Fürstenberg was not quite made because of both p-way and signal checks, with a top speed of 118kph, but Neustrelitz was reached 2 minutes early. Here I was invaded by three women from a collective, arguing furiously over their holiday rights just like militant shop stewards, and I gave up any attempt at tape-recording until they alighted at Demmin. I was intrigued, however, by their accurate forecasting of where we would be delayed and what we would cross at each delay point and their discussion of the likely lateness of the southbound *Meridian*, which we awaited at Neddemin for 10 minutes (they were right). I am sure they were not railwaywomen, however; they sounded from their conversation vaguely agricultural. The stretch from Neubrandenburg to Demmin took nearly 58 minutes for the 26 miles, including two dead stands totalling 14 minutes and four p-way slacks. We were now 17 minutes late and my intention of connecting at Stralsund for Bergen to pick up the *Berlinaren* (D317), which then runs non-stop from Stralsund Rügendamm to Neubrandenburg, looked doomed. By now a cold drizzle, constant checks and the realization I wasn't even going to make the D719, 6.02pm Stralsund to Pasewalk so I could cross to Neubrandenburg to pick up the *Berlinaren*, was making me a little depressed, but I found a perverse enjoyment in the exasperated roaring recoveries from each slowing and in the desolate smoke-filled landscape, and in the rugged wild riding that accompanied 103kph at Toltz-Rustow; 108 at Rakow; and 103 again at Zarrendorf. My notebook is full of barely readable scribblings like 'appalling ride', 'wild', 'stopped to let a workman's railbus go by', 'passing a freezing swamp', 'four-foot deep filthy snowdrifts still in the ditches'. It had atmosphere.

So we rolled into Stralsund 34 minutes late, 10 seconds after D719 jerked into motion and I found I had 2 hours to fritter away in a wet town with the *Mitropa* firmly shut. Two hours later I realised that I wouldn't have missed it for worlds! I fell in love with the place, its profusion of interesting buildings, its beautiful lakes in the misty dusk, the association between a last stronghold of pacifics peculiar to the area and a fascinating scenic town reminded me of my other great favourite, Lindau and its Bavarian 18.6s. I went to a fair in full swing in the little square under the *Marienkirche* (or was it the *Johanniskirche*?), ate my fill of all sorts of fripperies in the fair kiosks, jammed in between the local police and a group of sailors – I wasn't meant to be in Stralsund, of course, but I was becoming bold – and became mentally adjusted to a return to Berlin on the class 142-hauled 8.15pm ex Stralsund. I even persuaded myself that the journey would enable me to sort out my notes, plan the next day and get to bed that much earlier for some much needed and overdue sleep. 142.003-3 (one of half a dozen diesels of higher power than the standard 132s) duly ran punctually to Berlin. I watched 01.0530 leaving on the 12.03am from the Ostbahnhof and went to bed.

I decided to try the *Meridian* via Pasewalk again, this time on purpose – but first, as I was now in the habit of rising extremely early (when in Rome …) I got myself to Lichtenberg for D610, 6.10am Berlin-Stralsund, which appeared with eleven coaches, 338/345 tonnes behind 03.0058-2, which later settled down as regular loco for D613/D514. The start was fast with 115kph before Schönfliess on the Ring, but after a slack there and a p-way slowing to 20kph at Bergfelde, we coasted along in the low 70s to reach Oranienburg in 32 minutes 22 seconds, three and a half minutes early. I returned quickly to the Ostbahnhof on the diesel-hauled *Ost-See Express*, behind 132.514-1, and ate a rare breakfast.

Punctuality of the steam expresses had deteriorated and there was still no sign of D319 (off the night ferry from Malmö) by 9.30, when the 7.10am (previous day) Belgrade-Malmö, alias the *Meridian*, showed up with its rake of international coaches including the blue MAV ones. 03.0085-5 backed down onto a very full eleven coaches, 439/485 tonnes, and I acquired a compartment to myself in the front coach only by dint of accepting occupation of quite the filthiest compartment I had ever been in – littered with orange peel and empty beer bottles. The 44 minute booked

Oil-burner 03.0085-5 at Berlin Ostbahnhof with the D270 *Meridian* for Sassnitz and the ferry to Trelleborg, Sweden, 20 April 1979. (*Author*)

stop was massacred and we were given right away at 9.56am, 34 minutes late. We were checked to 40kph at Wühlheide and Springfühl and were brought to a halt for half a minute shortly afterwards, but roaring away to 110kph at Zepernick got us to Bernau in 32min 05sec. Then with one slight signal check and a p-way slack between Nechlin and Pasewalk, we took 68min 11sec for the 68.15 miles – 8 seconds more than 03.0046, with one less p-way slack and a marginally heavier train. Speeds – 102kph Rüdnitz; 117 Melchow; 100 permanent speed restriction at Eberswalde; 96 at Britz; 117 Herzsprung; 100/111 Angermunde; 110 Greiffenberg; signal check to 88 followed by 120 at Wilmersdorf; 116/106 Warnitz; 120 Seehausen; 96 permanent restriction at Prenzlau and a final 118 at Nechlin. The 30 miles from Bernau to Angermunde were passed in 30 minutes to the second and the 38.1 miles on to Pasewalk in a further 38min 11sec to the stand at the water column (Appendix 2, Table 10).

We stayed only long enough at Pasewalk to take water – 5 minutes – and left at 11.42. Progress north was similar to that of 03.0046 three days earlier, although one difference was that the weather was deteriorating fast and I was reminded of that other flat stretch of railway north of Papenburg and the sudden squalls and leaden skies that always took over from the blue skies of Rheine. The heathlands of Oranienburg-Fürstenberg and Eberswalde-Pasewalk also had their similarities with the Lingen-Meppen section of the Emsland main line and with the rugged three cylinder roar from 03.0085, I could shut my eyes and well imagine I was back on a Cologne-Norddeich D-Zug behind one of the vociferous Rheine 012s. 03.0085 accelerated hard to pass Anklam (26.25 miles) in 28 minutes 19 seconds, slowing to 40kph from its maximum of 110, then after more slacks, approached Greifswald emitting an ear-splitting roar at 116kph, whistle howling. As this steam-hauled named international express swept through the crowded platforms, I found this both exciting and in some odd sort of way, strangely moving – a real living anachronism that only I seemed to be appreciating as if it was being performed just for my benefit. Continuing at a steady 110-120kph, we came to a stand at a signal protecting Stralsund Rügendamm platform in 70min 53sec from Pasewalk (70 miles) and after standing there for 3 minutes, drew into the platform just 9 minutes late, a gain of 25 minutes from Berlin. 03.0085 was replaced by 03.0077 and I decided to explore the town in daylight (Appendix 2, Table 10).

The 2.57pm Stralsund-Leipzig, D717, sported Pasewalk's 01.0535-3 (alternating daily with 01.0530) on eleven coaches, 354/380 tonnes. The run was thoroughly competent throughout, on time or early at all points. The locomotive was clearly on top of its job, not needing pushing, achieving good but not outstanding times and speeds. The sharpest performance was to cover the 10.4 miles from Züssow to Anklam in 11min 10sec start to stop with a maximum of 114kph, very energetic although the engine was not flogged. Maximum speed after Pasewalk was 120kph, making Angermunde to Eberswalde, 16.25 miles, in 17 minutes 49 seconds and arrival at Lichtenberg was exactly on time.

A nice steamy half hour was spent watching two-cylinder coal-burning Pacific 03.2058-0 shunting a parcels train in the carriage sidings and then coal-burning

01.1518-8 slowly drawing out the stock for E314 *Gydania* and backing the coaches into the platform. The eight coaches, 321/350 tonnes were very full and I stood in the vestibule immediately behind the tender. I met the only other railway enthusiast I saw in the whole holiday here, an East German, who told me there was going to be a 'farewell to steam' from the Ostbahnhof depot in mid-May, double-headed by the depot's last standard 01 (01.2065) and 01.1518. He had tried to prime the driver to get the loco to make a noise as he was tape-recording also, but he was unsuccessful and I gather we had a normal run with this train with no excitement. 109kph between Springfühl and Karow was the high point and speed then drifted away to the upper 80s to Bernau. Bernau-Eberswalde, 13.75 miles, took 16min 45sec again maximum speed of 109, and the 16.25 miles onto Angermunde took 20min 8sec with a whispering 105kph at Herzsprung, where 03.0046 was roaring away at 120 with a substantially heavier load. The 01 looked splendid but the lack of energy in the running consoled me that in contriving to miss E314 most nights, I had probably not missed anything too spectacular. I returned from Angermunde on a late and empty D311, behind diesel 118.155-1, which according to the West German *Eisenbahn Kurier* 'ABC', did not exist.

My last full day on the Stralsund line – how was I to spend it? So far, I had had just two disappointments; a lot of good competent running had not produced any really fast speeds – no 'eighties' (more than 130kph) although the line speeds were only 120. And I'd set my heart on a run behind Stralsund's pet, the much decorated 03.0010-3 which had been my first sight of a DR Pacific, but after the first two days it had languished with its nose poking out of the Stralsund roundhouse, presumably under repair. I was now resigned to an attempt to get this loco on my last day in the GDR, by overnighting on the 12.03am Berlin and returning on D319, putting my return home schedule in jeopardy. I was not to know that 03.0010 would metamorphose into the coal-burning star of many *Plandampfs* in later years as 03.1010-2 (see chapter 16).

I decided to catch up on some sleep and catch the *Meridian* again. The strengthening vehicles were brought in tender first by the 03 diagrammed to haul the express from the Ostbahnhof – today it was 03.0090-5 performing the honours, an engine that did not appear to be in the best of condition. As I was still debating with myself whether to go, 03.0010 swept early into the station with D319. Rapid consultation of the *Kursbuch* (timetable) began to give me ideas, which crystallised as the *Meridian* also arrived early for once. 03.0090 was going to find timekeeping too easy.

I S-bahned to Warschauerbrucke, photographed 03.0090 waffling through the drizzle, then continued to Lichtenberg for the 10.18 express to Rostock. I noted 132.306-2 at the head end, then got down to the more serious business of buying presents for my children. The journey to Neustrelitz was uneventful, and I was deposited on the cold, wet, grubby and soldier-infested platform for the hour's wait until the arrival of D613 – probably longer if Saturday's experience with 03.0090 was anything to go by. So I walked round the town, added it to my list of places not to bother to return to, and sat on the platform with the Russian soldiers to wait and wait. First D613 was announced as forty late, then sixty … then a local for the single line to Neubrandenburg was despatched and I began to worry that even the 90 minute connection at Oranienburg was not going to be enough. Eventually, the train crept in shamefacedly and unannounced, 89 minutes late, beautifully poised to keep me on tenterhooks all the way.

I reappraised my priorities, confirmed that the whole point of the expedition this morning was to get a run behind 03.0010 and resolved to reduce my blood pressure by alighting at Fürstenberg and having another mini-exploration. Meanwhile, a short snippet with 03.0058-2 on eleven coaches, which ran from Neustrelitz to Fürstenburg efficiently enough.

At two o'clock, as I alighted, things began to improve. The drizzle stopped, the sun broke through and I found that the lake-encircled town was very attractive. My attempt to sunbathe on the banks of a lake as I ate my lunch was thwarted as the apparent access road led me straight into a Russian army camp, from which I hurriedly retreated, so I returned early to the station, still weighing the chances of 03.0010 being replaced by an Ostbahnhof diesel. I worried needlessly. Leibnitz's dictum that 'all was for the best in the best of all possible worlds', began to be a working hypothesis for this holiday. Right on the dot, D814 appeared round the corner behind the instantly recognised 03.0010. The load was eight coaches, 252/265 tonnes. It was a joy to accelerate out of the station, listening to a deep crisp even exhaust, passing Strelitz Alt at 120kph after a 30kph p-way slack, drifting into Neustrelitz in 16 minutes exactly for the 13.1 miles, 3 minutes early. Neustrelitz-Neubrandenburg was taken easily in 28 minutes 14 seconds for the 22 miles with a maximum of 108kph before and after a signal check to 10kph at Burg Stargard. The next section to Demmin produced nice noises, but the same delays as before from the rearranged timetable and I decided not to risk trying to get to Bergen to connect with the *Berlinaren*, but to play safe and wait for it at Neubrandenburg.

Stralsund's 'pet' oil-burning 03.0010-3 on arrival at Demmin with the 1.35pm Berlin-Stralsund express, 21 April 1979. This locomotive has been preserved in running order and converted to coal burning as 03.1010-2. (*Author*)

After returning to Neubrandenburg on a 110 hauled local, I spent 4 hours contemplating dead 41s (DR 2-8-2s), live 50s (DR 2-10-0s) and 01.0535 on depot, wandering round the city ramparts and eating a decent meal for once. 9.40pm came and went and eventually D317 was announced as 20 minutes late, which had expanded to thirty by the time it had negotiated the slack-infested northern fastnesses. 03.0085-5 was hauling seven coaches, 282/290 tonnes, and we departed 32 minutes late in a manner that had me flinging wide the window, grabbing my watch and hanging out, spotting the kilometre posts in the darkness.

The start was electric and we roared away up the bank to Burg Stargard at 80/87kph, passed in 7min 33sec, 112 at Cammin, 127 before Blankensee, 114 slowing to 102 through Neustrelitz (23min 23sec from Neubrandenburg, 22 miles away), 120 at Strelitz Alt, the same at Düsterforde, Fürstenberg, 35 miles, passed in 34min 18 sec, 112 at Drögen, then finally 131kph (82mph) at Dannenwalde, 129 at Altlüdersdorf and ... then the brakes slammed on as this was all obviously too much for the 110-hauled parcels train that had preceded us. We drew to a stand at Gransee in 45min 58sec for the 48 miles, an average speed of 63mph. There we stood for 6 minutes while the driver fumed, then roared off, signal checks at Buberow and Löwenburg, then we got a clear road and piled the speed on in a rip-roaring fashion, 120 at Gruneberg; 131 at Nassenheide; 128 at Fichtengrund; 120 Sachsenhausen; and another check to walking pace before Oranienburg passed in 72min 26sec (less than 60 minutes net for the 66.2 miles).

We continued to charge away from each signal check, 108/70* Bergfelde; 116/40* Schönfliess; 120 Springfühl; 50*/108 Wühlheide; still roaring like a demented thing past Rummelsburg at 112 and then – anti-climax – we joined the queue waiting to gain entrance to the Ostbahnhof, standing for 8 minutes at Warschauerstrasse, completing the journey, checks and all in 117 minutes 24 seconds, 43 minutes late — or about 88 minutes net for the 95 miles (Appendix 2, Table 10). My two objectives for the day had been met – 03.0010 and a fast run with 80s! If I had been game for more, 01.0530 was still awaiting the arrival of its train from Leipzig, but enough was enough, and anything else was likely to be an anti-climax, so I bade goodnight to the guards on night duty at Lenin's plinth well content.

My obsession with Stralsund's three cylinder 03s had the effect of virtually eliminating the Lutherstadt-Wittenberg two-cylinder coal-burning 03s from my planned schedule, so I decided to take up one of my emergency itineraries prepared when the Stralsund 03.00s were in doubt, and sample all the L-Wittenberg diagrams in one day. To this end I got myself to Berlin Schöneweide by 5.20am (and anyone who knew me then will know how hard that was!). I intended to catch D501 5.46am Schöneweide-Saalfeld, forgetting the existence of the 5.23am *Personenzug* (stopping train) to Halle, which was steaming gently in the platform with 03.2243-8. So to Schönefeld we trotted, a wee appetiser for later and 15 minutes less of 132.193-3 on D501.

I ate breakfast in one of the most hair-raising vehicles I have ever travelled in, with vicious side-play that went beyond the Pompey electrics at their worst. The train got later and later as we went south, and from Weissenfels I was well occupied by a beautifully eccentric seventy-year-old Saxon woman with an impossible accent, who told me all her travel woes and life history at a frantic pace that I could scarce follow and finally (I think) some slightly scurrilous and risqué stories. Not being quite sure that I was understanding properly meant that I had to be a little ambiguous in my reaction. By Rüdolstadt the lateness of the train and my exhaustion at following the aptly named Frau Keck (Mrs Cheeky!) caused me to do a bunk, and I had a sunny 20 minutes to wait by the river, during which time I photographed 01.0529 on the 9.3am Camburg-Saalfeld local and 44.0601-3 on a freight from Saalfeld.

D504 (Saalfeld – Berlin) arrived 3 minutes late behind two-cylinder oil-burning Pacific 01.0510-6 with thirteen coaches, 402/425 tonnes, which I took through to Leipzig. The running was not particularly inspiring, with many checks, both signal and p-way, and the locomotive seemed sluggish and needed punching hard. It produced fore-and-aft motion worse than any other 01 behind which I travelled and the same was experienced on another occasion behind this engine. We stopped for a train to clear the single line section at Uhlstadt for 4 minutes, and in between the checks, got a maximum of 88kph through Jena Paradies. Leaving Jena 13 minutes late, we suffered four long p-way slacks and then oscillated through Bad Kösen at an uncomfortable 105kph. Naumburg was left 17 minutes late and the final section from Weissenfels to Leipzig took nearly 38 minutes with p-way slowings all the way to Kotschau and then an aura of excitement as we eventually just made 110kph at Leipzig Leutsch. Arrival was 21 minutes late.

I continued through to L-Wittenberg behind another 132, getting later and later, and raced along the platform extension to find coal-burning 03.2176-0 heading a rake of seven bogie coaches that I saw rather a lot of. I have a log of P3516 from L-Wittenberg to Lückenwalde if anyone is really interested – the run was mainly remarkable for the consistency with which 75kph (48mph) was reached. However, the reasonable stock and repeated starts enabled good recording. I ate during the hour's stop at Jüterbog and used the 90 minute stop-over in Lückenwalde to thoroughly explore this grim and dusty town. Why had no-one painted the outside of their houses since 1939? I found a shop that sold the only DR railway magazine that I saw on the trip and bought a copy. I'm sure the GDR authorities wouldn't have been happy at tourists wandering freely around such a place. Back at the station, P3517 duly turned up on time behind the scheduled 03.2243 and the same seven standard bogie coaches, but had to wait for an express to pass and left 5 minutes late. The train ran quite energetically with good sound effects and touched 84kph between Klebitz and Zahne and 102 (!) after Jüterbog, arriving at Wittenberg on time.

I had nearly 2 hours to kill during which I fulfilled a strong urge to see the city and the Martin Luther-associated cathedral where the famous ninety-five theses had been nailed to the door, acting as the first catalyst for the founding of Protestantism. It was getting dark and drizzling gently and quite deserted – and most impressive. The sheer bulk of the church contrasted with the puny war memorial composed of an illuminated Soviet tank and the awesome silence in the eerie damp dusk was a memory I shall long retain. The sole movement was from an elderly woman tramp pushing a run-down pram – the only time I saw such a rebellious sight in the GDR. I walked back to the station completely at peace with the world.

Coal-burning two cylinder Pacific 03.2243-8 arrives at Lückenwalde with stopping train P3517 from Berlin Schöneweide to Lutherstadt-Wittenberg and Halle, 22 April 1979. (*Author*)

Back at the station, I found the same seven-coach set with 03.2155-4 steaming quietly at the head end. The locomotive was in good condition and after I had taken a (not very good) flash photo, I got into conversation with the crew – Driver Alfons Liehs and Fireman Werner Schmager, both of L-Wittenberg depot. They confirmed that the section to Jüterbog was being run by electric traction from the following month, the 03s going to store and the steam link being dispersed – Alfons was retiring and Werner was becoming a diesel driver on the Wittenberg-Dessau route on freight services with Russian built diesels of the 120 class. During the half-hour stop at Jüterbog, we had a long conversation which led to an exchange of railway literature and very nearly a footplate run, but unfortunately a security policeman was hanging around and we decided not to risk it.

As far as performance was concerned, it was a fairly normal run until Woltersdorf was passed, when I was interrupted by an amiable drunk, who found out I was English and regaled me most indiscreetly with the misdeeds of the GDR authorities, said how much he admired the UK and then asked of all things if I had any English soap – he had contracted eczema and was blaming East German soap! I actually had a bar of soap along with extra toilet rolls in case of emergency, thanks to advice from my intrepid forerunner to cart around washing utensils, loo paper etc., to make up for DR deficiencies, which I found to be a little hard on the DR, so I gladly donated one to him – which he took with compliments on the British way of life. Unfortunately all this was happening as we were rocketing around the Berlin Ringbahn at what I estimated was a speed well in excess of 100kph.

Next day, my original intention had been to journey south from Berlin on D563, the only D-Zug booked for an L-Wittenberg 03.2, then catch a local from Leipzig to Saalfeld, but I had confirmed that the Saalfeld-Sonneberg line still operated Class 95 2-10-2 tanks (T20 of Prussian origin). I therefore wanted to create sufficient time to get to Sonneberg and back, and sacrificed the steam run south for a further pilgrimage on D501 and another dreadfully early start. I crept out of the Berolina Hotel as though I was trying to avoid paying the bill and at least caught the local, 5.23am from Schönefeld, which was hauled by a filthy Pacific, 03.2058-0, and joined there a punctual D501 with 132.198-3. Another violent breakfast in its *Mitropa* followed, before a further friendly hour from Halle to Jena, having been joined by a young married couple and mother-in-law, who immediately raided the *Mitropa* and came back armed with beers and spirits – at nine o'clock in the morning! There was no way I was going to be allowed to miss the ensuing picnic, whether I liked it or not, and once my identity and nationality had been established, a celebration party took off. I was assumed to be conversant with all British pop songs (I prefer Mahler and Shostakovich!). I was offered an exorbitant number of Reichsmarks for my West German currency – in fact I exchanged some at the standard rate, which meant more bottles poured into my arms as further toasts were drunk. I staggered onto a revolving Jena platform with just enough wits left to realise I had to escape from this tidal wave of bonhomie, before I lost all trace of the day and my plans.

A bright red and black blur we passed at Camburg resolved itself into an ex-works 01.0529-6 with a seven-coach double-decker set on the 9.03am Camburg-Saalfeld local, which wafted me to Rüdolstadt midst a merry chattering noise and good accelerations to 90kph or so. At Rüdolstadt, D504 duly turned up behind 01.0510 again, so I let it go and sat down beside the mellow waters to sober up and eat some chocolate. P3004, 11.04am Saalfeld-Camburg local appeared on time behind 01.0520-5 and took me efficiently enough to Göschwitz where I connected with the 12.25pm Jena-Gera P-Zug, also booked for an 01.5; 01.0534-6 ran in almost at once. I'd hardly settled down to a good crisp climb, before we were in Stadtroda and we were all tipped out to continue by road. It was all very abrupt – 01.0534 had cut off before I fathomed what was going on. Into the 'bendy-bus' and off we swooped, my luggage falling all over the place, as we hared up hill and down dale and into Hermsdorf or Klosterlausnitz or both and then onwards in a dreadful train of six-wheelers hauled by the East German poor man's version of the V200, 118.132-0, which wandered down the hill and arrived at Gera 1 minute before the departure time of P5023, which was waiting behind 'bullet-nosed' 01.0505-6 – a replica of the Piko model in my loft. If this text seems a little breathless, it merely reflects my impression of the day so far, not helped by my alcoholic fog.

The new train of six-wheelers was jammed tight (I had to stand) and the coach windows were so filthy I could hardly see out, so I was thankful that I had rejected my earlier plan to take this local all the way from Leipzig. The 01 made pleasant noises up the bank above the grinding squeals of our primitive coach and I was pleased to get this loco – the only other 01.5 that had retained its bullet-nosed smokebox door was 01.0513, which stood on Saalfeld depot on the breakdown train the whole time I was there. One of the preserved 01.5s, 01.1531, has had one of these smokebox doors fixed to replace the DR standard version that graced all the others. I bailed out at a distinctly windy and chilly Weida – a dilapidated barn of a station – to await E402, a long rake of spotless DB coaches surprisingly pulled by 118.127-0 and pushed by 120.116-9, the latter trailing through to Gera. We passed E805 on the outskirts of Leipzig with 01.0521-3, which threw me – it was diagrammed for E807, which I intended to take from Leipzig back to Saalfeld – so it was no big surprise when I found 01.0510-6 again on the latter.

The 5.51pm Leipzig-Saalfeld loaded to thirteen coaches, 393/410 tonnes and a very young-looking crew were on the footplate of 01.0510. I was immediately aware on departure of the same pronounced fore-and-aft motion experienced with this loco earlier. A slow but noisy acceleration got the train going at 104kph by Leipzig-Plagwitz and held 98-102kph thereafter with a lot of pother and with a p-way slack to 40kph at Profen and a raucous 86kph at Bornitz. Zeitz (28.1 miles) was reached in 37 minutes 53 seconds, but 6 minutes late as a result of a late departure by the same margin. We stopped at Krossen with yet another p-way slack and then flogged along at a juddering 88kph, arriving Gera 9 minutes late. Gera to Weida (7.5 miles) took 17 minutes 4 seconds including a 45 second signal stop at Gera Zwötzen and hard running at 80/69 up the bank to Niederpölnitz, the summit being cleared at 56kph before the Triptis stop. We then drifted downhill in the dusk and ran into Saalfeld just as the 8.46pm P-Zug was roaring out with the three cylinder Jumbo 2-10-0, 044.0601-3, which

Rebuilt DR 01.0510-6 at Leipzig, ready to haul E807 back to Saalfeld via Gera, 23 April 1979. (*Author*)

seemed to be deputizing for one of the two 01.5s normally sub-shedded at Göschwitz. I checked the steamy atmosphere with 01s, 44s and 95s everywhere and retired to the Goldene Anker, well known to most enthusiasts, a little punch-drunk.

Dawn and another early rising and walk down through the town, already busier than the previous evening, to see what Saalfeld had to offer in daylight. I had hopes of a 95 or two, as I was planning a trip to Sonneberg. First, however, a quick run to Rüdolstadt and back before more serious business. The 5.53am Saalfeld-Camburg, consisting of four double-deck carriages and excessive power in 01.0509-8, ran smartly to Rüdolstadt. I had an outside hope of a 95 on the 6.45am Rüdolstadt-Saalfeld, which is booked through to Sonneberg, and was pleased when an ex-works 95.0045-5 brought the empty stock in from Saalfeld. What did surprise me was the appearance at about 6.40, of 95.0044-8, running light from the Jena direction, which promptly backed on to the other end of the train, and we set off for Saalfeld with 95s fore and aft! Great fun as I stood in the rear vestibule by 95.0045's smokebox and watched all the pumps and pistons pulsating as we trotted along in the low 60s (kph).

We got back to Saalfeld by 6.58 and by seven o'clock I was on E800, 7.03am Saalfeld-Leipzig via Gera, with 01.0521-3 – my fourth 'new' loco of a very young day. The load was a full twelve coaches, 356/385 tonnes, and departure was on time. A steady acceleration up the bank out of Saalfeld produced 51kph, clearing Unterwellenborn in 8min 27sec, but with a lot of slacks onwards during track 'doubling' operations, we took 25min 4sec to reach our first stop at Pössneck. Pössneck-Neustadt was very vigorous with 93kph through Oppurg, falling slowly to 70 above Neunhofen and a start-stop time of 9min 44sec for the final 5.6 uphill miles to Triptis with 65 at the summit was good going, with plenty of clear even exhaust. Thereafter it was easy-going, just reaching 96kph on the descent to Weida, arriving Gera on time. Just to prove the superiority of the 01.5s, 118.124-7 on the southbound E403 and the DB Nurnberg set, staggered up to Weida with a maximum of 45kph and could only achieve 42 on to Niederpölnitz. However, it was plain sailing downhill and we arrived back in Saalfeld shortly after the booked time of 10.15.

P18003, 10.34am Saalfeld-Sonneberg, was standing ready for departure with 95.0005-9 and five coaches, but with two transport police patrolling the platform and scrutinizing all joining the train. Trying to look as inconspicuous as possible, I joined the front coach and heaved a sigh of relief when 95.0005 yanked the train into motion punctually with me still on it. We wandered up the river valley on a glorious spring morning and had got to about Hockeroda before the police stirred themselves and undertook a check of personal papers. I handed my return ticket to the young lady guard and my visa (not valid for this *Bezirk*) to one of the officers at the same time and waited with bated breath.

I feared the worst when one of the policemen called the girl to have a look at my visa, but they handed it back with a smile, queried whether I had really obtained it in London, and wished me a pleasant trip, adding that everything was in order. They stayed on to chat for a while, told me which side of the train the best views were, and then settled in the next compartment of the open coach, to natter away in high pitched voices, thus giving my tape-recordings of the 95 an unusual background. I didn't time the journey, being much too busy taking in the views, hanging out of the windows trying to get decent shots on the most acute curves and doing some recording – not too publicly and not as we ran alongside the border fence. We reversed at Lauscha, glimpsed 5 minutes previously from a great height, and the police alighted for their lunch break before re-joining my return train, and 95.0005 ran round and took water. Thereafter we seemed to be threading our way through people's back gardens amidst the drying washing, clattering over makeshift bridges astride dashing streams and whistling furiously at large numbers of open crossings.

95.0005-9 leaving Lauscha after running round its train, P18003, 10.34am Saalfeld-Sonneberg, 24.4.79. (*Author*)

Ex-Prussian T20 2-10-2 tank, 95.0005-9 at Saalfeld with P18003, the 10.34am Saalfeld-Sonneberg, 24 April 1979. (*Author*)

T20 2-10-2T, 95.0036-4, at Sonneberg with the 1.32pm train from back to Saalfeld, 24 April 1979. (*Author*)

On arrival at Sonneberg, I half expected 95.0005 to run round, but lo and behold, another gleaming loco stood ready, complete with white-painted decorations, on a train of mainly six-wheelers, although a dirty orange 106 diesel shunter stood ominously close to the buffers of the rear coach. A quick sausage between the 1.10 arrival and 1.32pm departure and then 95.0036-4 was off, thankfully leaving the diesel slumbering behind us in the platform. Lots of school kids got on and off at regular intervals all the way to Lauscha, where our engine ran round and the police re-joined us with a merry salute. I taped the departure, roaring away straight up to the tunnel and onwards towards Oberlauscha, and we maintained speed in the upper 30s without any great striving after the initial rush out of Lauscha station. We passed 95.0044 slumbering on a local freight in Ernsttal station and came across 95.0014 with another, more substantial, freight lower down the valley – not a sign of the rumoured impending 118 or 119 diesels anywhere to be seen. And so we arrived triumphantly back in Saalfeld at 4.04pm, after over 5 hours of 95 haulage, a most relaxing and enjoyable day.

I had envisaged an inevitable diesel to Gera on E806, to meet the 5.51pm Leipzig, but there were plenty more surprises still left in store for me. After watching what I thought was a 'giesl' 52 in the marshalling yard, it emerged and showed itself as a spotless 2-8-4T, 65.1049. It was followed by a couple of 01s, (0519 and 0531) and 01.0505 romped in with the afternoon local from Pössneck. Then I suddenly noticed a 95 hauled local standing facing Gera and enquiry elicited the fact that it was the 4.55pm Saalfeld-Oppurg, which I proceeded to take to Pössneck ahead of E806. Another new 95 (my fifth of the day – how many diagrams are there?) 95.0004-2 on eight coaches, 165/175 tonnes, which I decided to time. We trotted up the bank to Unterwellenborn in 7min 15sec at 55kph, then progressed unhurriedly between p-way slacks at about the same speed, arriving at Pössneck inclusive of three stops totalling 2 minutes standing time, in 26min 17sec, only just over a minute longer than 01.0521 on E800 this morning nonstop!

I relaxed then to Gera behind 118.241-9 of Halle on E806 and arrived in good time to buy a real plum cake before seeking out the polished and decorated 01.0525-4, which had arrived on E807. The load was thirteen coaches 393/405 tonnes, and departure was on time. We had scarcely cleared Gera Süd when a series of brilliant lights flashed out a Morse message from the signal cabin and we were brought to a grinding emergency halt. There we stood for over 7 minutes, for no apparent reason, although I guessed we had left Gera with a door open. Recovery was swift, with 80 falling to 72 after Gera Rüppisch and Weida was reached 8 minutes late. Weida to Triptis took 16 minutes 37 seconds (9.4 miles) with the summit being passed at exactly 60kph and with considerably less fuss than 01.0510. After that I ceased timing as we gradually recovered time, rolling downhill to arrive at Saalfeld 4 minutes late and just in time to catch the 8.46pm (and perhaps an 044) to Rüdolstadt for dinner.

P5034 was waiting, however, with the Göschwitz-based 01.0534, which raced to Rüdolstadt with its light load. I then found the GDR equivalent of a pub, where I had a very pleasant and cheap dinner, with a friendly group of youths and girls in their twenties who turned out to be 'strolling players' putting on a Lessing comedy *Minna von Barnhelm* - oh, the memories evoked of the German Department at UCL! They toured about eleven towns in the Gera district with a repertoire of two or three plays at a time. This was a regular practice throughout the GDR and very commendable too. We talked of the inevitable pop music and football (Kevin Keegan), which appeared to be UK's main fame behind the Iron Curtain and then graduated onto politics. They were keen to know if their country's view of the UK was biased – unemployment, strikes, homelessness – and seemed to pity me for living in a country of perpetual fog! They took the view that governments of East and West presented biased images of the opposing bloc and painted a picture of their own country which was critical, especially of its bureaucracy and earnestness, but made it clear that they didn't approve of West German and American capitalist and materialist societies either. In fact, as far as government systems were concerned, they described themselves as cheerful anarchists!

As a group of actors, one area that they felt sore about, was censorship. We had quite a long talk about George Orwell, *1984* and *Animal Farm*. One of the group had managed to read *1984* and had been impressed and was keen to know about *Animal Farm* of which he had only heard, so I dredged my memory. Apparently the communists were much more concerned about lapsed and disillusioned communists than any outright opponent of the system – hence the fact that so many Soviet dissidents who were forced to flee to the West were equally critical of what they found. They were intrigued and sympathetic with my reason for visiting their country – they hadn't realized their transport system was quite such a museum piece although they were not surprised and said they would consider their travels in a new light in future!

Back to the station for P5041 10.22pm Rüdolstadt-Probstzella, which was waiting with 95.0044 and I was just snoozing off from the effect of a heavy meal and wine when a 44-hauled passenger train clattered into the opposite platform. Without further thought, I fell out of P5041 and into the other train, and as we roared out of the station I hastily consulted my timetable to see what I was on and whether I could get back to Saalfeld. Having established I was unlikely to get stranded, I turned my attention to P5038, 10.09pm Saalfeld-Camburg, which consisted of four double-deck carriages and 044.0601-3. This engine was working a variety of locals and was obviously covering the Göschwitz 01.5 turns with 01.0534. The train rushed into motion from each station – it seemed to achieve top speed before the platform was left – and then wooffled along at about 70kph. I decided I had better play safe by getting out at Zeutsch, the station after Orlamünde, and I got a beautiful tape there of the 44's departure complete with slip and frantic acceleration into the completely still and silent night – I seemed to hear it going for ever. After that I was quite unmoved by the last local from Jena to Saalfeld which came a few minutes later behind 110.544-4. At the end of this day I began to think that God must be a railway enthusiast!

I left you contemplating the theology of nostalgic rail travel in the bosom of the Anker Hotel, Saalfeld. Refreshed, and arising early like the locals, I crept from my hotel to see the dawn chorus of 01s — 01.0520 on the 5.53am to Jena and 01.0501 on the 6.21am to Gera. In addition, 01.0522 was in the yard, 0513 was on the breakdown train, 0524 was poking out of the roundhouse under repair, and 0529 was hovering for the E800. 01.0533 was lying in the yard, dead – either withdrawn or awaiting works. The only Saalfeld 01 I did not see in the three days was 0508. Then I saw another 95 on the 6.17am P5012, to Rüdolstadt so I chose this with 95.0043-0 with six coaches 155/170 tonnes – it was a workman's train for the Schwarza works – touching 69kph between stops. Back I see-sawed a few minutes later with 95.0004 at the front and 95.0043 aft, as on the previous day, maximum speed 64kph.

I now had to decide how I wanted to leave the Saalfeld area. The choice was 0529 on E800, 0510 on E802 or 0521 on D504. I had planned on catching the 2.02pm Eilzug from Halle to Nordhausen to traverse the Harzquerbahn, and in view of the current timekeeping of D504 and the tightish connection at either Halle or Leipzig, I decided to take E800 through to Leipzig. 01.0529-6, just ex-works anyway, had been further 'decorated' the previous day, with Saalfeld white running plate and bufferbeam edges. The load was twelve coaches, 356/390 tonnes. We left on time, climbed to Unterwellenborn in 7min 35sec at 51kph, then slacks to Pössneck, reached in 23min 45sec. We touched 90kph at Oppurg and the summit was cleared before Triptis at 62kph. We got to, and left, Gera on time, were held 6 minutes at Bad Köstritz to cross E403 and after a further 25kph p-way slack, reached Zeitz just over a minute late. We accelerated hard to 96kph by Bornitz only to catch the signalman out, as a 120-hauled coal train was still crawling into Reuden loop. After more checks, we sustained 100-105 through the Leipzig suburbs, although the riding of my coach was rough in the extreme. We terminated one and a half minutes late, having covered the 28.1 miles from Zeitz in 38min 7sec (33min net). We drew up in platform 1 at Leipzig Hbf alongside 01.0509 on P3020. I wandered along the concourse to see the 9.43am booked arrival of D563 from Berlin (a notoriously bad timekeeper) only to find it drawing in on the dot behind my favourite L-Wittenburg 03, 03.2155.

DR standard 2-10-0 50.3640-5 at Rothensee with P6448 Magdeburg to Oebisfelde [border with West Germany], 25 April 1979. (*Author*)

I decided to get to Halle as quickly as possible, in case anything interesting like the unique Halle-based Pacific 02.0201 or a steam-hauled train to Nordhausen was about – with my luck, I was beginning to get ideas above my station. A filthy electric, 242.115-4, took me to Halle and deposited me on a grey overcast day in a diesel filled city. I ate an early lunch, and came to the sober realization that nothing of interest was likely before the Harz railway. The more I thought about it, the stronger the urge to change my plans and get to Magdeburg for a coal-burning 01 to Halberstadt and perhaps a 50.35 2-10-0 to Thale or Wernigerode. So getting fed up, and feeling perhaps that the best of the holiday was over, I acted on the urge and caught D634 to Magdeburg hauled by mainline electric 211.048-4. With May Day looming up, Magdeburg was a mass of people, so I got rid of my luggage at the Hotel International and came back to the station at about two o'clock to see what was about. I concentrated mainly on the southern end of the station, looking towards Halberstadt and very nearly missed the fact that Oebisfelde had put out a 2-10-0, 50.3640-5 for P6448, 2.53pm Magdeburg - Oebisfelde via Haldensleben. I hastily checked I could get back by 4 o'clock and, deciding it was safe, boarded the train as far as Rothensee.

I enjoyed the steamy atmosphere there, taking photos of a freight hauled by 41.1144 and another of a 52 plodding slowly out of the marshalling yard. I was relying on an 18-minute connection back at Magdeburg out of an S-bahn train and I began to get worried as it failed to turn up. Then, 10 minutes after it should have appeared, a very late running international express, 132-hauled, hove into view and I gave up all hope of catching the 01.20 turn. But, surprise, it stopped – especially, it seemed, to pick up one S-bahn passenger. And it then proceeded to ignore passengers waiting at other S-bahn stations – I would still have missed the 4.3pm to Halberstadt if we had stopped. How jammy can you get?

We arrived back at Magdeburg at exactly four o'clock and I shot across the platform to find P8436, with four well-filled double-deck coaches and – relief –

Coal-burning two cylinder Pacific 01.2137-6 [now preserved in working order] on P8436 to Halberstadt at Magdeburg, 25 April 1979. (*Author*)

01.2137-6, clean and its smokebox door decorated with little May Day flags. I found a window seat upstairs in the first coach and after careful threading of the various junctions, I was in a good position to appreciate the vigorous exhaust that we were treated to over the next hour. The performance was surprisingly lively with 86 at Magdeburg-Thalmannswerk; 40* at Wolfsfelde; 105/45* Dodendorf; 106/45* Langenweddingen; 105/40* Blumenberg; 94/40*/108 Hadmersleben, reaching Oschersleben in 31 minutes 41 seconds.

We had a very long p-way slack to 10kph on departure, then barked away in an electric acceleration to 106/40* Nienhagen and 45*/106 Gross Querstadt – then finally we crawled for ages at walking pace through a p-way slack that had apparently been in place for over a year and meant no trains had ever arrived on time at Halberstadt during that period! Because of missed connections, we were told by the station foreman that we could join an empty stock train standing in the station – I hadn't the remotest idea where it was going to, but as it was hauled by Halberstadt's 50.3707-2, complete with May Day flags, I got in first and enquired afterwards. I found I was on the booked steam-hauled empty stock to Wernigerode for the 18.38 D-Zug, thence to Berlin, which goes back as far as Halberstadt with its 2-10-0. 50.3707 roared away on the seven-coach train and maintained a steady 64kph. Because of my last minute decisions, I had bought very few tickets on this day, and no ticket collectors came round other than on P8436, so a lot of these surprises were courtesy of the DR.

On arrival at Wernigerode, I found it was now possible to do what the timetable said was impossible – get a decent run on the Harzquerbahn after all. There were about four of the giant narrow gauge 2-10-2 tanks (the oil burning 99.02s or coal-burning 99.72s) in steam in the yard, including the sole 1933-built 99.7222. I bought a day return ticket in the gathering dusk – 'today?' said the booking clerk in disbelief – to Drei Annen Höhne, and joined empty P69755, 6.32pm to Benneckenstein, onto which a clean oil-burning 2-10-2T, 99.0231-3, backed, blowing off steam. My one apprehension in view of the booking clerk's surprise, my loneliness on the train and the fact that my visa was not cleared for *Bezirk* Halberstadt, was that I would be stopped by the lone policeman who came to check my visa before departure.

However, I need not have worried – he seemed very pleased to have a passenger and wasn't going to do anything to lose him – and he reassured me that he and the train crew were also going to make the return train connection at Drei Annen Höhne.

So we chuffed out of the station, along the road, and in and out of suburban gardens, before starting the climb in earnest. Once clear of the town, whistle blaring, smoke poured from the chimney as we squealed round tight curves into the woods. We then doubled back on ourselves as we scrambled up the hillside and made sure progress through the fir forest. After three quarters of an hour of spectacular scenery we arrived at the summit and drew up to the water column to await the 4.37pm from Nordhausen, P14410. This was heralded by a prolonged mournful whistle a long way off in the forest and eventually a bunker-first 99.0240-4 drew its train into the station. The descent to Wernigerode in the gathering dusk, the train snaking ahead giving prolonged sight of flashing wheels and rods, was accomplished all too soon, and I got out at the terminus, again the only passenger, having had a thoroughly splendid 50p's worth.

I was now keen to find something to eat – all these last minute connections ignored that aspect – but just as I found the open *Mitropa*, I discovered a two coach P16475, 8.57pm Wernigerode-Halberstadt, in the platform, with a tender-first 50.3632-2 ready to depart. The rumblings in my stomach were again ignored, and I went to stand in the darkened vestibule looking out at the smokebox of the 50, which was beautifully polished. Off we thumped into the darkness, a nice little unexpected pleasure. I had the train to myself yet again. On arrival at Halberstadt I at last satisfied my bodily needs and put up with an appalling run to Magdeburg on the one-stop P8479 10.44pm ex Halberstadt, with 132.385-6, which arrived eventually 45 minutes late at a quarter past midnight.

Having gone into the GDR via Helmstedt after all, I had left the Oebisfelde 2-8-2 41s for an early morning snippet. The time had now arrived to make that appointment, by getting up at the usual unearthly hour of 'five something', to catch the 6.06am Magdeburg-Rothensee with four double-deckers hauled by a 118 diesel hydraulic. That draughty station, in the middle of fields and gravel pits, was a little unwelcome at 6.30, especially as P9409, 4.17am from Oebisfelde, was 10 minutes late. However, it eventually turned up behind a disreputable 41.1289-2, its black and red paint indistinguishable as a dirty grey, but we took the commuters into the Hauptbahnhof efficiently enough. Having done it once, I decided to repeat it for good measure, and went to Neustadt, one station out, behind a 110 on a regular S-bahn train. I crossed platforms just in time to greet a punctual 5.46am Oebisfelde via Haldensleben, with a rather cleaner 41.1025-0. I did not time the 4 minute run – I just enjoyed experiencing steam commuter services in 1979. I then recovered my luggage and took the 7.46am D-Zug to Halle behind 211.031-0.

Arriving at Halle around 8.45am, I proposed to be really masochistic – to travel all the way to Berlin on a *Personenzug*, but getting there in time for a last run north on the 3.14pm Lichtenberg relief train to Stralsund. P3516, 9.10am Halle, left on time with a gleaming red 211.079-9. We weren't very punctual but I caught up with my reading matter, a well-recommended Paul Theroux account of a rail journey across

Asia, returning via the Trans-Siberian. Between Halle and Lutherstadt-Wittenberg I got from Calcutta to Moscow, I think – perhaps I exaggerate, it certainly seemed like it. Anyway, we still had a long time to waste at Wittenberg, where I could see a filthy 03 waiting to back down. At length the engine was identified as 03.2058-0 and I was pleased to find that the crew were Alfons Liehs and Werner Schmager again, and I was able to give them more magazines. We exchanged addresses and further photos. I received an invitation to breakfast from Werner, which was unfortunately not very practicable. Punctually at 11.03am we set off, but got no further than Blockstelle Labetz, before we were stopped with a 120-hauled freight in front. Bülzig was left 5 minutes late and we cut a few seconds from each section allowance to arrive at Jüterbog 3 minutes late with maximum speeds of 78, 80, 72, and 82kph. After a half hour wait where I was introduced to the young girl who was our guard, and had a Bockwurst bought for me, we jogged along to Lückenwalde, without exceeding 72, but arrived a minute early.

Finally we set off on the last lap, touched 100kph before Trebbin and then got caught up in a queue to get onto the Ring. We managed a brief last spurt to 102 past Genshagener Heide, then signal checks all the way to Schöneweide meant that we terminated 12 minutes late. Nearly every other train that could be seen on the Ring was at a stand, so things might have been a lot worse.

Lichtenberg station was heaving with Public Holiday crowds and the subterranean booking hall was jammed solid. The D10514 relief to Stralsund was backing into the station with a mere eight lightweight coaches to hold the awaiting hordes, so I let it go behind 03.0077-2. The crowd waiting for the regular train, D514, was even worse. Just before departure time it drew in behind 03.0058-2, with twelve coaches, 372/430 tonnes gross. All corridors were crammed and I just squeezed into a coach with access to a corridor window about two thirds of the way down the train. Although circumstances were not favourable, we got a very spirited run, with exhaust clearly audible from the seventh coach. Lichtenberg-Bernau took 21min 10sec with 100kph after Springfühl and 104 at Zepernick. At Bernau we stood for 4 minutes while the station staff, Japanese fashion, pushed everyone aboard and then ran the 13.75 miles to Eberswalde in 15min 53sec with a full 120kph at Melchow. We roared out of Eberswalde only to be brought to a dead stand after the first station (Britz) for just over a minute, while a 110 stood in the platform in our way at Chorin being watered by its driver. We continued with enthusiasm undampened taking 22min 41sec, including the stop, for the 16.25 miles to Angermünde where crews were changed and we were passed by 01.0507 on D717. The roars now became even louder, accelerating to 105 at Greiffenberg; 116 at Wilmersdorf; 125 at Warnitz; 122 at Quast; and 120 at Seehausen, stopping at Prenzlau in 24min 11sec (23.1 miles). The last 15 miles to Pasewalk took 19min 3sec including a p-way slack to 40kph at Nechlin and another 120.

I watched 03.0058 bark its staccato way out of Pasewalk after taking water and repaired to the crowded *Mitropa* for a quick meal and then observed D10719 relief arrive behind a 118 diesel instead of the expected Pasewalk 01.5. I therefore caught a 110-hauled local across country to Neubrandenburg and a long wait in the darkness until the arrival, 18 minutes late, of the *Berlinaren*, again with 03.0085-5. No fireworks

Two cylinder coal-burning Pacific, 03.2058-0, which hauled the author's D563 from Berlin to Leipzig on 26 April 1979, here in earlier days at Halle (Saale), circa 1978. (*Colin Boocock*)

this time, however. Competent, but nothing over 116kph and a lot of easy running with its comparatively light load, reaching the Ostbahnhof in 107 minutes 32 seconds, 102 minutes net and still 18 minutes late.

By now the lack of sleep on this holiday was beginning to take its toll, and although I was quite keen to take 01.0507 to Stralsund on the 12.3am from Ostbahnhof, I felt shattered and was almost swooning on the platform. One look at the enormous crowd awaiting D718 decided me and I tumbled into a late night S-bahn back to my home in the Berolina Hotel.

My final day in the GDR arrived. There was a plan. D563, 7.25am Schöneweide-Leipzig, due 9.43am, then *if* we were on time, the 9.45am Leipzig-Cologne as far as Hanover and the *Ost-West Express* to the Hook of Holland. Alternatively, 11.8am Leipzig-Duisburg and a tight connection to the *Rheingold*. Up late – a quarter past six – I even had a sort of breakfast and S-bahned for the last time to Schöneweide. At 7.10am the platform was packed, so I waited hopefully at the front end, craning round the crowds to catch a glimpse of the approaching train (rumour had it that the D563 was often a diesel at weekends rather than the diagrammed 03.2). A comforting billowing of white smoke appeared over the horizon and then a dark haze as the engine shut off steam, so I picked up my luggage and joined the rugby scrum. The familiar shape of 03.2058-0 ran in, its vestiges of former white painted decoration just visible, its front end bearing evidence of an attempted cleaning. I gave up any attempt to get a seat and positioned myself in the vestibule behind the tender where I managed to create and hold a space for myself and defend it against all-comers. The train was evidently long and full – that is all I could establish before departure. Later in the journey I managed to count the coaches (fourteen) and get an estimated weight (452/500 tonnes).

The start was inauspicious as we had a signal check to 15kph at Grunauer Kreuz and a p-way slack to 10kph approaching Schönefeld, converting an on time departure into a minute late start from the latter. We laboured up to 80kph, then had another p-way check to 15kph, before lurching off to the right on a mystery tour

A two cylinder coal burning 03.2 Pacific at speed on D563, Berlin Schöneweide – Leipzig, circa 1978. (*Werner Schmager*)

that I presume was the Genshagener Heide spiral, coming in to land with a thump at Birkengrund Süd at 100kph, 18 minutes 9 seconds from Schönefeld. 03.2058 was chattering very audibly now, with clouds of black smoke wafting over the mound of vibrating coal visible from the vestibule front windows. We gathered speed through Ludwigsfelde, reaching 105kph, just touched 110 at Thyrow and Trebbin before another p-way slack to 30kph at Woltersdorf, and passed Lückenwalde at 100 in 36min 9sec. Another long pre-electrification slack to 35kph at Forst Zinna followed and then a slow acceleration with this load to pass Jüterbog in 47min 51sec (37.5 miles) accelerating to 96 before falling only to 86kph at Blönsdorf summit. Down the other side of the bank we accelerated to 115 before shutting off steam and drifting through Bülzig, still doing 105-110.

We slowed for Lutherstadt-Wittenberg (57.5 miles in 67min 55sec) and then went out over the flooded Elbe quite hard, reaching 100kph at Bergwitz and passing a level crossing with a pleasing queue of cars as far as the eye could see! I admit we must have looked a fine sight from the road – a heavy express pounding through an open landscape, black smoke pouring forth (I think the fireman had a heavy job on this trip), whistle blasting. Up to Radis, speed gradually fell off to a minimum of 83 at the summit, not bad with this load, then we swept majestically downhill at a full 120kph at Muldenstein passing through Bitterfeld, unchecked, at 100kph, in 91 minutes 47 seconds (80.6 miles) 5 minutes early.

This sort of progress couldn't be allowed to continue and we got checked badly at Petersroda before being brought to a dead stand at Delitzsch for a full 6 minutes, teaching us a lesson not to run so early in future. When we got going again, it was hard work to accelerate up to 90kph in the suburbs of Leipzig and we rolled into the Hauptbahnhof 11 minutes late, in 132 minutes, 5 seconds, but only 108 minutes net for the 101.85 miles. I was rather proud of this effort from one of the last working coal-fired 03s, just a month before withdrawal, especially in view of the dire warnings I was given about the usual performance of this train.

After the check at Delitzsch, I had given up any thought of making the 2-minute connection into the Cologne train until I saw it standing in an adjacent platform, double-headed by two 211 electrics. As I was right at the front of D563, I decided to have a go, and as we screeched to a halt, I fell out of the train with my luggage, sprinted past the crowds waiting to join, took a last quick glimpse at 03.2058, and shot round the corner almost scything down an army platoon and grabbed at the last door of the D-Zug as it was being whistled away. Willing hands pulled me and my cases aboard and I collapsed into the corridor knocking one of the DB's metal rubbish bins into the four-foot, much to the merriment of a school party of young boys who were the other occupants of the corridor, just as the train jerked into motion. I managed to scramble up just in time to count D563's coaches, confirming backward glances made en route.

The guard took pity on my breathlessness and put me into a compartment reserved for war wounded, only to discover later that I was an English railwayman with loose DR change to get rid of, whereupon I was installed in an empty first class compartment and provided with a couple of bottles of beer. He then bemoaned the country's youth – Magdeburg football supporters had smashed up two excursion trains the previous evening – and fellow feeling between two railwaymen was complete. The train was routed via Dessau to Magdeburg, where our two electrics (211.095 and 211.096) were replaced by a less symmetrical pair – 132.189-2 and 118.080-1. The reason for all this power was that the load was seventeen heavy DB coaches. From Magdeburg onwards, when the train was forbidden to internal GDR citizens, I became painfully aware that it was full of weeping or moist eyed elderly West Germans who had been visiting their children and other relatives in the East.

The train was now some 40 minutes late, which made me grateful I had caught it at Leipzig as similar lateness on the next connection would have left me stranded on the continent overnight. Brisk border formalities at Oebisfelde consisted of a quick search under the seats by an Alsatian and no scrutiny of me or my luggage. To my surprise a DR girl came round offering to change any East German currency – I thought my remaining Reichsmarks were a loss – but she was helpful, left me a few coins suggesting I might purchase a few snacks from the *Mitropa* on Oebisfelde station (perhaps she was daughter of the licensee!). After that it was plain sailing – one DB diesel, 218.064-0 took over and we trotted through the spruce and scrubbed West German landscape to Wolfsburg and points west. I changed at Hanover into the Bad Harzburg-Hook train, tried to appear German as an unruly and 'hoity-toity' group of English private schoolgirls made loud chauvinistic comments about everything and everyone, and settled down to finish my travel book.

At Löhne, scene of a ghastly night in 1956 – recounted in *A Privileged Journey* – when our solitary coach was shunted every 10 minutes up and down the yard, I was joined by a middle-aged woman with whom I conversed in passable German for an hour or so, until we discovered we both had UK passports and lived within 5 miles of each other in Buckinghamshire.

After that I think I flaked out and slept through Holland, the channel crossing and the Harwich boat train. The end – a journey beyond all my expectations.

Chapter 14

Crewe

Jim O'Brien, London Midland General Manager, sent for me in the summer of 1982 and offered me the post of Chief Operating Manager of his Region. I was astonished, as I think were many others, but he had known me when he was Assistant General Manager of the Western Region and I was the Region's Management Services Manager. We had maintained contact during my higher profile time at the BRB when I led the Board's productivity team during critical negotiations with the top trade union officials. My High Wycombe neighbours were similarly impressed, until they heard that I was to be based at Crewe amid what they imagined were the North's dark satanic mills. I had to point out that outside the immediate confines of the town, there were cows and grass and trees and that generally Cheshire was acceptable as an abode, even for those who had never ventured north of the Watford Gap M1 service station.

My time as Chief Operating Manager, retitled Regional Operations Manager later, extended over the four years from 1982 to 1986, when I was offered a new and unique role at the BR Headquarters once more and began ten years of long-distance commuting from Crewe to Euston on a near daily basis. However, my immediate key responsibilities were to manage the safety, quality and economic operations of all trains over the whole Region which then included the West Coast Main Line to Birmingham, Crewe and North Wales, Liverpool, Manchester and Carlisle, the former Lancashire & Yorkshire lines west of the main Pennines, and the Midland main lines from St Pancras to Derby, Nottingham, Sheffield and Carlisle via Settle. I was assisted in the process by a staff of 25,000 and a budget of £35 million. Many of my roles lay outside the scope of this book, but these are covered in *The Toss of a Coin,* where I explore these issues and my later time in charge of safety policy at the BRB in some depth. However, there are some of my activities in this role that may be of interest to readers, even if my only 'steam' exposure was in the auditing of an occasional steam special on my patch and a couple of forays overseas when I was able to couple conferences or meetings in Europe with a last fling at the dwindling remaining steam there.

The Region's management was dispersed – Operations in Crewe, Mechanical Engineering at Derby and General Management at Euston, so the GM's Monday morning 'Prayers' were essential for all of his team. After my first meeting I returned to Crewe on the 6.05pm Euston-Preston and Blackpool and noted AL6 electric 86.259 *Peter Pan* at the head end. We got only as far as Wembley before we came to a halt and an ominous silence reigned. Eventually, after a delay of 70 minutes, 87.028 *Lord President* appeared from Willesden Depot only a mile away, coupled on ahead of the failed locomotive and we continued north. Leaving Rugby, we suddenly ground to a halt again and it transpired that 87.028 had now expired, and worse, had experienced brake problems that proved impossible to release. Eventually, we were hauled back into Rugby by an 86/3, leaving the two disabled electrics on the Down Main just beyond the Birmingham line flyover and the new loco ran round and got us to Crewe just before midnight. Enthusiastic in my new duties, I offered help to the guard and went through the front half of the train explaining what had happened and offering to take messages – it was before the days of mobile phones. By the time I alighted at Crewe, I had fifty-eight messages to pass on from the Crewe booking office phone – the front coach was full of French children going for exchange visits to families all over Cumbria and two gentlemen implored me to advise their wives of the reason for their delay, as they would not otherwise be believed!

The next Monday evening, I caught the 6.05 again and 86.259 was once more the loco – and it failed en route yet again. Crewe Control realised that this loco was my bête noir and started warning me (and my wife) when that loco was in danger of appearing on a train I was due to take. When, a couple of years later, the GE Section demanded four 86s for crew training to Norwich, Crewe Control, with some irony, selected 86.259 and 86.416 *Wigan Pier* and I gather one of them pulled the wires down in Liverpool Street station the first time the loco set foot in it. I subsequently had a number of perfectly adequate runs behind 86.259, including cab rides as I made it my principle to ride with drivers as much as possible – they used to complain that they only saw management when they were 'on the carpet'. *Peter Pan* has since metamorphosed into *Les Ross* after the Birmingham DJ that now owns it, via some ridiculous interim name, and I had the pleasure recently of supplying Les with the details of its nefarious past. However, as indicated in chapter 17, it performed perfectly on my last excursion with it.

In the early 1980s, we were testing the three Advanced Passenger Train (APT) sets – one based at Crewe for crew training and tests and one at Glasgow, which, with the London set, initiated passenger trials. I travelled in the cab of the Crewe train with members of the ASLEF Trade Union and we had an excellent run – in fact, comfort in the cab seemed superior to that in the train. At least we were not subject there to any of the signs of nausea that some early passengers complained of. Cyril Bleasdale, the Director InterCity, asked us to arrange a non-stop high speed run to Glasgow to demonstrate what the unit could do and I was the Operator in charge of the run, saddled with the responsibility of ensuring no signal delays. All was going well until we approached Stafford, when we came to a halt before a red signal protecting the line from Birmingham. I was about to be subjected to a barrage of banter from the engineers present when Ken Burrage, the Regional Signal Engineer discovered that the stop was caused by a track circuit failure and I was let

Preserved ac Electric 86/2 locomotive, 86 259, formerly *Peter Pan,* now named *Les Ross* after its Birmingham DJ owner, at Preston after hauling an enthusiasts' special from Birmingham New Street, April 2010. (*Author*)

off the hook. Despite this, we raced north in a record time of 3 hours 52 minutes from London to Glasgow, a time still to be beaten by a Pendolino unit (for log, see Appendix 1, Table 13). Unfortunately the Glasgow unit, which seemed more prone to failure than the others, broke an axle at high speed during a Board high profile test run and shortly afterwards the tilt train system was abandoned in the UK until the Italians picked up where we had stopped.

I was in charge of operations over the Settle & Carlisle and in March 1983 I was invited by York Museum's Engineer, John Peck, to join his party at Leeds in the saloon behind 46229 *Duchess of Hamilton*, and ride the footplate from Hellifield to Garsdale. We had a heavy fourteen-coach load of 565 tons gross and, with Driver Ken Iveson and Fireman John Brown of Skipton and Inspector Arthur Morris of Preston, we left Hellifield 14 minutes late. The train had arrived at Leeds behind 45407 from Carnforth 8 minutes late. We accelerated to exactly 60mph at Settle Junction and held a steady 38mph through Stainforth and Horton-in-Ribblesdale with full regulator and 30 per cent cut off. Steam pressure

From the footplate of 46229 *Duchess of Hamilton* as an enthusiasts' special leaves Hellifield, March 1983. (*Author*)

Advanced Passenger Train 370 006 at Crewe, 1983, during a test run – this train is now exhibited at Crewe Heritage Centre. (*Author*)

was spot on 250psi and we began to blow off, so the driver dropped the lever to 35 per cent and we accelerated to 45mph and held that on the long 1 in 100, easing to 30mph over Ribblehead viaduct. Driver Iveson increased the cut off to 40 per cent as he opened up after the viaduct slack and we accelerated slightly to 34mph on the final 1 in 100 to Blea Moor Tunnel and drifted down to Dent just 2 minutes late. We crawled into Garsdale station searching for the location of the water hose and stopped just one minute late. The full log and working is shown in the Appendix 1, Table 12.

I had an enthusiastic Loco Inspector, Phil Bassett, based in Birmingham who persuaded me – with not a lot of difficulty – to check the safety of these trains by riding on the footplate from Banbury to Marylebone. In March 1985, the motive power was 35028 *Clan Line* with eleven coaches, 360 tons gross. We had Driver Brian Axtell and Fireman Brian Tagg of Marylebone and Inspector Peter Crawley of Euston. We took on 5,000 gallons of water at Banbury and set off 10 minutes late with steam pressure fluctuating between 220 and 245 psi. A slight signal check to 36mph slowed us at Aynho Junction and we climbed the 1 in 200 to Ardley fairly easily with 25 per cent cut off and 220 psi, only achieving 44mph. We took the downhill stretch with liberal interpretation of the speed limit despite my presence – I think they wanted to demonstrate to me the ridiculousness of the 60 limit – touching 75 after Bicester, when I was handed the shovel. I fired from Bicester to Ashendon Junction, and maintained pressure at 220 psi, during which time we'd observed a 20mph p-way slack, then opened up with 35 per cent cut off and half regulator achieving 42 at Brill Tunnel at the summit of the 1 in 200 gradient. After Ashendon Junction, the steam pressure took a nosedive to 170 psi – was it belatedly my fault? Possibly it was the result of the first real pressure put on the locomotive as full regulator and 25 per cent cut off was used on the rising gradient to Princes Risborough, increased to 27 per cent on the final stretch of 1 in 88/100 to Saunderton, where speed had dropped from 60 at Ashendon to 41 at the summit. It was easy after that, however, as we drifted downhill through West Wycombe, steam pressure recovering to 200

35028 *Clan Line* at Marylebone with the enthusiasts' special that the author rode from Banbury, March 1985. (*Author*)

The author at the controls of 35028 *Clan Line* on arrival at Marylebone, March 1985. (*Author*)

psi. We were on time at High Wycombe where we stopped to take on a further 1,600 gallons of water. The fireman, after discussions with the Inspector, altered the damper setting and we had no trouble with steaming for the rest of the journey, arriving at Marylebone 4 minutes early.

Later that year, in November, Phil Bassett took me himself on 4498 *Sir Nigel Gresley* with a heavy twelve-coach, 460 ton load. We had Driver Trevor Barrett, and Fireman Brian Tagg once more. The train arrived very late from the Eastern Region at Banbury (it had started from York) and we left 69 minutes late after filling the tender with 4,250 gallons. We were again checked at Aynho Junction and recovered to 48mph at Ardley summit with three quarters regulator and 30 per cent cut off. We then crawled to a stand at Bicester waiting for the 5.40pm Paddington DMU to come off the single line. Departing 91 minutes late, I was offered the driver's seat and regulator and to this day I'm convinced Phil was anticipating that I'd exceed the '60 limit' and strengthen his case for that limit's abolition. I had my friend, train timer Alistair Wood, in the train behind, so I knew every speed would be meticulously recorded. I quickly adjusted the cut off to 15 per cent with full regulator as we accelerated to exactly 60mph at Ashendon Junction, brought the regulator back to half to maintain this speed, to Phil's obvious chagrin, and then opened up to full regulator again as we hit the rise after Haddenham. I must admit we slightly exceeded the limit just reaching 64 at that point but I increased the cut off to 25 per cent as we approached Princes Risborough at 58mph and I enjoyed myself in the darkness pulling the cord for a long blast on the chime whistle as we hurled ourselves through the waiting crowds on the platform. The steam pressure was rock solid at 225 psi and we maintained 54mph on the final part of the climb to Saunderton. I had gained 15 minutes on schedule from Bicester to High Wycombe without excessive speed and I was very proud of myself! I handed the driver's seat back to Trevor Barrett after Wycombe and just enjoyed the pleasure of the effortless run into London. 4498 was in excellent mechanical condition, was economical and rode well, although the safety valves lifted at around 230 psi instead of the designed 250. The full logs of 35028 and 4498 are also in Appendix 1, Table 12.

There were other enjoyable occasions to which I was invited as the LM's senior Operations representative. My family were guests at the Crewe Works Open Days, when my children particularly enjoyed climbing aboard the various locomotives displayed. I was also introduced to Ian Allan's Great Cockrow 7¼inch gauge railway at Chertsey – over 4 miles of track fully signalled to BR standards. I'm told that new signalling innovations, including the 'flashing yellow' indication were first tried out here. I was given charge of Richard Stokes' GW *Mere Hall*, Mike Johns' K3 and John Butt's un-rebuilt *Royal Scot* on various visits – all by courtesy of colleagues alongside whom I'd worked. This could be quite a test of enginemanship when it was possible to really mess up the busy schedule by running short of steam. I'm pleased to say I did not disgrace myself, apart from giving John Butt a scare when, on the first trip with 6100, I discovered rather late that the brake valve operated in the opposite direction to the other locomotives and we sailed round the first curve rather too near the safety margin for comfort. I also have a shot of my 12-year-old daughter,

John Butt with his 7¼in gauge model of 6100 *Royal Scot*, on the Great Cockrow Railway at Chertsey, 1984. (*Author*)

The author receiving instruction from Mike Johns on Richard Stokes' 7¼in gauge model of GW Modified Hall in BR mixed traffic livery, 7915 *Mere Hall*, 1984. (*Author*)

Helen, driving a Black 5 with Malcolm Southgate, the LM General Manager, and Cyril Bleasdale, then InterCity Director, as passengers – unfortunately too blurred for publication!

Throughout my time at Crewe, I was the officer in charge of the Royal Train when it started on the LMR and when the queen herself was on board. The arrangement between regional managers was that the officer from the originating region would see the train through to destination, so most fell to me (London/Euston departures) and the Western Region man (for Windsor starters). I could and did delegate the 'mini-royals' as specials for other members of the Royal Family were known, to one of my other officers. I would average five to ten trains a year, usually starting from Euston in the late evening, stabling overnight at some remote and secret siding location and proceeding unhurriedly in the morning to the nearest station to the queen's first engagement. Timekeeping on this last leg was absolutely essential and I took pride in the train drawing to a stand as the second hand crept towards the twelve of the appointed minute. I only failed once – I'd gone north to Glasgow with 87.023 *Highland Chieftain* as our engine (that and 87.024 *Lord of the Isles* were my regulars – 87.002 and 87.005 were also used from time to time). We were timed via Birmingham New Street to spend some pathing time and avoid the rush of West Coast night mail and newspaper trains, and when we drew punctually to a stand, I was informed that 87.035 *Robert Burns*, waiting to drop on our rear, had just failed. 87.023 therefore ran round and we departed 6 minutes late, which we soon made up and arrived punctually at our stabling point, some half hour from Glasgow Central.

External view of officer's saloon 2911 on the royal train at Crewe, 1984. (*Author*)

Inside the Royal Train Officer's Saloon, [office area used by Winston Churchill as mobile office during the Second World War] 2911, 1984. (*Author*)

Inside the Royal Train Officer's Saloon [Officer's day accommodation], 2911, 1984. (*Author*)

87 024 *Lord of the Isles* on the Royal Train at Crewe, 1984. (*Author*)

It was in January and there was an extremely heavy frost overnight and I was alarmed to see that our relief train crew had not arrived at their rostered time. When they did arrive they found they were unable to raise the pantograph of the electric loco and soon there were men in orange jackets swarming all over it. Then we found the semaphore signal controlling the exit from the siding was frozen in the 'on' position and no-one could free it. I lost patience with the efforts to release 87.023's pantograph and decided with the Scottish Inspector that we'd recouple the Class 47 that had drawn us into the siding and propel us to Central station, with the main crew in the front loco to control the brakes. We eventually set off and I calculated that we'd be at least 20 minutes late at our destination. This was relayed to the Queen's secretary and I awaited events, my heart in my mouth. I suddenly noticed that we were being propelled at a fair pace – the speedometer in my saloon indicated 75mph, whereas I had thought we were restricted to 40mph in propelling mode. Before I could take breath, I realised we were crossing the Clyde and just managed to get a message to the queen that we were now arriving less than 10 minutes late. I was told subsequently that Prince Philip was totally unready, still in his shirt-sleeves at a computer, although apparently the queen riposted that she was ready as she had her hat on!

On another occasion we'd left our stabling point in north Cheshire on time, but had to run the gauntlet of the West Coast main line at line speed between Warrington and Wigan before bearing off to Southport, our destination. This meant our 47 had to sustain 80-90mph on this stretch and I had not realised that the queen was taking breakfast during this period. We hit the 70mph curve after Warrington at Winwick Junction at just over 60 and got an immediate frantic phone call from the royal dining saloon imploring me to slow the train as the queen thought we had been derailed.

A few minutes later we hit Golborne Junction at 84mph against the permitted 90 and I got a further irate call to say that the queen had spilt coffee down her dress and was having to change to a new outfit. The dining table in the royal saloon ran lengthways down the centre of the coach and so she rolled with the curve. The expected visit to the Tower did not materialise, but I soon got an understanding with the queen's officials that they would advise the railway when the queen would be having a meal so that the train schedule took this into account and did not require the train to exceed 50mph. In this case, it would have been difficult as the Sovereign does not like delaying ordinary passengers and we couldn't have occupied the main line at the lower speed between Warrington and Wigan in the morning peak without substantially affecting other trains.

I have to say that the duties of the officer in charge of the royal train usually were an easy task, as certainly everything on the LMR was planned down to the last detail. However, I was never relaxed until we had deposited the royal party at their destination, in case anything went wrong and urgent high profile decisions had to be made. On one occasion, I had to get Jim Summers, my Scottish Region counterpart, up at two o'clock in the night to check our route availability from Carlisle to Aberdour via Perth instead of via Edinburgh as the police had had a phone call advising that there was a bomb on the Forth Bridge. Having got the all clear from Jim and told that the engine would run round outside Perth station, a footman rang to ask when the Corgis would be able to uncross their legs as the stabling time had disappeared with the diversion. We therefore rerouted the train into a Perth platform at five o'clock to allow the footman to walk the dogs. When we stopped the still air was rent with howling dogs for the police had turned up with Alsatians who were having Corgis for breakfast!

It was pleasant on the home run. After the royal party had alighted I would travel back with the empty stock as far as Crewe – the train went on to Wolverton where it was stabled. On one occasion, returning from Glasgow in mid-morning, we ran into Carlisle station middle road just as I was being served lunch on a silver platter by the royal restaurant crew. The platform at Carlisle was full of passengers awaiting the London service that was due to overtake us, and seeing me in state everyone began to wave to me. I practised my royal hand wave – I've no idea who they thought I was, but I'm sure most told their children that they'd seen royalty.

In 1985 and the first six months of 1986 I was much occupied by safety and train punctuality issues and a major reorganisation which eliminated the Divisional level structure and developed the Business Sectors – I was very busy developing and bedding in the major changes in my department. I also undertook some radical analyses of safety and punctuality, which led to quite significant changes in the way we managed both, adopting a much more proactive and analytical approach and methodology. I guess as a result of these studies, I was sent for by David Kirby, Board Member for Operations and Engineering, and asked to accept the position of the Board's first Quality & Reliability Manager. 'Why me?' I asked in some innocence, to receive the riposte, 'Well, as Operating Manager of the West Coast Main Line, you know more about failure than anyone else.' I hope he was joking.

Chapter 15

Quality & safety management, British Railways Board and more opportunities to visit Europe

Four-phase electric locomotive 40110 *Nice* on which the author rode on a *rapide* from the Belgian border to Paris Gare du Nord, July 1986. (*Author*)

So I knew more about failure than anyone else, did I? I discovered that my appointment owed much to pressure from non-executive Board Members who came from industries where reliability and quality management was accepted as routine and a basic management concern. Apart from the application of reliability management techniques in some technical design departments, most BR management was not conversant with the latest thinking on these issues and it became apparent very quickly that I was being left to discover for myself what might be relevant and of value to the industry. Go to France and Germany, I was urged. Find out what they do!

It was strange to move from the responsibility for an annual budget of £35 million and a constant series of events and pressures to which I had to respond, to a situation where, initially, I had a part time secretary only, an empty office with no files and the ball in my court to determine how to fill my days. So I acted on the suggestion given to me by David Kirby and organised meetings with operations and engineering managers in the SNCF and DB. Arrangements were made for me to ride in the cab of an electric locomotive from the Belgian border to Paris and then to travel in the cab of a DB locomotive on the left bank of the Rhine to observe the impact of cab radio. The SNCF loco was one of the ten quadruple system Co-Co electrics, 40110, described by the inspector as *très fragile*, but we performed perfectly, with the strict adherence to absolute punctuality that SNCF was known for at that time. I tried in vain to establish the techniques SNCF management used to ensure their punctuality performance, but my question did not seem to be understood. It was apparently self-evident that trains had to run to time, but SNCF managers could point to no analyses or justification of reliability investment. It was just taken as a 'given' without question.

As I stepped from the cab of 40110 at the Gare du Nord, the inspector asked if I was free the following day. As I was not returning to the UK until the *Flèche d'Or* the following afternoon, he suggested I showed up at the Gare de Lyon at 7am and he accompanied me in the cab of a TGV to Lyons and back with a 1 hour coffee break in a city café there. I was back in Paris by midday! The precision was exemplified by his statement that there were 6 seconds recovery time between each signalling section, which allowed the TGV to run on less than full power for over 50 per cent of the journey if there were no delays.

TGV units at Paris Gare de Lyon including unit 14 in whose cab the author returned to Paris on the 10am from Lyons, July 1986. (*Author*)

184

View from the cab of TGV 14 on the approach to Paris Gare de Lyon on the 10am from Lyons, July 1986. (*Author*)

The author in the cab of TGV unit 27 working 7am Paris-Lyons-Marseilles, July 1986. (*Author*)

I had an enjoyable trip in the cab of Co-Co electric 103.128-5 from Mainz to Cologne and the value of the radio system was shown when we received a message about the failure of level crossing gates approaching Bonn. As a result, we were not stopped to be warned, but acknowledged the message and proceeded over the crossing at 5mph losing only a couple of minutes in consequence.

I found little supporting evidence in the DB either for their quality policy, which seemed to be based on building in substantial spare capacity regardless of cost. As well as the provision of spare stock and locomotives to cover unforeseen incidents, equipment was utilised way below its capacity or over-engineered. As an example, I was told that the V200 diesel hydraulics built in 1953 were normally only run by drivers in notch 4 (of a 7 notch controller) except on an InterCity or EuroCity train running late. As a comparison with the British culture, the WR 'Warships' based on the DB design, spent most of their journeys from Paddington to the West of England being worked to their limit in notch 7. Although there are no V200s still in service on the DB, examples can still be found – sold to the Swiss, Greek and Saudi Arabian railways. In contrast, the British examples were all withdrawn from service by the early 1970s, even though they were built four years later than their German predecessors. The British were famed at getting a quart out of a pint pot and this was exemplified in the lesser subsidy that BR received from the taxpayer compared with its continental neighbours, and the passenger business wanted to extort the maximum advantage from its new resources to boost revenue, but BR paid the price in significantly reduced reliability and lack of standby cover.

I guessed that there was a balance between the continental obsession with quality at any cost – or the cost of this not even quantified – and the British culture of paring everything to the bone under the pressure of successive governments. I decided that I'd have to look at other industries for guidance and spent a more useful time exchanging ideas with British Airways and the oil industry and being introduced to the concept of TQM (Total Quality Management), the philosophy of which was the value of spending more time in planning to get it right first time, to avoid the greater cost of correcting error. The priority is to collect information in detail about performance, analyse the data thoroughly and look to see where corrective action will produce the greatest impact for the least expenditure of resources.

A railway quality conference in Malmö, Sweden, for two days in September 1986 gave me the opportunity to revisit East Germany en route home – to have a last glimpse of DR steam and visit Werner Schmager, the ex-steam pacific fireman I met in 1979 and more recently a steam 52.80 (austerity 2-10-0) driver as well as a driver of class 120 Russian built diesels. I had been invited to his home near Lutherstadt-Wittenberg. The conference with European railway colleagues, studying SJ staff motivation and quality, ended mid-afternoon on Wednesday 24 September, leaving me a few hours to explore Malmö in dazzling sunshine, buy the cheapest camera I could find (not easy in Sweden) to replace my Canon which had lost a vital reflector – a disaster I still cannot explain – and enjoy a spectacular sunset on Malmö beach, looking at the Copenhagen skyline 50km away.

At 8pm I repaired to Malmö Central station, stocked up with food for the night, watched the overnight *Lapland Express* depart behind two Rc4 electrics and joined the six motley coaches waiting in platform eight to form the D319 *Sassnitz Express* – a DR Malmö-Berlin day coach; two *Mitropa* sleepers for Berlin; a Czech couchette for Prague and Budapest and two SJ vehicles for the local run to Trelleborg, one a very ancient baggage van. After a short argument with the DR attendant over the fact that London had managed to reserve me a sleeper, and provide a railway ticket, but had omitted to give me a sleeper ticket, I managed to negotiate a lower price (£20 instead of £50) for a second-class sleeper instead of first. Therefore a second berth was made up in my compartment, but as no-one occupied it, honour was satisfied all round!

For the half-hour jogtrot to Trelleborg, SJ provided their very latest aluminium liveried Rc5 1377, in contrast to D316 seen later at Trelleborg about to set off to Malmö behind two ancient 'connecting-rod' electrics. The first remarkable performance of the trip then took place, following a delay whilst hordes of wagons of timber were shunted onto the ferry 'Trelleborg' as follows:

Loco:	SJ shunting electric 498	
Load:	4 DR/CSK vehicles + 8 wagons of timber	
Location:	Trelleborg Yard	
Loco att'd to train:		22.21
Train drawn back off 1377:		22.22
2 SJ coaches detached:		22.22 ½
1377 exit from head of train & reverse to siding:		22.24
Begin propelling movement to ferry:		22.24 ½
To dead stand in berth on ferry:		22.28
Departure of ferry (7min late):		22.32

May I just add that the propelling movement to the ferry was made with four passenger vehicles leading, followed by eight wagons loaded with timber – I don't remember a performance to rank with this, but I have my suspicions about how many rules we broke in the process!

After a very smooth crossing on SJ's flagship, we arrived in Sassnitz on time at 2.20am and we had been drawn off by DR 0-6-0 diesel shunter 106.947 and were at a stand on dry land at 2.30, less than 10 minutes after the ferry's engines were switched off. Clearly the port arrangements on both sides of the crossing were slick from much practice. Customs were friendly in the extreme and raised no objection to the cassette I had recorded for Werner of various DR, DB and BR steam locomotive noises. I had been told by the consulate in London that video cameras and privately made cassettes were the only taboo items for import. The only comment made re the DR recordings was 'Wasn't that a bit difficult to make?' I assumed at the time he was referring to the problem of isolating locomotive noises from all the other railway sounds, but subsequently I wonder if he was not indicating tactfully that making tape recordings in East Germany was illegal for foreigners.

Our 106 now began a series of reversing moves that totally confused my sense of direction, then set off towards the town of Sassnitz round a curve that went on and on, so that I had no idea whether we'd done 180 or 360 degrees or started on a second circuit! Arrival in Sassnitz station facing the opposite direction to DR mainline diesel 132.436 and a few mainline coaches did not make the right connection in my brain, until we began to reverse to the rear of the 132. Seven years previously it would have been oil-burning Pacific 03.0010-3! Sigh!

We joined the electrified railway at Neustrelitz and duly arrived at Berlin Lichtenberg (nearly) on time behind electric 211.045. Upstairs, Lichtenberg looked no different to my 1979 trip, except for the 'knitting' overhead. Downstairs, there was a vast new booking hall, but that was no help as I joined the queue awaiting the moneychangers – unfortunately I managed to get behind a whole coachload of Russians, all with especially complex group warrants etc., that took 45 minutes to sort out. My first queue! Moral: learn patience or suffer high blood pressure.

I had intended to S-Bahn to the Alexanderplatz to complete formalities there, but one experience of queues was enough, and I wanted the maximum time with Werner, so I stayed put and caught D713, thirteen coaches and electric loco 211.041. We picked up the 5-minute late arrival of the train at Lichtenberg, and began to run out of the morning mist into glorious September sunshine on the Ringbahn, when a series of 'popping' noises from the loco and a juddering halt nowhere near any signal alongside the Wühlheide freight humpyard indicated the worst. Twenty minutes of total silence and lack of movement had me calculating the effects of a much shorter stay at Wittenberg, when suddenly another couple of 'pops' and 211.041 sprang back to life. We ran into Schönefeld 19 minutes late, got stopped for a track machine to cross in front of us at Glasower Damm, 20 minutes late at Luckenwalde, dead stand for signals again amidst the Russian army at Forst Zinna and got into Wittenberg 25 minutes late.

To my pleasure and relief, I was met at the station by Werner who had commandeered the only taxi for miles around, whisked off past a chalk storage silo which had managed to explode the previous weekend covering half the city in chalk dust (comical as no-one was hurt), and reached Griebo, Werner's home village miles out in the country. A pleasant day was spent eating and drinking, exchanging reminiscences, eating and drinking, looking at railway memorabilia, eating and drinking, meeting the family and pets, eating (and drinking), and, to cap it all, enjoying his summerhouse – a whole *Baureihe* (class) 52 cab, curtained and upholstered, purchased with winnings from the state lottery! Despite the numberplate visible (52.5765-2), the cab actually comes from 52.7323. Does sitting in it all afternoon, drinking schnapps, eating apples, listening to 03.2155 on the tape recorder, and talking to Roselinde, Werner's wife (DR equivalent to a TOPS clerk) constitute a run behind 52.7323?

I had calculated times to reach Jena in time for a hopeful Class 41 2-8-2 run to the Goldener Anker at Saalfeld, but hospitality was so lavish, and time ran on so fast that I was persuaded to leave departure to the last moment – walking with Werner to the local station 10 minutes away on the Dessau-Wittenberg line. A P-Zug would give a 20 minute connection into a Berlin-Halle-Leipzig train which in turn would give a 25 minute connection at Halle to D507 Berlin-Saalfeld and a 10 minute connection at Jena with P5039. Werner had staked his reputation on the punctuality of the P-Zug, only to have it rudely shattered, when the girl on duty informed us that it was over 30 minutes late and hadn't left Dessau yet. Werner shouted 'Stay there!' and fled, reappearing 5 minutes later on his motor scooter, together with his future son-in-law similarly equipped. My cases were strapped on, pannier style, to one scooter, while I was balanced on Werner's pillion for a hair-raising 15km run at top speed (for this mode of transport), mainly over cobblestones! We made it with 3 minutes to spare, for D1715 and 211.060 was about the only train I saw on time that day.

I was now introduced to a new, and as I discovered, totally typical phenomenon in the form of a coach that was disgustingly filthy inside and out, and whose windows were jammed open. We all heaved and shoved to no avail, except for making ourselves filthy too. Luckily the sun still shone, but it was breezy as we bowled, or rather lurched, along at 120kph. The general camaraderie that had developed as we all strove together was enhanced as a 2 year old made eyes at a packet of wine gums I was devouring, so he was – with his mother's grudging consent – fired in the best tradition of 'little and often' all the way to Halle!

The connection was comfortably made at Halle to D507, which ran in on time behind brand new electric 243.091. At Camburg, the train went downmarket to 119.180, which burbled to Jena where, in the gloom, sat four ancient DR coaches and a very subdued 41.1180-3. You can have details of the run if you want - suffice to say, we left

Werner Schmager, a Deutsche Reichsbahn fireman, with the cab of DR 'austerity' 52.7323 [masquerading as 52.5765-2], which he bought with money he won in the State lottery, acting as his summerhouse in Griebo near Lutherstadt-Wittenberg, which the author visited in September 1986. (*Author*)

on time, got stopped for 2 minutes at signals before Göschwitz and then just held time (picking up the odd half minute in running and losing it again at stations), so we arrived at Rüdolstadt Schwarza 5 minutes late, there to await a local off the single line from Saalfeld for 14 minutes (booked). We got a little running at just under 100kph between Kahla and Orlamünde, but most maxima were in the 80-90kph range. 41.1180 was nice and steamtight, and showed no stress over its lightweight load (156 tonnes).

Relieved that I had at least got to Saalfeld and that the Göschwitz 41s hadn't all expired before the end of the Summer service, I enjoyed the oily scent and warm glow from the cylinders on arrival at a deserted Saalfeld station, before it made off for the shed, and I made my way over the Saale, under the arch and into the square – to be allocated the same familiar bedroom I'd had in 1979.

Up on Friday, 26 September at 6.30am, I had the luxury of a breakfast, before arriving at the station at the unusually civilised hour of 7 o'clock – my dawn chorus of 01.5s long since migrated – and looked in vain for any engine for the 7.20 P5014 to Jena. There was a thick mist, and at about 7.15 hopeful steam noises were heard, followed a few seconds later by the dull glow of the lights on the tender of 41.1225-6 as it backed onto the train. Rows of BR 119s continued their slumber whilst our 41 commandeered the only train going anywhere (the rush hour was long since over). Our load was four double-deck coaches, which 41.1225 whisked up the valley crisply enough, time slightly in hand throughout – maxima 92kph before Orlamünde; 90 before Kahla; 90 again after Kahla; 90 again before Göschwitz and Jena Paradies. Eventually we were held for a minute on the mainline, waiting to cross into the 'slow' platform at the Saalebahnhof, and stopped 1 minute late.

I had now constructed a programme that required me to return to Saalfeld to announce my presence to the state authorities – a bureaucratic obligation required within 24 hours of setting foot in the GDR and the Saalfeld office was only open on Fridays from 9am to midday – before retracing my steps to Göschwitz on P3004 (11.28 Saalfeld) to pick up 41.1225's next leg of the diagram to Gera and back. A cup of coffee from a cracked cup in the Jena *Mitropa* – transport caff would be more appropriate – and I went back upstairs to join the throng awaiting D501 – 09.24 Jena (ex-Berlin Schöneweide). However, I was no sooner on the platform when the PA burst into life and gave an estimated arrival of 30 minutes late – groans reverberated round the platform. I then decided the P-Zug booked to follow D501 would just give me time for the formalities at Saalfeld, when *that* was reported 40 minutes late. I now had to decide between obeying police regulations for foreigners and continuing behind the BR41.

Having decided, with little inner struggle, to do the latter, I spent a pleasant couple of hours 'doing' Jena, the sun bursting through the mist to cheer everyone up. Back in good time for P6017 (12.23 Jena-Gera) I found 41.1225 had beaten me to it and I selected the only bay in the first coach where the window winder actually worked, so I could enjoy '*41-gesang*'. This meant the window that appeared to have a bullet hole in it, with ominous cracks spreading to all corners. It didn't really matter though, because the other coach windows were almost too filthy to see out of, and with luck I could spot kilometre posts through the bullet hole!

DR 2-8-2 41.1225-6 at Jena with a P-Zug for Gera, one of the last DR passenger trains scheduled for steam haulage, September 1986. (*Author*)

Promptly at 12.23, without waiting for the booked Berlin connection – D503 was also running 30 minutes late – off we went. We waited at Göschwitz for 14 minutes (7 minutes overtime) waiting for the 132 hauled local from Weimar, but not for P 3004 from Saalfeld, so even if D501 had been on time, I could well have lost out by returning to Saalfeld to register with the police. The next half-hour was pure delight – 41.1225 was driven hard uphill through tree-covered hills, gloriously arrayed in their autumnal splendour, all glowing in the sun. The climb starts immediately from Göschwitz, and we chattered along steadily, accelerating to 71kph before the Neue Schenke stop. Then it was 77 before Stadtroda, then a temporary speed restriction (TSR) to 40kph, followed by the curving climb through the trees, eventually reaching a rousing 75kph before stopping at Papiermuhle.

Restarting on the gradient, we worked very hard to achieve 65kph at the summit, before a crawl at 15kph over dodgy earthworks into Hermsdorf-Klosterlausnitz. Most of the population was waiting for us there, and so we left with our four coaches packed to the gunnels. Our last bit of uphill work was achieved at 56kph, then we flowed downhill at 97, before grinding to a halt – we were too fast for a Jena-bound BR 120 diesel on a heavy freight banked by a 110 which was occupying the single line ahead. Because of this and the overtime at Göschwitz, we were 11 minutes late into Gera, but I calculate our loco and crew had saved at least another eight minutes delay by their hard work. Gera had made a poor impression on me before, with its weed

191

infested station (still true) and industrial approach from the north, but I had an hour to wander round the city and found it much better than my expectations. A lot of hard work in restoring buildings had taken place in the GDR over the previous seven years, although as *Bezirkstadt*, Gera was obviously an administrative show place. The town centre, and odd nooks and crannies, were lavishly endowed with fountains and flowerbeds all resplendent in the sun.

Back at Gera Hauptbahnhof, 41.1225, having turned, was standing with the same four coaches, which were rapidly filling up with the other half of Hermsdorf-K's population. Climbing out of Toppeln on the steepest stretch (where all freights were banked) we sustained 58kph until abruptly brought to a stand by signals. And there we stuck for 32 minutes – looking out at a beautiful pastoral scene – whilst I assumed a previous train had passed out. When we eventually moved, it became clear that long stretches of single line just can't cope with the traffic now moving – H.K was saturated with heavy freights all waiting impatiently for something to move.

Thirty-five minutes late from Kraftdorf, we made mincemeat of the rest of the schedule on the climb, with 60kph exactly at the summit and 90 as we rolled into Hermsdorf-Klosterlausnitz, now only 25 minutes late. We cut station time and left 21 minutes late, now with room to breathe, and after a careful negotiation of the 15kph TSR, allowed speed to rise to an exhilarating 101kph round the wooded curves, having the privilege of not having to stop at Papiermühle in this direction. This got our lateness down to 17 minutes at Stadtroda, where we stood for a minute after right away whilst the driver had a literal physical needs break against the tender bogie, hidden from the platform but not from peering eyes in the train. The train terminated at Göschwitz alongside a platform of Russian soldiers standing in formation, so I tried hard to ensure my photography of 41.1225 could not be misinterpreted. Two stored 41s (41.1055/1125) stood derelict as a backdrop.

A BR114 took me to Jena Paradies where I alighted and sat down with a good book in the sunshine on the banks of the Saale. A wander round revealed a bossy lady directing over a tannoy a group of kids only a few feet away in a gymnastics routine ready for display at the city 750th anniversary celebrations, and a tramway being double-tracked and extended down a chestnut tree-lined avenue. I wore out a lot of shoe-leather looking for somewhere to eat and eventually flaked out in a deserted churchyard alongside the grave of Karl Zeiss, founder of the German camera/optics firm that 'is' Jena. Suddenly from within the depths of the adjacent *Friedenskirche* (Church of Peace) – the old university church – music burst forth and I sat for half an hour or more in the dusk, as the sole audience of an organ recital. When it was time to go, I walked past the old houses that formed part of the university buildings, past ghosts of Goethe, Schiller, not to mention my old UCL German Department.

I was not very confident of a 41 on P5039 this evening, as the previous day's leg of the diagram had been a 119. I was therefore pleased to see 41.1150-6 waiting for me, although the station staff discovered a defect in the third coach – it must have been bad – and the rear two coaches were detached, leaving a featherweight train only. Two Russian soldiers waiting for the D-Zug, intrigued by the steam locomotive, came across and asked me if it was going to Saalfeld, and much to my surprise and gratification, chose to travel to Saalfeld behind steam. We'll convert the world yet! One can't really say much about loco performance on such a train – 78 tonnes – except that the driver took it almost too easily, with exhaust beats being almost inaudible after the first hundred yards. We were 2 minutes late into Rüdolstadt Schwarza to await the 110 off the single line, and got into Saalfeld on time. As the 10.09pm Saalfeld (a 41 diagram) was in fact a 119 diesel, I decided to catch up on sleep.

Saturday morning was misty and with the outstanding visit to the *Anmeldungsamt* still weighing heavily on my conscience, I repaired to the station to see P5014. However, a BR 119 diesel stood at its head (the rest of its diagram is SX), so I made a rare pedestrian excursion round Saalfeld itself, via the banks of the river, finishing up at the *Gertrudiskirche*. After my morning constitutional, I checked the 8.34SO from Saalfeld, in case the Göschwitz 41 had slipped a turn, watched 41.1225 being coaled and watered for something, but another 119 backed onto the train, so I decided I had to face the music with the local bureaucratic authorities. Even at 9am prompt a small queue had formed, but I duly faced up to the German maiden wielding absolute power, and for the first time on this holiday tried to look more ignorant of affairs than I was. Having pleaded that the office was closed (which it was at a suitable '41-free' time) I was admonished that I could be fined for not reporting within 24 hours, but shoulders were shrugged and I received my visa back duly cleared, not only for Saalfeld, but for Halle also, a useful bonus.

Back to the station, where 41.1225 had attached itself to a freight in the yard, so it was D504 and the quickest way of getting to Halle. 119.104-8, the Bw Probstzella *Jugendlok* (what do the young people of Probstzella do with 'their' loco - clean it? - maintain it? - hold jumble sales to pay for it?) had the somewhat dubious challenge of achieving this, and with a moderate load of ten coaches and a van, produced a long plod up the Saale valley at a steady 96kph. Once again, the coaches on this important express were absolutely filthy with all the windows jammed – the frames of mine were warped. Passing Göschwitz I noticed 41.1273 standing dead outside the depot, and another inside, as well as a party of twenty German photographers, cameras at the ready, looking decidedly glum as the succession of 119 hauled trains passed them. They'd have to settle for 41.1225 and its freight and the dead 2-8-2s on shed.

Despite our ineffective burbling, the schedule clearly anticipated this, and we were in Camburg only 1 minute late. The engine change was efficiently executed, and a brand new and gleaming electric 243.160-9 hooked on. Tempo now changed and we swept up to the permitted 120kph very rapidly, stopping at Naumburg and Weissenfels. We suffered a TSR to 15kph through Grosskorbetha, and looking out of the window I became aware of a desolate landscape, deteriorating by the second. The misty sunshine of Saalfeld was now pure mist, dank and cold; we seemed to be in the middle of a weed infested marshalling yard with nothing but rows of wagons with tanks and army vehicles – like being in the middle of an army building site. Everything in sight was smothered in a dirty grey chalky dust, and a foul stench pervaded even through the jammed windows heralding a chemical works sprawling across the landscape, spewing its pollution in all directions.

The train rushed by a hideous, derelict, vandalised works station (Leuna Werke Nord) trying to get the hell out of this hole as fast as possible, but signals brought us to a grinding halt in the middle of another marshalling yard, before allowing us to creep into Merseburg station at exactly midday. Midnight would have been more appropriate – oh, Merseburg of *Zauberspruche* fame, look what dabbling in magic has done to you! (The Merseburger 'spells' were a set of mediaeval German incantations and proverbs.) Permitted by the chief witch to extricate ourselves from this hell-on-earth, we swept past coal trains stranded in all directions, waiting entrance to Halle (Süd) yard and got into the Hauptbahnhof just over a minute late.

I dumped my luggage with the very obliging staff of the Hotel Stadt Halle, got an (unfortunately erroneous) message that a lady from the German Philharmonic Orchestra was waiting to meet me at the bar, and took lunch, not in the sumptuous hotel restaurant, but at the decidedly downmarket Halle self-service *Mitropa*. The food was adequate but all the crockery was chipped, the flimsy cutlery was bent as if a hundred Yuri Gellers had been at work and queues wound sinuously round the food area, bottle-necked at one check-out where an ancient crone dispensed her change with grubby fingernails. My plan was to use Halle as the launching pad for Nordhausen and the narrow gauge Harzquerbahn, but I'll leave you for a short while queueing in the dingy *Mitropa*!

I left you in the insalubrious interior of the Halle *Mitropa* on Saturday morning 27 September 1986. On the assumption you have not gained food poisoning by proxy, we'll continue our journey, as the object of this piece of masochism was to be ready to take E854 (14.02 Halle – Leinefelde) as far as Nordhausen and get a complete run across the Harzquerbahn. The Eilzug nine lightweight coaches with 119.081-8 was spectacularly unspectacular, nearly maintaining point to point times, firstly with a plod across the level to Roblingen at 96kph, then beginning the long climb to Blankenheim, sustaining 70kph before Lutherstadt-Eisleben, and faltering to 49kph at the summit itself. The descent could tempt nothing more than 100kph and arrival in Nordhausen, on a disappointingly grey and misty day, was 3 minutes late. The day was so gloomy and nondescript, that I wished it would make up its mind one way or the other, and wondered if exposure to the low mountains of the Harz would produce some decisiveness on the part of the weather. It did!

A wander across to the adjacent, deserted, Schmalspurbahn (narrow-gauge) terminus found the first really clean train I had come across in the GDR – seven cream and red Harzquerbahn upholstered coaches, with open verandas, and 2-10-2T 99.7243-1, gleaming and simmering quietly at the front end. A few shoppers and schoolchildren joined around four o'clock, and at 4.08pm P14408 duly sprang into life. The first few kilometres through the Nordhausen suburbs produced little excitement – just a trundle, some nice hooting, and the exit of most of our passengers. At Ilfeld, reached in half an hour, the Harz really begins, but first we had to wait for a late running train from Hasselfelde, with bunker-first 99.7241, which collected most of the passengers waiting on the island platform.

I took a photograph of the meet, the first splash of rain descended, and as we accelerated 5 minutes late onto the real start of the climb, aiming at a cleft in

DR metre-gauge 2-10-2T 99.7243-1 on the Harzquerbahn departing from Eisfelder Talmühle in pouring rain, on a through train to Wernigerode, September 1986. (*Author*)

the wooded hills straight ahead, the rain turned into a steady downpour, maintained throughout our passage of the hills. We reached Eisfelder Talmühle efficiently enough, demonstrating a healthy bark from the front end, and stood a minute overtime, taking water. I had been travelling immediately behind the locomotive, but I moved back three coaches and stood on the verandah in order to get a good view and photos on the numerous curves. On our restart, curving sharply round a stream bed, our thunderous exhaust did not necessarily denote success, as furious slipping occurred on rails made wet for the first time in weeks coupled with the first leaf fall. Our driver was not one for caution, however, and just kept the engine at it until the wheels gripped again. Despite one or two anxious moments, we made it past Tiefenbachmühle, and there were a few hundred yards of (steeply graded) straight track, where, I noted, we accelerated harshly, 'sounding like a "King" tackling Dainton'. It was a glorious thrash, and I was getting soaked, enjoying every minute of it.

Then the valley narrowed further and became tortuous, and the gradient, if anything, steepened and 99.7243 just wouldn't take it – after slowing for one of the worst bends, we all but stalled. Our driver attempted to keep us going but a wide-open regulator merely produced spectacular smoke effects, cinders and noises that must have been heard in Eisfelder Talmühle. Then, just as I was fearing that we were really stuck, 99.7243 managed to scrape round a final bend and get a grip on another couple of hundred yards of straight which we tore into, getting up to 45kph very quickly. We now had enough momentum for the next set of reverse curves, and our driver had no intention of risking braking this time, so we hung on for grim death – although my notes say the train was doing 45kph, the loco was doing 80! It sounded like a machine gun at the front end.

The next 10 minutes were most exhilarating as we roared through the sopping pine forest, obviously intent on regaining time lost lower down the bank and then, suddenly, we broke out of the forest and the mist, and here on this remote mountain top was a town – or rather, what looked more like a city – with buildings as far as the eye could see, plus a very large church; Benneckenstein – how do they exist up here in winter?

Despite our problems, we had actually regained a minute on schedule. We stood for a minute to exchange pleasantries with the solitary member of station staff, a blast on the 'Merchant Navy' hooter, and off we roared again, still upwards for the first kilometre or so, my log recording 60/30 – again a differential speed distinction between the loco and train wheels! Heaven knows what strain this was putting on loco, rails and couplings.

Then, over the top, steam was shut off and black smoke tumbled out of the chimney into the dank forest, not to mention adding a further layer of filth to the cinders already caked on my wet clothes. Out of the mist came an immaculate row of suburban bungalows and chalets – goodness knows who lives there; perhaps commuters to the city of Benneckenstein, in the aptly named village of Sorge (Anxiety). Off we went again, over the undulating line, keeping closely to the mountain contours, roaring and slipping through the swirling mist and into the evening dusk. On the next stretch of line we ran parallel to the East/West German border for a few hundred yards, alongside the cleared space and wire fence patrolled by Alsatians barking furiously at the train. The nearest pine tree to us was now ten yards away in the German Federal Republic, and sparks from the loco descended indiscriminately on the two countries, as well as on the roofs of the sixth and seventh coaches of our train.

The next place was called Elend (Wretched) – I am not sure whether this is a commentary on the weather, past experiences of numerous engine drivers or politics of the day – and it appeared in the middle of a Somme-like no-man's land. From the buildings visible (just) it seemed to be a spa and health resort. One border guard observed one elderly man joining our now deserted train under the watchful and efficient eyes of the young woman stationmaster (banished here to avoid some scandal in her village, perhaps) and off we barked again – now my notes say 'like a Black 5 climbing the West Highlands at 35-40mph' – to the 540 metre summit, then mournfully howling through the forest as we approached Drei Annen Höhne, where we were due to pass the last Wernigerode-Nordhausen through train. Sure enough, as we emerged from the gloom, there stood the original 99.7222 (the 1931 prototype of the 1950s built class), waiting patiently for us.

After all the excitement and ferocity of our uphill efforts, the descent to Wernigerode high on a ledge on the steeply wooded hillside, was cautious in the extreme, and we actually dropped time until we cut out some station stops through the streets of Wernigerode, finally arriving 3 minutes late, after a fascinating but somewhat emotionally and physically draining experience.

There was no time to hang around in Wernigerode and savour the experience, however, as the D-Zug for Berlin was waiting to be whistled away. That duly went off behind a 119, and the following local – 112.529-3 and four double-decker coaches – trotted to Halberstadt punctually. Arrival there was too late to take advantage of any of the booked steam workings, but I was anxious to see if there were any signs of life in the depot – and, sure enough, my first sight was of the triangular headlights of a 50.35 2-10-0 as it blasted away, light engine, back onto shed. However, as this was the last day of the summer service, would it be resurrected the next day?

99.7236-5 on a Wernigerode to Brocken metre-gauge train passes another 99.72 at Steinerne Renne, 22 March 2004. (*Colin Boocock*)

I confirmed my reading of the *Kursbuch* – that the seasonal Eilzug to Halle ran every conceivable day of the year except Saturday evenings starting from today; noted with some amusement and sense of superiority at least half a dozen angry passengers arguing with the booking clerk because they had misread the timetable, and resigned myself to a tortuous all-stations journey of 2½ hours back to Halle. Having attended to my needs from the all-hours *Mitropa*, I watched various complex shunting moves taking place in the station – on a drizzly, misty evening redolent of BR in the 1950s and 60s, with steam oozing from coach pipes all over the place, unfortunately not from any steam locos.

The 8.34pm P-Zug to Aschersleben eventually acquired the expected 110 (110.865-8 of Güsten) and I buried myself in a book until we were tipped out in the destination town, to allow the (non-existent) semi-fast train to overtake us. Aschersleben station – what a dump! No working toilets, no refreshments, no platform facilities at all – not even a train! Just darkness, drizzle and a gaggle of disconsolate passengers, all destined to be stranded in Halle at midnight. I wandered round the town in the dark, heard some distant revelry, but concluded most citizens were at home watching telly. I also concluded that the town deserved a station somewhat better than that provided by DR. I finally committed myself to the 10.27pm Aschersleben-Halle P-Zug with 110.057-7 and slumbered all the way to my bed in the Hotel Stadt Halle, pausing only long enough to remove the grime deposited on my person by 99.7243.

My plan for my final day, 28 September, the first Sunday of the new winter timetable, was to take the 7.44am Eilzug Halle-Wernigerode, and spend most of the day on the Harzquerbahn with time to see if any of the early evening Halberstadt passenger turns were steam. I set my alarm in good time, but was a bit surprised when I got up to find I was too early for breakfast, even on a Sunday. Anyway, breakfast was dispensable, so I lugged my suitcase through the deserted street to the all-night *Mitropa*, ignoring the huge digital florescent clock on the building opposite which said 6.23am.

An army of station staff was sticking up the new winter timetable sheets, when I noticed the station clock said 06.38 and enlightenment came. The GDR had changed their clocks overnight to winter-time and I had just foregone the extra hour in bed! I was still kicking myself when I realised a train for the Wernigerode direction was being announced, so I wandered up the platform and saw a filthy 132.041 run in from Leipzig with Sundays only P4430, 6.45am Halle-Thale. I decided to get into the warmth of the train, rather than put up with a cold and misty Halle any longer, and we duly shot off through the suburbs in a hell of a hurry, in marked contrast to my experience with 119-hauled services.

After 20 minutes or so, the sun attempted to break through, but our 120kph dash was short-lived as we were constantly checked, arriving at Aschersleben 11 minutes late. During this journey I had been busy with the *Kursbuch*. Taking my early rise as inspiration rather than error, I attempted to look for variations to my itinerary. By the time we reached Wegeleben, after more checks and a level crossing failure, I had constructed a programme that included the Selketalbahn (totally unknown to me) with a choice in the late afternoon of steam on Halberstadt-Thale locals or if steam had disappeared with the summer timetable, a last trip on the Harzquerbahn to Drei Annen Höhne and back. At Wegeleben, our Class 132 hooked off and ran round the train, picking up 4 lost minutes, and we set off down the single line to Quedlinburg, with me standing in the now-rear vestibule, watching black smoke hover over the dead straight track on a perfect Sunday morning, blue sky appearing as if a magic wand was being waved. My only companion was a small boy who, as the 132 ran round, kept shouting to his dad that perhaps we'd have a 'Dampflok, vielleicht ein Nul-Zwölfter!' What a thought! Anyway, what does a seven year old from East Germany know about 012s? In exhaust terms, 132.041 was certainly making a passable imitation.

I had over an hour to wait in Quedlinburg, and as I staggered off the train, my first sight was a pall of smoke rising from the siding next to the platform. A quick dash enabled me to watch 50.3606 setting off, tender first, towards Wegeleben with a pick-up freight – so I knew the Halberstadt 50s had not died with the summer timetable. Thus heartened, I left my luggage in the ornate and lofty booking hall and set off over the river to augment my meagre breakfast. No luck on this score, but what did I find? Quedlinburg was an incredible place – a seventeenth-century town, total and complete, dumped into the twentieth century. When I found a street full of timbered overhanging buildings and cobblestones, I fired off my camera – then I turned a corner, and found another, and another and so on, each better than the previous one. There was no road traffic, so I felt I was transported back three centuries. All the houses had carved messages conveying the date of building (1650 -1690 exclusively), the names of the original owners and a text or domestic message.

In fact, I was so intrigued that I almost overdid the exploration and had to run back to the station to catch the 9.39 local service to Aschersleben via Gernrode and Frose, which was standing in the station with 112.406-4. This was a mixed train consisting of five coaches, one brakevan and six wagons, with which we toiled uphill through numerous apple-orchards at a steady 25kph. At Bad Suderoda, a wagon of brown coal was surprisingly full of about twenty boy soldiers. What were they doing? Training to be miners? And at Gernrode I alighted into dazzling sunshine and made for the narrow gauge tracks next door. What a sight beheld my eyes – a dead Mallet 99.5904 lay immediately in front, 99.5906 was shunting some ancient carriages in the yard and my train, P14463 10.07am Gernrode-Stiege puffed into the station with 1897-built Mallet 99.5902-4 with two decrepit four wheel coaches and a van.

Everyone hung all over this friendly little railway, and I chose the veranda immediately behind the locomotive, along with about four others, including the guard, so that we could see into the footplate through the huge open back cab windows. It was the nearest thing to a footplate ride without actually being in the cab – all the controls could be seen, indeed, most of the way when he wasn't stoking, the fireman was exchanging pleasantries with the guard. The boilerplate (Hanomag 1929) could be clearly seen.

At 10.07 promptly we jerked into motion, a quick blast on the whistle, and out of the trees straight across the main road and into the apple orchards. Across a couple of fields and into the wood, and we were onto the hour long thrash through the spectacularly autumn-tinted leaves, climbing high up the valley – my senses overwhelmed with the noises of steam, the smoke pouring into the sparkling trees, the glimpses of lakes seen distantly and the steady clanging of shovel on metal as the fireman got stuck in. And after just over an hour's glorious run, we squealed our way round the curves by the main (and only) road into Alexisbad, and halted opposite 99.6102 waiting with the 11.16 back to Gernrode. While 99.5902 took water, I wandered up the track and shot the Stiege train leaving with spectacular exhaust.

I had an hour in the sunshine at the station café, before another Mallet, 99.5906-5, rolled in, also early, with the 11.00 Gernrode-Harzgerode (P69711) and I repeated the experience behind the locomotive as we curved sharply away from the Stiege line, and climbed through pinewoods alongside the Alexisbad-Harzgerode road, watching the trail of black smoke hanging over the valley behind us, and hooting loudly each time we decided to cross the road to easier geography on the other side! Another lake appeared on top of the hill and all too soon we were running into the terminus. A quick pose for photographs, the passengers dispersed and 99.5906 scampered round, ready to descend with now myself as sole passenger. There were a few places where energy was still required, but my main memory is rounding one of the many sharp curves and watching 99.5906 drifting, the rich brown smoke billowing lazily off the chimney top, smothering the beautiful landscape with a pungent odour. We rolled back into Gernrode at lunchtime.

Metre-gauge Mallet 99.5906 at Harzgerode on arrival with the 11am from Gernrode, September 1986. (*Author*)

Metre-gauge Mallet 99.5902 leaving Alexisbad with the morning Gernrode – Stiege service on the Selketalbahn, September 1986. (*Author*)

Mallet 99.5902 takes water at Alexisbad before departing for Stiege on the Selketalbahn, September 1986. (*Author*)

I had three quarters of an hour to wait, but the attraction of staying at the *Schmalspurbahnhof* (narrow-gauge station) with its pretty little garden, fountain and park benches was greater than searching for lunch in the town, so I picked up some windfall apples and pears, and watched 99.6102 and 99.5906 preparing their trains and departing over the main road. 99.6102 nearly scared an elderly woman driver out of her wits, as she only noticed the train when she was almost on the crossing and for a moment hesitated transfixed like a rabbit caught in headlights.

The 2.17pm P-Zug for Quedlinburg bowled in late with orange painted 106.661-2, which, despite being a shunting locomotive, had a greater turn of speed than the 112 coming – it was downhill though. I reacquired my luggage and made my way back to Halberstadt behind a couple of 112s, having to change again at Wegeleben. At the latter station, another 50 (50.3556) was busy shunting its freight, and although it was a welcome sight, I realised I had now seen two of the four working 50s that covered a seven loco diagram, reducing the odds of steam on the passenger legs. However, as we entered Halberstadt, several 50.35s were noted in steam, so I decided to try for Thale rather than selecting the Harzquerbahn option.

The first booked steam was the 4.07pm ECS to Thale (stock of D649, 6.40pm Thale-Berlin), which, even as I was thinking about it, backed into the station, propelled not by one 50.35 but two! I expected to see one cut off for one of the other turns, but a quick review of the various diagrams I had brought confirmed that, on Sundays only, this ECS was actually booked to be double-headed by two steam locos. I, with a German enthusiast, approached the smart young girl guard to ask permission to join the train to Thale, and to my chagrin, met with a very firm 'no'. I remonstrated a little and we were joined by the young girl's companion who was going up to bring

The Selketalbahn station at Gernrode with departing metre-gauge train for Alexisbad and Harzgerode with 0-6-0T 99.6102-0, September 1986. (*Author*)

a Sundays Only P-Zug back – she tried her hardest to shift the first girl, but totally without success – she seemed petrified of getting into trouble, because the bosses' office was opposite the platform, and someone might see us joining.

Why are all the attractive girl guards on DR so officious, and the plain ones jolly and co-operative? I found the same at Jena when I asked permission to take a photo of 41.1225 from off the platform end from a perfectly safe traincrew pathway. However, as the younger girl was in charge, there was nothing the older girl could do, except shrug her shoulders and apologise. So I had to be content with taking a photograph of 50.3552-2 and 50.3553-0 as they pounded out of the station with the train of D-Zug coaches. For a moment I wondered if the other locos seen in steam on shed – 50.3520 and an absolutely filthy and half dismantled (one smoke deflector missing) 50.3557 – would grace the 16.48 to Aschersleben (no, a BR 110) or the 17.11 to Thale (no, a 119) but as I rode out behind 119.181 on the latter, I had to accept that there is a limit on how far one can push one's luck, and certainty of a steam return should have satisfied me. The 119 duly droned up to Thale uneventfully, arriving a minute early and the arrival there confirmed what I had anticipated – that 50.3552 was standing ready for departure with the Sundays only P8439 Thale-Magdeburg, with 50.3553 in the same platform behind it on D649.

I decided to return to Halberstadt behind both locos, so I quickly joined P8439 after taking in the well-maintained and white paint decorated 50.3552-2, complete with snowplough. This loco was ex-works after a light repair in August – its last 'heavy' was in 1982 – and it had made a fifth 50.35 available to Halberstadt for the seven-day diagram. Our five coach train was not going to test the locomotive, especially as the start from Thale is steeply downhill, but the engine quickly accelerated to around 75kph through the streets of Thale, and then kept going across the open landscape, with speed rising to 90, passing Neinstadt in 4 minutes 20 seconds and eventually reaching a top speed of 95kph before shutting off steam for the Quedlinburg stop. The start to stop time was 10 minutes 5 seconds, as booked, for the 10 kilometres.

After watching 50.3552 pound away from the station, I had another pleasant wander round the ancient town in the dusk, on a balmy and beautifully warm evening, in the sure knowledge that a steam hauled D-Zug awaited me. I got back to the station in good time, and found gathered throngs all going back to Berlin after a weekend at home or visiting relatives and relished all the trappings of anticipation as the *Schnellzug* was announced. The three triangular lights appeared in the distance, and, on the dot, 50.3553 bustled into the station. I found a niche for myself in the packed train in the front vestibule, where I could hear the acceleration of the loco, and catch sight of the kilometre posts in the reflection of the coach lights behind me. Acceleration was brisk to 90kph, then we eased off and my impression is still mainly of looking back and watching the swirling exhaust as I tried to catch sight of half hidden posts. We passed the first station, Ditfurt, in 6 minutes 37 seconds, easing to 80kph through the station, worked up to 90 again, then braked to 45kph for the long curve round onto the mainline at Wegeleben (10 minutes 38 seconds). A final 87kph and we drew slowly into Halberstadt in 18 minutes 46 seconds for the 18 kilometres

– a loss of one and a half minutes on a very tight schedule. Timekeeping really demanded higher speeds than the 2-10-0 was authorised for, or a very fast approach unchecked into the junction at Halberstadt.

50.3553 was in good condition and also bore the remnants, somewhat faded, of smokebox decoration and I stayed whilst its coaches were shunted out of the station and it 'whoomphed' off to the shed. I was about to take a half-hour sojourn in the *Mitropa*, when 50.3606 appeared in the yard with a freight, and I had a pleasant 20 minutes watching it shunting, then departing with its long train in the Magdeburg direction.

I was going to leave you at this point, but I joined the Wernigerode portion of the Berlin train that appeared about 10 minutes late and crammed into the corridor to travel as far as Magdeburg en route for home. I sat on my case in the front coach amid more good looking young girls than I'd seen in one place for a long time! The 132 duly delivered us to Magdeburg where I alighted to a station that looked down and out after a hectic Sunday. A tramp was amusing passengers by filling a left-luggage locker with about twenty empty beer bottles, and I made my way up onto the platform while the crowds thinned out.

Then the noises of the night took over – a steam loco a long way off hauling a heavy freight, the steam pipes laid between the running lines creaking and jumping as the heating system was switched on, and crickets, the noise of swarms of crickets filled the night air.

Back to reality and my new role to improve the quality and reliability of British trains, although my experience in East Germany indicated a quality manager there would have had a field day – assuming he had some cash to invest and willing human resources. I found a challenge awaiting my return. The East Coast timetable had begun to fall apart and I was asked by John Prideaux, InterCity Director, and John Nelson, ER General Manager, to assess whether the plan or its implementation was at fault. The conclusion I came to was that acceleration in the schedules had removed unnecessary recovery time, but the completion of the electrification work the previous year meant that the ECML timetable had luxuriated in surplus recovery time for several months and that a miscellany of lost time for operating and engineering reasons had been hidden – only to be revealed as this time was stripped out. We identified some twenty-five reasons for regular lost time and began the task of analysing each and counting the cost of correcting them, to establish priorities we could plan and budget for.

This led to a request for me to be the main speaker at the German Railways Operating Conference in Bamberg in 1988, when I was asked to address their Board Member and senior colleagues for three 45 minute sessions on the system I had developed on the West Coast Main Line in 1986 and refined for the ECML study. An interesting aside is that I prepared three 45 minute presentations in English and had them professionally translated for me to deliver them in German. On my first run through rehearsal I found each of my talks took a full 70 minutes to say the same thing in German and I had to be ruthless in using the blue pencil. The end result was satisfying, however, and DB adopted my 'punctuality budget' system for its whole

EuroCity and InterCity timetable two weeks later. I dined out for years on how I told the German Railways how to run their trains on time! Despite my success there and on the East Coast, I never did succeed in persuading my successor on the West Coast to adopt the system also!

In December 1988 BR suffered the tragic multiple train crash at Clapham Junction. I was asked by David Rayner, the Board Member to whom I now reported, to use the techniques I had developed for reliability management to evaluate BR's safety management systems and compare with best practice in British industry. I also chaired a team of operators and engineers, collating the evidence to brief BR's legal team at the Judicial Inquiry ordered by the government on the accident, following a similar public outcry after the King's Cross underground station fire the previous year. I spent six months doing this in 1989 and then attending the Inquiry each day, spending a day giving evidence myself on the quality and reliability systems, such as IS 9000, then being applied by a couple of BR's engineering departments. BR gave the Inquiry the commitment to review its safety management systems and when it was over, we appointed a senior consultant from Du Pont to work with me – I was the pilot study project manager to look at his findings on the West Coast Main Line.

The result was far-reaching, although not necessarily the basis for a book aimed mainly at railway enthusiasts. Suffice to say that over the next three to four years we turned BR's thorough but basically reactive approach to safety to one that put the emphasis on prevention, using techniques such as risk assessment and the knowledge gleaned from academics such as Professor James Reason at Manchester University and Jens Rasmussen of Denmark in human factors and human error. We compiled the first annual Safety Plan for BR, which set objectives for passenger, public and staff safety, underpinned by a number of safety improvement programmes, which received ring-fenced funding from the government.

This led to enquiries from railway systems worldwide on safety management – especially from Commonwealth countries whose railways had been built by the British. As a result, I found myself making presentations at international safety conferences and attending an annual seminar for safety specialists, which we initiated with the Japanese and New Zealanders. I was asked to provide advice from BR to the railways of Australia, New Zealand, South Africa, Canada and Hong Kong and attended quarterly meetings in Europe with my opposite numbers from Germany, France, Switzerland, Holland and Belgium. I mentioned the first safety conference in Japan in 1990, which inspired the annual seminars thereafter. The Japanese do these things in style – vast conference hall, 500 attendees, lavish gifts. After the conference, David Rayner and I were invited to visit the JR driver training school to see their simulators and both of us were introduced to the controls of a cut down EMU to drive to a half hour realistic video unfurling on a wide screen in front of us. This was part of a safety briefing all Japanese drivers received which included testing in an emergency situation. All we knew was that we would be faced with some emergency during our 30-minute drive to which we would have to react. After a few minutes, passing through a station at 60mph, a person threw himself off the platform in front of me, committing suicide. I braked fiercely – not that I could avoid him – and went through the emergency procedures when the train came to a stand. It was so realistic that I found that I was trembling with the shock! David then took over and a quarter of an hour later he had collided with a JCB on an ungated farm crossing.

From the mid-1990s I was invited as only one of two industry managers – the other was from Shell in The Hague – to share experience with safety science academics from Europe and the USA. We met annually at the Werner Reimer Institute, a large conference centre in beautiful grounds in the spa town of Bad Homburg, a few miles north of Frankfurt-am-Main. My job and that of Kurt Visser, the Shell Manager, was to provide case histories from our industries, which would be discussed in the light of the theories and research they were presenting and to challenge the practicality and usability of their ideas. The main point of mentioning it here was to say that it gave me both the opportunity and excuse to add a few days to my time in Germany as the conferences in May 1993 and 1994 coincided with the steam locomotive *Plandampf* events in former East German territory between Bebra and Erfurt, Erfurt and Meiningen and Erfurt to Dresden and Görlitz. On parade, working scheduled expresses, semi-fast and local trains over the routes, were four Pacifics of renown – a traditional two cylinder standard pacific of the Deutsche Reichsbahn of class 01, 01.2137, the East German postwar rebuild of this class, 01.1531, a light axleweight version, 03.2001, and a three cylinder Pacific, streamlined when built, de-streamlined after the war and rebuilt with an all welded boiler in the 1950s, 03.1010, which is one of preservation's fastest locomotives – allowed 140kph (87mph) – and has recently been 'twinned' with Britannia, *Oliver Cromwell.*

Khyber Pass Railway Armstrong Whitworth 2-8-0 2216 at the water stop half way between Peshawar and Landi Khotal with the Chartered Institute of Transport special train, 1996. (*Author*)

Australia's Western Railway preserved metre-gauge steam 4-8-2 W945 *Banksiadale* at Perth on a tourist circular run via Freemantle, September 1989. (*Author*)

My overseas safety consultancy work also gave me an occasional opportunity to indulge my enthusiasm. In Western Australia I was able to join a regular round trip tour in Perth and Freemantle behind 3ft 6in gauge 4-8-2 No.W945 *Banksiadale* and during my time in Canada doing work for the Canadian equivalent of the Railway Inspectorate, I was encouraged to take a trip from Ottowa to Montreal to meet the Via Rail managers. I was put in the cab of diesel electric 6424 on a huge load of four 'tilt' coaches, with a few desultory passengers; the trip was mainly memorable for the number of open crossings over which we screamed with horn blaring, and the number of times the driver and inspector pointed out beaver dams being built in streams and wet lands beside the track which – unless dismantled – would flood and damage the permanent way.

In 1996 my former General Manager and Chairman of the Chartered Institute of Transport, Cyril Bleasdale, invited me to the AGM of the CIT in Pakistan to make a presentation on the adaptability of my safety cost benefit work to environmental management. After the AGM and conference was over, the Pakistan hosts arranged for the party to make a special trip to the Afghan border at Landi Khotal on the Khyber Pass Railway. Our special train, guarded with riflemen at each coach door and seated on the bufferbeam of the front locomotive, was topped and tailed by two First World War Armstrong Whitworth HS 2-8-0s, numbers 2216 and 2277, which steamed up the rugged mountains and experienced several reversals.

In 2000, I was asked to lead a small team to undertake the three-year review that the Hong Kong Mass Transit System (MTRC) commissioned. We spent three weeks looking at the network on which the citizens of Hong Kong relied and judged them against their mission statement – to be the best and safest system in the world. The company had to be efficient – a 5 minute delay warranted a paragraph in the local media and a 20 minute stoppage would cause a headline article! We eventually surfaced with seventy recommendations, which both surprised and concerned our hosts, but we were recommending a perfectionist case only because of the MTRC's avowed ambition.

Around the same time, and after my retirement from Railtrack in 1996, when it transferred from government to private ownership, I was an Associate Director/Consultant with International Risk Management Services, a small UK organisation carrying out high level railway safety commissions. We had bid for an Irish government contract to review the safety systems and infrastructure of CIE, the Irish national railway and were called to make a presentation to the Irish Railway Inspectorate on the day that I was committed to chairing the Railway Children charity AGM in London, which had been widely advertised and needed to go ahead on that day. The Irish government personnel were good enough to transfer our presentation to 4pm to allow my company to charter a light aircraft to pick me up from London City Airport immediately at the conclusion of the charity AGM. It was all down to split second timing, whisked by taxi to the airport, the light aircraft propellers already turning, with a car waiting for me at Dublin. I felt a bit like 007 until, just after take-off, I realised that in my haste I'd omitted a toilet stop and flew over the Irish Sea with my legs crossed, as there were no facilities in the tiny aircraft! I am pleased to say that we got the contract.

Relationships gained during that exercise have subsequently paid dividends in the support given by key people in Iarnrod Eireann to the Railway Children charity – including rail tours for the charity to Sligo with the last two single cab GM diesels and in April 2010, a tour to bid farewell to the last Mark III coaches in the country.

Members of the CIT AGM conference on the bufferbeam of Pakistan Railways 2-8-0 2277 during the water stop on the Khyber Pass Railway special, 1996. (*Author*)

Chapter 16

Plandampf – Germany 1993-4

Opportunities to indulge my enthusiasm for mainline steam had been few and far between since my intensive couple of weeks in the German Democratic Republic in 1979. As Chief Operating Manager of the London Midland Region from 1982-6, I had been kept pretty well occupied, although I allowed myself, under a little gentle persuasion from my Traction Inspectors, to undertake an annual safety check on the footplate of one of the steam specials – 46229 on the Settle & Carlisle, 35028 and 4498 on the Banbury-Marylebone route. However, I missed the everyday atmosphere of the steam railway and my occupational and family duties certainly did not allow for tours of India or China, which might have been the only source of such experiences at that time.

I was involved in the total review of BR's safety management systems after the 1988 Clapham train accident, and in 1990 became BR's Head of Safety Policy. This meant my involvement in various overseas conferences with other railways, notably in Australia, New Zealand, South Africa and Hong Kong, but more regular trips to Europe to share research with my opposite numbers in France, Germany, Switzerland, Holland and Belgium, also with the Union of International Railways (UIC) at their headquarters in Paris. During this period I became aware of the regular *Plandampf* events held in both West and East Germany, supported by both German and British enthusiasts (David Sprackland in the UK springs to mind as one of the main instigators). The concept is to diagram selected steam locomotives to timetabled trains over a two-three day period, to run to the normal diesel schedules and with regular bone-fide passengers as well as offering *Plandampf* runabout tickets for enthusiasts for the duration of the event. Some of the early events were in the Trier/Rheinland area but gradually became more ambitious especially in the newly opened up states of the former East Germany.

As recounted in the last chapter, one of my regular and extremely pleasant commitments during the 1990s was an invitation to join a group of safety science academics at their annual conference in the beautiful spa resort of Bad Homburg, a few miles from Frankfurt-am-Main. These were normally held in May and I noted with interest that the May 1993 event nearly coincided with an ambitious *Plandampf* on the Bebra-Erfurt mainline. The conference finished at lunchtime on the Saturday (May 8) and I realised that, with only a small diversion, I could take advantage of the remainder of that Saturday and enjoy the complete workings on the Sunday – the event had started with full steam operations on the Friday. So, after farewells to the academics, I boarded a scheduled Frankfurt-Leipzig express, D2756, which ran punctually to Bebra where normally a DR 232 diesel would drop on to the rear for the border crossing and climb to Hönebach and on to Erfurt and Leipzig. However, on this date, this was one of the scheduled steam workings between Bebra and Erfurt and I was both pleased and relieved to see polished 01.1531-1 poised ready to back onto the eight-coach train. This locomotive was formerly one of Saalfeld's oil-burning reboilered 01s, restored to coal-firing since the oil crisis in the early 1980s, refitted with one of the conical smokebox doors that these splendid looking pacifics had, and renumbered to the computerised coal-burning allocation numbers.

After the general fuss and milling around of enthusiasts, passengers and townsfolk bringing their small children to see the fun, we set off in earnest and on time. We went thundering through Ronshausen on the climb to Hönebach Tunnel at a steady 58kph, but then had a series of bad track slowings which plagued the route at this time and meant timekeeping, whether by steam or the regular diesel hauled trains, was difficult. In between the slacks we touched 102kph at Hörschel as we approached our first stop at Eisenach, in just over 45 minutes, but only 1 minute

Deutsche Reichsbahn rebuilt two cylinder 01.5 Pacific, 01.1531-1, hauls D2756 Frankfurt-am-Main-Leipzig between Bebra and Erfurt during the 1993 *Plandampf* event, here climbing to Hönebach Tunnel, 8 May 1993. (*Author*)

late on a fairly slack schedule. Further slacks between Eisenach and Gotha, where I alighted, meant a late arrival of 6 minutes despite touching 110kph after Fröttstadt. A half hour wait at Gotha, and standard DR 1925 designed 01.2137-6 swept into the station on time with the eight-coach Cottbus-Eisenach D2752. After this service stopped at Fröttstadt, windows were flung wide as we roared up to a maximum of 120kph before a 40kph long slack made our arrival a couple of minutes late — just 23 minutes 32 seconds including the station stop for the twenty-nine kms (18 miles). I alighted at Eisenach in order to pick up the diagram of the third German pacific in action that weekend – my erstwhile favourite Stralsund 'pet', formerly 03.0010-3, now converted to coal-burning 03.1010-2. The wait was just another convenient half hour and my intention was to run through to Erfurt, check into my hotel and find an evening meal. 03.1010, duly burnished and in excellent order, was waiting in Eisenach station, with just six coaches, 250 tonnes gross, on D2659, the 7.14pm Eisenach-Cottbus D-Zug. It departed glowing in the evening sunshine and promptly spent several minutes traversing a very long temporary single line section at no more than 30kph through Wutha, then opening out to a full throated three cylinder roar before a brief stop at Fröttstadt and 110kph on the short 9 minute run from there to Gotha. The p-way slack had cost us at least 6 minutes and we roared away from Gotha with clear intention of time recovery, reaching 115kph in less than 4 minutes when we ground to a halt to await V200.033 (not quite a *Plandampf* but a DB preserved diesel) coming off yet another temporary single line for track repair purposes. We waited less than a minute however, and then – after slow running through the track works – it was pandemonium from the front end, the exhaust echoing around the still evening air, back from the brilliant yellow fields full of rape-seed flowers. 116kph at Neudietendorf, just 5 minutes after the regulator was opened, and we ran into Erfurt just 6 minutes late, where 03.1010 handed over to an electric locomotive for the onward run to Weimar, Leipzig and Cottbus.

My only full day during this *Plandampf* event was Sunday the 9 May, so I had to take full advantage of it. I had received details in advance of the trains booked for steam haulage and the diagrams planned for the three pacifics, and had worked out the following somewhat hectic roster for my own tour of duty:

5.58am N8554 Erfurt – Eisenach (3 coach + 2 vans) – 01.1531-1
7.09am D2653 Eisenach – Gotha (7 coaches) – 01.2137-6
8.15am D2758 Gotha – Bebra (9 coaches) – 03.1010-2
10.19am D2753 Bebra – Gotha (9 coaches) – 01.1531-1
12.15pm D2754 Gotha – Eisenach (7 coaches) – 01.2137-6

This intensive 'see-saw' would then be followed by a trip from Eisenach past the Wartburg on the single line to Meiningen, allowing me to watch various train movements around Eisenach, and the hope to pick up a couple out of the Prussian Railways P8 4-6-0, the Baltic tank class 62, or the DR 50.35 that were operating shorter distance trains. After a turnround at Wasungen, a small country station, I'd be back in Eisenach by 4.30pm in time to pick up again on the mainline schedule of:

5.09pm D2755 Eisenach – Gotha (8 coaches) – 01.2137-6
(D-Zug from Frankfurt/Main to Frankfurt/Oder)
6.15pm D2752 Gotha – Bebra (10 coaches) – 03.1010-2
9.15pm N8569 Bebra – Erfurt (5 coaches) – 03.1010-2

What were the highlights? Firstly, astonishment that everything worked to plan, no failures, no late running so extreme that any connections were missed. Secondly, another glorious May day with warm sunshine throughout that made you glad to be alive. Thirdly, locomotive running performance of the highest order, with no time loss debited to the steam locomotive although the large number of track slowings caused some late running.

I got to Erfurt station at dawn, to find a typical DR local train, three coaches and a couple of vans, with super power 01.1531-1 oozing steam between each coach as the steam heating awakened the creaking coaches. We stopped at every single station en route to Eisenach – a 1-hour journey, with rarely more than 5 minutes between stops and speed accelerating to around 80-85kph between stations, needed to keep time. I concluded that these local trains, presumably booked for a 232 diesel normally, were much harder to time with steam than the expresses, and we'd dropped 7 minutes to Gotha, admittedly with a couple of minutes station overtime and one 15kph signal check. We cut station time at Gotha and departed 1 minute late and just about held point-to-point times to Eisenach, a 2-minute loss accounted for by another temporary speed restriction. This sort of train was ideal for those more intent on tape-recording than performance logging.

01.2137-6 on the 7.09am from Eisenach back to Gotha performed efficiently enough, losing 3 minutes on the 22 minute schedule for the 29 kilometres because of the 30kph single line slack, top speed 102kph. I was looking forward to the next leg, when 03.1010-2 would have a good run with a more substantial load – nine coaches, 322 tonnes tare/340 tonnes gross. The train was one of the regular Cottbus-Frankfurt-am-Main interval expresses and was well filled – indeed most enthusiasts filled the corridors while I took an empty corridor side corner seat in a compartment occupied by three nuns. They were clearly enjoying themselves and as we roared through the beautiful countryside, one of them suddenly wound down the main half window and they drank in the ear-splitting sounds of the pacific as it excelled itself, running the 29 kms to Eisenach in 20 minutes 45 seconds (18 minutes net – even time) with a top speed of 122kph. Leaving Eisenach on time, we reached 120kph by Herleshausen, less than ten minutes out and despite more single line working including a dead stand, were just over a minute early into Bebra. I shall not forget in a hurry the sight of the three elderly nuns trying with one hand to hold on to their wimples which were attempting to fly off in the fierce draught while running at 120kph and balancing their totties of something medicinal (?) in their other hand! And laughing like schoolgirls at the same time!

After this shock to the system, I calmed down by watching 44.1486 shunting in the sidings at Bebra while 03.1010 retreated among the electrics on the depot and 01.1531-1 appeared and stood ready for the next Frankfurt/Main-Frankfurt/ Oder Schnellzug. The train was a heavy nine-coach train, 358 tonnes tare, a very full 385 tonnes gross, and heads were hanging out of every window in the front three coaches. An initial 66kph past Ronshausen fell to 56 before Hönebach tunnel and then four bouts of single line working for engineering work and a 20kph signal check made us 12 minutes late into Eisenach. Although we recovered 5 minutes of lost time at Eisenach, we did labour after the long slowing past Wutha and failed to get above 93kph, before arriving 13 minutes late at Gotha. This was probably the poorest performance of the event, although there was no net time loss.

Midday at Gotha and the platforms were crowded with weekenders going back to Frankfurt and points west, 'normal' passengers far outweighing the enthusiast fraternity. It was therefore a joy to watch the incredulity of the awaiting hordes as 01.2137-6 swept into the platform virtually on time, with D2754 (Cottbus-Frankfurt/ Main). The seven-coach train was full and standing and despite a special unscheduled stop at Fröttstadt, we only dropped 3 minutes on the 20-minute schedule (net time 17 minutes well under even time) by dint of sustained high speed running between 124 and 127kph for over 5 minutes.

Standard DR 01 Pacific 01.2137-6 rushes into Gotha station, ignored by an intending passenger, with D2752 Cottbus – Eisenach, as part of the 1993 *Plandampf*, 8 May 1993. (*Author*)

Coal-burning three cylinder DR Pacific 03.1010-2 [formerly Stralsund's oil-burning 03.0010-3] runs into Eisenach station with a stopping train from Bebra to Erfurt, *Plandampf,* 9 May 1993. (*Author*)

It was now time to use the interval available to visit the Eisenach *Mitropa* although there was so much to see. 50.3688 had arrived on a local from Meiningen and 44.1486 had arrived from Bebra, had shunted out a heavy freight and now departed thunderously for Bebra again. Next 03.1010 ran in smoothly with a Bebra-Erfurt stopping train. In the meantime, ex Prussian P8, 38.1182-5, sidled down to the four coaches that had just arrived from Meiningen in order to form my next trip – the 2.04pm N7729 local from Eisenach to Meiningen via Bad Salzungen. The P8 was in the form that many of the DB P8s finished their days in the Crailsheim/Stuttgart area – with small 'witte' smoke deflectors but original Prussian small bogie tender. I made myself comfortable in an empty compartment and chewed my baguette and ham as we slogged up the steep grade past the towering Wartburg castle to our left, falling to 34kph at the summit.

Our departure had been 6 minutes late awaiting a (non-steam) connection and lateness had grown to 10 minutes by the first stop, Förtha, awaiting access to the single line, but after that it was plain sailing and we lost no further time to Bad Salzungen where we were able to cut our booked time and leave punctually. The longest section between stations after the first climb was only 7 minutes and the P8 accelerated its light load up to 80kph between stops capably enough. At a small rural station called Wasungen I decided it might be wise to alight rather than risk a frantic train crossing at the next station, and anyway, the area was pleasantly wooded and made a good photographic background.

Sure enough a few minutes later I was able to photograph Baltic tank 62.1015-7 emerging from the trees with the five coach N7732, 3.15pm Meiningen-Eisenach. Running was very similar to that of the P8, although we lost 3 minutes at Marksuhl awaiting access to the single line and the last section from Förtha to the Wartburg tunnel was clearly not timed for steam capability – the 4-6-4T worked hard to maintain 45kph on the gradient and despite 96 down the other side dropped a couple of minutes to arrive in Eisenach 9 minutes late.

Another half an hour wait and it was another sprint from Eisenach to Gotha, D2755 connecting the two Frankfurts, with 01.2137-6 yet again. The eight-coach, 340 tonnes gross load was enough to tax the 01 with the usual long p-way slack and we dropped 3 minutes on the 22 minute schedule without exceeding 100kph. Now for the last round trip – to Bebra and back to Erfurt, both with my favourite 03.1010-2. The train was the heavy ten-coach D2752, from Cottbus to Frankfurt-am-Main, packed tight that Sunday evening and weighing a full 440 tonnes gross. It was a good omen that it arrived only 2 minutes behind schedule and it was obvious from the start that we were in for something exceptional. The 10 minute sprint to the first stop, Fröttstadt, was completed on schedule and then we winged it for Eisenach

Ex DR 4-6-4 Baltic Tank, 62.1015-7, emerges from the woods at the rural Wasungen station with the N7732 3.15pm stopping train from Meiningen to Eisenach, as part of the *Plandampf* 9 May 1993. (*Author*)

with sustained high speed running at 128-132kph from Mechtenstadt-Sättelstadt to Schönau before the obligatory slowing onto the single line at Wutha. The twenty-nine kms had taken only 25 minutes including the Fröttstadt stop and I reckoned it was another net 17 minutes for the 18 miles start to stop. Departing 5 minutes late, we thundered out of Eisenach reaching 80kph in just under 3 minutes and then ran at a steady 120kph until the temporary speed restriction to 60kph before Gerstungen, after which we had to climb steadily to Hönebach tunnel from the east. We settled to a sustained 77kph, plunged into the tunnel at 72 and freewheeled down the other side of the bank at 110kph. Despite a slow entry to the west side of the station, we had regained a minute and were just 4 minutes late where we handed over to the DB 103 electric at Bebra.

I now had time for a leisurely evening meal, watched 03.1010 being coaled, watered and turned, and waited for it to gracefully couple up with the five coach all stations local to Erfurt – the parting shot of this *Plandampf*. Darkness fell as we departed and it was a joy to open the window wide to the mellow air, few enthusiasts or genuine passengers paying attention to this stopping service. Merry noises were heard as the Pacific blasted away to overcome the tight timings and the effects of the p-way slacks and we were a couple of minutes late at Gerstungen where we waited to catch our breath, leaving on time. An immediate mile long 30kph speed restriction and 4 minutes station overtime at Hörschel put us nearly 10 minutes late into Eisenach and after that it was a real struggle, flailing away in the darkness, unable to see mileposts, losing time steadily as the speed restrictions took further toll. By Fröttstadt, our lateness had grown to 16 minutes but then we got second wind and raced away between stops to 100kph and more, with an estimated 110kph just before Gotha. We finally wended our way into Erfurt just before midnight, with me virtually the only passenger and I spent a few minutes in the dim lighting of the station absorbing the hiss of steam, the oily smell, the pant of the air brake – a scene so 'ordinary' in many ways that it did not seem like a special day, but a time warp back to the 60s and 70s. Ah well! Back to my Erfurt hotel bedroom and sweet dreams!

The following year, 1994, I had a further opportunity to sample the *Plandampf* experience. It was going to be a complex week though, with sleep opportunities even fewer than usual. I had a meeting at the Paris HQ of the Union International de Chemins de Fer (UIC) on Monday and Tuesday, 2 and 3 May, and found that these coincided with another DR based *Plandampf* event. Before my UIC meeting I could savour two days of booked steam services on the Dresden-Görlitz and Dresden-Zittau mainlines, and after the meetings I could catch up on the last two days of a similar event in the Thüringenwald, based around the Erfurt-Arnstadt-Saalfeld-Meiningen routes.

On Friday 29 April, a punctual Lufthansa flight deposited me in Frankfurt-am-Main in a central European heatwave in good time to catch the sleeper from there to Warsaw and Moscow, D451, 11.58pm ex Frankfurt. DB electric 110.391-0 left the station on the stroke of midnight with twelve coaches (486 tonnes tare) including a Polish (WARS) sleeping car in which my berth was situated. The door rattled, the Polish sleeping car attendant gave me a toothbrush and a plastic cup, but no water, but long before Fulda I was fast asleep.

01.2137-6 takes over D451, 11.58pm Frankfurt-am-Main – Moscow sleeping car train, at Dresden Neustadt as the first run in the DR 1994 *Plandampf* between Dresden and the Polish border at Görlitz, 30 April 1994. (*Author*)

I awoke on the Saturday morning to a misty sunrise over a flat landscape near Riesa, and by 7am we were snaking our way round the western leg of the triangle avoiding Dresden Hauptbahnhof (Hbf), across the Elbe bridge into Neustadt station just 5 minutes late. I humped my case and camera bag out of the sleeper along the platform to a first-class coach nearer the front of the train, now apparently thirteen coaches, 524 tonnes tare/550 tonnes gross, and spied a wisp of steam in the distance. Reassured, I watched DR standard Pacific 01.2137-6 back down onto this international express, and couple up observed by a small band of fellow participants and a larger gaggle of genuine passengers and bystanders who wondered what on earth was going on. At the back, a bleached red 232.533-0 attached itself to provide electric heating and some initial banking up the steep grades for the first dozen miles – after that it just applied enough power to provide no drag on the train engine as 550 tonnes was quite enough for a single 01 to time an international express without the weight of the heavy 232 diesel as well.

At this point I have to say that later in the day I managed to lose my notebook – one of three misfortunes that befell me. I had already left my reading glasses on my desk at home and had had to buy a spare pair at the Heathrow chemist. Therefore the first few logs are remembered with approximate times and speeds only. We departed Dresden Neustadt right time at 07.27 and hammered out through the industrial suburbs into wooded hills at a steady 60kph, reaching a maximum of 90kph at Arnsdorf before a couple of p-way speed restrictions and single line working before Bischofswerda. Then the 01 opened up to reach 110kph, and the sun broke through the mist as we negotiated the long curve into Bautzen station, arriving a full 6 minutes early. We waited time, then negotiated yet another temporary single line, 30kph slowing with a maximum of 90kph, arriving at Löbau on time. The line speed for most of this route was only 100kph with a small section at 120kph between Bischofswerda and Bautzen. At Löbau the end of the platform beyond the perspiring 01 jutted onto a viaduct and swarms of black flies were hovering round the bushes in the heat. After photographing the departing train and listening to its exhaust beats echoing back from the wooded hill ahead, most of us found a small snack bar outside in the cobbled station yard and ate a bockwurst as breakfast in the heat haze – 9am and the temperature already in the upper seventies Fahrenheit.

A 20 minute wait saw us back in the station to pick up D456 Warsaw-Dresden, which drifted in on time behind a two cylinder 03.2 hauling a lightweight international express of only three coaches; apparently a defect on the booked rolling stock had reduced the formation including the loss of the buffet. The *Plandampf* crowd crammed into the already overfull train and blocked the corridors, all windows lowered to the maximum! Preserved 03.2204, based at Cottbus, whirled its featherweight 125 tonnes load up to 102kph before the first station – Breitendorf – but then a long speed restriction to 40kph past Kubshütz made us 5 minutes late into Bautzen and station overtime whilst further crowds tried to pack themselves into the reduced formation made us 7 minutes late away. For some reason we then made a special additional stop at Bischofswerda and despite yet more single line working for engineering work, with a last minute dash past Arnsdorf at 104mph, we were only 9 minutes late on arrival in the cavernous Dresden Hbf.

The DR seemed to be undertaking very extensive engineering work at this time, investing a significant sum to bring the former DR up to DB standards. I had seen this the previous year during the Bebra-Erfurt *Plandampf* and the Dresden-Bautzen section in particular had two sections of single line working and a further 40kph speed restriction – all long. Not only were delays encountered because of these restrictions, but late running meant delays often waiting access to the single line sections. In the circumstances, I'm very surprised the DR authorities had agreed to the *Plandampf*, although the steam locos seemed to be as successful at reducing the delays to a minimum as the diesel hauled services. I discovered that because of the limited track capacity, some locals between Dresden and Bautzen had been cancelled, hence the additional stops inserted to some expresses.

Dresden Hbf on this Saturday morning was a very steamy place. 03.2204-0 stood proudly at the buffer stops in the main train shed. Baltic tank 62.1015-7 was belching sulphurous smoke just inside the overall roof at the head of a local to Arnsdorf. Three-cylinder 03.1010-2 was taking water at a column just outside the main shed, prior to backing on to four coaches forming a D-Zug to Görlitz standing on the upper level platforms. Bone fide passengers looked bemused as though they had dropped into a time warp.

01.2137-6 battles out of Dresden with the 550 ton D-Zug D451, approaching Arnsdorf, 30 April 1994. (*Author*)

Two cylinder Pacific 03.2204-0 on arrival at Dresden Hbf with D456 from Warsaw, *Plandampf*, 30 April 1994. (*Author*)

I joined D1853, 11.42am Dresden Hbf-Görlitz, with 03.1010-2 and four coaches, 175 tonnes gross. We left the Hauptbahnhof and Neustadt on time and showed energy whenever we could with a slightly over the top 112kph before Arnsdorf and 104kph after all the engineering work just before Bautzen. We took 50 minutes 30 seconds start to stop for the 56 kilometres from Neustadt, a loss of nearly five minutes on a section with a low line speed as well as all the engineering restrictions. We ran the 22 kilometres on to Löbau in 19 minutes 59 seconds, with a top speed of 112kph and yet another 40kph single line section, lost another minute in station overtime and then hot-footed it for Görlitz, the final 24 kilometres taking 20 minutes 30 seconds, top speed 110kph, but with a 50kph restriction through Reichenbach and a 20kph signal check approaching the terminus. We arrived 6 minutes late.

We arrived behind the steel fencing of the customs barrier blocking access to the platforms serving trains for Poland, and I ventured into the sweltering and deserted town – now Saturday afternoon – like a morgue with all the shops closed from midday. I found an ice-cream kiosk and walked through the park occupied only by a courting couple and a pair of small girls playing an inept game of shuttlecock in which neither managed during my passage of the park to return any hit of the other. I crossed a main road on which a long queue of cars and lorries waited in total absence of movement to get onto a bridge which formed the frontier to Poland and I walked through another leafy park to the customs house before retracing my steps past the same players to the main tram-lined street and station.

The three cylinder Pacific had turned and was now standing at the head of the same four coaches forming D1854, 2.47pm Görlitz-Dresden. We left on time and completed the 24 kilometres to Löbau in 18 minutes 27 seconds, with a top speed of 104kph and 60kph slowing through Reichenbach. There we waited for nearly 10 minutes for the arrival of 03.2204 off the single line section, and then covered the 22km to Bautzen in 16 minutes 45 seconds, maximum speed 110kph. The 03.10 was in beautiful condition, with a perfectly even roar, heard to great effect on these two runs in the constant accelerations to permitted line speed. I photographed the 03.10 leaving Bautzen, left my luggage in the station lockers for another couple of hours' exploration. DR reboilered 2-10-0, 52.8056, was plinthed in the forecourt and I passed it making tracks for the old town glimpsed from the approach viaduct via a fountain in which the local children were cooling down. Below a road viaduct was a millrace, a couple of baroque castles and mediaeval cottages, and on the hillside on the skyline, various spires, turrets and towers projected above the horizon.

The old part of the town was undergoing much restoration (like the railway) and the square round the cathedral and the main castle was resplendent. Bautzen seemed to be a very attractive city, deserted on this sunny afternoon. I got back in good time to see D1852 (4.57pm Görlitz-Dresden) run in on time behind 03.2204-0, took a photo with the zoom lens, lined up for a second as the brown smoke rolled from the chimney as the train drifted up the platform – and the shutter refused to operate. I shook it, tested the batteries, ran for the train and got in, flustered and frustrated that once more my camera had packed up at a highly inconvenient moment.

Baltic Tank 62.1015-7 at the head of a local train to Arnsdorf at Dresden Hauptbahnhof, *Plandampf*, 30 April 1994. (*Author*)

03.1010-2 stands at the head of D1853, 11.42am Dresden Hbf-Görlitz, at Dresden Hauptbahnhof, *Plandampf*, 30 April 1994. (*Author*)

The run to Dresden hardly permitted the 03 to demonstrate its capabilities, although the many additional stops allowed it to show off its starting prowess and throw its exhaust echoing off numerous station buildings. We departed just over 1 minute late, touched 109kph by the first station, Seitschen, but then substituted for a cancelled local train by stopping at Bischofswerda, Weikersdorf, Grossharthau and Arnsdorf. We then roared away, accelerating our four-coach train to112kph down the grade to Dresden, arriving at Neustadt 9 minutes late.

It was then at Neustadt that the next (and final) misfortune befell me, in that in my hurry to leave the train and attempt an abortive photo of the 03, I left my notebook and pen in the compartment. By the time I had waited to see 03.2001-0 arriving 25 minutes late with a train from Zittau and caught the next local to the main station, I had missed my chance to recover my log book. I abandoned any further attempt to repair my camera, and managed to find a kiosk open that sold 'throwaway' cameras, and bought a couple to tide me over until the main shops reopened after the weekend.

I took a taxi to the Touristenhotel just outside the old city, and left my luggage thankfully in the student hostel type room, before going 'on the town'. I stripped down to my shirtsleeves, found the tram system back to the Hauptbahnhof, and set off after a quick bite to walk through the city centre to the Elbe. I had not checked the weather, however. Unnoticed by me, in the twilight, the blue skies had given way to storm clouds and the heat had become even more oppressive. I had walked barely half a mile before there was a crash of thunder and the heavens opened. I dashed from awning to awning until, near the *Altmarkt*, I gave up and worked out the complex tram system and found the right pick-up point. Even then, after a long wait (many of the trams were cancelled because of extensive road works – the whole former GDR seemed to be a building site) I thought nemesis had arrived when the local police seemed to be escorting our tram driver away – but it turned out he was seeking their assistance to eject an elderly drunken woman from the front seat!

I slept at last and woke, prompted by my alarm, at 5.30am on Sunday, May Day. Breakfast was served in the Tourist Centre opposite at 6am precisely – not a second earlier despite the queue of the *Plandampf* crowd, bleary-eyed and hopeful, standing a few minutes earlier before a resolutely shut door. I bolted my rolls and jam and lugged my baggage aboard the sole taxi that I had commandeered in good time to join the first local to Arnsdorf that was shuffling in to the upper level on a very bleak morning – the temperature must have dropped twenty degrees overnight – behind the 4-6-4T, 62.1015-7. We departed at 6.49am on the dot at a brisk pace, stopping briefly at Dresden Mitte and arriving at Neustadt station a minute early. This place now became very steamy as 03.2204 was blowing off steam furiously on the 7.15 Eilzug to Zittau, and 03.1010-2 ran in light engine from Altstadt depot and passed through the station positioning itself to take over D451 for Görlitz and points east to Warsaw and Moscow. The sleeping car express from Frankfurt drew in punctually behind a 143 electric and as soon as the train came to a stand, a 232 diesel buffered up to the rear to provide heating and a bit more assistance than had been given to the 01 the previous day. The train was eleven coaches weighing 448 tonnes tare, 470 tonnes

After turning, 03.1010-2 is ready to return to Dresden on the 2.47pm departure on D1854, Görlitz, 30 April 1994. (*Author*)

gross, and departure was on time, the climb out past the industrial district being achieved at a steady 72kph and a full 120kph being reached after Bischofswerda and the succession of engineering slowings. Bautzen was reached a triumphant 8 minutes early and the run onto Löbau was made punctually without any further fireworks. The 03.10 was worked very hard and emitted its usual satisfying roar, but assistance from the rear diesel was more apparent, especially in recovering from the single line engineering slowings.

The forecourt at Löbau was as cold today as it was hot yesterday, so we all huddled in the small waiting room. David Sprackland, the *'Plandampf* maestro*'*, had managed to 'book' himself on two footplates at once and offered the arriving 01 to a colleague who had helped him with organizing administrative work, or myself. In reality, by the time 01.2137-6 had swept into the station, and photos had been taken, the right away whistles were shrilling. Both of us had luggage and frankly were not suitably dressed, so we scrambled aboard the four-coach D456, Warsaw-Dresden. We kept time to Bautzen, with a maximum speed of 112kph, then a special stop at Bischofswerda and the usual engineering slowings made our arrival at Dresden Neustadt 7 minutes late. I bailed out here this time as I had promised myself a run as far as Bischofswerda on the Zittau semi-fast. This was formed of five newly liveried *Interregio* coaches and a resplendent 03.2001-0, adorned with large smoke deflectors and burnished boiler bands. The train was E4487, 11.15am Dresden-Zittau and it ran crisply stopping at Arnsdorf with maxima of 98 and 102kph before and after this stop. Arrival in Bischofswerda was on time.

A half hour exploration of Bischofswerda on a raw Sunday morning did not enable a favourable comparison with other towns visited, and I was glad that the margin before the return journey was so small. The Zittau-Dresden Neustadt train, E4486, arrived punctually behind 03.2204-0, but was held for 10 minutes awaiting a diesel hauled train off the temporary single line section to Arnsdorf. There were no additional stops this time and the 03 and its light four-coach train lost no further time despite the single line working and a signal check outside Neustadt station.

I was going to have to terminate my involvement in this part of the *Plandampf* as I had to catch the 4.45pm Intercity express to Frankfurt and an overnight sleeper service from there to Paris to be ready for my UIC meeting on Monday morning. However, I still had a couple of hours spare, so I decided to pay a brief visit to the Altstadt loco depot. I needed to catch a local to the Hauptbahnhof (it turned up behind 62.1015-7 without me even trying to get steam) and then took a taxi through bleak dual-carriageways and cobbled back streets to the depot and there found a hive of activity. There were queues of the general public and a pall of black smoke hung over the depot as a number of locos were being serviced as well as exhibited.

DB standard 2-10-0, 50.1849, was squealing over the sharply curved sidings with a footplate full of excited but nervous children. Small 0-6-0 tank 89.6009 was doing a similar turn over a shorter stretch of track at a more sedate pace. 03.2204 was coming on shed for coaling and watering and pacific 01.1531 was lurking in steam somewhere. 2-8-0s, 58.261 (ex-58.1111) and 58.3047, were simmering in the roundhouse, with 2-6-2, 23.1113, dead alongside. A couple of Saxon locomotives, the Meyer 0-4-4-0T 98.001 and the mighty 2-8-2 19.017, were stabled on a centre siding. At the other end of the shed, in the second roundhouse, stood 0-8-0T 92.503 and two Prussian 4-6-0s, the P8 38.1182-5, and long withdrawn and preserved olive green S10.1, 1135 (ex 17.1055), alongside a number of venerable electric locomotives – E77, E71 and E17 among them – and the diesel three-car *Fliegende Hamburger* set in purple and cream. What a feast!

It was then back to modern reality – IC 652 *Georg Philipp Teleman* with a 143 electric to Leipzig, another after reversal to Erfurt, a 232 to Bebra and 103.117-8 to Frankfurt. Then a TEN sleeper for the overnight journey to Paris, leaving with 103.215 at the front and a dual voltage 181.209-8 trailing to take over after an early reversal – but I was asleep. I only awoke as we swept past Meaux on the outskirts of Paris where we arrived 3 minutes late behind 15025 *Toul*. I was back in the heatwave and after the grind of the UIC meeting, it was pleasant to relax in a café near St Michel at 11pm with the temperature still eighteen degrees Celsius. And to look forward to the next day when the meeting would finish at lunchtime, enabling me to return to Frankfurt and Erfurt, ready for another couple of days' *Plandampf* on the scenic and heavily graded Erfurt-Arnstadt-Meiningen route.

The next day, Tuesday, 3 May 1994, I finished my UIC meeting at 12.30, too late to catch the 12.58pm to Frankfurt but much too early to wait for the 5.16, so I decided to go via Strasbourg, Karlsruhe and Mannheim on the Paris-München EC67 *Marie Curie*, which left Paris Gare de l'Est at 1.44pm in glorious sunshine. I trusted that this routing would give me more time in Frankfurt for a return visit to the I-City

Preserved Saxon 2-8-2 19.017 on exhibition at Dresden Altstadt depot Open Day & Gala during the 1994 'Plandampf', 1 May 1994. (*Author*)

buffet there and remove any worries about connecting to D451 sleeper back to Erfurt (the same Dresden –Warsaw –Moscow sleeper caught the previous Friday night that was then scheduled for steam haulage between Dresden Neustadt and Görlitz).

SNCF 15065 *Vaires-sur-Marne* headed fourteen corail vehicles and ran efficiently through the green countryside while I took a leisurely and not unduly expensive lunch in the dining car. We arrived in Nancy a minute early at 16.28, were held unusually overtime, and, shortly after departure, came to a screeching halt in the middle of nowhere. Much scurrying by the train staff heralded the fact that someone had pulled the communication chord and I began to worry about connections in Germany. Eventually it transpired that somebody in the rear coach had had a heart attack, and we crawled forward to Lunéville where we were met by an ambulance.

We were fortunate in the end to be only 23 minutes late arriving in Strasbourg, and the DB dual voltage 181.205-6 continued to pick up time through Baden Baden, arriving at Karlsruhe 17 minutes late. The I-City train to Cologne had gone, but I rushed across the width of the station to just catch a four-coach local hauled by 141.221-2 on the 7.10pm *Nahverkehrzug* (commuter train) to Mannheim, calling at all stations through very undistinguished countryside made even more featureless by the miles of noise screening fencing alongside the high speed stretch. A quick connection at Mannheim to IC 553 *Pfälzer Wald*, behind yet another dual voltage electric, 181.224-

7, (the train had come from Saarbrücken) and we arrived at Frankfurt-am-Main 2 minutes early, and in good time to enjoy some delicious fruit tarts I had discovered the previous week in the buffet, before making my way to the now familiar PKP sleeping car on D451 waiting alongside the post office activity on platform 1. It was the same venerable vehicle, the same berth, the same waterless sink – but a different Polish attendant who appeared to be unable to speak German. He preferred to have a go in execrable English. The upshot was that I had great difficulty in persuading him that I wanted to alight at Erfurt at 3.45am as his list showed me booked through to Leipzig. I thought I had made myself eventually clear, but I was wrong.

D451 left punctually at 11.58pm on 3 May – only eleven coaches this time – behind DB electric 110.333-2. I slept at once and duly awoke in good time to my alarm, and ready by 3.30, I went in search of the attendant to retrieve my ticket and passport. I couldn't find him anywhere. After 5 minutes of near panic, I discovered him ensconced in a sleeping compartment with a woman in very suspicious circumstances! Muttering under his breath, he kept repeating that I was going to Leipzig and I kept saying louder and louder in any language I could muster that I was getting out at Erfurt, NOW!! Grudgingly he gave me back my documents and I alighted onto the warm and deserted Erfurt platform alongside 232.052-1, which had brought us from Bebra 3 minutes early.

I discovered very quickly that the only waiting room – like so much else in the former East Germany – was under repair and unusable. Unwilling to park myself in the open for a couple of hours, I worked out that I could catch the 4.28am N-Zug to Arnstadt in time for a comfortable connection with the 5.09 return which itself formed the set for the steam planned 6.05 to Saalfeld. 232.345-9 burbled to Arnstadt and the 5.09 return turned out to be an extraordinary train. Firstly, it was the only train I have ever travelled on (or indeed seen) that was triple powered with three different forms of traction! Secondly, it had nearly as many traction units as coaches! The formation of the train from the front was:

232.379-8
143.193-1
Four former DR double deck coaches
41.1185-2 (tender first).

What is more, on our short journey all three traction units were under power – indeed, the 41 was chuntering very merrily at the back, clouds of white smoke hanging in the crisp early morning air. Despite all this, we somehow managed to drop 2 minutes on schedule, only partly explained by a momentary check as we drew into Erfurt station.

The same set now formed the first officially planned steam part of the *Plandampf* programme called *Der Berg ruft* ('The Mountain calls'). The 41 gleamed in the still clear sunrise, and a few event participants began to show up. The 41 was comfortably on top of its job, and ran within booked time all the way until the last stop before Saalfeld-Bad Blankenburg – where it waited nearly 4 minutes for a late running diesel hauled train to cross. Speed between stops was mainly around 80kph although we were clearly climbing between Stadtilm and Singen, when a very noisy 74kph was maintained. After that we drifted downhill easily, with 90kph on the last stretch as we tried to recover from the Bad Blankenburg delay, arriving 3 minutes late.

I had the option of returning to Erfurt on the return working of 41.1185-2, with the coaches off the 8.50am arrival from Arnstadt, due behind 01.1531-1, but this relied on a 7-minute connection at Erfurt to an I-City train to Leipzig to make certain of connecting with the scheduled steam 12.22pm Leipzig-Arnstadt-Würzburg D-Zug. I was highly dubious about this connection and when there was no sign of the 01.5 on the inward working, I decided to take no chances and caught a double-headed 219 (renumbered 119s to avoid duplication with DB classes) hauled direct train to Leipzig. IC 804 *Hans Sachs*, the 8.55am Saalfeld-Berlin, was rather a grandiose description of 219.073-4 & 219.069-2 and their four coaches, but they ran smoothly enough to convert a 6 minute late departure into a 2 minute early arrival in Leipzig. I kept my eyes peeled for the late running 01.5 and eventually glimpsed it coasting on the far bank of the Saale river, about 12 minutes late. I'm told that 41.1185 made up time and duly made the Erfurt connection, but at any rate, I avoided a lot of anxiety. The vast empty concourse of Leipzig and its twenty-plus platforms glistened cathedral-like in the dusty sun rays, and I took advantage of the time available to purchase a replacement camera for my defective Canon T50 and the two 'throwaways' that had served me well.

I walked to the end of the platform in the hot sun and peered to see if I could see any sign of steam, and after an anxious quarter of an hour a plume of smoke could be glimpsed behind some buildings on the horizon. A few moments later, a black tender could be seen inching its way towards the station, and the 03.2 with its original style tender and large smoke deflectors stood poised to back on to the late running Cottbus-Würzburg express. The six-coach train ran in 15 minutes late behind a 143 and 03.2001-0 backed smartly down, cylinder drain cocks hissing noisily, alerting the casual passengers to the unusual sight of a steam Pacific in the midst of electric expresses and push-pull suburban trains rushing in and out of the station.

The 03 was coupled up so swiftly and the station work conducted so efficiently that our departure was almost on time. The staccato exhaust from the Pacific leaving the station alerted the unsuspecting casual passengers and heralded straightaway that the driver meant business. A quite exceptional run followed. The noise from the front end turned people's heads upwards from the streets below, their back gardens or from their bedroom windows and those of us in the train got a sharp reminder of the days when smuts in the eye were a common hazard! One of the pleasures of the *Plandampf* programme is watching the reaction of ordinary people going about their business, suddenly confronted by a roaring, snorting beast belching black smoke over the town. Best of all are the faces of impatient motorists waiting at level crossings as they realize the nature of the thundering train bearing down on them. The young children get excited and elderly folk stop and stare wistfully at the vision from their youth. This journey from Leipzig was a particularly rich experience of this

Preserved two cylinder 03.2001-0 at Leipzig Hauptbahnhof at the head of the 12.22pm D2155 Leipzig-Würzburg, as part of the Erfurt-Arnstadt-Meiningen *Plandampf*, 4 May 1994. (*Author*)

phenomenon. In the next compartment, a small boy of three or four travelling with his mother could not believe what was going on, and spent most of the time hanging out of the open window mesmerised until the inevitable smut got lodged in his eye, and the experience began to pall rather rapidly.

The train was D2155 Cottbus-Würzburg and was formed of six coaches, 224 tonnes tare, 245 tonnes gross. We had already reached 104kph by the suburbs of Leipzig-Leutsch and 112 before an 80kph restriction at Militz, then speed was piled on with a maximum of 122kph between Kotschau and Bad Dürrenberg. With a slack to 75kph through Grosskorbetha, we stopped at Weissenfels in 26 minutes 33 seconds from Leipzig Hbf. We then roared away achieving a full 120kph in the 9 minute 40 second run to Naumburg, the 54km (virtually 34 miles) from Leipzig being completed in 36 minutes 13 seconds including the Weissenfels stop! Another acceleration to 120kph before the Apolda stop followed but the next section was spoiled by a check to walking pace to pass a message from the signalman at Ossmannstedt to the driver, so that we took 30 minutes 27 seconds for the 41km (25.5 miles), including the Apolda stop. Despite this delay, we were still running on time and on the next section to Erfurt, the driver pushed his willing steed to a steady 125kph (other timers made it a full 128kph, or 80mph) between Hopfgarten and Vieselbach before our rapid entrance took Erfurt by surprise and we were stopped outside the station for half a minute. Even so, we had completed the 14 miles in 17 minutes, 1 second or about 15 minutes net. Our early arrival allowed us to alight and photo 41.1185 passing the 03 in the rain, which had replaced the sunshine of Leipzig. It had been a thrilling experience as the engine roared through the countryside at top speed, whistle shrieking, smoke swirling everywhere.

A small boy, excited and enraptured by the sight of 03.2001-0 at the head of D2155 [until he got a smut in his eye] leans out of the carriage window as the express leaves Weissenfels station, where he and his mother joined, 4 May 1994. (*Author*)

We continued at a slightly more sedate pace with a maximum of 104 before a dead stand at signals at the Neudietendorf Junction, but arrival at Arnstadt, now in torrential rain, was still on time. I took a taxi in the murk through streets ripped apart by sewer and telecommunication infrastructure renewals to Hotel Anders – a newly modernised, family-run establishment that met best western standards. After I had checked in, the rain eased up a little, and armed with umbrella, notebook and my newly acquired camera, I retraced my way through the old town centre – a 25 minute walk to the station.

D2157, an express from Stralsund to Würzburg, was scheduled for steam haulage through to Meiningen each day of the *Plandampf* arrangements, and on this day, as pacific 01.1531-1 was diagrammed with an eight coach train (325 tonnes gross), a banker was provided to assist to the summit of the line at Oberhof. The train ran in a couple of minutes late behind a 143 electric and, while the 01.5 backed on to the head end, 2-10-0 50.3688-4 buffered up to the rear. The climb through Gehlberg to Oberhof through the dripping trees was thrilling in the extreme, with both ends of the train and their hard working locomotives almost continuously in view on the winding route. I was about three coaches from the rear, but the noise from the 01.5 at the front was deafening and I was very surprised that it kept its feet as the weather deteriorated even more as we neared the summit. The climb was completed in spectacular style, with speed sustained at 77kph on the lower reaches and 69kph near the summit, and the overall time from Arnstadt to Oberhof of 28 minutes 45 seconds turned a 3 minute late departure into a 4 minute early arrival. Timekeeping then fell apart as we had to wait for a late running diesel-hauled train before we could access the single line and drift downhill to Zella-Mehlis, Suhl and Meiningen. The line's curvature meant we did not exceed 97kph and we were 7 minutes late into Meiningen.

The air was fresh and the trees glistened in the reflected sunlight after the torrential rain as I made my way through Meiningen's 'English Park' to the castle and square in the old part of the town in search of a substantial meal – luckily fulfilled. The timing was just right and an amble back through the same park, complete with folly and lake, found 01.1531-1 turned and heading the last local back to Erfurt, framed by a gaudy rainbow etched against the black sky that dominated the northern hills. Despite the light load (three coaches) and superfluity of power available, there was still plenty of opportunity for graphic noises and volcanic exhaust on the climb to Oberhof. The departure from Suhl was especially dramatic, leaving the station on a viaduct high above a main road junction, threatening to cause a road accident as drivers caught sight of a huge steam engine charging the steepest part of the climb to Zella-Mehlis. We had left Meiningen 8 minutes late (waiting a connection) but the sustained 74kph on the steepest part of the climb meant we had regained all but 2 minutes by the summit. We rocketed downhill round the curves under light steam at an uncomfortable 107kph and arrived at Arnstadt just 1 minute late.

Next day (Thursday May 5) I arrived early at Arnstadt station on a misty morning promising more rain, and caught the 7.49am N-Zug from Arnstadt to Saalfeld, four coaches and 01.1531-1 again. Timekeeping was fairly simple and speeds were low between the frequent stops. We were delayed 2 minutes at Singen by a large party of schoolchildren joining the train and ran up to the early 80s (kph) down the Saale valley arriving at Saalfeld 2 minutes late. Our set, minus one coach that the 01 removed, formed E4400 9.06am Saalfeld-Erfurt and 03.2001-0 dropped onto us as soon as we stopped. The three coach train provided no obstacle as far as Rottenbach, where we were early, but after a 20kph engineering slack at Paulinzella we almost slipped to a standstill on the steep gradient and wet rails, eventually recovering amid sudden bouts of slipping to 46kph. Even so we arrived right time at Stadtilm and then drifted downhill to Arnstadt.

Back in Arnstadt in the cool wind and showery rain, I watched an N-Zug depart for Meiningen with a 228 diesel and decided to walk to the depot to see what was going on there. I meandered under the bridge by the main road and then took a long straight but narrow and tree-lined road. Patches of blue sky were beginning to appear, lighting up the dull red paintwork of a row of stored 228 diesels hiding behind the trees, which were outside the depot on a siding awaiting their fate. I discovered a gate leading into the depot and soon found myself peering down at 91.6580 belching smoke during fire cleaning. 50.3688 was under the coaling stage next to it. I found a way down to the roundhouse and there discovered 38.1182-5 inching its way forward onto the turntable. Prussian T20 2-10-2T 95.1027-2 was also in the roundhouse, dead, having suffered a failure and was under repair (91.6580 was covering its *Plandampf* turns). There were a couple of other dead tank engines in the roundhouse as well (a 74 2-6-0T and an 0-6-0T class 89). In the meantime, the class 50 came round for turning and coaling under an ancient hand operated grab crane.

Preserved Prussian P8 4-6-0 38.1182-5 rumbles onto the turntable at Arnstadt during the 1994 Erfurt-Meiningen *Plandampf*, 5 May 1994. (*Author*)

Arnstadt depot during the *Plandampf* with T20 2-10-2T 95.1027-2 which had failed and Prussian static exhibit 2-6-0T 74.231, 5 May 1994. (*Author*)

After a lengthy and nostalgic sojourn in the depot, I returned to the station and took a photo of a departing freight double-headed by 50.3688 and 91.6580. I then travelled to Meiningen on a three-coach N-Zug and large diesel 232.345-9 which managed to lose 22 minutes on the schedule, mainly through tardy trains at single line crossing stations. I was aiming to experience a run behind a Jumbo three-cylinder 2-10-0, 44.1093-2, which was diagrammed to work the seven-coach N6823 2.58pm Meiningen-Leipzig as far as Erfurt. I intended to take the 44 as far as Oberhof, returning with the Stralsund-Meiningen Schnellzug. The 44 accelerated well and kept time apart from a 4-minute wait at Dietzenhausen crossing a late running semi-fast. The big 2-10-0 sustained 60kph between stations on the climb with its 265 tonnes gross train, and 43kph above Suhl on the steepest part of the climb. This was more than enough for timekeeping and we arrived in soaking rain early at Oberhof.

The clouds seemed permanently settled over the hills above Oberhof and the surrounding pine forests were lost in swirling mist and drenching rain. The light was dwindling rapidly, I watched 44.1093 waffle off into the tunnel and then walked up the road to above the tunnel mouth, where there was a phalanx of photographers under a motley selection of brightly coloured umbrellas. Suddenly a thunderous noise burst through the gloom and two hard working steam locos could be heard, shutting off steam just before they came in sight. 50.3688 eased into view at the head of a long freight and drew round the curve up to the water column. Photography seemed a waste of time, although I snatched one shot of 50.3688 arriving on the freight train. After taking water, the two locos whistled up (91.6580 was the banker), and all the photographers had raised their cameras in readiness when the freight suddenly reversed into a siding out of sight to clear the line for a service passenger train. Multiple exasperation! As far as I was concerned, the light was already too far gone for my cheap substitute camera.

I returned to the station to await the D-Zug, which emerged from the tunnel 6 minutes late with 41.1185-2 and eight coaches, 325 tonnes gross – apparently the 41 was trusted to bring its load up the gradient without a banker. The rain resumed its relentless dominance and it was plain sailing for the 41 down the gradient reaching 103kph between stops. The sun now shone again in Meiningen, just as it had the day before, and I took another satisfying meal in the same restaurant before joining 41.1185-2 again on the last stopping train (N6840) to Erfurt. The 41 glowed in the evening sunset against the dark cloud background and the 2-8-2 made mincemeat of the schedule with its three-coach, featherweight train. The only real effort was to accelerate up the grade to 67kph after Suhl on the steepest grade before Zella-Mehlis. After Oberhof, the train glided downhill at a steady 90kph until Gräfenroda, where there was a 3-minute delay crossing D2159. A final 96kph before Arnstadt Süd and it was all over. Well nearly! Every year they say this *Plandampf* will be the last one, but even in 2007, there seems to have been one somewhere with a 52.80 2-10-0, and the narrow gauge Harz and Selketal railways keeping the steam flag flying. I think I'll leave it at this with my memories, but perhaps other readers might be tempted to seek out another 'final *Plandampf*' event!

Three cylinder freight 'Jumbo' 2-10-0 44.1093-2 at Meiningen with N6823, the 2.58pm stopping service to Leipzig, which the 2-10-0 will take as far as Erfurt, 5 May 1994. (*Author*)

Chapter 17

Special Trains, 1968-2010

UK steam was finished. That was what we all thought. In the summer of 1968, I took off for a fortnight of 'big' steam in France, 241P Mountains on the Le Mans-Nantes and Bourbonnais routes, former PLM Pacifics on the boat trains to and from Calais. I did it again in November, steam and snow with 241P 8 and 241P 24 on the Bourbonnais, more Pacifics in the raw cold at Amiens, and a final fling in the summer of 1969 with the few remaining Mountains alongside the River Loire.

There was one brief respite. An Irish preservation society had advertised a weekend excursion called the *Brian Boru* in the spring of 1969, and I took the ferry from Holyhead to Dun Laoghaire and caught the *Enterprise* behind a 1955 built Metrovick Co-Co (A59) to connect with the special which was starting from Belfast Great Victoria Street station the next morning. Sky blue GNR(I) 4-4-0 171 *Slieve Gullion* was the attractive motive power on a light train of five coaches, 160 tons gross. A 7 minute late departure – changing a vacuum pipe – had become 12 minutes by the time we reached the border at Dundalk, despite 72mph at Lurgan and 76 descending from Adavoyle, but after customs we were held to depart behind a DMU local and a series of signal checks, and two p-way slacks made us 40 minutes late at Dublin (Amiens Street – now Connolly). 171 was clearly struggling towards the end of the run and we discovered later that a gland had blown out shortly after leaving Dundalk.

At Dublin, 2-6-4 tank number 4 backed three more coaches for the Dublin enthusiasts to join us for the run via the main line to Cork. We were booked to be double-headed with 171, but the engine was failed there and after the gland was packed, it ran light to Dublin to join us the next day. The powerful tank engine performed with vigour and kept to the schedule throughout, with a top speed of 73mph between Limerick Junction and Mallow. Next morning, 171 had reappeared and, with No.4 bunker first as pilot, we were treated to a run past up Rathpeacon bank, having been bussed out to a suitably photogenic spot. At 9.50am, some 25 minutes late after tardy buses on congested roads returned us to Cork (Kent) station, we set off for real, with No.4 as pilot, to the top of the bank at Rathduff, then 171 tried a solo effort, before falling foul of the errant gland almost immediately

Preserved NCC 2-6-4T No.4 takes water at Portarlington on the Dublin-Cork leg of the *Brian Boru* railtour, May 1969. (*Author*)

Preserved GNR[I] 4-4-0 171 *Slieve Gullion* at the head of the *Brian Boru* two day rail tour from Belfast to Cork on arrival at Dublin Connolly [Amiens Street], May 1969. (*Author*)

and struggling to Limerick where we were 40 minutes late – 10 minutes of that attributable to 171's shortcomings. Then nemesis – No.4, which had caught us up and was being turned ready for double-heading us back to Dublin, managed to derail its pony truck on the throat to the engine shed, blocking 171 in as well and putting the rest of the tour in jeopardy. It was eventually rerailed and 171 released and the authorities decided to send us back via the main line instead of via Ennis and Athenry because of our lateness, the ailing 171 and the loss of No.4. The load was reduced to six coaches and 171 set off, its gland repacked temporarily once more, until we stopped at Ballybrophy to take water. Then No.4 appeared out of the ether and attached itself as pilot, bunker first as the authorities found the derailment on Limerick shed had been caused by poor track and thin tyres on the tank's pony truck. To our surprise the authorities decided No.4 could resume duties as long as the pony truck was trailing! We resumed our booked route from Ballybrophy, now running an hour late. The two engines disappeared to shed at Dublin and a few of us due to return to Belfast wondered what would happen next. Apparently, No.4 derailed again on shed and 171's gland packing had failed once more and it was with considerable surprise that we found our special continuing to Belfast at eleven o'clock at night with four coaches and both steam engines. We left 3 hours late and arrived at Belfast at ten to three in the morning after a very atmospheric run, stopping frequently in the pitch darkness behind an all stations DMU north of the border, the train swathed in steam – it was beautifully warm if nothing else!

That was it, then. I got married in September 1969 and settled to domestic life, whilst commuting daily on foot through the park in Bridgend to catch the train to Cardiff – I was then Divisional Train Planning Officer in Marland House at Cardiff. In 1971, two new things happened – my daughter, Helen, was born and 6000 *King George V* was resurrected from Bulmer's Sidings and made a successful return to BR metals, paving the way for a resumption of steam on the main line in the UK. I now had to balance my dual responsibilities of job and home with the opportunities afforded to engage in my hobby. I sought 'leave' for a long weekend tour in West Germany in 1972 – an LCGB tour by ship from Harwich to Emden and a tour on the lines around Friesland and the Ruhr behind DB three cylinder pacifics and 2-10-0s and then, that October, I joined a tour at Newport for a run over the North & West behind 6000 to Hereford and the lone double-chimneyed Jubilee, 5596 *Bahamas* on to Shrewsbury. For the first decade or more, steam engines were restricted to 60mph for insurance reasons on BR and 6000 could only show what it could do on the uphill sections. Llanvihangel Bank was taken easily with its 330 ton load, with 36mph on the steepest 1 in 82 section, accelerating to 42mph at the summit. 5596 ran under very light steam to a water stop at Ludlow and was then opened out climbing very noisily to Church Stretton with a minimum of 46, arriving 8 minutes early in Shrewsbury.

In 1973, the year my second daughter, Catherine, was born, I made just one day excursion, in October behind 4472 *Flying Scotsman,* an engine I'd nearly had in its final double-chimney form on the East Coast mainline, turning it down for a Gateshead

A4 (60005) instead. A heavy load, including 4472's second tender, 530 tons gross, was taken very noisily from Tyseley to Didcot. The start out of Leamington was very laboured but by Fenny Compton I could hear every exhaust beat very clearly from the fourteenth coach! After that, we loped through the countryside at the 60mph limit, stopped in the middle road at Oxford awaiting a path and arrived at Didcot 16 minutes late, where we were set loose around the GW depot.

In 1974, I got permission for two days off as well as a week in Germany to experience the three-cylinder oil-burning 012s on the Rheine-Emden-Norddeich line. I picked up at Newport a special that had started from Northampton – 4079 *Pendennis Castle* on ten coaches, 395 tons gross. Still restricted to 60mph, we ran easily except on the climbs through Cwmbran, to Llanvihangel and to Church Stretton – the latter bank was surmounted very creditably at 37mph at the summit. However we were badly delayed outside Shrewsbury because of a derailment at Sutton Bridge. The return journey southbound over the same route with 4472 was dire. We were stopped at Sutton Bridge Junction just 4 minutes out of Shrewsbury to pull brake chords – more 25in to 21in vacuum problems, perhaps. When we restarted it was apparent 4472 was winded and we crawled in the low twenties up the long grade to Church Stretton, falling to 18mph at the summit, although with the extra tender the trailing load was now 465 tons gross. Coasting downhill through Church Stretton, 4472 began to blow off steam, but progress after Hereford was pedestrian. It was clear that in a rerun of the 1925 exchange, 4079 was again the victor.

October 1974 saw me behind 6000 again on the North & West, this time southbound, leaving Shrewsbury 20 minutes late after arrival of the special from Euston via Crewe. The load was eleven coaches, 410 tons gross, and hill climbing was energetic enough for timekeeping despite three severe p-way slacks – probably bridge clearance problems, until two dead stands outside Hereford made us half an hour late there. The King detached two coaches and crimson 5690 *Leander* backed on and worked the nine coach 335 ton load to Oxford. Despite working hard, we dropped nearly 10 minutes to Worcester, but then time recovery began, we fell to a minimum of 27mph on Chipping Campden Bank and after a water stop at Moreton-in-Marsh, we exceeded our 60mph speed limit, reaching 72 at Handborough and arrived 25 minutes late.

After a farewell to West German steam at Rheine in January 1975, I was 'permitted' one rail tour a year by my infant daughters and in June1975 I joined a Nottingham-Ravenglass rail tour at Carnforth, where V2 4771 *Green Arrow* and B1 1306 *Mayflower* were waiting for the train, which arrived half an hour late behind 4472, after a diversion in the East Midlands following a derailment. The pair took it in turns to perform, with the B1 doing all the initial work, to Ulverston, after which the V2 burst into syncopated life. Between them, they recovered most of the lost time, albeit without exceeding 55mph on the coast run. After a pleasant jaunt on the 'Ratty', the pair turned an 18 minute late departure into a 5 minute late arrival only at Carnforth – but it was the B1 doing all the work, throwing sparks high into the air as the V2's brick arch had collapsed.

B1 1306 *Mayflower*, paired with V2 4771 *Green Arrow* at Carnforth waiting for the Nottingham-Ravenglass rail tour, which arrived 30 minutes late behind 4472 *Flying Scotsman*, June 1975. (*Author*)

In April 1976, I went ambling round the East Anglian countryside with S15 30841 taking over from a Class 37 at Manningtree, which ran across the Fens to March via Stowmarket and Ely, touching a surprising 68mph at Soham. A pair of Brush 31s took over at March and drew us on to Loughborough for a run over the Great Central with Black 5 45231. A couple of months later I sampled the weird combination of LNWR Jumbo 2-4-0 No.790 *Hardwicke* piloting 92220 *Evening Star* from Carnforth to Leeds City – the pair racing through Keighley at an illegal 73mph with a heavy thirteen coach 480 ton load. 4472 left Leeds 25 late with a reduced load – eleven coaches, 420 tons gross – and managed to drop another 25 minutes, although this included a wait of 10 minutes at Knaresborough awaiting a DMU off the single line. However, 15mph up Horsforth bank out of Leeds was hardly scintillating and it took us 96 minutes to get from Leeds to York via Harrogate. Later in the day 45407 and 61306 double-headed us back to Carnforth and excelled themselves by arriving 11 minutes early.

1977 saw me on a special from Hereford to Chester behind 6201 *Princess Elizabeth* returning from Chester with 6000 and in September my son, Christopher, was born. In March 1978 I had a day out in Scotland with 60009 *Union of South Africa* from Edinburgh to Aberdeen and back, out via Dundee and Montrose and back via Dundee, Perth, Stirling and Falkirk. We were hampered by the 60mph limit but the noise was nice – both the three-cylinder exhaust when working uphill and the chime whistle. A further run with 4771 round the circle from York to Leeds was followed by the one run with Royal Scot 6115 *Scots Guardsman* in LMS black livery, plenty of sparks flying in the November murk. After a fairly bright start to Sheffield, it palled horribly on the climb to Totley Tunnel, barely sustaining 16mph with its twelve-coach load, then stopped at Grindleford Box for a blow-up and to allow the fireman some respite, going into the tender to drag coal forward. It managed to take 106 minutes from Sheffield to Guide Bridge, from whence it retired to Dinting and other workshops for thirty years before re-emerging in Brunswick Green to do great work over the Northern Fells.

I abstained from steam in 1979 and had just one tour in 1980 – an interesting Northern tour starting 40 minutes late from Manchester Piccadilly with 40.020 to Guide Bridge where two of the Woodhead route electric locos, 76.011 and 76.021 (ex 26011/21), climbed through Woodhead Tunnel at a steady 48mph with the 420 ton train. No further time was lost and another 40 (083) took us the short distance from Rotherwood Junction into Leeds. There the combination of 4771 (again) and the beautiful crimson Midland Compound, 1000, as pilot, recovered a quarter of an hour to Hellifield and a further 5 minutes onto Carnforth with a nice 72mph after the 'other' Clapham Junction. 4498 *Sir Nigel Gresley* was waiting to take us back to Manchester Victoria via Blackburn. An A4 is not the ideal motive power for such a route full of slacks and we were losing time, taking it very easily past Clitheroe with the fire giving trouble, clinkering up. We stopped at Blackburn to take water and clean the fire and left 34 minutes late. With full steam pressure restored, we roared up through Sough Tunnel at 34mph, regaining 12 minutes in the first dozen miles and touched 75mph at Clifton Junction before arriving at Manchester twenty 20 minutes late.

In 1981, I was drawn like a moth to the flame by the prospect of a Lord Nelson on the Settle & Carlisle. If you have read my descriptions in *A Privileged Journey* of my experiences with the class on Southern commuter trains, you will know that I was harbouring a sense of awful foreboding at what might take place, especially when I saw that the load from Carlisle on this wet January day was a heavy thirteen

Midland Compound 1000 and V2 *Green Arrow* pause for a photo-shoot at the 'other' Clapham Junction, having taken over the Manchester originating railtour at Leeds from a pair of Woodhead electrics and a class 40. They would take the train on to Carnforth, where 4498 *Sir Nigel Gresley* would return the railtour to Manchester Victoria, 1980. (*Author*)

coaches, 510 tons gross. I was used to straining to hear a slight waffling noise as we shuffled out of Woking towards London and it was indeed a novelty to really hear 850 *Lord Nelson*'s thunderous exhaust as we lifted this load out of Carlisle. We made respectable time to Appleby – 'roared' (!) out and got stuck into the climb through Crosby Garrett and Smardale, when there was a shuddering in the train, the brakes began to leak on and speed fell to 12mph, with great lumps of burning coal falling onto the luckily sopping turf. 'Here we go again', I thought, 'out of steam already.' We stood for 5 minutes at Kirkby Stephen with the blower on and a volcanic show of black smoke rising heavenwards, when we restarted with the most ear-splitting din I've ever heard from a 'Nellie' and held 29mph at Mallerstang, accelerated to 38 on the gradient easing, then topped Ais Gill at 28mph and arrived at Garsdale, unbelievably only 1 minute late. We left there 7 minutes early after watering and coasted down the bank arriving at Hellifield 4 minutes early. This run is a total mystery to me. There is no doubt that we ran out of steam at Kirkby Stephen, but the recovery after only 5 minutes was awesome, although I and the fire brigade are heartedly glad that the moors were sodden. I'm told that this was a test to see what load the Nelson could be allowed over this route. I'm not sure what lesson they drew from the experience. 44767 *George Stephenson*, the Black 5 with Stephenson's Link Motion, took over the full 13 coach load at Hellifield and after a dead stand at Settle Junction, was driven all out on the 2 miles of 1 in 100 through Giggleswick and accelerated on the gradient to 37mph, a phenomenal effort for a class 5 power classification.

In May 1982, I rose early in anticipation of a run over the Settle & Carlisle with my favourite Southern locomotive, 777 *Sir Lamiel*. To this day I have a guilty conscience over this trip. The night before, as friends left our house late, their car unfortunately ran over and killed our five-month old kitten. I buried the poor thing and left early in the morning before the children were up, not realising the extent of grief that my wife was left to cope with – three wailing children for most of the day apparently. I was therefore oblivious of all this as 777 backed onto our train at Carlisle just before midday for the southbound run. We had ten coaches, 395 tons gross and ran hard to Appleby topping the 1 in 132 after Cotehill at 46mph, 64 in the dip after Lazonby and then 47 minimum at Langwathby at the top of the 1 in 132/110. We arrived in Appleby 6 minutes early, but a slow running water column meant we were 12 minutes late away. We accelerated to 53mph before Ormside Viaduct, then fell to and held 34mph to Mallerstang, 32 at Ais Gill and arrived at Garsdale just 4 minutes late. 777 primed on leaving Garsdale and we took it easily until we passed through Blea Moor Tunnel, then coasted down to Settle in the mid-60s before a very long p-way slack to 20mph at Long Preston made us 9 minutes late at Hellifield. 45407 did the honours onto Carnforth and turned a half hour late departure into a 5 minute early arrival at Carnforth – but that was because we omitted the photographic stop at Clapham Junction as the light had grown poor and we were running late.

In 1985 it was the 150th Anniversary of the Great Western Railway and there were a number of special runs to celebrate this – not all of them successful. However, on 1 September I joined an excellent run from Plymouth to Bristol on the *Great*

Western Limited, double-headed by a pair of Castles, 5051 *Dryslwyn Castle* (formerly *Earl Bathurst*) and 7029 *Clun Castle*. The load was eleven coaches, 440 tons gross, and departure was just a minute late. The start out of North Road was very measured, but the pair took Hemerdon with some ease, surmounting the 1 in 42 at 22mph, gaining 2½ minutes on the climb, and, with both locomotives blowing off steam, topped Dainton at 24mph, now nearly 10 minutes early. The engines were watered at Newton Abbot and departure was 9 minutes late. Clearly, the schedule was absurdly easy for we were on time by Exeter without any rush of blood round the coastal section and then, after a 20mph p-way slowing at Collumpton, we cleared Whiteball at 53mph and coasted down the other side at 70mph until stopped for 10 minutes at Silk Mill Box as we'd activated a hot box detector. After a quick examination of both locos, it was established that the heat from the passing engines had fooled the machine and we were able to resume, Taunton being reached six minutes late in consequence. Without anything over 65mph, we were 4 minutes early by Bridgwater and went via Weston-super-Mare for pathing purposes. Finally, both engines were given their head and sustained 75mph from Yatton to Nailsea and a final 2 minute stand for signals outside Temple Meads could not stop them arriving nearly 5 minutes early.

5051 *Earl Bathurst* [renamed *Dryslwyn Castle* for this run] and 7029 *Clun Castle* power up Dainton Bank regaining time on a GW 150 Anniversary Train from Plymouth to Bristol, 1 September 1985. (*Author*)

The author with Driver Callum McRaild in the cab of K1 2005 during the run on the *Jacobite* to Mallaig, July 1987 (*Author*)

1986 was a fallow year as far as UK specials were concerned – although it was eventful in that I moved on from Regional Operating Manager at Crewe to being BR's first Reliability and Quality Manager. Although not really a special and therefore falling outside the scope of this chapter, I was invited by a former LMR Area Manager, by then at Fort William, as a sort of farewell to my Operating job, to enjoy a footplate run on one of the *Jacobite* regular runs from Fort William to Mallaig and back. I went with Driver Callum MacRaild, Fireman Graham Lloyd and Inspector Colin Ross on Black 5, 44932 – the hardest work was climbing with its six coach 215 ton gross train from Glenfinnan Viaduct up gradients averaging 1 in 50 at an earsplitting 28-30mph, whilst blowing off steam simultaneously. The 1 in 48 to Beasdale summit was finally cleared at 24mph. Unfortunately, that only presaged a long wait at Arisaig (whose beautiful surroundings compensated us) as a scheduled DMU from Mallaig was running 25 minutes late. The following year, I was invited again and took my place on apple-green liveried K1, 2005. With the same driver, we almost duplicated 44932's speeds before Lochailort and then recovered from a dead stand there to 24mph at Beasdale summit.

I came back to renewed interest in UK specials in 1995 when the spectacular 'locomotive trial' over Shap was conducted with the three main contenders for BR's most powerful pacific, 4498, 46229 and 71000. I rode on two of those behind 46229 and 71000 – the latter the clear winner on this occasion. The runs were well publicised at the time, so I'll not go into a full description here. Suffice to say that the noise and excitement as 71000 took its eleven coaches up Grayrigg at over 60mph and roared over Shap Summit at 54mph was stupendous.

From the footplate of 'Black 5' 44932 as it climbs the 1 in 48 of Beasdale Bank at a steady 24mph with the *Jacobite*, July 1986. The author had just moved on from his position as Regional Operating Manager LMR and one of his former Area Managers, now AM Fort William, organised this footplate trip. (*Author*)

A similar trip was arranged the following summer, when the *Jacobite* was hauled by apple-green K1 2005, which is also seen climbing Beasdale Bank at an identical 24mph, July 1987. (*Author*)

In 1998 I enjoyed a special of a different sort, when Virgin Trains provided an ex-works HST for guests at the first Railway Children charity ball held that year at the National Railway Museum. Power car 43098 was named *The Railway Children* at Euston before departure by Sally Thomsett (Phyllis in the famous film of the same name) and we went via Birmingham and the cross-country route to York to stay in Virgin territory.

I'd retired from BR and Railtrack employment by 1996 although I continued undertaking safety consultancy work for another five years or so. This gave me even more time to follow my main interests, although by this time the building of the charity for street children living on or around railway stations in the world was taking priority. However, in 1999 I couldn't resist the proposed run with a King over Shap. If I thought 6024 was going to give 71000 and 46229 a challenge, I was unfortunately wrong, as poor coal and a congealed and dirty fire after a long pathing and water stop at Barton & Broughton caused 6024 to stagger over Grayrigg at not much more than walking pace and stall altogether half way up Shap. It was remarkable that after a 20 minute stand with blower hard on and vigorous efforts by the fireman with the long pricker (despite the overhead lines) the King was able to restart the 480 ton train without assistance and without a slip in the pouring rain, although we were now nearly 2 hours late. The fire was thoroughly cleaned at Carlisle and the return run was at a very high level of performance. Leaving Carlisle 90 minutes late, 6024 stormed to Shap in just over 38 minutes with a minimum of 48 at Shap station and 50 at the summit, touching 85 on the descent through Tebay and another 84 before Oxenholme, pulling back 10 minutes of lost time before the water stop at Carnforth.

Sally Thomsett, one of the stars of the 1970's film *The Railway Children*, names Virgin HST power car 43098 *Railway Children* after the charity at Euston station, before taking guests to the first Railway Children Ball, May 1998. (*Author*)

A further 83mph on the level at Brock reduced our lateness further (we had cut nearly 30 minutes off our watering time at Carnforth also) and we left Preston 39 minutes late. We were well out of our path, however, and were sidelined at Springs Branch for the 6.15pm Carlisle to pass us. Our fire was now deteriorating and we took it easily to Crewe arriving 3 minutes under the hour late.

Also in 1999 a special train went from King's Cross to York in connection with a possible launch of an initiative called 'Rail 2000' – the proposal for a major exhibition based on Shildon Museum at which Railway Children was to be a key partner. This did not come to fruition. However, I travelled in the cab of Deltic D9009 *Alycidon* as far as Peterbrough – a noisy and exhilarating experience – and saw 45407 take the special on from York to Darlington. A couple of special events that did take place in 2000 and in which I participated were the 'Steam Weekend on the Met' and a run over the North Wales coast line behind 5029 *Nunney Castle*. The 'Met' excursions on the late May Bank holiday were very happy affairs with WR 0-6-0T 9466, LM 2MT 2-6-2T 41312, K1 62005, and B12/3 61572 all performing with vigour up the bank from Rickmansworth to Amersham.

The *Ynys Mon Express* in October took place in gale force winds and torrential rain. This was no hindrance to 5029 and its ten-coach, 385 ton load on the outward run facing into the gale, with 76mph being achieved between Crewe and Chester and magnificent running at a steady 78-82mph between Holywell Junction and a 30mph restriction through Prestatyn, recovering from a long signal check at Saltney Junction that had cost us 12 minutes. We were only 6 minutes late into Llandudno Junction where we were meant to replenish our water supply but could coax nothing from the supply available so we took it easily on to Holyhead, especially on Anglesey, where flooding of the track forced us to walking pace. We arrived 11 minutes late at Holyhead Harbour station.

Our return was more problematical. Despite all the external rain water, our loco had problems in obtaining a sufficient supply to top up the nearly empty tender and that delay, then a loss of path, meant we left Holyhead 51 minutes late. More flood restrictions and signal checks made us 56 minutes late at Llandudno Junction where we were more successful in finding a working fire hydrant and left 48 minutes late. We were clearly following a service train and kept speeds to the mid-60s to avoid further checks and arrived at Crewe exactly 51 minutes late – as we had been leaving Holyhead.

In April 2002, I enjoyed a trip behind 6233 *Duchess of Sutherland* on its Crewe-Carlisle home territory. The Duchess, in the capable hands of Bill Andrews and Frank Santrian of Crewe, performed in an exemplary manner, arriving on time at Barton Loop with a maximum of 79mph before Acton Grange Junction and 62mph minimum at Boars Head with its 430 ton train. We left Carnforth Loop 5 minutes early, held to 51mph at Grayrigg before a 15mph long p-way slowing at the top, accelerated to 78mph by Tebay and fell to 49 at Scout Green, then actually accelerated again to 53 at Shap summit. With 77 through Plumpton, we were threatening to arrive at Carlisle extremely early, but we were forced to wait for 60009 departing 14 minutes late with a special on the Settle & Carlisle, and arrived exactly 1 minute early. A similar exemplary return saw us 2 minutes early into Carnforth Goods Loop and then a somewhat erratic playing with the schedule restarting from Carnforth 21 minutes early, waiting at Preston for the 4.06pm Glasgow Voyager to pass, then signals approaching Crewe, but we were still 4 minutes early at the end of the day.

2003 was a barren year as far as rail excursions were concerned but I was tempted by a two day special in May 2004 to celebrate the seventy-fifth anniversary of the *Golden Arrow*. The twelve-coach, 480 ton gross load was hauled into Victoria by a class 66, which was meant to bank the train, hauled in full Golden Arrow regalia by 34067 *Tangmere*, but at the end of the platform the diesel ground to a halt because its TPWS equipment tripped at the signal at the platform end and 34067 stalled on the climb to Grosvenor Bridge. After a 15 minute wait, 66249 was able to resume and got us going again and we romped away to 73mph at Penge before two signal stands at Bromley South and Petts Wood Juction as we were out of our path. We recovered with great vigour, roaring (do Bulleid Pacifics roar?) over the summit of the 1 in 120 at 68mph, touched 78 on the descent from Knockholt, followed by a full 84mph at Hildenborough and a sustained 81 on the level through Paddock Wood and Marden before the first water stop at Headcorn, where we were almost on time. However, the road water tanker failed to show up and we were rescued by the local fire brigade, although we exceeded our allowance as water pressure was low. Another 78 before Ashford was the end of the high speed, but a routing via Canterbury West, Sandwich and Deal was interesting and to accelerate our heavy load from a dead stand (signals again) just before Deal station up the 1 in 70 through Walmer to Martin Mill to a rousing 45mph was first class, although, because of the various delays and setbacks, we were 20 minutes late at Dover Priory

and managed to miss the ferry to Calais! A splendid thirty-six hours was then spent in France with former PLM Pacific 231K 8 literally flying the flag all the way from Calais Ville to Paris and back, with diversions round the Paris Ceinture lines with a somewhat short of steam 2-8-0 140C 231 and a stop at Noyelles on the return to experience the light Baie de Somme railway. Then, after the crossing back to Dover, nemesis – 34067 after its excellent performance the previous day, was found on servicing after the run to have leaking tubes and was

34067 *Tangmere* at the head of the seventy-fifth Anniversary *Golden Arrow* before departure from Victoria, May 2004. (*Author*)

Vintage Train's 4965 *Rood Ashton Hall* at Knowle & Dorridge before departure with the Christmas luncheon round-trip to Coalville, 17 December 2004. The author was invited to the footplate on the return leg at Nuneaton and successfully fired the engine to the Tyseley terminus. (*Author*)

failed. Our run home to London behind a grey freight 37, 37.689, was a punctual anti-climax.

Another special I joined in 2004 doesn't qualify for inclusion as no steam power was involved – although a fair bit of energy was expended as it was the Railway Children's *Three Peaks Challenge* – the train sponsored by Network Rail, EWS and Virgin with other rail associated companies providing free services and fifty teams of four ascending Snowdon, Scafell Pike and Ben Nevis in 36 hours. The train was variously hauled by 90031 *The Railway Children Partnership*, the royal 67006, and a pair of 37/4s over the West Highland. We made £180,000 for the charity.

Finally, I joined Tyseley's Christmas lunch special for a run around the Midlands behind the excellent 4965 *Rood Ashton Hall* which was easily on top of its job and on which I was invited to renew my firing skills on the last leg from Nuneaton back to Tyseley after a very full lunch including Christmas Pudding (but no wine – I had been pre-warned!). I found it surprisingly easy to maintain pressure as we barked away from Nuneaton up the 1 in 123/126 to Stockingfold Tunnel, just falling from 47 to 44mph at the summit and sustaining 65mph on slightly rising gradients at Washwood Heath. The load was a featherweight 195 tons, however.

In 2005, my sole outing was on an Irish Rail special from Dublin to Sligo and back, behind the last two single cab GM diesels, 124 and 134, in aid of Railway Children, but in 2006 I was invited to another high profile special to Glasgow, during which I was to receive a very generous donation for the charity from the authors and publishers of the book written to celebrate the centenary of Glasgow Central station. The occasion was, of course, the seventieth anniversary of *Princess Elizabeth*'s record braking 1936 runs, which we were to replicate – as far as we could with current speed limitations – between Preston and Glasgow. The load was only seven passenger coaches, but the addition of unpowered 67012 trailing made the gross load 345 tons behind the tender. On the 16 November, therefore, we left Preston 8 minutes late,

Preserved Princess Royal 6201 *Princess Elizabeth* stands at Preston with its support coach ready to take over the special train commemorating the seventieth anniversary of its record breaking run from diesel locomotive 67012, 16 November 2006. (*Author*)

which we turned into a 35 minute early arrival at Oxenholme having omitted the scheduled and unnecessary pathing stop at Carnforth, after sustained speed in the mid-70s from Garstang onwards. We left Oxenholme a full three quarters of an hour early, accelerated up Grayrigg Bank to 42mph near the summit, when we were slowed, being turned into the loop there for a 10 minute stop to let a Voyager pass. We accelerated hard to pass Tebay, still 31 minutes early, at 74mph and dropped to 45 at Scout Green as we faced a fierce side wind. We passed Shap summit at 33mph in 7 minutes, 7 seconds from Tebay and ran into the loop behind the platform at Penrith half an hour early to take on both coal and water. Leaving on time, we touched 77mph on the descent to Carlisle arriving 3 minutes early and leaving 2 minutes late. With a 79 at Gretna junction, we roared up the 5 miles of 1 in 200 to Kirkpatrick at a minimum of 70mph to another pathing stop at Lockerbie on time. We left on time, got up to 74 at Wamphray before the climb to Beattock Summit, passed Beattock station, having already gained 4 minutes on schedule at 68mph and did not fall below 45 on the main climb before arriving at the Summit loop in 16 minutes 32 seconds from Beattock station, 6 minutes early. We took water at Abington, stopped at Carstairs to pick up a pilotman and ran easily to Glasgow Central threatening to arrive 12 minutes early until a signal stop on the bridge over the Clyde outside the station made us just 2 minutes early in.

The return journey the next morning was a similar punctuality tour de force. Despite a 13 minute late departure because of late arrival of the stock (our diesel overtime fuelling), we were already 16 minutes early by Law Junction having gone via Bellshill and Wishaw, and drew into Carstairs Up Goods Loop 21 minutes early. After taking water again at Abington and leaving 7 minutes late behind a tardy Voyager, we sailed onwards, ignoring a pathing stop to let a Pendolino pass until Quintinshill, and then, despite the usual stop outside Carlisle, we were 7 minutes early in, where 6201 cut off and went to Upperby for coal and water. We fell to 37 at Shap Summit, passed in 41 minutes 55 seconds from Carlisle, and were still 9 minutes late into Oxenholme Goods Loop. The rest was easy. Leaving another pathing stop at Carnforth just 3 minutes late, we raced for home and sustained 75-78mph from Bay Horse to Barton and Broughton, arriving at Preston exactly on time.

There was a final lull in my excursions until May 2009, when Bob Meanley of Tyseley invited me to be his guest on a couple of runs over Shap with rivals 46115 *Scots Guardsman* and newly restored double-chimney Castle, 5043 *Earl of Mount Edgcumbe*. On 9 May, the special arrived on time into Crewe from Birmingham behind Les Ross' blue 86.259 (known in my LM operating days as *Peter Pan,* when it had been my bugbear, failing twice spectacularly on my return from General Manager meetings in London on successive weeks). However, on this occasion it performed in an exemplary manner, reaching Preston from Crewe in the scheduled 41 minutes. A beautifully polished 46115 set off from Preston with eleven coaches, 425 tons gross, with some difficulty and 4 minutes late, having to set back, and then slipping and we dropped a couple of minutes to Lancaster despite reaching 78 at Oubeck and were 8 minutes late into the Carnforth water stop. We left on time and were going well by Oxenholme, which we passed at 60mph, and went over Grayrigg at an excellent 46mph, passing Tebay at 78, now 6 minutes early ready for a record attempt at Shap, matching its performance a few weeks earlier on another special. However, at that very moment we ran into heavy squalls of rain and the Scot lost its feet at MP 53, and again at Scout Green where we had fallen to 33mph. We fell further to 29mph at MP 37.5 before recovering to 34 through the final rock cutting to Shap summit and were still 3 minutes early into our pathing stop at Penrith, with a maximum of 77 at Clifton.

The return run as far as Carnforth was superb. We passed Penrith at 73mph in 23 minutes 13 seconds, already 2 minutes up, and then roared away to a minimum of 53 at the top of the 1 in 125 to Shap, 57 through Shap station and 51 at the final summit. We passed the summit in 36 minutes 45 seconds, the record with a 4-6-0 on this load and well up with the best Pacific runs. We ran easily downhill with nothing over 72, passing Tebay 8 minutes early, coasted down Grayrigg and after a 2 minute stand on the main line at Carnforth awaiting a path to cross to the Down Goods Loop, we ran in 3 minutes early. We were held awaiting the road behind a late running Virgin train and then things deteriorated. With nothing over the mid-60s and signs of a dirty fire and steaming problems around Brock, we were brought to a stand by signals at MP 3 and were 21 minutes late into Preston, where we handed over to 86.259 once more. We now had to wait six weeks to see how 5043 would fare amid the speculation following previous bad experiences with both 6024 and 5029 on the fells. 7029 had fared well in 1967, but with only a very light train.

This time, on June 20, a Brush type 47 had brought the rail tour excursion more or less punctually from Birmingham and the steam locomotive took over at Crewe. 5043 *Earl of Mount Edgcumbe* backed on with its support coach making a ten-coach train weighing 383 tons gross, and with Crewe driver, Bill Andrews, at the regulator and with owner Bob Meanley's son, Andrew, as fireman, we set off hopefully for the north, GW enthusiasts' hearts in their mouth after so much previous disappointment on this route and with the comments of all GW denigrators' words ringing in their ears! The initial part of the run was fine, as had been 6024's before its disgrace. We were running at 78mph within 10 miles of the start, having already overturned a 2 minute late departure into two early past Weaver Junction where we obeyed a 40mph p-way slack, were up to 75 again by Bamfurlong, climbed the 1 in 104 to Boars Head with a minimum of 63mph, then ground to a stand at Euxton Junction as we were running too early. Despite this brief signal stand, we crawled through Preston 4 minutes early and ran at a steady 75-76mph from Brock to Oubeck, before a couple of severe signal checks which prevented us showing off to the crowds on Lancaster station. With a crawl into the Carnforth Down Goods Loop we were still a minute early.

5043 left the train to go onto Carnforth depot to take on water and after waiting for a Virgin train to precede us, we departed 2 minutes late for the real test. We barked strongly up the 1 in 134 to MP 9.5 at 42, then touched 68 before the climb to Grayrigg began. We passed Oxenholme now 2 minutes early at 58mph, with two-thirds regulator and 28 per cent cut-off according to Bob Meanley who was on the footplate, and topped Grayrigg summit at 46mph. We accelerated swiftly through the Lune Gorge to 78 at Tebay, now 6 minutes early, and with the same regulator opening, cut-off was advanced to 33 per cent at Scout Green, hardly excessive, but enough to avoid falling below 40mph and accelerating to 44 on the last level quarter mile to the summit board. We were stopped just after Shap station to be warned of emergency track repairs and then sailed downhill in the mid-70s to arrive, after a crawl up Carlisle platform, just 1 minute late. Smirks on the faces of GW fans were perceived and a number of pints were bought by the confounded doubters in various Carlisle pubs that lunchtime!

The King had recovered its reputation on the southbound climb to Shap, and 5043 showed that its morning run was no short-lived wonder, and very nearly matched 46115's southbound Shap run, passing the summit in 37 minutes 5 seconds at 54mph, still blowing off steam from time to time on the ascent. With 77 down the bank, we were seven early as we passed Tebay and a full 78 at Oxenholme led to us being 9 minutes early there, before a 10 minute stand on the Up Main waiting passage over to the Down Goods Loop at Carnforth meant we were just a minute late in.

A couple of minutes late departure from Carnforth was recovered by Preston with a glorious spell of running nearly touching 80 at Brock, before grinding to a halt in Preston station for half an hour as all trains were at a standstill because of points failures around the station. Despite this being the end of nearly 300 miles of steaming, 5043 was still game, with steam to spare, as we sped up to 79mph after we had regained the fast line at Balshaw Lane. A slight signal check before Warrington, then the upper 70s again before a 50mph slack at Weaver Junction (now 27 minutes late), then another rousing 75 at Hartford before a crawl to walking pace past Crewe Coal Yard Box and threading our way across the throat at the north end of Crewe station to platform 12, where we arrived 28 minutes late – the lateness caused solely by the points problems at Preston. 47.580 coupled on ahead of 5043 for the home run to Tyseley, but I left at this point, well satisfied with the day and the vindication of GW locomotives' reputation on the northern fells.

Chapter 18

The Jingpeng Orient Express

I'd seen photos. Photos of massive double-headed freights pounding through an arctic landscape. A brand new railway in 1995 with semaphore signals, oil lamps and steam engines built in the late 1980s. It was remote, alien, difficult. Then an opportunity arose. Tim Littler's travel company in Altrincham teamed up with Steam Railways' Nigel Harris to advertise the first group visit to the Jingpeng pass in 2002 using a special tourist train – said to be Mao Tse Tung's own until converted for tourist use as the country opened up to overseas visitors. It was expensive of course, but the children had grown up and fled the nest. My middle daughter had been living in Kenya for a number of years and had married an American teaching at an international school in Nairobi. I made my peace with Pat, my wife, by promising her an appropriate number of flights to Kenya to equal my expenditure on the Chinese railtour, and – in the end – she almost fulfilled her part of the bargain.

There were seventy-two passengers on this most exclusive and ground-breaking rail tour and we flew initially to Beijing and for a couple of days became typical tourists visiting Tiananmen Square, the Forbidden Palace and the other major famous sites on every visitor's list of 'must-sees'. There were said to be thirty five star hotels in this paradise for the proletariat and the city – on the surface – was like so many other glamorous first world cities. Then, on the second day, we boarded a coach to take us to our first railway visit, a 2ft 6in narrow gauge limestone railway just 45 minutes by road from the centre of Beijing. Well, that was what the brochure said. After a further 30 minutes or so, the bus driver admitted that he was lost, the Dahuichang railway not being on the normal tourist trail, and we finished up following a cyclist through narrow slumlike alleyways before alighting at a dilapidated limestone unloading plant in which a couple of ancient rusting narrow-gauge 0-8-0s stood oozing steam and Dickensian decrepitude at the head of a set of primitive unbraked hopper wagons. While we watched the incongruous vision of nineteenth-century technology just an hour away from Beijing's twenty-first century infrastructure, one locomotive shuddered into movement and began to propel its raft of hoppers into the corrugated shed over the gap where each hopper was upended in turn to spew its stone in a thundering cloud of white dust. When the shunter wanted to halt the raft of hoppers he merely thrust his metal pole between the spokes of one of the hopper wheels and the wagons would come to a sliding slithering squealing halt.

Meanwhile, the other locomotive, without any visible sign of identity, set off from the siding, where the empties had been accumulating, up the hill to the limestone quarry about 2 miles away for the next load. These two trains see-sawed for the next couple of hours, while we gaped at the sight and scattered round the

Chinese limestone railway 0-8-0 2ft 6in narrow gauge locomotive at Dahuichang, 45 minutes from the centre of Beijing, March 2002. (*Author*)

Two stored 0-8-0 narrow gauge locomotives at the small corrugated iron shed at Dahuichang limestone works, March 2002. (*Author*)

252

area taking innumerable photos. Someone discovered the little tin engine shed and two more dead locomotives of the same type – the standard Chinese narrow gauge loco – inside. One had clearly not moved for months as there appeared to be a bird's nest in the wire mesh acting as a filter over the engine's smoke stack. Eventually, as dusk began to fall, we tore ourselves away from this scene – now alas no more as the quarry and limeworks closed a couple of years later. We made our way back to our five star hotel, checked out and were chaperoned to the main railway station and ensconced in the 'soft class' waiting room to await permission to join our special train. No train-spotters allowed here and, I noted, also none of the street children that one would have found swarming round a major station in India. It was more like an air terminal, with passengers being invited to board their trains and released from the appropriate waiting area only when their train was platformed and ready.

Our thirteen-coach train, some 715 tons tare, consisted of a kitchen car with a dining saloon either side, a lounge and bar car and then the passenger vehicles arrayed either side of that. Each vehicle had its own female attendant fetchingly and most unsuitably attired in a pale pink jacket uniform and – I gathered later – each of these reported to a manager who in turn reported to the Train Manager and other hierarchy of officials. These, with the catering and train crew staff, meant that our seventy-two passengers were to be served by seventy Chinese Rail staff throughout the tour – a ratio that did not seem exactly productive and certainly might have accounted for part of the cost, although it may have been part of the Chinese government's policy to ensure full employment and therefore a disincentive to rebellious acts. I made myself comfortable in my cabin, not unlike the compartments in the Orient Express – in

One of the carriage attendants arrayed in the tourist train uniform of pale pink overcomes her curiosity by climbing onto the dirt of the cab of QJ 6992, exploring the unaccustomed steam haulage of the thirteen coach special train, March 2002. (*Author*)

China Rail JS 2-8-2 6403 begins the climb from Chengde exchange sidings to the steelworks with a load of coal, March 2002. (*Author*)

fact our train tour was entitled *The Jingpeng Orient Express*. We adjourned to one of the dining cars for our first dinner on board and partook of a variety of Chinese dishes with only chopsticks to handle – the wide variety of meat and fish became the same wide variety at every lunch and dinner for the menu itself never varied, except when we were out for the day in the photo-shoot minibuses, when we were each provided with the standard Chinese packed lunch of noodles, hard-boiled egg and apple.

A standard DF4 diesel electric loco, No.1589, took our entourage gently through the night to Chengde, the site of the Emperor's Summer Palace, but our goal was rather different. The China Rail main line connects here with an industrial branch high into the hills where a major steelworks is located and freight to and from the exchange sidings was handled in March 2002 exclusively by steam. The locoshed at the summit of a long heavily graded section, through the streets of Chengde and then into the hills, services a number of JS 2-8-2 locos and the more modern SY light axle 2-8-2s, which were being built new, mainly for industrial systems right up to the year 2000. Trains of coal for the steel works start from the exchange sidings with a JS or SY, and, after bisecting the town, stop outside the prison where normally two bankers of the same types are added to attack the 1 in 33 gradients to be surmounted.

We were bussed with our packed lunches to a hillside where the locomotives would be working flat out and we waited and adjusted our cameras while a series of trains stormed up the incline, one of them literally setting the scene alight as the sparks from the labouring locomotives caught the dry grass. This was said to be the last location in the world where steam banking locomotives were regularly used, and the more remarkable in that most trains were charging the hills with two. Three JS, 5634, 6227 and 6403 were seen going up and down the line and SYs 0532, 0533, 1029, 1522, 1753 and 1765, the latter two built in 1998. We moved on to the yard and loco depot at the entrance to the steelworks and found it to be a hive of activity, with around three freights shunting or being prepared at any one time, as well as seeing two or three locos under the coal stage, taking water or having their fire cleaned. In the steelworks itself SY 0872 was shunting, but there was a line of dead JS and SY locomotives awaiting repair or scrapping.

JS 2-8-2 drawing a load of oil tankers out from the Chengde steelworks exchange sidings whilst two SY 2-8-2s wait to proceed with trains of coal, March 2002. (*Author*)

A 1998 built SY 2-8-2 1765 tackles the 1 in 33 to Chengde Steelworks banked by JS and SY 2-8-2s at the rear, March 2002. (*Author*)

While we were awaiting the next sortie from the city, we noticed a number of people, including children, scouring the line with sacks. We deduced in the end that they were gathering unburnt coal that had been thrown from the hard-working engines' chimneys and that they would make briquettes from this dust to sell as fuel in their villages. We returned to the city and watched an SY, belching black smoke, thundering over a busy level crossing in the main street and learned that a new line was being constructed to avoid the main centre, much to the relief of the local population, I imagine. A little further on, near the junction with China Rail, a bridge crossed a large frozen river on which a few children were skating in the gathering dusk as we watched yet another JS rumble tender-first across the ice with a string of empty coal wagons.

JS 2-8-2 6403 crosses the ice-bound river in Chengde city centre with a train of empties from the steelworks for the China Rail network, March 2002. (*Author*)

We ambled northwards that evening after another meal in the dining cars and some adjourned to the bar car where one enterprising enthusiast was teaching the resident Chinese pianist to play the Blues – and very professionally she managed it too. In the morning, we awoke to cold clear skies and found we were in a town called Tongliao where the northern terminus of the JiTong Railway line is found – so called from the cities at either end of the 943 km long line – Jining Nan and Tongliao. There had been a report that our first steam locomotive would be attached here, but it was a bright orange diesel electric, DF3, number 0037, that buffered up and rumbled us a short 15 minute journey to Zhelimu where we stopped, the diesel disappeared and everyone alighted in anticipation. There, the huge twelve wheeled tender of the gigantic QJ 2-10-2 appeared, a colossus. It turned into No. 7164, a late member of the class, built in 1987, one of the specially decorated engines normally diagrammed to the passenger trains – there was a daily stopping passenger train each way over the whole line that took 24 hours and required three engine changes en route. This one had a string of Chinese characters along the smoke deflector sides and I assumed it was named in some way. I submitted a photograph I took to Ivor Warburton, a senior railway manager with that rare attribute, knowledge of Mandarin Chinese(!) and he told me that the inscription read *Go safely and run to time*, not quite in the same league for romanticism as *Flying Scotsman, Wild Swan* or *Sir Lancelot*.

It was said that these locomotives were restricted to 50 miles per hour and we duly set off across the plains at a steady 40-45mph for the first hour or so, until we stopped at a crossing point to pass a double-headed freight – a pair of QJs, the front one of which was another 'decorated' engine, 6632. Later we sat for half an hour at a station called Pingaudi while a freight ahead cleared the long single line section and stopped again at Zhunstariwushi (I think that was its name) to pass the northbound passenger train, hauled by QJ 6996 which was running 6 minutes early according to the timetable we'd perused at Tongliao. We'd now taken 3 hours to

QJ 2-10-2 7063 heads the *Jingpeng Orient Express* special train on the JiTong Railway through the barren hills of Inner Mongolia between Chabuga and Lindong, March 2002. (*Author*)

travel 110 kilometres and proceeded at a faster pace (touching a reckless 46mph at one point) into a landscape where the supposed flat earth yawned in chasms of brown soil, gashes amid the yellowing grass. We came upon the first engine change point, Chabuga, where we interrupted our midday meal, much to the consternation of the dining car staff, and even more, the women car attendants who insisted on rubbing down the carriage handrails after every passenger had alighted, a process that frustrated many of our camera enthusiasts who were concerned that they would not be in time to photograph our retiring 7164. This engine duly chugged off into the distance and backed into the engine servicing point while another QJ, unnamed and undecorated this time, 7063, built in 1986, attached itself to our thirteen coaches.

After an hour or so of passing over the plains of northern China with only a few straggling silver birches in the way of vegetation, we began to climb through low hills and the exhaust from the locomotive became evident. We gathered speed until we had reached 48mph – our highest so far – and sustained a steady 41mph on the climb, but there was no sign I could decipher on the track to indicate the gradient. We drew to a stand at a village called Lindong to pass another double-headed freight and noticed a pagoda standing isolated on a bare hill. After a 10 minute stop, during which our locomotive took water, we continued in the mid-40s to our first major destination of Daban, where we all decamped and made for the engine shed which is the maintenance depot for many of the hundred or so 2-10-2s that were the sole power for the JiTong.

Some forty of these QJs were based at Daban for servicing as well as heavy maintenance, and many of these were moving around the depot being coaled and watered, ready for their next duties, in addition to a couple we found in the workshops and a row of about half a dozen stored out of service and awaiting the cutter's torch. One was actually derailed and on the ballast and would be dismantled where it stood. As the JiTong was the last major concentration of these relatively modern locos,

257

Daban depot, home to around forty of the JiTong Railway's QJs, and the main maintenance workshop for the whole fleet of around a hundred. Failed or damaged locomtives were just abandoned to await breaking up whilst other engines including the tourist train's 6992 await their next turn in the background, March 2002. (*Author*)

whenever one had an incident or failure needing an expensive repair, the engine would be laid aside and a replacement purchased from the large remaining stock underemployed on the main CR network, made redundant through electrification and the cascading displacement of diesels.

After a stop at a local hotel for a shower, we returned to the station for dinner on the train and a night ride over the spectacular mountain section between Daban and Haoluku. We were shunted up the platform by another QJ, 6984, the loco minus smoke deflectors as were a number of other QJs used only as yard or station pilots, and awaited a new loco to set out for the mountain section. Then we hit a problem – a political problem. The Chinese railway authorities had decided to cancel the night programme despite it being part of our contract. Presumably, they could not see the point and had decided to economise, thinking that the passengers would not complain as they would be sleeping anyway. Clearly they did not understand the thought processes of British railway enthusiasts! A number of hardy souls decided to support our tour organisers by going 'on strike' on the platform and refusing to re-embark until the authorities relented and reinstated the programme as advertised. The tour operator was concerned that climbing down at this stage might encourage the Chinese to make further modifications at our expense and dug their heels in, despite the obvious risks. In the end, a compromise was reached and 7063, duly serviced and turned, took us back to Chabuga overnight, and left us in Lindong for a day's photography that began at dawn.

It was for such occasions that I'd raided Milletts in the UK for thermal underwear, gloves and balaclava, and an insulated jacket that made me appear as Michelin Man. We had been warned to expect minus twenty degrees Celsius with a wind chill factor making it feel like minus forty with dire warnings about camera battery life in these extreme conditions. In fact it had been the mildest winter for forty years and as we

A QJ 2-10-2 heads a southbound freight away from the station of Lindong past the pagoda, one of the very few that survived the destruction caused by the 'Gang of Four' and their anti-intellectual and anti-religion campaigns of the 1960s, March 2002. (*Author*)

climbed to the pagoda standing dramatically on the bare hillside that we'd noticed the previous day, several of the party began to feel overdressed and clothing began to be discarded. As the day progressed and the sun rose high above the barren hills, temperatures rose to nearly 15 degrees centigrade and as long as we sheltered from the wind off the Gobi, we could pretend we were in an English Spring.

Most of us gathered by the pagoda – because of its remoteness it was one of the few that survived the onslaught of the Gang of Four and their anti-intellectual and anti-spiritual crusade – and got a panoramic view over the village in the distance, a frozen river and acres of greenhouses growing cucumbers and other salad foods. We also had an excellent view of the station and could contrast the trains in the valley with the ancient pagoda in the foreground. All of us, that is, except for John Cameron, former British Rail non-executive Board Member and owner of 60009, who, great walker that he is, set off over the barren hills as if it was his own grouse moor. We basked in the unexpected sunshine and watched the freights move below like Hornby models – a train drew up to take water roughly every hour or so and we returned to the station to watch the daily southbound passenger train roll in behind 7010, passing 7037 waiting to depart northwards with a heavy freight. We then moved to another location overseeing a sweeping curve below a brooding hillside. We stayed long enough to photograph our own train returning empty stock from Chabuga where it had been serviced, and it was touch and go as the sun began to sink and the shadow of the hill grew closer and closer to the track – 7063 and our special just made it in time.

We had dinner on the train on the return to Daban and waited with bated breath to see if last night's stand-off was to be repeated. We had made our point, however, and promptly at midnight, a Daban based QJ, 6992, exchanged places with 7063. There were few asleep as we set off for the most spectacular part of the route,

259

QJ 7010 rushes into Lindong station with the daily stopping passenger train from Jining to Tongliao, while QJ 7037 waits to proceed southwards with a freight for Ben Hong marshalling Yard where diesel traction will take over, March 2002. (*Author*)

A QJ 2-10-2 heads a heavy coal train away from Lindong towards Chabuga, March 2002. (*Author*)

the central section through mountains that rose to 8,000 feet, although we were already at a high altitude. These mountains were eroded and rounded, barren orange earth, but looking eerie and menacing in the moonlight. Because of the need to economise in the line's construction – the province had to bear the cost – there were few tunnels; just a steady 1 in 90/83 gradient from Reshui in the north to the summit at Shangdian, 45 minutes of twisting looping track threading the mountains accompanied by a continuous thrash from the 2-10-2, or, in the case of freights, two 2-10-2s. Then the line dropped at a steady 1 in 90 through the Jingpeng pass and town and evened out to Haoluku, where the engines from the mountain section exchanged for a Baiqi QJ, which would have been turned and serviced there. I took few notes of this night trip, just listening to the exhaust and watching the lights of our train as we snaked round the various horseshoe bends, but I noted that we arrived 35 minutes early.

A pair of QJs, 6274 leading, storm out of Haoluku towards the mountain section to Daban, the leading engine 'blowing down' steam on the run, a common practice on this railway, March 2002. (*Author*)

We watched the dawn over Haoluku and 'did' the servicing point – just three other QJs as well as 6992 – and ate breakfast before returning in daylight to Daban at 9.10am. We sauntered at 35-40mph on the level and got to Jingpeng 34 minutes early where we alighted to take photos of a crossing freight with QJs 6517 and 6986. We then began the climb in earnest, passing the little village of Xiakengzi at an ear-splitting 18mph and the famous curved elegant concrete viaduct at Si Mingyi at 21mph. As the gradient eased slightly at Hadashan, we accelerated to 28mph, then settled to 20mph all the way to the summit at Shangdian, where our 3 minute early departure had grown to a 16 minute early arrival. We then dispersed by minibus for the afternoon, taking photos of trains on the viaducts – and elsewhere. The

A pair of QJs climb slowly up the Jingpeng pass onto the famous Si MingYi curved viaduct with a northbound freight, March 2002. (*Author*)

261

vehicle used a newly built stretch of motorway for a few miles passing unopened standardised petrol stations all waiting for the inevitable traffic to come as prosperity increased. However, at the present, the only other vehicle we encountered on the motorway was a donkey cart and its perambulating driver.

We wandered at one stage into one of the villages by a dried up river bed and stared at the tiny brick one-room houses, each with its small enclosure in which a pig or a few chickens would be snuffling. There was poverty here, but not the destitution or gross inequality that I'd seen in India. And the children stared at us 'big noses' as Westerners were known, pampered children, valued as the country's one-child policy makes each the centre of attention and hopes for each multi-generational family. There was a sense of space, of timelessness as we waited and watched the trains and the villagers watched us with curiosity. As long as you had a zoom lens, you could spend some 30 minutes or more with the train visible as it snaked around the landscape. At one point, we could see three different levels and watched mesmerised as a pair of light engines traversed in front of our eyes three times before disappearing as specks into a tunnel near the summit. The people were more secretive – we found it hard to get more than a superficial glimpse into their lives. As the sun set, the earth and concrete glowed orange and we were bussed back to Daban and our train.

We had a further night ride over the mountain section with the busy 6992 and returned at dawn once more, gaining 36 minutes on the first section passing 7041 and 7143 at Jingpeng station and then climbing at a steady 23-24mph to Shangdian gaining a further 15 minutes. Freights were busy this morning, for we passed 7009 and 7112 at Xiakengzi and 6388 and 7012 were waiting for us in the loop at Shangdian. When we set off down the gradient, we passed 6638 and 6878 in the loop at Liudigou and kept the train under control between 25 and 35mph round the double horseshoe bend before Reshui. We passed yet another pair of QJs just before Daban and arrived just over 2 hours after leaving the summit, now 40 minutes early.

We now had time for a thorough visit to Daban depot, during which many members of the group were persuaded by the local capitalists to purchase movable momentoes of the withdrawn QJs rusting at the back of the shed. Once more we left the shed, fittingly, at the setting of the sun, and

QJ 6992 pauses for photos at the Shangdian summit of the JiTong Railway on the *Jingpeng Orient Express* and is admired by local Chinese children, March 2002. (*Author*)

QJ 6992, the motive power for the Jingpeng *Orient Express,* hauls the train round one of the many curves in the mountain section of the railway between Daban and Reshui, March 2002. (*Author*)

joined 6992 for the last run over the mountain section to Haoluku. We sustained 22-23mph on the 1 in 83 with our 730 ton train (about the same engine/train weight ratio as the double-headed freights), falling to 16mph on the double horseshoe, recovering to 21 and falling away again to 18 at the summit. Presumably working to the freight schedules and allowing for non-existent pathing times to cross freights, we were again 45 minutes early into Jingpeng and passed the fast daily DMU – a sort of 'Virgin Voyageur' – shortly afterwards arriving at Haoluku in darkness, where a new QJ (at last), 7043, was waiting to take us through the late evening to Baiqi.

We left Haoluku with some energy, throwing sparks into the darkness and running in the upper 40s for 3 hours, arriving at the next engine change point, Baiqi, at midnight. 6633 now took over, although at 3am it was not a priority to study the engine, but we found it in Ben Hong marshalling yard the following morning, the point at which steam is replaced by a diesel for the last section to Jining Nan. We spent the morning in the yard watching shunting by

QJ 6992 on the *Jingpeng Orient Express* on the double set of horseshoe curves between the summit and Reshui, March 2002. (*Author*)

another deflector-less QJ, and departures for Baiqi and points north behind several QJs, including 'our' 6633 which, in daylight, we discovered to be a much decorated passenger engine. Watching the Chinese staff at work was of interest also – clearly 'Health & Safety' has not raised its head here yet. A group of men were unloading a raft of coal wagons by hand, nothing but coal dust swirling in the bitter wind, without any protection from the choking filth. Others were dashing around the tracks between moving trains. As a former railway safety manager it probably was just as well that I could not speak Chinese.

We finally returned to the station to pick up the daily all stations passenger train to Jining Nan. It came bustling in on time behind a much-decorated QJ, 6304, which, unfortunately, cut off here to be replaced by DF4 diesel 7304 to Jining Nan where we were repatriated with our special, now headed by another DF4 to take us to Hohhut and Baotou for sightseeing as a further QJ area we had intended to visit had been dieselised in the preceding months. On the way back to Beijing, we glimpsed three QJs shunting a p-way depot and one SY, 1027, shunting at Chang Ping, then it was back to sightseeing with an inevitable visit to the Great Wall – interesting, but crowded with tourists, so unlike the remote part of the country we'd visited, only known to rail enthusiasts in the Western world.

Now it's back to reviving memories with the superb books of photographs of the last Chinese steam – books such as *Extreme Steam* by Steve le Cheminant, Vernon Murphy and Michael Rhodes and *China – the World's Last Steam Railway,* a photo essay by John Tickner, Gordon Edgar and Adrian Freeman. And, of course, my own photographs.

The 'decorated' [propaganda] QJ 6633, used for passenger work, which hauled the *Jingpeng Orient Express* the previous night between Baiqi and Ben Hong, returns northwards with a freight from Ben Hong Yard, March 2002. (*Author*)

264

Chapter 19

The Railway Children Charity

I have mentioned the Railway Children charity a couple of times. After my first consultancy trip to Australia in 1989, under the guise of Transmark, to look at the application of quality management to Western Australia Railway's freight business, I returned via Bombay. My family had sponsored the education of a girl and her younger brothers in that city through Save the Children and I asked if it would be possible to visit her and her family as I passed through. Arrangements were duly made and I arrived at Bombay International Airport at midnight and must have been the last person off the Jumbo jet as I found myself at the end of a 2-hour immigration queue in a stifling sultry building without (then) air conditioning. After a novice's frantic and panicky attempts at finding my way to a taxi and my hotel on Marine Drive in the south of the city, I got to bed around 3am, feeling nauseous – I had unwisely taken my anti-malaria tablets on an empty stomach. I tossed and turned and at seven o'clock I could stick it no longer and got up. Unable to face breakfast, I dressed, took a few deep breaths on the promenade facing the Arabian Sea and debated with myself what to do next, as I was not due to meet the girl and her family at the Save the Children agency in Colaba, on the Eastern coast side of the city until ten o'clock.

I decided to fill in the time by walking across the city to my destination, the flat of a couple who belonged to the Theosophical Order of Service and acted as Save's agents in managing over 700 sponsorship grants. After half an hour or so, I was lost until I stumbled across Churchgate railway station. I entered the crowded concourse to scrutinise my street map and as I was doing so, I was accosted by a small girl, probably around six or seven years of age, begging. I had no small change, so I waved her away, when to my shock, she brought out a plaited whip from behind her back and started lashing herself across her naked shoulders. I stood there stupefied, like a dummy, when she repeated her actions. I was feeling fragile anyway and emotionally I couldn't cope. I fled the scene and when I'd pulled myself together, I thought, 'I can't leave her like that', and I went back. I've no idea what I thought I was going to do and in the event I couldn't find her again on the chaotic concourse.

As I went on my way, my mind was racing to explain what I'd just witnessed and I soon realised that this girl was the exploited victim of some unscrupulous adult who was using her to extort cash from gullible tourists like me in return for a meal or so a day. I am still haunted by the eyes of that girl and when the truth of the situation dawned on me, I got sufficiently angry to search for organisations, which would protect such vulnerable children. To cut a long story short, on my return I got involved initially with Amnesty International UK's 'Working Group for Children' and a few months later, became their representative on a newly formed Consortium for Street Children, a group of a dozen or so British non-government organizations (NGOs) working for street children internationally.

A few weeks later, the then Prime Minister, John Major, offered the Consortium a launch and reception at No.10 Downing Street and I got involved in the discussion on how to use the occasion. When the debate turned to the causes of children coming to the street, I doodled a simple risk assessment of being a street child on the back of an envelope as I listened – a Fault Tree highlighting root causes and an Event Tree which explored consequences. The Fault Tree highlighted three key immediate causes: children coming from destitute families searching for earning opportunities; children running from abusive situations, physical and sexual; and children abandoned or neglected for a variety of reasons. Rarely was poverty a root cause on its own. It was usually coupled with the experience of violence or abuse and often went back to the root causes that were behind families in trouble – conflict; health breakdown such as the AIDS pandemic; natural catastrophes such as earthquakes, hurricanes and floods causing family disruption; economic collapse; and loss of employment opportunities. All these put immense strains onto families and created the scenarios in which some children suffered traumatic experiences with which they were unable to cope. When children opted for escape to the street they were then met with the urgent needs of finding food, shelter and friends and I explored the actions they took to satisfy those basic needs, often with consequences that made them further rejected by society.

I asked each of my colleagues round the Consortium table what their NGO's intervention strategy was, and to my surprise found a glaring gap. Whilst large international NGOs like UNICEF and 'Save the Children' did little work directly with 'detached' street children, their partners worked in both urban slum and rural situations on preventative measures – education and health care in particular. 'Amnesty' was working on extreme consequences when the behaviour and life style of the children made them victims of violence and abuse, especially from the police and other agents of 'normal' society. I had identified that the first few days – or indeed hours – after a child has turned to the street and travelled to some city are a key risk time in that child's life. As BR's Head of Safety Policy, I had been introduced by the BT Police to two Salvation Army Officers, who patrolled the large London railway termini in the 1980s and early 90s, looking for runaway children at risk. They told me that they had picked up 3,600 under 16 year olds in the ten years of their mammoth self-imposed task – an average of one every evening. They also said that a young teenager alone there had on average ten to 20 minutes before they'd be targeted by a pimp, paedophile or drug dealer. In the last few years such children are not as obvious, as the introduction of stricter barrier control, CCTV cameras and extra

The author, David Maidment, at the launch of the Railway Children charity on Waterloo concourse, backed by an exhibition of photos *Children of Bombay* by Dario Mitidieri, 31 May 1995. (*Author*)

police presence has caused the children to avoid London and go where they are less easily recognised. Anyway, as a result of my discussions at the Consortium, I explored the opportunities to intervene with these children, to offer support before they were abused, exploited or corrupted, and came to the conclusion that the transport terminals of the world – railway stations in Asia and Eastern Europe, bus stations in Africa and Latin America – were obvious places to make a first contact. I therefore persuaded some of my railway colleagues to raise money to work in partnership with local organisations that would go out onto the platforms and offer help to the children as soon as possible, backed by drop-in centres where the children could obtain immediate food and health care while longer-term options were explored with them. On May 31 1995 this came to fruition and the 'Railway Children' charity was born on the concourse of Waterloo station 'under the clock'.

Over the last twenty years the charity has grown to a £3 million a year turnover organisation, working in India, East Africa and the UK, reaching out and offering help to over 45,000 children a year. Whilst the charity receives donations from the general public and Trusts such as Comic Relief and the Big Lottery, over half of its income since the beginning has come from individuals and companies associated with the railway industry. Since privatisation, not only are the train companies and Network Rail supportive, but also the numerous equipment suppliers and providers of legal, financial and consultancy services have become major donors. Events such as the annual Railway Ball at the Grosvenor House Hotel, the annual 'Three Peaks Challenge by Train' event (sponsored by companies in the industry) and numerous

The platform school at Ahmedabad station run by Railway Children's Indian partner, *Sarjan*, 1998. (*Author*)

Two young slum children scavenge for coal and cinders from the ashpan of Darjeeling Himalayan locomotive 791, at Darjeeling, January 2001. (*Author*)

English Welsh & Scottish electric locomotive 90031 named *The Railway Children Partnership* by 'Railway Children' actresses Sally Thomsett and Victoria Taylor, Old Oak Common Open Day, May 2000. (*Author*)

other fundraising initiatives have been supported by individuals and companies and this includes a number of Britain's heritage railways. Any profits or royalties from the sale of this book will also be donated to the charity.

At the first Railway Ball, which was held at the National Rail Museum, our guests were taken to York via Birmingham by a Virgin HST set, one power car of which (43098) was named *Railway Children* by Sally Thomsett (Phyllis in the original film of that name). EWS donated a nameplate from a class 47, *Lady Diana Spencer*, to the charity, which was subsequently auctioned for £10,500. Since then there have been three other locomotive namings after the charity – 90031 at the Old Oak Open Day in 2000, Class 442 EMU 2411 at Waterloo and more recently East Midlands HST 43082 at a Leeds Neville Hill Open Day.

Of particular interest to railway enthusiasts will be the 'Three Peaks Challenge'. A special train (the first one left Euston hauled by EWS' 90031 *The Railway Children Partnership*) takes up to 200 members of fifty teams – mostly from the various rail companies – to Bangor for a night climb of Snowdon (weather permitting), with the train taking the tired and often soaked passengers on to Ravenglass for a special train on the Ravenglass and Eskdale Railway to Boot for a 5 mile walk to the foot of Scafell Pike and a daylight climb. After a pub dinner, the weary climbers travel through the night to Fort William, where our intrepid teams scale Ben Nevis at 5am, returning (hopefully) to pick up the special train, which gets back to London on the Saturday evening.

Ravenglass & Eskdale Railway 0-8-2 *River Irt* on arrival at Dalegarth with the Railway Children teams who walked to Wastwater and climbed Scafell Pike as one of the fundraising 'Three Peaks Challenges'. (*Author*)

A couple of years ago, the Tyseley depot celebrated its hundreth anniversary with a widely publicised Family Day and the London Midland depot management and Bob Meanley at the Vintage Trains centre there donated £1 of the entrance fee and ran raffles and other collections for the charity. £15,000 was raised and when a number of heritage railways in the West of England decided to collaborate over their recognition of the GWR's 175th anniversary in 2010, the Railway Children was invited to participate in the various commemorative events – Open Days, Gala Events and special GW Rail Tours. Vintage Trains of Tyseley invited 'Railway Children' to run raffles on excursions throughout the spring and summer and after some charity volunteers covered the Crewe-Kensington railtour on 6 March with 6201 *Princess Elizabeth*, I joined the *Moonraker* special from Solihull to Salisbury with Bob's 5043 *Earl of Mount Edgcumbe* in early April. I was preoccupied on the southbound run taking over £470 in raffle ticket money and on a rain-swept platform in Salisbury – reached on time at noon – with 5043 as backdrop, I was interviewed on camera for a DVD that Roger Hardingham of Kingfisher Videos was making for the GW175 anniversary. After finding the winners of the raffle on the return trip, I started to take notice of the engine performance and after an unusually brisk transit of the Basingstoke to Reading connection, we were held for 5 minutes at Reading West awaiting line clear across to the Relief Line at Scours Lane. We quickly accelerated and ran at a steady 75mph from Goring to Moreton Cutting where we slowed for the Didcot stop to allow a South Wales passenger to make his connection. We duly arrived at Hinksey Up Loop to take water and during another swift passage from Oxford North to Banbury I received an invitation conveyed from Bob who was firing 5043 to join him and Driver Ray Poole on the footplate from Banbury.

Ex-GNR J52 0-6-0T 68846 on the East Somerset Railway in support of a railway gala in aid of Railway Children. (*Author*)

5043 *Earl of Mount Edgcumbe* at Banbury towards the end of the *Moonraker* rail special, where the author joined Bob Meanley on the footplate for the return to Tyseley, 3 April 2010. (*Author*)

During the short stop there to set down more passengers, I climbed into the cab, finding Bob strenuously raking the fire as a combination of suspect coal and the formation of clinker after steaming for over 12 hours was having a deleterious effect on the boiler pressure, which was hovering around 180lb psi instead of the optimum 225psi. Despite the low pressure we set off with vigour, passing Cropredy at 60mph and leaving steam on after Fenny Compton so that we accelerated rapidly to a full 80mph before easing. All this time, our boiler pressure fluctuated between 160 and 200psi, but we still cleared Leamington in under even time from Banbury and despite a check to 10mph at Warwick, we stopped at Warwick Parkway 5 minutes early. It was now raining and we struggled to start on the 1 in 95 out of Warwick Parkway where we'd made a booked stop. Eventually we held the rail with much sanding and opened out blasting over Hatton summit at 40mph. After stopping to set down more passengers at Knowle & Dorridge we arrived at our destination 1 minute early. Bob had worked hard to retain pressure and he commented that a single-chimney Castle would not have made such good time with poor coal and low pressure (for log, see Appendix 1, Table 14).

A couple of weeks later I enjoyed a fabulous day out with my raffle team on the *Bristolian*, with 5043 re-enacting its previous spell on the 105 minute scheduled train back in 1958. A group of us, at the invitation once more of Bob Meanley and Vintage Trains, joined the *Bristolian* at Paddington, an eight-coach train including a GUV, converted to hold additional water tanks to allow Castle 5043 to run non-stop to Bristol. The down run was excellent and we arrived at Bristol in glorious sunshine 12 minutes early in 133 minutes from Paddington, having manoeuvred our way between HSTs without being brought to a stand, with the able help of First GW staff on board with radios and computers regulating our progress. I left my team to handle the raffle on the return urging them to waste no time going through the train – rumour had it that the return run might be something rather special – and it was, with a vengeance. We set off with *Bristolian* headboard and the historic '473' headcode displayed and accelerated up to Badminton in true *Bristolian* style and then reeled off the next 100 miles at an average of nearly 74mph – a remarkable feat for a locomotive whose maximum speed was 75mph. Perhaps we crept at times to 77-78mph, even a momentary 80 through Hullavington, but thanks to First Great Western's close monitoring, and the chance location of other services that might have delayed us and 5043 and her crew's excellence, we got a clear road throughout, stayed on the main line and entered platform 1 at Paddington triumphantly in 2 seconds under 110 minutes, only five minutes outside the *Bristolian* schedule when speed was not circumscribed, and some 46 minutes early! (See log, Appendix 1, Table 15).

There are certain impressions that will stay in my mind for ever: standing at the end of platform 3 at Temple Meads looking at 5043 in full *Bristolian* regalia, headcode 473, just as I'd stood there fifty-four years earlier looking at 5063

5043 *Earl of Mount Edgcumbe* at Bristol ready to depart on the Up Bristolian to Paddington, which it completed in 109 minutes, arriving 44 minutes ahead of schedule. (*Author*)

The Railway Children raffle team led by Stan Judd, at Bristol TM on arrival with the down *Bristolian*, 17 April 2010. (*Author*)

before taking an old Midland Compound to Wickwar to see a great aunt; standing in the corridor of the first coach hearing 5043 give full throat as we accelerated hard to Chipping Sodbury Tunnel and the sparks illuminating the inside of Sodbury Tunnel; storming past Swindon station at 74mph, whistle screaming; hurtling through Didcot at 78mph, now 20 minutes early, anticipating we might beat a competitor for the main line at Reading; and the continuing exhilaration as we tore through the suburbs at a steady 75-77mph. The only people unhappy were the restaurant car crew who were still serving dinner to passengers as we drew in to the terminus ... It was a memorable day for all concerned. Tony Streeter, former editor of *Steam Railway,* told me that he'd never travelled on the old *Bristolian* – 'You have now,' I replied.

Apparently it was all so easy on the footplate – Bob Meanley reported that the regulator's second valve was just cracked open and that cut-off was fixed at 15 per cent nearly all the way. An increase to 17 per cent produced acceleration immediately to 80mph, so the cut-off had been brought back to 15 per cent again. The engine, had it been permitted, could easily have run the eight coaches (one over the normal *Bristolian* load) at 90mph on the level. And on top of this we had collected over £1,000 in the raffle and David Atkin had sold £600 worth of commemorative first day covers depicting the *Bristolian* for the Railway Children. That was certainly a win/win experience for all concerned.

Railway Children was the beneficiary of further GW175 events through the summer and autumn of 2010 – present at the Steam Galas at Didcot, Swindon and Toddington and on other steam rail tours, including 6201 *Princess Elizabeth* through to Swansea in place of the unavailable 70013 and another fabulous performance by Tyseley's 5043 on the Settle and Carlisle which raised £530 on the outward journey raffle – a record for one set of passengers – and culminated in a stupendous climb to Ais Gill on the return, when the Castle hauled 470 tons (including the trailing type 47 which was confirmed as providing no power at all) scaling the summit at 42mph with 50 per cent cut-off, full regulator, both injectors on and blowing off steam, the estimated drawbar horsepower exceeding 2,000 for the first recorded time on a Castle locomotive (Appendix 1, Table 16). I think that is a good place to leave this story …

Perhaps a final postscript – in the summer of 2013, I was invited to have a 'Railway Children' stand at the Network Rail National Plant Exhibition at Long Marston. Rail Media, a company producing a rail industry monthly magazine, bought 150 copies of my history of the charity, *The Other Railway Children*, and presented them to the other exhibitors, who donated over £12,000 to the charity during the two day event. Finally, I was invited to join everyone at a demonstration and found myself – after an introduction by Network Rail's Steve Featherstone – asked to unveil the nameplate of Colas Rail Freight 66850 standing gleaming there. I assumed there was about to be a fifth locomotive named *Railway Children,* but when the curtain drew back I was astonished to find the nameplate read *David Maidment OBE*. When the Minister of my local Methodist Church announced this to the Sunday morning congregation (he was a bit of a rail enthusiast) he wondered whether this was the railway equivalent of 'sainthood'!

Steve Featherstone from Network Rail and Stephen Haynes of Colas Rail Freight present the author with a replica nameplate of 66850, which he has just named at the Network Rail Plant Exhibition at Long Marston, June 2013. (*Rail Media*)

Appendix 1
Train 'log' tables, UK 1962 - 2013

Table 1: Waterloo-Yeovil Junction with an un-rebuilt Battle of Britain
34086-83D (ex-72A)
219 Squadron
11-410 tonnes gross, reduced to 8-295t from Salisbury
7.0pm Waterloo-Exeter Central
3.4.64

Waterloo	00.00		T
Vauxhall	03.35		
Queens Road	-	56	
Clapham Jcn	07.06	46*	
Earlsfield	09.18	56	
Wimbledon	11.34	sigs 35*	
New Malden	14.35	62	
Surbiton	16.41	70	
Hampton C Jcn	17.52	77	
Esher	19.20	sigs 40*	
Walton	22.32	64	
Weybridge	25.25//27.15	sig stand	
Byfleet	30.09	58	
Woking	34.25	63/ sigs 55*	
Brookwood	38.06	65/68	
MP 31	-	67	
Farnborough	42.57	75	
Fleet	45.40	83	
Winchfield	48.15	85	
Hook	51.58	pws 28*	
Basingstoke	57.30	72	
Worting Jcn	59.55	69	
Oakley	61.52	72	
Overton	64.38	83	
Whitchurch	67.26	86	
Hurstbourne	68.50	90	
Andover Jcn	72.50	85	
Red Post Jcn	-	81	
Grateley	77.13	74	
Porton	82.00	87/92	
Tunnel Jcn	86.42		
Salisbury	89.37	(75 net)	
	00.00		4L
Wilton	05.36	55/62	
Dinton	11.18	76	
Tisbury	15.13	71/69	
Semley	20.10	62	
Gillingham	23.53	76	
MP 107.5	-	65	
Templecombe	29.43	84	
Milborne Port	32.23	58	
Sherborne	35.38	80	
Wyke Crossing	-	83	
Yeovil Junction	40.47		2L

Table 2: Up Bournemouth Belle (4.40pm Bournemouth Central)

	35022 - 70A		35016 - 70A		34098 - 71A	
	Holland-America Line		Elders Fyffes		Templecombe	
	12 Pullmans 500t		12 - 500t		11 - 445t	
	8.8.64		5.9.64		1.4.67	
Southampton Central	00.00	1L	00.00	T	00.00	1L
Northam Jcn	03.47 10*		03.30 10*		03.29 10*	
St Denys	06.02 47		05.50 36		05.25 40	
Swaythling	07.58 49		08.20 44		08.43 48	
Eastleigh	12.12 pws 15*		13.09 pws 15*		10.23 56	
Shawford	19.03 48		19.34 47		- 52	
Winchester	23.05 51		23.49 50		20.50 pws 15*	
Winchester Jcn	25.45 52		26.40 50		24.01 47	
Wallers Ash	- 54		30.04 53		27.27 51	
Micheldever	33.19 53		34.10 55		31.38 54	
Roundwood	- 54		- 57		- 53	
Wootton Box	- 67		- 68		37.58 65	
Worting Jcn	41.39 63*		42.14 60*		40.11 65*	
Basingstoke	43.53 71/78		44.24 81/83		42.27 68/73	
Hook	48.22 79		48.38 80		47.01 80	
Winchfield	50.18 80		50.23 88		48.52 82	
Fleet	52.53 82		52.45 86		51.20 88	
Farnborough	55.25 79		55.05 85		53.45 86	
MP 31	- 75		- 83		- 84	
Brookwood	59.37 83		58.50 90		57.43 81/87	
Woking	62.38 72*		61.27 84/89		60.53 sigs 60*	
Byfleet	64.52 79		63.47 pws 15*		63.15 72	
Weybridge	66.57 72		68.03 52		66.31 pws 35*	
Walton	68.57 sigs 38*		70.12 73		69.13 63	
Esher	72.15 65		72.30 78		71.48 71	
Hampton C Jcn	73.17 67		73.25 77		72.48 70	
Surbiton	74.27 69		74.24 74		73.55 68	
New Malden	- 66		- 72		75.56 72	
Wimbledon	79.03 65		78.50 62*		78.38 sigs 30*	
Clapham Jcn	82.37 40*		82.19 42*		82.50 55/40*	
Queens Road	- 54		- 54		- 56	
Vauxhall	86.03		85.48		86.25 sigs 15*	
Waterloo	90.17 (84 net)	1L	89.45 (82 net)	T	90.17 (81 net)	7E

Table 3: Woking-Waterloo, 1965-66 (Commuter runs)

	34041 - 70F (71B)	34006 - 70E (72B)
	Wilton	Bude
	11 - 390t	12 - 445t
	6.4am S'ton Term	(Sun) B'mouth via Havant
	10.5.65	6.3.66
Woking	00.00	00.00
Byfleet	04.20 62	04.40 63
Weybridge	06.38 70	07.14 59
Walton	08.23 75	09.20 68
Esher	10.40 72	11.48 70
Hampton C Jcn	11.42 sigs 60*	12.47 71
Surbiton	13.03 62	13.54 68
New Malden	15.18 64	15.57 68
Wimbledon	19.25 sigs 20*	18.18 67
Earlsfield	22.01 52	20.12 54
Clapham Jcn	24.15 40*	22.35 35*
Queens Road	- 48	- 50
Vauxhall	27.48	26.19
Waterloo	31.03 (28 net)	29.19

	77014 - 70C	34019 - 70D (71A)
	(Standard 3 2-6-0)	*Bideford*
	6 - 220t	11 - 390t
	6.39am B'stoke	6.4am S'ton Term
	22.11.66	30.12.66
Woking	00.00	00.00
Byfleet	04.13 64	04.13 73
Weybridge	06.48 59	06.28 71
Walton	08.56 73	08.12 79
Esher	11.35 sigs 45*	10.16 82
Hampton C Jcn	14.04 sigs 5*	11.05 80
Surbiton	17.08	12.15 sigs 62*
	00.00	
New Malden	04.15 58	14.40 55*
Wimbledon	07.02 67	19.58 pws 15*
Earlsfield	08.54 sigs 50*	22.06 59
Clapham Jcn	11.03 40*	24.08 40*
Queens Road	- sigs 30*	- 57
Vauxhall	15.40	27.28 sigs 5*
Waterloo	19.22 (28 net)	32.05 (27 net)

Table 4: Southampton-Waterloo, 1967

	34044 - 70F (71B)		35013 - 70A	
	Woolacombe		*Blue Funnel*	
	11 - 400t		11 - 400t	
	2.34pm B'mouth		11.17am Weymouth	
	28.2.67		9.6.67	
	Driver Hooper (70A)		Driver Saunders (70A)	
Southampton Central	00.00	8L	00.00	1L
Northam	03.27	10*	03.50	10*
St Denys	05.25	44	05.19	44
Southampton Airport	08.21	55	08.25	54
Eastleigh	09.51	61	10.04	56
Shawford	13.50	61	14.21	58
Winchester	16.55	62/ sigs 10*	18.00	sigs 50*
Winchester Jcn	22.22	pws 15*	20.47	pws 15*
Wallers Ash	26.12	48/53	-	38
Weston Box	27.53	63	-	51
Micheldever	29.56	67	32.31	55
Roundwood	-	68	-	52
Wootton Box	34.47	75/78	-	62/ sigs 50*
Worting Jcn	36.37	65*	41.40	62*
Basingstoke	38.58	73/76	44.08	68/81
Hook	43.10	84	48.31	86
Winchfield	44.46	92	50.08	93
Fleet	46.57	95	52.13	97
Farnborough	49.07	94/90	54.57	sigs 64*
MP 31	-	86	-	pws 40*
Brookwood	52.42	84	60.07	77
Woking	56.08	sigs 60*	63.00	sigs 70*
Byfleet	58.30	75	64.39	83
Weybridge	61.35	pws 15*	66.43	86
Walton	66.05	58	68.13	88
Esher	68.42	69	70.08	90
Hampton C Jcn	69.38	72	70.54	90
Surbiton	70.41	74	71.45	92
New Malden	72.53	sigs 50*	73.34	68*
Wimbledon	75.50	61	78.30	sigs 0* (Raynes Pk)
Clapham Jcn	79.28	40*	82.59	60/40*

Queens Road	-	58	-	60
Vauxhall	82.53		86.15	
Waterloo	86.08 (72.5 net)	2E	89.35 (76 net)	5E

Table 5: Cardiff-Shrewsbury, 1963
4.40pm Cardiff-Liverpool
6922 *Burton Hall* 89A (84G)
6 coaches 208/215t
26.4.63

Cardiff	00.00		T
Rumney River Bridge	-	62	
Marshfield	07.40	71/79	
Gaer Junction	11.48//12.50		sig stand
Newport	16.12		
	00.00		T
Maindee North Jcn	01.55	56	
Caerleon	04.05	59	
Ponthir	05.45	63	
Llantarnam	06.06	56	
Llantarnam Jcn	08.10	56/53	
Pontypool Road	11.50		9E
	00.00		T
Little Mill	02.33	62/56	
Nantyderry	05.10	68/64	
Penpergwm	07.37	70/62*/60	
Abergavenny Mon Rd	10.40		
	00.00		T
Abergavenny Jcn	02.50	36	
Llanvihangel	07.37	46/67	
Pandy	10.05	64	
Pontrilas	15.08	61*/58	
St Devereux	18.38	62	
Tram Inn	20.53	65	
Red Hill Jcn	24.16	38*	
Rotherwas Jcn	26.50	50	
Hereford	29.26		7.5E
	00.00		T
Barrs Court Jcn	02.48	sigs 2*	
Shelwick Jcn	04.49	54/62	
Moreton-on-Lugg	07.31	68/70	
Dinmore	10.31	62	
Ford Bridge	13.13	71/67	
Leominster	15.18	68	
Berrington & Eye	18.10	73/67	
Woofferton	20.50	74	
Ludlow	25.08	66/pw 2*	
Bromfield	29.25	46	
Onibury	32.11	60/62	
Craven Arms	35.15	70/66	
Marsh Farm Jcn	-	64/57	
Marshbrook	39.50	57	
Church Stretton	42.38	55/62	
Leebotwood	46.02	68/64*	
Dorrington	48.40	72	
Condover	50.43	66	
Sutton Bridge Jcn	53.45//54.02	sig stand	
Coleham	55.15//55.36	sig stand	
Shrewsbury	58.45 (50.5 net)	9E	

(6922 ex-works, 21.3.63, no clear reason for being driven so hard.)

Table 6
11.40am Euston-Windermere *The Lakes Express* **to Weaver junction, 1L27**
6.7.63
46254 *City of Stoke-on-Trent* **5A**
12 coaches, 413/430t

Euston	00.00	(Banked to Camden No.1 by 44839 - 21A) 1L	
Camden No.1	03.42	23	
Queens Park	09.02	pw 25*/42	
Willesden Junction	11.58	pw 26*	
Wembley Central	16.44	52	
South Kenton	-	56	
Harrow & Wealdstone	20.36	61/ pw 50*	
Bushey & Oxhey	25.30	59	
Watford Junction	26.53	68	
Kings Langley	30.99	66	
Apsley	35.26	pw 3*	
Hemel Hempstead	37.53	46/53	
Berkhamsted	42.00	62	
Tring	45.51	70	
Cheddington	50.55	77/ pw 10*	
Leighton Buzzard	56.15	63/74	
Bletchley	61.59	80	
Denbigh Hall Sdgs	-	pw 28*	
Wolverton	70.01	74	
Castlethorpe	72.02	75	
Roade	76.37	68	
Blisworth	-	80	
Heyford Box	-	83	
Weedon	-	82	
Welton	89.18	72/70	
Hillmorton Box	93.40	77/ sigs 5*	
	96.29//96.48	sig stand	
Rugby	101.00	pw 5*	T
Brinklow	109.19	65	
Shilton	112.20	69	
Bulkington	-	75	
Attleborough	116.16	78	
Nuneaton	117.17	82	T
Hartshill Box	-	81	
Atherstone	121.25	76/84	
Polesworth	124.40	85	
Tamworth	127.20	81/70*	
Coton Xing	-	73	
Hademore	130.28	71/66	
Lichfield	133.00	62	3E
Armitage	138.05	65	
Rugeley	141.09	62/65	3E
Colwich	144.05	72	
Shugborough Tunnel	147.02//147.45 sig stand		
Milford & Brockton	149.25	pw 20*	
Stafford	158.02	48	3L
Great Bridgeford	-	60	
Norton Bridge	163.54	68	
Standon Bridge	-	72	
Whitmore	172.15	70/68	
Madeley	174.28	83	T
Betley Road	176.53	87	
Basford Hall	179.54	sigs 36*	
Crewe	182.15//189.58 sig stand	(11.25 Euston ahead)	6E/1L
Crewe Coal Yard	-	51	
Coppenhall Junction	196.20	58/71	
Winsford	200.20	79	3E

Minshull Vernon	-	82	
Hartford	204.24	sigs 18*	
Acton Bridge	208.55	57/62	
Weaver Junction pass	211.04	67	5E

After this, there were three dead stands for signals at Warrington and severe checks outside Wigan making us 14 minutes late there where I left the train. I timed 46229 on 27 July and 46238 on 24 August on the same train and although punctuality was better – 2 minutes early at Preston with 46229 and 10 late with 46238 – neither performed with the vigour or high speeds of 46254. This run suffered eight p-way slacks and three dead stands for signals before Crewe and was still 6 minutes early there! Net time is almost impossible to calculate – I estimate around 150 minutes for the 158 miles to Crewe.

Table 7

3.48pm TThSO Crewe-Glasgow (Crewe-Carlisle)
1.8.63
46235 *City of Birmingham* **5A**
6 coaches, 187/200t

Crewe	00.00		18L
Coppenhall Junction	08.17	sigs 10*/54	
Winsford	12.25	75	
Hartford	15.57	74/71	
Acton Bridge	18.17	62	
Weaver Junction	20.15	64	
Norton Crossing	-	80	
Acton Grange Junction	25.10	sigs 5*	
Warrington	28.49	(Special stop)	
	00.00		
Dallam Branch Sdgs	02.56	48	
Winwick Quay	04.25	54/ sigs 15*	
Golborne Junction	-	55/67	
Springs Branch	17.33//18.40	sigs stand	
Wigan	19.58	15* to Slow Line	
Boars Head Junction	24.06	46	
Standish Junction	25.32	49/64	
Euxton Junction	31.57	75	
Leyland	32.46	74	
Preston	38.55	sigs 3*/ sigs 10*	
	42.10//42.27	sig stand	
Barton	48.36	68/74	
Brock	-	sigs 20*	
Garstang	55.45	sigs 5*/54	
Bay Horse	62.13	74	
Oubeck	65.48	75/ sigs 15*	
Lancaster	70.10	pw 20*	
Hest Bank	74.55	70	
Bolton-le-Sands	76.00	75	
Carnforth	77.25	84/81	
Burton & Holme	81.35	76/sigs 40*	
Milnthorpe	84.14	67	
Hincaster Junction	86.07	71	
Oxenholme	89.23	68/64	
Lambrigg Crossing	-	62	
Grayrigg	96.30	59	
Low Gill Junction	98.13	76/79	
Tebay	101.13	84/89	
Scout Green	103.44	67	
Shap Summit	106.30	62/ sigs 50*	
Shap	108.25	73	
Thrimby Grange	-	78/81	

Clifton & Lowther	114.17	83	
Eden Valley Junction	-	85	
Penrith	118.43	pw 15*	
Plumpton	123.25	82	
Calthwaite	-	87/94	
Southwaite	127.30	75/78	
Upperby	-	sigs 25*	
Carlisle	136.15	(99 minutes net)	1L

Table 8

1.00pm Leeds City-King's Cross (from passing Grantham) *The West Riding*
15.6.63 (Last day of steam into King's Cross)
60107 *Royal Lancer* **34A**
11 coaches, 382/420t

Grantham	00.00 *pass*	63	4L
Great Ponton	03.26	62	
Stoke Summit	05.26	62	
Corby Glen	07.54	82	
Little Bytham	11.21	93	
Essendine	13.52	85/87	
Tallington	16.33	89	
Werrington Junction	20.54	90	
New England	-	54/sigs 12*	
Peterborough	26.47		T
	00.00		T
Fletton Junction	03.46	38	
Yaxley	06.52	65	
Holme	10.08	60*	
Connington Box	-	67	
Abbots Ripton (Leys Summit)	16.07	55½	
Huntingdon	20.36	77½	
Offord	23.03	64*	
St Neots	27.09	63/77	
Sandy	33.31	75	
Biggleswade	35.57	73	
Arlesey	39.25	72/76½	
Three Counties	40.35	74	
Hitchin	43.43	72/66	
Stevenage	47.00	62½	
Knebworth	50.15	72/67	
Welwyn North	52.59	74	
Welwyn Garden City	56.56	sigs 5*	
Hatfield	60.18	58	
Potters Bar	65.15	70	
Hadley Wood	67.09	72	
New Barnet	68.26	71	
New Southgate	71.10	58*	
Wood Green	72.45	60	
Finsbury Park	75.43	54/25*	
King's Cross	82.20	(78 minutes net)	1E

The last run of one of the oldest A3s (double-chimney and DB smoke deflectors) on the last day of steam on the ECML south of Peterborough.

Table 9

9.15am Paddington-Worcester
26.10.63
7032 *Denbigh Castle* 81A
8 coaches, 273/310t

Paddington	00.00		1L
Westbourne Park	03.08		
Old Oak Common	05.22	54	
Acton	07.03	61	
Ealing Broadway	08.35	pw 48*	
Southall	12.23	53	
West Drayton	16.32	72	
Slough	21.12	77/73	
Taplow	24.34	75	
Maidenhead	26.08	76	
Twyford	31.58	74	
Reading	37.15	(36 mins net)	T
	00.00		0.5L
Tilehurst	04.27	58	
Pangbourne	07.21	70	
Goring	10.25	65/71	
Cholsey	13.46	76	
Moreton Cutting	16.29	73/ sigs 49*	
Didcot East Jcn	18.20	34*	
Appleford Halt	21.30	55	
Radley	25.21	60	
Kennington Jucn	28.46	sigs 38*	
Oxford South	32.09//32.40	sigs stand	
Oxford	34.38		2E
	00.00		0.5L
Wolvercot Jcn	05.30	46/40*	
Yarnton	06.52	54	
Handborough	10.41	59	
Finstock Halt	15.23	70	
Charlbury	16.54	68	
Ascott-under-Wychwood	20.25	72	
Shipton	21.33	73	
Kingham	24.50		3E
	00.00		T
Adlestrop	04.52	64	
Moreton-in-Marsh	10.13		
	00.00		
Blockley	05.03	56/71	
Chipping Campden	06.58	65/84	
Honeybourne	10.42	100	
Littleton & Badsey	12.27	102/88	
Evesham	14.58		
dep	00.00		1L
Fladbury	06.53	56/pw 5*	
Pershore	11.00	64	
Stoulton	13.17	66	
Norton Halt	16.17	pw 50*/67	
Worcester	20.12	(16 mins net)	1L

Loco inspector and passenger on footplate.

282

Table 10: Glasgow-Aberdeen 3 hour trains, 1963-4

8.25am Glasgow *The Grampian* **and 5.30pm Glasgow** *The Saint Mungo*
Timed from Stirling or Perth

	8.25am Glasgow 60094 *Colorado* 65B 13.6.63 7 coaches, 255/270t			5.30pm Glasgow 73152 65B 13.6.63 7 coaches, 255/270t			8.25am Glasgow 44721 63A 20.6.63 7 coaches, 255/270t			5.30pm Glasgow 60010 *Dominion of Canada* 61B 8.1.64 7 coaches, 255/270t		
Stirling	00.00		3L	00.00		4L	00.00		2L			
Cornton	03.18	56/60		03.28	56		03.13	61½				
Bridge of Allan	04.21	56		04.35	54/47		04.17	55				
Dunblane	06.33	54½		07.15	42		06.32	51/47				
Kinbuck	09.47	47		11.40	34		10.01	45				
Greenloaning	12.53	68		15.26	67		13.20	70				
Blackford	16.47	64		19.25	63		17.02	67				
Gleneagles	19.21	pw 34*		21.50	pw 44*		19.27	pw 43*				
Auchterarder	21.34	66/pw 21*		24.10	59/pw47*		21.26	78				
Dunning	26.01	76		28.06	73		24.35	83				
Forteviot	28.13	80		30.28	71		26.43	75				
Forgandenny	30.24	81		32.54	70		29.03	73				
Hilton Junction	31.56	72		34.35			30.42	72				
Perth	34.53		1L	37.57		5L	33.35		1.5E			
	00.00		1L	00.00		6L	00.00		T	00.00		14L
Almond Valley Jcn	-	48		-	48		-	53		03.17	57½	
Luncarty	06.08	58½		06.56	51		05.58	62		06.53	63	
Strathord	06.55	60		07.52	54½		06.53	65		-	64	
Stanley Junction	09.14	54½		10.29	47		08.50	60½		08.57	66/73	
Ballathie	-	61		12.50	62		10.52	77		11.03	76	
Tay Viaduct	-	72		-	65		-	81		-	80	
Cargill	13.23	pw 23*		14.59	pw 29*		12.15	76		12.34	74	
Burrelton	16.59	59		18.46	55		14.02	77		14.30	79	
Coupar Angus	19.02	73		20.59	72		15.43	82		16.23	76	
Ardler	21.06	72		23.04	73		17.33	78		18.23	78	
Alyth Junction	22.58	75		24.55	72		19.16	77		20.15	79	
Eassie	26.19	75		28.18	77		22.26	76/78		23.36	82	
Glamis	28.06	71		29.57	80/76		24.10	74/72		25.24	76	
Kirriemuir Jcn	30.27	73		32.04	82		26.24	75		27.35	81	
Forfar	33.46		3L	35.02		9L	29.32		2.5E	31.06		13L
	00.00		6L	00.00		8L	00.00		T	00.00		13L
Clocksbriggs	04.01	65		03.50	66		04.16	63		03.55	65	
Auldbar	06.23	73		06.08	74		06.41	70		06.26	74	
Guthrie	08.00	58*		07.48	67*		08.25	62*		08.05	75/62*	
Glasterlaw	09.58	70/67		09.34	74/69½		10.21	66/65		10.01	74/70	
Farnell Road	12.50	73/68*		12.13	80		13.10	69*/75		12.50	77/70*	
Bridge of Dun	15.42	64/60*		14.37	72*		15.51	68*		15.36	71/63*	
Dubton	18.15	64		16.51	75		18.11	68		18.07	71	
Kinnaber Junction	19.25	60		17.58	65		19.22	60		19.17	65	
Craigo	21.23	75		19.51	73		21.23	70		21.20	73	
Marykirk	23.08	64		21.39	60		23.15	61½		23.10	68	
Laurencekirk	26.06	62/68*		25.06	53/65		26.30	58/63		26.11	65/75	
Fordoun	28.55	71½		28.08	65		29.42	65		28.53	80/70½	
Drumlithie	32.38	60/57		32.26	51		33.34	60/56		32.35	68/66	
Carmont	34.28	64½		34.28	62		35.22	66		34.14	70	
Dunnottar Box	37.07	58*/64		37.06	72		37.53	70		36.43	80/64*	
Stonehaven	40.10		4L	39.55		6L	40.57		1E	39.55		11L
	00.00		2L	00.00		5L	00.00		2E	00.00		9L
MP 228	-	50		-	44½		-	44		-	55	
Muchalls	05.55	71/65		06.31	66/62		06.48	67/63		06.07	78	
Newtonhill	07.02	pw 20*		07.40	pw 17*		07.54	pw 17*		07.04	72/75	
Portlethen	11.09	53		11.47	48		12.57	49		09.10	70/76	
Cove Bay	14.43	62/54*		15.45	61		16.36	60		12.08	63*	
Craiginches South	18.05	60/55*		-	70		-	66		-	74	
Ferryhill Junction	19.55			20.26			21.02			17.58	sigs 15*	
Aberdeen	21.46		T	22.18		4L	23.01		2E	19.14		5L

283

60010 and 60094 were good 'average' runs for A3 and A4 Pacifics on this train. 73152 was substituting for a 61B A4 which had failed on the Up run. Presumably 44721 was also a last minute substitution for the 65B A3 or A4. The Black 5 holds the honours for the Perth-Forfar mile a minute run, thereafter was driven more easily as it was running early. 73152 was weaker on the banks, but was driven hard making a terrific din, especially when speed rose to 82 before Forfar.

Table 11: South Wales-London with 2 x Cl 37s, 1966

8.20am Swansea High Street-Paddington (from Cardiff)
10.5.66
D6877/D6892 86A (in multiple)
11 coaches, XP64 stock.

Cardiff General	00.00		1L
Marshfield	06.58	69/85	
Gaer Junction	10.38		
Newport	12.36		0.5L
	00.00		1L
Bishton	-	84	
Magor	07.55	80	
Severn Tunnel Jcn	10.23	30*	
Severn Tunnel West	11.55	74/84	
Severn Tunnel East	15.22	72	
Pilning	16.39	69/sigs 20*	
Patchway	22.05	48/sigs 30*	
Stoke Gifford West	23.29	66	
Winterbourne	25.26	73	
Coalpit Heath	26.33	75	
Chipping Sodbury	29.38	81	
Badminton	33.05	82. pw 24*	
Hullavington	40.48	76/90	
Little Somerford	43.46	100	
Brinkworth	45.29	98/100	
Wootton Bassett	48.26	80/72*	
Swindon	55.05	sigs 35*/ 65	
Marston Sidings	-	65/sigs 50*	
Shrivenham	60.47	84	
Uffington	64.18	95	
Challow	66.17	98	
Wantage Road	68.06	102	
Steventon	70.57	103	
Didcot	73.22	pw 64*/87	
Cholsey	76.33	96	
Goring	78.55	99	
Pangbourne	82.26//83.39	Track circuit failure	
Tilehurst	87.16	60	
Reading	91.18	10* slow past derailment	
Twyford	97.01	84	
Maidenhead	101.31	98	
Taplow	102.37	100	
Slough	105.05	102	
Langley	106.27	100	
West Drayton	108.28	80 eased	
Southall	111.41	79	
Ealing Broadway	114.23	72	
Acton	115.36	68	
Westbourne Park	119.11		
Subway Junction	122.11//122.48	sigs stand	
Paddington	125.47	(105 minutes net)	12L

GM Gerry Fiennes was concerned at the underpowered WR expresses and allocated 2 Cl 37s in multiple (series D687X-D689X) with the XP64 stock, the prototype Mark IIs, for a couple of S.Wales-London expresses for a fortnight until the 37s began to fail as they were not designed for continuous high speed.

Table 12: Footplate runs - ROM LMR Safety Audits 1983-5

1Z38 Charter Euston-Carlisle (Footplate, Hellifield-Garsdale)
12.3.83
46229 *Duchess of Hamilton* **5A**
14 coaches, 535/565t
Driver Ken Iveson, Fireman John Brown, Skipton
Inspector Arthur Morris, Preston, Engineer in charge John Peck, York NRM

46229 took over the train at Leeds from 45407, which arrived from Carnforth 8 minutes late. Travelled in NRM support coach with John Peck from Leeds to Hellifield.

Hellifield	00.00		250 psi, full reg, 45% cut-off	14L
Long Preston	02.55	42/55	Full regulator, 15% cut-off	
Settle Junction	05.09	60	Eased, full reg, 15% cut-off	12L
Settle	07.15	54/48	250 psi, full reg, 15% cut-off	
Stainforth	-	42	20% cut off	
MP 240	-	38	30% cut-off, blowing off steam	
Horton-in-Ribblesdale	-	38/42	35% cut-off	
Horton station	-	44/46	250 psi, full reg, 30% cut-off	
Selside	19.00	43/45		
Ribblehead Viaduct	-	32*	eased	
Blea Moor	26.20	34/20*	40% cut-off, slip in tunnel	6L
Dent	35.22	45/20*	230 psi, ½ reg, 30% cut-off	2L
Rise Hill Tunnel	-	45	225 psi, ¼ reg, 30% cut-off	
Garsdale	42.30	5*	slow to water hose	1L

2,000 gallons of water used Hellifield-Garsdale. Loco in superb condition, crisp, sure-footed in misty damp conditions, very smooth riding. No safety concerns.

4.20pm Stratford-on-Avon-Marylebone Railtour (Footplate from Banbury)
3.3.85
35028 *Clan Line*
11 coaches, 360t
Driver Brian Axtell, Fireman Brian Tagg, Marylebone
Inspector Peter Crawley, Euston

Banbury	00.00		Water, 5000 galls.	10.5L
	-	35/44	245 psi, ½ reg, 30% cut-off	
Kings Sutton	07.40	50	220 psi, 20% cut-off	
Aynho Junction	09.48	sigs 36*	200 psi, shut off/ 30% cut-off	
Ardley Tunnel	-	42	210 psi, 25% cut-off	
Ardley Summit	-	44	225 psi, 27% cut-off	
Ardley	17.02	53/63	200 psi, shut off	
Bicester North	-	75	210 psi (DM firing)	
Blackthorn	-	AWS 30*	200 psi, ½ reg, 30% cut-off	
Brill	-	46/pw 20*	220 psi, 35% cut-off	
Brill Tunnel	-	42	220 psi (DM ceased firing)	
Ashendon Junction	34.35	50	200 psi, 25% cut-off	
Haddenham	-	60	170 psi, full reg, 25% cut off	
Ilmer Halt	-	58/48	180 psi, ½ reg, 25% cut-off	
Princes Risborough	45.00	45	210 psi, 27% cut-off	9.5L
Saunderton Summit	-	42	190 psi, full reg, 27% cut-off	
Saunderton	49.27	58	180 psi, shut off, coasting	
West Wycombe	52.50	56	200 psi	
High Wycombe	56.35			T

1,600 galls used Banbury-High Wycombe. Loco in some difficulty for steam. Damper adjusted at High Wycombe and no further difficulty experienced. Loco ran under easy steam from Beaconsfield to Northolt Junction, speed in low 60s, arrived Marylebone 4 minutes early. No safety concerns.

Table 12 (cont'd)

12.00pm York-Marylebone Railtour (footplate from Banbury, scheduled dep. 5.06pm)
23.11.85
4498 *Sir Nigel Gresley*
12 coaches, 435/460t
Driver Trevor Barrett, Fireman Brian Tagg, Marylebone
Inspector Phil Bassett, Euston

Train arrived very late from ER behind 4498. 4,250 galls taken on at Banbury. Timings to nearest ½ minute.

Banbury	00.00			69L
Kings Sutton	07.00	51/53	230 psi	
Aynho Junction	10.00	sigs 30*	210 psi, shut off	
Ardley Tunnel	-	42	220 psi, ¾ reg, 25% cut-off	
Ardley Summit	-	46/42	230 psi, 30% cut-off (slipping in tunnel)	
Ardley	-	55	200 psi	
Bicester North	24.00//43.00	sigs stand (waiting 17.40 Pdn DMU off single line)		72L/91L
	-		180/240 psi, 3,500 galls left.	
Blackthorn	-	56	230 psi (DM firing from Bicester)	
Brill	-	pw 20*		
Brill Tunnel	-	25	230 psi, full reg, 25% cut-off	
Dorton Halt	-	50	15% cut-off	
Ashendon Junction	-	60/56	230 psi, ½ reg, 15% cut-off (DM driving from Ashendon Jcn)	
Haddenham	-	64	225 psi, full reg, 15% cut-off	
Ilmer Halt	-	56	Full reg, 25% cut-off	
Princes Risborough	-	58		
Saunderton Summit	-	54	225 psi, full reg, 25% cut-off	
West Wycombe	-	60	easy, coasting	
High Wycombe	77.00	35*	225 psi (DM ceased driving)	76L
Beaconsfield	83.00	60/56/40*	Full reg, 25% cut-off	
Seer Green	-	54	½ reg, 15% cut-off	
Gerrards Cross	89.00	sigs 25*		
Denham	-	60	½ reg, 15% cut-off	
West Ruislip	-	60	(1,750 galls left)	
Northolt Junction	99.00	20*/38	240 psi	72L
Sudbury	-	pw 20*	240 psi	
Neasden	112.00	40*	Full reg, slipping.	
Dollis Hill	-	45	175 psi	
Marylebone	124.00			75L

4498 in good condition, rode well, accelerated well on full regulator and 15 per cent cut-off, steaming freely, blowing off at 230-240psi. No safety concerns.

Table 13: APT Record Run - Euston to Glasgow Central

4.35pm Euston-Glasgow APT
12.12.84
370.006/7 (49.003/6 power cars)
2+8 chs

Euston	16.35		T
Camden	16.37	TSR 20*	
Willesden Jcn	16.41.5		0.5 L
Watford Jcn	16.47.25		0.25L
Tring	16.54		T
Bletchley	17.01.25		0.25L
Hillmorton		TSR 50*	
Rugby	17.20.25	60*/TSR 20*	1.25E
Nuneaton	17.29		2E
Tamworth	17.35.5		2E
Lichfield	17.38.5		2E
Armitage		TSR 50*	
Milton & Brockton		sigs 20*	
Stafford (South)	17.49.5//17.51.75	sigs stand (TCF failure)	
Stafford	17.53.25	80	2.25L
Norton Bridge	17.56.75		2.25L
Crewe	18.08		2.5L
Warrington	18.22		2.5L
Wigan	18.28.5		2.5L
Preston	18.37	35*	2L
Lancaster	18.48.5		1.5L
		TSR 40*	
Carnforth	18.53.5		0.5L
Oxenholme	18.59.75		0.25L
Penrith	19.17.25		0.25E
Carlisle	19.28.5	20*	0.5E
Gretna Jcn	19.34.25		1.25E
Lockerbie	19.44		0.5E
Beattock	19.50.5		3E
Beattock Summit	19.55.25	120	3.25E
Carstairs	20.07		3.5E
Glasgow Cen	20.27.25		5.25E

3 hours 52.25min record run , with 4 x TSRs and a signal stand.

Table 14: *The Moonraker* (GW175, Solihull-Salisbury)

Solihull to Salisbury and return, Saturday 3 April 2010
'The Moonraker'
5043 *Earl of Mount Edgcumbe* 84E
9 coaches, 350/375 tons

Departed Solihull at 07.38 on time, called at Dorridge, Warwick Parkway, Banbury, took water at Hinksey Up Loop and arrived in Salisbury at 11.57 on time. (Took Railway Children raffle en route, raising £470.00)

Return Journey.			
Salisbury	16.05	sigs Andover/Whitchurch	T
Basingstoke	16.55	25*	3L
Bramley	-	68	
Reading West	17.12//17.17	sigs stand	
Scours Lane	-	20* to Relief Line	
Goring	-	75	
Cholsey	-	75	

Didcot Parkway	17.33		T
	17.39		1L
Radley	-	60	
Hinksey Up Loop	17.56	(water)	T
	18.27	(waiting line clear)	4L
Oxford station (Middle)	18.29	15*	4L
Oxford North junction	18.30	(pathing)	3L
	18.40		T
Wolvercote Junction	18.45	60	1L
Kidlington	-	64	
Tackley Box	-	65	
Heyford	18.51	75	1E
Aynho Junction	18.59	70/50*/ sigs 25*	1E
Kings Sutton	-	65	
Banbury	19.07		1L

On footplate from Banbury (Bob Meanley acting as fireman)

Banbury	19.10	Clinker forming, fire irons used		2L
Cropredy	-	50	180 psi, full reg, 25%	
MP 74	-	60/64	160 psi	
Fenny Compton	19.20	75	200 psi, full reg, 18%	1E
Southam Road	-	80	eased	
Fosse Road	-	75/70		
Leamington Spa	19.29	40*	160 psi	6E
Warwick	19.32	sigs 10*	180 psi	
Warwick Parkway	19.35			5E
	19.39	slipping on gradient & wet rail		3E
			225 psi (blowing off)	
Hatton	19.45	38/40	full reg, 30%, 210 psi	2E
Lapworth	-	50/ sigs 20*		
Dorridge	19.55	180 psi		T
	20.00			2E
Widney Manor	-	50	160 psi/180 psi	
Solihull	20.07	(slow to platform) 200 psi		1E

Firing of poor quality coal was heavy, pressure seemed to recover when fire burnt through or when the draught on the fire was heaviest. After some 12 hours of steaming, clinker was forming from Banbury onwards. Loco rode well, had very even beat and seemed strong despite the periods of low boiler pressure.

Table 15: *The Bristolian*, **Bristol to Paddington via Badminton (GW 175)**
The Bristolian, **Saturday, 17 April 2010**
5043 *Earl of Mount Edgcumbe* **84E**
8 chs, 288/315 tons
Driver Andy Taylor, Firemen, Alistair & Bob Meanley

Bristol Temple Meads	00.00		T
Dr Days Junction	02.50	26	¼ E
Stapleton Road	04.33	40	
Narroways Hill Jcn	05.12	36	¾ E
Horfield	-	27	
Filton Junction	10.09	31/ sigs 13*	T
Bristol Parkway	13.50	36	¾ L
MP 110	16.04	56	
Westerleigh Junction	18.57	63	T
Sodbury Tunnel	22.14	67	
Badminton	25.37	62	
Hullavington	30.28	78/80	6E
Little Somerford	33.54	78	
MP 87	-	75	

Wootton Bassett	39.21	66*	8½ E
Swindon	44.17	74/72	11¾ E
MP 75	-	77	
Shrivenham	48.48	77	
Uffington	52.44	78	14¾ E
Challow	54.39	80/78	15½ E
Wantage Road	57.30	78	19½ E
Steventon	60.54	sigs 64*/70	
Didcot	63.33	78	20½ E
Cholsey	67.08	78	
Goring	70.00	75	
Pangbourne	72.34	77/78	
Tilehurst	74.48	75	
Scours Lane	-	sigs 41*	
Reading	77.43	49	25¼ E
Sonning	-	66	
Twyford	82.26	74	25½ E
Ruscombe Sidings	-	78/80	
Maidenhead	87.41	79	28¼ E
Taplow	89.03	76	
Burnham	90.15	77	
Slough	92.13	77	30¾ E
Langley	93.59	74	
Iver	95.10	76	
West Drayton	96.22	77	
Heathrow Airport Jcn	98.00	73	33 E
Hayes	98.14	73	
Southall	99.42	76	35¼ E
Hanwell	-	76	
West Ealing	101.41	75	37¼ E
Ealing Broadway	102.23	74	
Acton	103.35	73	39 E
Ladbroke Grove	105.48	42*	40¼ E
Paddington	109.58	(106 mins net)	44 E

Report from Bob Meanley on footplate: 5043 worked with 2nd valve of regulator just cracked and 15 per cent cut-off. Increasing cut-off to 17 per cent produced acceleration to over 75-80mph and engine brought back to 15 per cent.

Table 16: *The Pride of Swindon* **Carlisle-Crewe via Settle & Carlisle (GW 175)**

15.00 Carlisle-Crewe/Tyseley
5043 *Earl of Mount Edgcumbe* **84E**
10 coaches + 47.773 trailing (dead)
470/503t
Driver Mick Kelly, Fireman Alastair Meanley

Carlisle	00.00		4 ½ L
London Road Jcn	02.27		1L
Petterill Bridge Jcn	03.10	blowing off	1L
Scotby	08.27	32	
Cumwhinton	10.41	38	
Howes Sidings	12.21	40/43	1L
Cotehill	-	43 blowing off	
MP 300	-	42	
Armathwaite	19.22	53	
Barton Wood	-	59/57 blowing off	
Lazonby	24.47	68	1E
Little Salkeld	27.39	64	

Langwathby	29.17	57 blowing off	
Culgaith	32.56	62	2 ½ E
New Biggin	-	57	
Long Marston	37.37	63 blowing off	
MP 278	-	62/58 easy	
Appleby	40.27		6E
	00.00	Water	13 ½ E
Ormside Viaduct	-	50/56	
Ormside	05.15	53	
Helm Tunnel	-	47 blowing off	
Griseburn	09.25	42/40	
Crosby Garrett	-	42/45	
Smardale Viaduct	13.28	49/43 blowing off	
Kirkby Stephen	16.26	41	11E
Birkett Tunnel	19.30	42/41	
Mallerstang	-	44/47 50% cut off	
Ais Gill	26.07	44 ½	13E
Garsdale	29.20	57/60	12 ½ E
Dent	32.50	63/40*	
Blea Moor	39.25	52/60	13E
Batty Moss Viaduct	-	20*	
Ribblehead	42.05	30* blowing off	13E
Selside	-	57	
Horton-in-Ribblesdale	-	60 easy	
Settle	54.05	60*	
Settle Jcn	56.14	60*/64	15E
Long Preston	-	5* sigs	
	62.20/64.50 sigs stand		
Hellifield	67.28		11E

As loco was still blowing off steam, Driver Kelly opened up to 50 per cent cut off for the last mile to Ais Gill summit and accelerated on the 1 in 100 gradient, giving a calculated (by Mike Notley) IHP of 2,230, and EDBHP of 2,030, the highest ever recorded power output for a Castle and equal to the best King records. Mike Notley was travelling in the cab of 47 773 at the rear and confirmed that no power was applied at all by the diesel.

Appendix 2
Logs of journeys abroad, 1962-1979

Speed Conversion

Continental 24 hour clock used throughout and all speeds in the following tables are quoted at kilometres per hour. Conversion to miles per hour:

Kph	Mph	Kph	Mph	Kph	Mph
10	6	60	37.5	95	59
20	12.5	65	41	100	62
25	15.5	70	44	105	65.5
30	19	75	47	110	69
35	22	80	50	115	72
40	25	85	53	120	75
45	28	90	56	130	81
50	31				
55	34				

Table 1: SNCF Paris(Est)-Troyes-Chaumont-Mulhouse, 1961-2

08.23 Paris (Est)-Bâle Train 43
16.8.61
231 G 21 Troyes (Paris-Troyes)
231 G 144 Belfort (Troyes-Mulhouse)
13 chs, 508/535t

08.25 Paris (Est)-Bâle Train 43
13.7.62
241 P 21 Noisy-le-Sec (Paris-Chaumont)
241 A 7 Chaumont (Chaumont-Mulhouse)
13 chs, 483/510t

							km
Paris (Gare de l'Est)	00.00		2L	00.00		T	0
Pantin	07.31	74		06.10	88		
Noisy-le-sec	11.08	84		09.05	103		1:200F
Rosny-sous-Bois	14.24	86		11.28	109		
Nogent	16.55	103		13.48	pw 35*		1:167R
Villiers-sur-Marne	19.56	90		19.50	60		
Êmerainville	25.15	74		25.12	76/91		1:143R
Boissy	27.53	110		-	115		
Gretz-Armainvilliers	32.09	120		31.20	113		
Verneuil l'étang	39.58	76		39.08	105		1:200R
Nangis	51.03	78/84		48.34	107/112		
Maison Rouge	58.21	77		54.23	95		summit 1:200R
Longueville	63.12	128		59.13	113/101*		1:167F
Flamboin	66.44	124*		63.10	112		
Hermé	68.59	101		65.28	107		L
Melz	72.05	100		68.21	109		
Nogent-sur-Seine	75.51	93 **eased**		71.35	110		110
Marnay-sur-Seine	79.48	90		74.51	105		
Pont-sur-Seine	81.32	92		76.25	110		1:500F
Romilly-sur-Seine	87.39	91		82.00	103		129
Chatres	93.25	103		87.45	98/103		1:333F
Vallant-St Georges	96.18	100		90.48	92		
Savières	100.43	110		95.26	106		
Troyes arr	110.39		½ E	105.30		5 ½ E	166 (104 miles)
(231 G 144 on)	00.00		1¼ L	00.00		T	
Rouilly	10.08	82		07.58	107		
Lusigny	14.54	100		11.57	111/108		
La Villeneuve	22.05	90		21.26	pw 25*		
Vendeuvre	26.02	79		25.21	100		
Jessains	33.37	123		31.53	114		

Arsonval	36.24	107		35.00	100*/114		
Bar-sur-Aube arr	39.31		1¼ E	38.32		3½ E	
	00.00		½ L	00.00			221
Bayel	10.22	76		07.58	100		
Clairvaux	14.30	82		11.00	110		
Bricon	26.32	75/69/85		19.55		112/100/109	
Chaumont arr	38.33		T	29.38		9½ E	262 (164 miles)
	00.00		1L	00.00	(241 A 7 on) T		
Foulain	10.11	115/100		09.50	108/102		
Vaisignes-sur-Marne	14.46	96		14.14	100		1:167R
Rolamport	18.33	100		17.40	110		
Langres arr	25.36		½ L	24.10		2E	
	00.00		¾ L	00.00		T	296
Culmont-Chalindrey arr	12.38	93	1¼ L	11.05	94	1E	
	00.00		1¼ L	00.00		T	307
Hortes	07.47	120/137		07.06	114/105*		1:167F
Charnoy	11.12	133		10.49	111/101*		(15 kms)
La Ferté	13.18	118		13.12	108		
Vitry-Vernois arr	18.12		½ E	18.13		1¾ E	
	00.00		¼ L	00.00		T	
Jussey	09.49	110		08.42	107		
Pont d'Ateliers	18.03	118		17.07//18.00 Spl stop			
Pont-sur-Saone	23.14	88/80		26.05	77		
Vaivre	27.56	116		30.57	110/106		1:167F
Vesoul arr	31.56		¼ L	35.02		3L	
	00.00		1½ L	00.00		3L	380
Colombier	09.31	61		07.53	75		1:167R
Crévenay-Saux	15.33	72/108		12.58	82/ pw 50*/110		
Lure arr	27.55		2¼ L	26.00		2L	
Lure	00.00		2¼ L	00.00		2L	410
Ronchamp	13.17	63/72		12.05	69		
Champagny	18.56	100		17.33	76		1:250F
Bas Evette	25.56	110		23.47	110		1:167F
Valdoie	27.39	120		-	112		
Belfort arr	31.07		T	29.36		1½ E (Load reduced to 9 chs, 316/330t)	
	00.00		1L	00.00		3¾ L	442
Petit-Croix	11.03	108		09.18	112		
Montreux-Vieux	12.28	105		10.42	100		
Valdieu	14.00	105		12.21	105		1:167R/F
Dannemarie	16.51	123		15.28	109/ pw 24*/106		
Altkirch arr	22.24		T	24.11		6L	
	00.00		¼ L	00.00		6L	
Walheim	03.50	100		03.29	100		
Illfurth	06.10	107/99		05.44	109/93*		
Zillisheim	08.08	106		07.27	112		
Hasenrein	-	sigs 22*		-	108		
Mulhouse arr	13.11		1E	12.47		3¾ L	491 (307 miles)

231 G 21 and 231 G 144 were both PLM Pacifics modified by Chapelon − 231 G 144 still had its PLM large tender, 231 G 21 had SNCF standard tender. 241 A 7 was the only double chimney 241 A. The two Mountains accelerated quicker and were faster uphill, the Pacifics were driven harder downhill. All were 120kph maximum except 241 A 7 which was limited to 110kph.

Table 2: SNCF - Mulhouse-Chaumont-Paris (Est), 1961-62

Train 42 (Bâle) Belfort-Paris (Est)
20.8.61
241 A 58 Chaumont (to Chaumont)
241 A 63 Chaumont (from Chaumont)
15 chs, 586/625t
16 chs, 628/675t from Troyes

Train 42 (Bâle) Belfort-Paris (Est)
24.7.62
241 A 18 Chaumont (to Chaumont)
241 P 26 Noisy-le-Sec (from Chaumont)
13 chs, 470/500t
14 chs, 508/545t from Troyes

							km
Belfort	00.00		½ L	00.00		1L	0
Valdoie	06.58	53		-	56		
Bas Evette	10.18	70/75		09.31	72	1:200/167R	
Champagny	17.34	92/99		16.16	90/115		
Ronchamp	21.43	112		19.50	105*/118		
Lure arr	28.04		½ L	26.18		1E	
	00.00		3L	00.00		T	32
Crévenay-Saulx	13.47	106/113		19.11	87/ pw 35* 9long)	1:250R (8 kms)	
Colombier	17.23	116		22.56	115		
Vesoul arr	21.57		3L	27.41		5 ½ L	
	00.00		3L	00.00		5 ½ L	62
Vaivre	05.25	88		04.50	80/87		
Pont-sur-Saone	11.29	96/115		10.35	72/109	summit 1:167R	
Pont d'Ateliers	16.37	106/113		17.22	pw 15* (long)		
Jussey	24.56	108		28.55	107		
Vitry-Vernois	31.26	105		35.06	112		
La Ferté	36.30	99		39.32	118		
Charnoy	39.12	92		41.53	105		
Hortes	44.09	69/61		46.10	85/72	summit 1:167R (15 kms)	
Culmont-Chalindrey arr	52.58		2L	53.54		5 ½ L	
	00.00		1L	00.00		5 ½ L	135
Langres arr	13.14		T	10.58	107	3 ¾ L	
	00.00		2L	00.00		4 ¾ L	146
Rolampont	08.58	102		08.30	107/95		
Vaisignes-sur-Marne	12.18	106		11.57	108		
Foulain	-	112/77		16.03	115/85	1:167R	
Chaumont arr	25.31		2 ½ L	23.42		2 ¾ L	
(241 A 63 on)	00.00		3 ½ L	00.00	(241 P 26 on)	3L	180 (112.5 miles)
Bricon	10.15	108		08.43	112/105/119		
Clairvaux	19.18	112		17.55	96*/107		
Bayel	22.32	106		20.52	115		
Bar-sur-Aube arr	27.30			26.25			
	00.00			00.00			221
Arsonval	06.02	93		04.57	111		
Jessains	09.33	85/82		07.59	106/112	1:167R	
Vendeuvre	17.18	117		13.53	108/101*/106		
La Villeneuve	20.43	120		20.00	pw 25*/90		
Lusigny	27.15	115		29.13	pw 23*/106		
Rouilly	31.28	111		33.15	112		
Troyes arr	38.12		½ E	39.15		T	
	00.00		T	00.00			276
Savières	12.33	100		10.52	112	1:333R	
Vallant-St Georges	17.23	105		15.23	108/94	1:500R/F	
Chatres	20.26	110		18.13	107	1:333R	
Romilly	25.46	108		23.35	111	1:500R	313
Pont-sur-Seine	31.39	105		29.15	110/106	L	
Marnay-sur-Seine	33.23	105		30.52	105		
Nogent-sur-Seine	36.59	105		34.11	102/107		332
Melz	40.35	107		37.38	105		
Hermé	43.38	111		40.39	109		
Flamboin	46.04	108		43.05	104		
Longueville	50.41	96/74		47.43	83/74		
Maison Rouge	58.22	67		55.05	67/72	summit 1:167R	

Nangis	66.00	110		62.05	100	(17.5 kms)
Verneuil l'étang	75.56	113/102		71.58	110/112	
Gretz-Armainvilliers	84.52	98		81.03	80 easy	
Boissy	89.42	105		-	85	
Emerainville	91.59	108		88.43	90	
Villiers-sur-Marne	-	110		93.45	50*/83	
Nogent	98.53	112/ pw 10*		96.44	100	
Rosny-sous-Bois	-	pw 10* (long)		99.23	75 easy	
Noisy-le-Sec	108.53	92		102.29	78	
Pantin	113.05	96/sigs		105.53	80	
Paris (Est) arr	119.03 (113 net)	2 ¾ L		113.20	½ E	442 (276 miles)

241 A 18, 58 and 63 all standard Est Mountains with heavy loads. 241 P 26 had so much time in hand by Longueville that it drifted under easy steam for the rest of the way arriving meticulously at the appointed hour.

Table 3: Calais to Amiens, 1962, 1968.

08.09 Paris (Nord)-Calais Mme (Amiens - Boulogne Ville)
25.7.62
231 K 46 Calais
13 chs, 523/550t

08.10 Paris (Nord)-Calais Mme (Amiens-Boulogne V)
25.7.68
231 K 16 Calais
16 chs, 642/700t

				km			
Amiens	00.00		T	0	00.00		T
St Roch	05.05	70			05.12	65	1:200F
Dreuil les Amiens	-	94			09.37	pw 70*	1:200R
Ailly-sur-Somme	10.43	107			-	90	L/1:200F
Picquigny	13.15	115			13.53	110	L
Hangest	16.53	122			17.34	118	
Longpré	20.06	120			20.51	116	
Long le Catelet	-	122			22.03	116	
Fontaine-sur-Somme	22.40	120			-	120	
Pont Rémy	24.33	118			25.04	122	
Abbéville	28.55	120/110*		45	29.37	125/115*	
Port le Grand	33.07	115/109			33.46	118	
Noyelles	36.03	122			36.36	115/118	
Ponthoile Romaine	38.40	124			39.17	122	
Rue	40.58	122			41.41	116 eased	
Quend Fort Mahon	43.30	122/115			44.28	112	
Conchil le Temple	46.04	124			47.16	109	
Rang du Fliers Verton	49.18	109		85	50.58	96/103	1:250/1:500R
St Jossé	52.00	120			54.09	100	1:280/1:500F
Etaples	55.06	105/111		96	57.58	96/91	L
Dannes Camiers	59.12	100/78			62.58	85/65	
Neufchatel	63.06	115			68.23	61	1:133R (4 kms)
Hesdigneul	66.01	pw 20*			-	100	1:143/1:133F
	66.35//66.53	sig stand					
Pont de Briques	72.13				74.19	88	
Boulogne Ville arr	76.23 (72 mins net)	123 1½ E		78.17 (77 mins net)		T	
		(77 miles)					

231 K 46 was in superb condition, machine titulaire; 231 K 16 was 'run of the mill' in the last year before withdrawal, but ran superbly to Rue with this 700 tonnes load, then eased to avoid early running.

19.19 Calais Maritime-Amiens (Paris) Train 32
24.7.68
231 K 27 Calais
141 R 1201 Boulogne (Pilot to Boulogne only)
15 chs, 638/690t

				km
Calais Ville	00.00		23 ½ L (Late arrival of cross channel ferry)	0
Les Fontinettes	03.52			
Fréthun	07.32	96		8
Pihen	11.04	85		
Caffiers	14.10	83		1:125R (12 kms)
Le Haut Banc	17.27	108/90*		1:125F (9 kms)
Marquise Rinxent	19.35	105/93*		25
Wacquinghem	23.32	115		
Aubengue	25.03	103		1;125R (2 kms)
Wimille Wimereux	26.14	110/95*		35
Boulogne Tintelleries	29.28	109		1:167F
Boulogne Ville arr	31.33		20L (141R 1201 detached)	
	00.00		21L	42 (26 miles)
Pont de Briques	05.10	95		1:167F / L
Hesdigneul	07.41	94/82		
Neufchatel	11.24	72		1:143/1:133R
Dannes Camiers	15.31	120/125		1:133F
Etaples	19.19	122		69
Bifarcation Le Tréport	-	124		
St Jossé	22.30	115		L
Rang du Fliers Verton	25.11	115		80
Conchil le Temple	28.59	113/116		1:280R (1 km)
Quend Fort Mahon	31.06	118		L
Rue	33.49	117		
Ponthoile Romaine	36.14	118		
Noyelles	38.55	118		
Port le Grand	-	117/119		
Abbéville	46.10	118		120
Pont Rémy	50.54	113/110		
Fontaine-sur-Somme	53.03	106		
Long le Catelet	54.33	107		
Longpré	55.58	110		
Hangest	61.32	109/ sigs 20*		
Picquigny	68.18	90		
Ailly-sur-Somme	-	95		1:200R (1.5 kms)
Dreuil les Amiens	72.18	pw- 80*		
St Roch	-	96		1:200R (1.5 kms)
Amiens arr	80.02	(72.5 mins net) 22L		165 (103 miles)

PLM pacifics were provided with a pilot for Caffiers Bank as far as Boulogne, which restricted speed theoretically to 100kph. After Boulogne 231K 27 with this very heavy load was allowed 120kph. The signal check at Hangest cost at least 6 minutes.

Table 4: Kaufbeuren-Kempten, 1961

13.48 München-Lindau (Genf) D96 *Rhône-Isar*
18.8.61
18.610 Lindau (18.523 built Maffei 1927)
9 chs, 352/395t

				km	
Kaufbeuren	00.00			T	0
Biessenhofen	05.57	78			
Ruderatshofen	08.59	90			
Aitrang	12.09	82			
Günzach	20.05	pw 45*			
Wilpoldsried	26.40	130/90*			
Betzigau	28.37	105			
Kempten-Hegge arr	35.16			5E	43
(27 miles)					

08.39 Lindau/Oberstdorf-München E689
18.8.61
18.602 Lindau (18.547 built Henschel 1931)
11 chs, 426/445t

Kempten Allgäu	00.00		½ L
Betzigau	08.22	67	
Wilpoldsried	10.39	85	
Günzach	19.39	66/110	
Aitrang	28.19	70*/85	
Ruderatshofen	31.39	100/40*	
Biessenhofen	36.39	T	
	00.00		
Kaufbeuren arr	07.09	T	

Table 5: Lindau to München, 1962

09.33 Lindau-München Hbf (00.55 Genf), D91
17.7.62
18.614 Lindau (18.532 built Henschel 1930)
6 chs 228/240t

				km	
Lindau Hbf	00.00		T	0	
L-Aeschach	03.15	48			
Oberreitnau	10.54	50/64			
Rehlings	14.28	60/69			
Schlachters	16.13	80			
Hergensweiler	18.56	90/85			
Hergatz	22.42	101		23	
Wohmbrechts	24.16	82			
Heimenkirch	31.07	74/ pw 43*			
Röthenbach	36.49		1 ¾ L		
	00.00		¾ L		
Harbatshofen	07.40	52/ pw 38*/82			
Oberstaufen	14.47		2 ½ L		
	00.00		3L		
Ratholz	07.47	96/80*			
Bühl	11.12	96			
Immenstadt	13.11		2L	72	
	00.00		½ L		
Seifen	05.14	70*/100			
Oberdorf	08.11	75*/95			
Waltenhofen	11.31	78*			
Kempten-Hegge	14.15		¼ E		
	00.00		T	89	
Betzigau	09.22	70/ pw 30*			
Wilpoldsried	11.25	100			
Günzach	19.00	80/62			
Aitrang	26.10	97/68*			
Ruderatshofen	28.27	95			
Biessenhofen	31.40	105/85*			
Kaufbeuren	35.58		T	132	
	00.00		T		
Leinau	05.05	88			
Pforzen	06.56	103			
Beckstetten	10.05	96/84*			
Buchloe	15.43		¾ L		
	00.00		1 ½ L	152	
Igling	06.36	101			

					kms
Kaufering	09.15	pw 46*			
Schwabhausen	16.48	105			
Geltendorf	19.20	95			
Grafrath	25.25	87/96			
Fürstenfeldbruck	31.28	90			
Puchheim	35.57	103			
Aubing	38.47	95			
Pasing	41.02	100		213	
Mü-Laim	43.00				
München Hbf	47.16		1 ½ E	220 (137.5 miles)	

Table 6: Hamburg to Köln, 1962 (Oil-burning 012 Pacifics)
Köln to Aachen, 1962 (Coal-burning 03.10)

08.26 Hamburg Hbf-Köln D94
20.7.62
01.1079 Osnabrück (to Osnabrück)
01.1068 Osnabrück (from Osnabrück)
12 chs, 409/445t

				kms
				0
Hamburg Hbf	00.00		2L	0
Veddel	05.46	72		
Hamburg-Wilhelmsburg	07.52	84		
Hamburg-Harburg arr	14.02	sigs 15*		
	00.00		T	
Bk. Glüsingen	-	pw 24*		
Hittfeld	11.39	72		
Klecken	15.50	79		
Buchholz	19.44	104		
Sprötze	22.22	120		
Tostedt	25.50	107/116		
Königsmoor	29.16	122		
Lauenbrück	32.58	120		
Scheessel	35.56	116/120		
Rotenburg arr	41.23		2L	
	00.00		1L	
Sottrum	07.49	105		
Ottersberg	12.03	115		
Sagehorn	15.53	118		
Bremen-Oberneuland	18.57	120		
Bremen arr	27.13	122	1E	
	00.00	Sigs.	9 ½ L	
Bremen-Hemelingen	06.17	99		
Dreye	09.10	109		
Kirchweyhe	11.27	107		
Barrien	13.54	105		
Syke	16.00	90		
Bramstedt	19.30	105		
Bassum	21.52	115/106		
Twistringen	26.40	116		
Drentwede	30.23	122		
Barnstorf	33.15	128		
Drebber	36.37	120		
Diepholz arr	41.10		8 ½ L	
	00.00	Slipping	9L	
Lembruch	08.02	103		
Lemförde	12.06	110/104		
Bohmte	18.27	116		
Ostercappeln	22.49	94		
Vehrte	27.01	82		

Station		Time	Speed/Notes	Loco	Dist	Notes
Belm		-	110			
Osnabrück	arr	34.59		8L		(01.1079 off)
		00.00		8 ¾ L	240	(01.1068 on)
Hasbergen		07.48	103		(176.5 miles)	
Natrup-Hagen		10.41	106/104			
Lengerich		13.38	120/ pw 82*			
Kattenvenne		18.05	120			
Brock-Ostbevern		21.03	122			
Westbevern		22.10	122			
Sudmühle		26.39	120			
Münster	arr	31.10		7L		
		00.00		6 ½ L	290	
Hiltrup		06.31	106			
Steiner See		07.52	115			
Rinkerwald		10.23	120			
Drensteinfurt		13.22	120			
Bockum-Hövel		19.33	106/115			
Hamm Hbf	arr	23.33		5L		
Hamm		00.00		4 ½ L	326	
Wiescherhöfen		05.10	104			
Bönen		08.05	118/104			
Unna		12.46	pw 45*/77		345	
Holzwickede		18.56	50*/96			
Schwerte	arr	27.00		4 ½ L		
		00.00	Sigs.	7 ½ L	361	
Bk. Steinhausen		-	pw 40*/65			
Westhofen		05.12	pw 70*			
Hohensyburg		07.32	103			
Hagen	arr	13.22		10L		
		00.00		9L	374	
Hagen-Haspe		05.38	60			
Gevelsberg		10.03	60			
Ennepetal-Milspe		11.54	60			
Bk Martfeld		14.03	61/90			
Schwelm		15.21	111			
Wuppertal-Oberbarmen		18.49		6 ¾ L		
		00.00		6 ¾ L	401	
Wuppertal Barmen		02.42	60			
Wuppertal-Unterbarmen		04.08	80			
Wuppertal-Elberfeld		06.07		7L		
		00.00		6L		
Wuppertal Steinbeck		02.00	47			
W-Zoo-Garten		04.25	88			
W-Sonnborn		04.55	93			
W-Vohwinkel		06.15	103			
Grüten		10.05	sigs 45*			
Haan		12.10	106			
Solingen-Ohligs	arr	14.31		5 ½ L		
		00.00		5 ½ L	419	
Solingen-Landwehr		03.27	106			
Leichlingen		05.05	120/sigs 22*			
Opladen		09.30	85/109			
Leverkusen-Schleebusch		11.50	112			
Köln-Mühlheim		-	80*			
Köln-Deutzerfeld		21.45//22.33	sigs stand			
Köln Hbf	arr	26.18		T	447 (279 miles)	

298

18.55 Köln-Aachen (Oostende)
20.7.62
03.1013 Hagen-Eck (reboilered 03.10)
13 chs, 517/550t

				km	
Köln Hbf	00.00		7L	0	
Köln-Ehrenfeld	05.29	82			
Köln-Stadion	08.09	83			
Lövenich	09.49	85/90			
Grosskönigsdorf	12.42	88			
Horrein	15.51	115			
Sindorf	17.39	120			
Buir	21.57	103			
Bk Merzenich	-	102			
Düren	27.27	90*/104		39	
Langerwehe	33.27	99/110			
Nothberg	36.34	pw 60*			
Eschweiler	39.04	pw 55*			
Stolberg	42.25	100			
Aachen-Rothe Erde	47.48	pw 20*			
Aachen Hbf arr	51.24	(46 mins net)	3L	70 (43.75 miles)	

Two good typical runs with oil-burning 3 cyl 01.10 (012) Pacifics on the 'Rollbahn' – the Hamburg-Köln run regularly worked by these locos until taken over by V200 diesels in the mid-60s. There were several sections at or near even time – Rotenburg to Bremen, 43 km in 27mins 13 secs (59mph average); Bremen-Diepholz, 69.7 kms in 41mins 10 secs (63mph average); and Osnabrück to Münster, 50.2 kms in 31mins 10 secs (60mph average). The 03.10 (coal-burning loco) was a case of 'all-out' with this load – the noise was deafening.

Table 7: SNCF, Brittany, Summer 1968-9

08.00 Paris (Montparnasse)-Granville SO, Train 403 (from Dreux to Argentan)
27.7.68
141 P 228 Argentan (Chapelon 2-8-2)
12 chs, 415/445t

					km
Dreux	00.00		T		0
St Germain-St Rémy	08.53	61/ 106		1:100R/ 1:111F	
Nonancourt	12.15	89		1:100R	
KM 105	-	100/96		1:125R	
Tillières	19.07	107	1½ E	1:143F	
Verneuil-sur-Avre	24.42	99	2E	1:125R	26
Bourth	30.21	105		1:200R	
St Martin d'Ecublei	35.23	109/100*	2 ½ E	L	
L'Aigle	38.53	pw 60*			50
Rai-Aube	42.48	101	2E	L	
St Hilaire-Beaufai	45.25	105		L	
St Gauburge	48.28	99	2 ½ E	1:125R	
Planches	51.18	105		1:250R	
Le Merlerault	54.49	101*/107	3E	1:100F	
Nonant le Pin	57.31	110/104*		1:143F	
KM 180	-	110		L	
Bifurcation de Surdon	63.05	60*			91
Almèneches	65.35	99			
KM 96	-	110			
Argentan arr	72.33		3½ E		116 (72.5 miles)

Although 141 P 228 was in externally poor condition, it ran well on this Summer Saturday holiday express and averaged 60mph exactly over the 72 miles from Dreux to Argentan, while remaining within its 110kph (69mph) limit. It was replaced at Argentan by 141 P 108 of the same depot for the run on to Granville,

stopping more frequently on the undulating route, on time or early throughout. Probably the hardest piece of work was to accelerate the 445 tonnes train from a pway slack of 22kph after Vire up the 1:100 of nearly 8 miles to a steady 90kph.

10.05 Paris (Montparnasse)-Les Sables d'Olonne & Pornic, Train 953 (from Le Mans to Nantes)

	20.7.68 241 P 5 Le Mans 15 chs, 605/650t			28.7.68 241 P 12 Le Mans 18 chs, 740/800t		
						km
Le Mans	00.00		½ L	00.00		T 0
St Georges Etival	08.30	96		08.59	96	1:500/333F
Voivtres	10.39	107		11.18	106	L / 1:250F
La Suze	13.56	112		14.43	112	
Noyen	19.27	95		20.12	104	1:200R (5 kms)
Avoise	24.09	108		24.37	120/110	1:200/167F (4 kms)
Juigné-sur-Sarthe	27.58	96		28.06	95	1:200R (5 kms)
KM 255	-	86		-	106	
Sablé	31.08	125		31.04	110	49
KM 264	-	115/120		-	118	1:200F/1:200R
Pincé-Précigné	35.56	126		35.55	120	
Morannes	38.37	115		39.03	107	1:250R (5 kms)
La Porage	41.54	120		42.27	111	1:200F (2 kms)
Etriché Chateauneuf	43.58	115		44.34	111	L
Tiercé	46.20	111		46.58	110	1 in 333F
KM 292	-	107		-	106	1:200R (4 kms)
Vieux Briollay	-	120		49.45	116	1:200F
St Sylvain Briollay	50.57	110/118		51.33	115	
Ecouflant	53.45	pw 22*		54.22	118/111	
Angers Maitre Ecole	59.10	80		56.50	107	
Angers St Laud arr	61.27	(58.5 mins net)	T	59.37		2½ E 97 (60.6 mls)
	00.00		½ L	00.00		1E 0
La Pointe Bouchemaine	06.42	112		07.20	107	1:300/400R
Les Forges	08.55	124		09.40	112	
La Possonnière	11.15	115		11.52	112	1:200R/1:200F
St Georges-sur-Loire	13.40	121		14.39	112	
Champtocé-sur-Loire	17.58	121		18.56	113	1:500R/1:500F
Ingrandes	20.55	120		21.52	115	
Montrelais	-	112		23.58	113	1:400R
Varades	25.28	111		26.17	114	L
Anetz	-	111		29.27	115	
Ancenis	32.03	111		32.42	112	
Oudon	37.06	111		37.39	111	
Clermont-sur-Loire	-	108		39.35	112	
Le Cellier	-	108		40.46	108	
Mauves-sur-Loire	42.22	111		42.48	107/114	
Thouaré	45.03	108		45.28	115	
St Luce	-	107		46.56	115	
Bifurcation Chateaubriant	-	105		-	easy	
Nantes arr	52.37		2E	53.08		3E 88 (55 miles)

Both machines ran very sweetly with enormous loads, no fuss, both driven relatively hard to accelerate and then steadily once speed around 110-120kph achieved. Maximum speed for 241 P locos was 120kph. Both sections require 60mph average speed to keep time.

19.18 Nantes-Paris (Montparnasse) Train 10762 Supplementaire
17.8.69 (Sunday)
241 P 16 Le Mans
12 chs, 449/475t

18.00 Le Croisic - Paris Montparnasse Train 762
21.7.68
241 P 33 Le Mans
17 chs, 624/680t

				km				
Angers St Laud	00.00		10L	0	00.00			1½ L
Angers Maitre Ecole	02.59	90			02.49	75		
Ecouflant	06.03	117			08.21	pw 20*	1:200R	
St Sylvain Briollay	08.51	122			11.57	108	1:200F	
KM 294	-	110			-	107	1:200R	
Vieux Briollay	10.39	115			13.52	118	1:167F	
Tiercé	13.20	120			16.38	119	1:200F/1:200R	
Etriché Chateauneuf	15.35	122			18.56	121	1:333/400R	
La Porage	17.34	122/119			21.05	118	1:200F	
Morannes	20.42	122			24.17	115	1:333R/L	
Pincé Précigné	23.40	124			27.20	118	1:333F/L	
KM 264	-	120			-	111		
Sablé	28.08	116		48	31.58	115	1:250F	
KM 255	-	112			-	108	1:200/167R	
Juigné-sur-Sarthe	30.16	122			35.07	112		
Avoise	-	125			38.18	120	1:167R	
Noyen	38.25	117			42.33	115	1:200F/1:200R	
La Suze	43.27	125			47.57	124	1:200F	
Voivres	-	122			51.23	125	L	
St Georges Etival	48.54	116			53.31	115/120/ sigs 30*		
Le Mans arr	54.54		5L	97	60.48	(56 mins net)		2L
				(60.6 miles)				

241 P 16 was just ex-store, with an Inspector on the footplate. The train left Nantes just over 13 minutes late because of poor operating at Nantes and ran the 55 miles to Angers in 52 minutes exactly regaining 3 minutes without exceeding 120kph. The train managed to average 66mph between Angers and Le Mans with 475 tonnes gross on an undulating road on a relief train on a Sunday with a loco just ex store!

241 P 33 the previous year just kept the 60mph schedule with the one severe pw slack at the beginning with nearly 700 tonnes. This was the Sunday evening train from the coast (worked by an État pacific from Le Croisic to Nantes) for which Train 10762 was the relief, the following year, when Train 762 was diesel hauled. 241 P 33 accelerated very hard from the pway slack until the summit at KM 292 and then ran without apparent undue exertion thereafter. It would not have been possible to regain the slight late start without exceeding the 120kph speed limit.

18.00 Le Croisic-Paris Montparnasse Train 762 (from St Nazaire to Nantes)
28.7.68
231 D 511 Nantes
9 chs, 350/395t

				km	
St Nazaire	00.00		2L	0	
La Croix de Maen	03.18	80			1:250F
Montoir de Bretagne	05.36	111			1:250R
Donges	09.36	120			L
KM 472	-	122			
Saveney	15.46	76*		25	
KM 465	-	107			1:333R/L
KM 463	-	120			
Cordemais	21.38	116/124			1:333F
St Etienne de Montluc	24.30	117/122			L
Couëron	28.28	120			
KM 441	-	pw 80*			
La Basse Indre	31.26	90			
Chantenay	34.57	98			
Nantes arr	39.00	(37 mins net)	3L	64 (40 miles)	

Another 60+mph schedule for a Sunday evening holiday express, one of the last remaining État Pacifics worked hard and just failing to keep time because of the pway slack. The engine accelerated very hard from the St Nazaire stop and after the Savenay slowing. 231 D 511 and all the remaining État pacifics were withdrawn the following month, 231 G 558 being preserved.

Table 8: SNCF - The 'Bourbonnais', 1968

18.57 Paris (Gare de Lyon)-Clermont Ferrand, Train 1109
16.11.68
241 P 8 Nevers
13 chs, 546/590t

Gien	00.00		T
Km 157	-	75	1:125R
Briare	08.38	122	1:200F
Chatillon	11.23	119/122	1:200R
Bonny	15.07	124/119*	L/1:200F
Neuvy	17.53	120	L
Myennes	22.21	120/124	
Cosne arr	25.32		½ E
	00.00		T
Villechaud	06.17	109	1:200R
Tracy Sancerre	08.39	118	L
Les Girarmes	09.10	122	
Pouilly-sur-Loire	13.31	115/119	1:167R
Mesves Bulcy	16.29	120	1:167F
La Charité	20.10	112	1:200R
La Malche	-	125	1:200F
Tronsanges	24.24	116	1:333R
Pougues les Eaux	27.03	120/111	1:200F/1:143R
Fourchambault	30.26	125/120	1:200F
Vauzelles	33.06	p-way 10*	
Nevers arr	38.01		2E

18.57 Paris (Gare de Lyon)-Clermont Ferrand, Train 1109
23.7.68
241 P 24 Nevers
10 chs, 411/450t

18.57 Paris (Lyon)-Clermont Ferrand, Train 1109
15.11.68
241 P 24 Nevers
12 chs, 506/550t

								km
Nevers	00.00		¾ L		00.00		1½ L	0
Saincaize	09.36	109/84*			09.27	107/80*		
Mars	15.35	115			15.14	120	1:250R	
St Pierre le Moutier	-	109/120			19.25	105	1:200R	
Chantenay St Imbert	24.26	116			24.44	115	1:200F	
Villeneuve-sur-Allier	29.55	115			29.43	120/128	L	
Moulins arr	40.27		¾ E		39.48		1E	60
	00.00		T		00.00		T	
Bessay	10.16	120			11.02	116		
La Ferté	-	115			14.18	115/118		
Varennes-sur-Allier	18.12	120			20.13//20.39 sigs failure			
	-	115			22.44//24.05		1:250R	
Créchy	-	118			-		L	
Billy Marcenat	-	111			-	115		
St Germain des Fossés arr	27.59		1E		35.50		7L	
	00.00		T		00.00 Take water		9L	101
	-	112			-	105		
Vichy arr	10.26		½ E		10.57		9L	
	00.00		½ L		00.00		9½ L	111
Hauterive	05.28	94/100			05.20	100	1:200R	

St Sylvestre	-	96			-	80	1:91R
Randan Tunnel	11.11	100			-	83	1:91R
Randan	12.12	112			13.51	115	1:125F
St Clément de Regnat	15.32	108*			-	107*	
Thuret	-	120			-	115	1:143F
Surat	-	112			-	120	1:143R
Ennezat Clèrelande	-	105*/ sigs 20*			-	112	1:143F/R
Riom arr	28.58		2E		29.33		7L	
	00.00		T		00.00		8L	152
Gerzat	06.12	122			05.45	122	1:200F/125R	
Clermont Ferrand arr	12.25		2 ½ E		11.52		5L	166
							(104 mls)	

18.57 Paris (Lyon)-Clermont Ferrand, Train 1109
26.7.68
241 P 8   Nevers
13 chs, 546/600t

Nevers	00.00		¼ L
Saincaize	10.30	106/ 83*	
Mars	15.32	125	1:250R
St Pierre le Moutier	19.27	117	1:200R
Chantenay St Imbert	24.30	120	1:200F
Villeneuve-sur-Allier	29.50	108/122	L
Moulins arr	38.45		3E
	00.00		½ E
Bessay	11.07	111/117	
La Ferté Hauterive	14.16	115	1:250R
Varennes-sur-Allier	18.56	120	L
Créchy	-	122	
Billy Marcenat	-	115	
St Germain des Fossés	28.15		1¼ E
	00.00	100*	
Vichy arr	11.18		½ E

00.24 Clermont Ferrand-Paris (Lyon), Train 1116
27.7.68
241 P 22   Nevers
14 chs, 565/600t

St Germain des Fossés	00.00		½ E
Billy Marcenat	-	100/112	1:250R
Créchy	07.22	120	L
Varennes-sur-Allier arr	11.30		
	00.00		
La Ferté	07.41	95/115	
Bessay	10.45	122	1:143F
	19.52/24.50	sig stand	
Moulins arr	28.50		
	00.00		5 ¾ L
Villeneuve-sur-Allier	-	110/118	
St Pierre le Moutier	21.51		
	00.00		
Mars	-	120	
Saincaize	11.32	80*/118	
Nevers arr	19.10		¾ L

The first run (previous page) in November 1968 shows 241 P 8 at its best, when it was the regular engine for the Nevers-Morêt-Nevers sections of Trains 1110 and 1109. The next two runs show 241 P 24 south of Nevers on Train 1109. The main feature of the first run was the phenomenal climb to Randan tunnel, 7 miles of 1:91

303

– the average speed over this gradient was 61mph (98kph), the same speed being maintained throughout the climb. The same loco with an extra two coaches, 100 tonnes, achieved 80mph (128kph) on the level before Moulins and would have kept time easily but for the signal failure at Varennes-sur-Allier. 241 P 8 with thirteen coaches, 600 tonnes gross, ran Nevers-Moulins start to stop in 38 minutes 45 seconds, gaining over 3 minutes with a top speed of 78mph (125 kph) on the level at Chantenay and ran at a steady 120-122kph between Moulins and St Germain-des-Fossés but I alighted at Vichy in order to pick up the overnight Clermont Ferrand-Paris sleeper (Train 1116), 241 P 22 with fourteen coaches, 610 tonnes gross. Despite a 5 minute signal stand before Moulins, it arrived virtually on time into Nevers.

08.35 Clermont Ferrand-Paris Montparnasse, between Nevers and Morêt les Sablons, Train 1110

	23.7.68 241 P 23 Nevers 13 chs, 546/590t			15.11.68 241 P 8 Nevers 13 chs, 546/600t			17.11.68 241 P 8 Nevers 12 chs, 506/550t		km
Nevers	00.00		T	00.00		10L	00.00	T	0
Vauzelles	04.24	65		04.54			03.59	1:143F	
Fourchambault	07.05	111/99		07.49	108/99		06.50	116/102	
Ponges-les-Eaux	10.53	112		11.40	115		10.37	118	1:200R/143F
Tronsanges	13.34	115		14.27	110		13.23	115	1:330F
La Malche	15.09	120		16.10	120		-	122	
La Charité	17.47	105		18.40	108		17.38	107	1:125R 26
Mesves Bulay	21.26	115		22.19	122		21.22	120	1:200F
Pouilly-sur-Loire	24.31	110		25.22	114		24.26	113	1:167R
Les Girarmes	26.53	127		27.43	122		26.50	124	1:250F
Tracy Sancerre	29.13	125/115		30.02	125/116		29.19	115	
Cosne arr	34.57		2E	37.43	(slow in)	11L	35.15	2E	58
	00.00		T	00.00		11L	00.00	T	
Myennes	05.02	100		06.10	65* SLW		04.58	80* SLW L	
Neuvy	09.44	122/113		14.49//15.12 sigs SLW			16.00	pw 15* (long) L	
Bonny	12.29	120/115		21.28	99		19.28	110	1:167R
Chatillon	16.27	123		25.41	120		23.25	124	L/1:167F
Briare	19.09	107		28.25	122/112		26.08	120/109	1:200F/1:200R
Gien arr	25.48		1¼ E	34.20	(26 mins net)	18L	32.11	(25 mins net) 5L	99
	00.00		T	00.00		18L	00.00	4 ½ L	
Les Choux	09.25	99/122		08.48	111/122		08.21	120	L
Nogent	13.09	111/118		12.34	118		12.09	118	1:200F/167F
Solterre	16.14	116		15.37	123/120		15.13	115/120	L
Montargis arr	24.22		0.5E	23.27		16 ½ L	23.17	3L	
	00.00		T	00.00		16L	00.00	2L	135
Cepoy	05.07	106		04.58	100		05.13	105	1:167F/200R
Ferrières	08.43	118		08.45	118		08.48	122	L
Dordives	11.43	120		11.47	123		11.48	125/120	L
Souppes	13.59	120		14.05	120		14.14	115 (blizzard) L	
Bagneaux	17.08	124		17.18	122		17.36	108* (blizzard) L	
Nemours	19.18	125		19.31	120		19.52	124	L
Bourron	23.20	120/115		23.37	122		24.04	115/117	1:200R
Montigny	25.07	120		25.31	122		26.02	109	1:167F
Morêt les Sablons	30.51		4E	30.37		11½ L	31.35	1½ E 186	

(116 miles)

The first run was in the summer with the normal load, punctilious timekeeping throughout. 241 P 23, along with 241 P 3 which performed similarly three days later, was withdrawn the following month. The two runs with 241 P 8 were run in bitterly cold weather with snow on the ground. On the first of these, 241 P 24 had arrived from Clermont Ferrand 10 minutes late with the full 13 coach train throughout – the Monday morning booked formation, having suffered a severe p-way slack and signal check. Both runs with 241 P 8 suffered engineering work between Cosne and Gien, on the Monday single line working was still in force, but the Thursday it was a long 10mph pway slack, both costing around 7-8 minutes. After the slack, 241 P 8 shot off, exhaust sounding like a machine gun. On the last run, the section between Montargis and Morêt was traversed in a white-out blizzard, tearing through the fir forest in the swirling snow and smoke. 241 P 8 had been brought back from store and given a light overhaul and was in excellent condition.

	Left time	Left speed	Left notes	Right time	Right speed	Right gradient/notes	km
08.35 Clermont Ferrand-Vichy (Paris) Tr. 1110 23.7.68 241 P 24 Nevers 10 chs, 411/440t				**16.35 Marseille (00.24 Clermont Ferrand) Paris, Tr.1116** 24.7.68 141 R 1214 Nevers (coal burner) 15 chs, 603/650t			
Clermont Ferrand	00.00		1L	00.00		T	0
Gerzat	06.08	126		-	118/65*/111	1:125F	
Riom arr	11.43	sigs 15*	2L	13.12		2L	
	00.00		2L	00.00		1¾ L	14
Ennezat Clèrelande	06.22	122		06.37	106	1:143F/143R	
Surat	08.02	125		-	102	L	
Thuret	09.39	115		10.37	102		
St Clément de Regnat	12.09	106/104		13.22	96	1:125R	
Randan	15.37	98		17.08	87	1:125R	
Randan Tunnel	-	108*		-	108	1:100R/91F	
St Sylvestre	19.01	105*		20.50	96*	1:91F	
Hauterive	-	107*		-	105/96*		
Vichy arr	26.37		½ E	29.48		T	55 (34 mls)

241 P 24 was Never's most common Mountain (with 241 P 8) for the Clermont Ferrand-Nevers section in the summer. This was a typical run over the 1:125 to Randan Tunnel. 141 R 1214 was a replacement for a 241 P and was restricted to 100kph, although higher speeds were recorded over the first section. The climb to Randan was equal to a 241 P with this load.

Table 9: Rheine-Emden-Norddeich, 1973-74

	Left time	Left speed	Left notes	Right time	Right speed	Right notes	km
08.41 Münster-Norddeich, D1337 23.7.73 012.075-8 Rheine (3 cyl oil-burning 4-6-2) 10 chs, 397/415t				**08.41 Münster-Norddeich, D1731** 13.7.74 012.066-7 Rheine 10 chs, 375/400t			
Rheine	00.00		18L	00.00		1L	0
Deves	05.52	90		05.47	80		
Salzbergen	07.25	104		07.11	107		
Leschede	12.10	122		11.50	122		
Elbergen	15.29	105*/107		15.06	104*		
Lingen	19.49	122		19.23	118		31
Holthausen	22.15	120		21.48	120		
Geeste	24.15	128		23.53	120		
Meppen	29.31	128/116*		29.38	120/100*		52
Hemsen	32.08	112/118		32.32	sigs 68*		
Haren	35.03	127		35.57	109		
Lathen	39.03	133		40.13	128		
Kluse	42.39	136		-	131/127		
Dörpen	44.39	111*/120		46.28	120/104*		
Aschendorf	49.27	124		51.27	120		
Papenburg	52.52	sigs 42*		54.09	112*		98
Steenfelde	57.27	100		57.28	118		
Ihrhove	59.15	112/100*		58.55	120/96*		
Leer arr	64.01	(60.5 mins net)	14L	63.46	(62.5 mins net)	3E	115
dep	00.00		12 ½ L	00.00		½ L (72 miles)	
Neermoor	06.49	105/110		06.12	107		
Oldersum	-	118		10.27	120		
Petkum	-	120		-	120		
Emden Bw	-	easy		14.48//18.15	sigs stand		
Emden Hbf arr	18.25		12L	22.20		4L	141 (88 miles)

Both trains had a schedule of 68 minutes for the 72 miles, which both completed in 63-64 minutes (ave. speed 67-68mph) although net times of 60.5-62.5 mins = 69-71mph average start to stop. 012.075, running late, was pushed very hard and well exceeded the line limit of 120kph. 012.066, overhauled in 1973, was a fixture on D1731 in 1974, was in good condition and ran hard, but not thrashed like the previous run.

	19.04 Norddeich-München, D730 20.7.73 012.104-6 Rheine 7 chs, 273/285t		19.04 Norddeich-München, D730 22.7.73 012.077-4 Rheine 7 chs, 273/290t		19.07 Norddeich-München, D730 14.7.74 012.081-6 Rheine 7 chs 272/285t		km
Leer	00.00	2 ½ L	00.00	5L	00.00	8L	0
Ihrhove	05.39	120	06.06	116	05.44	116	
Steenfelde	-	122	07.41	125	07.19	120	
Papenburg	10.53	sigs 42*	11.06	sigs 65*	10.42	pw 60*	17
Aschendorf	14.29	107	14.51	109	14.05	120	
Dörpen	19.38	104*/118	19.59	105*/116	19.06	104*/116	
Kluse	21.53	120	22.16	124	21.18	124	
Lathen	25.53	124	26.05	125/127	25.17	125/115	
Haren	30.10	120	30.18	122	29.42	110/120	
Hemsen	32.48	125	32.53	128	32.24	123	
Meppen	35.22	101*	35.26	105*	35.02	100*	63
Geeste	41.29	113	41.26	120	40.40	123	
Holthausen	43.45	115	43.33	122	42.46	125	
Lingen arr	47.00 (44.5 mins net) ½ E		46.29 (44.5 mins net) 1½ L		45.51 (43.5 mins net) 3¾ L		84 (52.4 miles)

This very sharply timed sleeper train (52.4 miles in 50 minutes) was consistently achieving net times around 44-45 minutes (average around 70-72mph), 012.081 achieved a start to stop average of 68.6mph actual including the moderate p-way slack at Papenburg. 012.104 was withdrawn shortly afterwards and was exhibited for several years at Carnforth; 012.077 had achieved three runs averaging over 60mph consecutively on the same day; and 012.081 was recently given a light overhaul and was in excellent nick, beat very staccato and even.

	D714 16.55 Rheine-Norddeich 20.7.73 012.055-0 Rheine 7chs, 259/275t		07.07 (Suns) Rheine-Norddeich 14.7.74 012.100-4 Rheine 8 chs, 293/300t		D714 16.50 Rheine-Norddeich 23.1.75 012.081-6 Rheine 6 chs, 220/245t		km
Rheine	00.00	4L	00.00	4L			0
Deves	05.08	101	05.07	99			
Salzbergen Box	-	109	06.30//08.21 sig stand				
Salzbergen	06.33	120	11.02	9L			
			00.00	9L			
Leschede	11.18	128	05.53	104/122			
Elbergen	14.22	105*/118	09.22	96*/107			
Lingen	18.57	5L	14.30	8 ½ L			
	00.00	4 ¼ L	00.00	7L			31
Holthausen	04.19	111	04.17	108			
Geeste	06.35	127	06.34	114			
Meppen	13.02	4 ¼ L	14.11	8L			
	00.00	4 ½ L	00.00	8L	00.00	5 ½ L	52
Hemsen	04.38	105	04.25	115	-	113	
Haren	07.39	122	08.10		06.12	120	
			00.00				
Bk 274	-	122	-	105/115	-	118	
Lathen	11.53	124	07.01		10.40	120	
			00.00		-	116/120	
Kluse	-	120	06.05	108	14.52	120	
Dörpen	17.58	105*/115	08.34	112/96*/105	17.04	96*/122	
Aschendorf	22.58	120	14.32	9L	22.14	108*	
			00.00	9L	-	pw 65*	
Papenburg	26.46	3 ½ L	05.28	90 9 ½ L	26.47	4L	98

306

Papenburg	00.00		4L	00.00		9½L	00.00		4½L
Steenfelde	-	106		05.11	99		04.23	120	
Ihrhove	06.29	125		07.02	101/96*		05.55	124/96*	
<u>Leer</u>	11.07		4L	12.23		12L	10.42		4¼L	115
	00.00		1½L	00.00		9L			
<u>Neermoor</u>	06.07	108		08.23	79				
				00.00					
Bk Rorichum	-	115		-	90				
<u>Oldersum</u>	10.03	122		07.40					
				00.00					
Petkum	12.33	124		05.16	88				
<u>Emden Hbf</u>	17.01		1½L	11.09		13½L				141

(88 miles)

Three hard running services where the 012 s were thrashed to their limit. D714 was a 'mile a minute' schedule between all stops and on the standard seven coach load, the 012s could just about maintain schedule provided no out-of-course delays, but there was little in hand. By 1974, this service was steam only on Saturdays. The 07.07 Sunday only semi-fast train to Norddeich was an incredible train – booked for five coaches and with mile-a-minute schedules over very short distances, 012.100 was three (empty!) coaches overload and was worked flat out from Rheine to Papenburg with a noise level so harsh that I retreated to the third coach with my tape recorder to avoid distortion. After that, the boiler was beaten and the crew had to ease to allow steam pressure to recover.

Table 10: German Democratic Republic, 1979

						km
07.10 Beograd-Berlin Ostbhf-Stralsund-Sassnitz, D270 *Meridian* 18.4.79 03.0046-7 Stralsund (3 cyl oil-burning 4-6-2) 11 chs, 439/475t			**(09.22 Berlin Ostbhf diverted via Pasewalk)** 22.4.79 03.0085-5 Stralsund 11 chs, 439/485t			
Berlin Ostbahnhof	00.00	9L	00.00		34L	0
Warschauerbrücke	03.20		02.59			
Rummelsburg	07.03	78	06.42	76		
Wühlheide	11.08	56*	-	45*		
Springpfühl	13.19	80	12.42	80		
	-	88	17.05//17.29 sig stand			
Karow	20.54	96	24.45	80		
Berlin-Buch	22.35	105	26.25	100		
Röntgental	-	105	27.45	101		
Zepernick	-	easy	28.57	110		
<u>Bernau</u> arr	28.11		32.05			
dep	00.00		00.00			44
						(27.5 mls)
Rüdnitz	05.43	105	05.39	102		
Biesenthal	08.34	112	08.33	113		
Melchow	-	115	-	117		
Eberswalde	14.52	105/95*	15.10	99*		66
Britz	17.23	108	18.04	96		
Chorin Kloster	20.08	112	21.00	102		
Chorin	-	118	22.40	111		
Herzsprung	26.05	120	27.11	117		
Angermünde	28.47	96*	30.00	96*/111		92
Greffenberg	34.21	105	35.45	108/ sigs 87*		
Wilmersdorf	36.27	120	38.33	120		
Warnitz	40.43	115	43.03	116		
Seehausen	43.31	107	45.53	106/120		
Prenzlau	51.55	pw 22*	52.05	96*		129
Dauer	56.58	122	56.56	111		
Nechlin	59.46	126	59.57	116		
	-	pw 42*/ 80	-	pw 42*/83		

Pasewalk	arr	68.03	(water)		16E	68.11	(water)	13L	153
									(95.6 miles)
	dep	00.00			T	00.00		12L	
Sandförde		06.25	83			05.57	92		
Jatznick		08.44	104			09.02	99		
Ferdinandshof		13.00	105			13.27	105		
Borckenfriede		16.53	107			17.32	107		
Ducherow		20.13	115 / sigs 30*			20.57	107/110		
Anklam		30.27	82/40*/65			28.19	40*		195
Klein Bünzow		38.50	90			36.49	pw 65*		
Züssow		43.42	99/ 70*			41.51	99/70*		212
Gross Kiesow		48.06	112			45.56	109		
Greifswald Süd		53.18	109/115			-	112		
Greifswald		54.32	115			52.09	116		230
Mesekenhagen		57.13	113			-	112		
Jeeser		-	109			57.49	108		
Miltzow		62.54	96			61.09	96		
Wüstenfelde		66.14				64.18			
		73.09//74.38	sig stand			70.53//73.40	sig stand		
Stralsund Rügendamm		77.35			2E	76.31		9L	261
									(163 miles)

14.57 Stralsund Hbf-Pasewalk (Berlin Lichtenberg) D717
18.4.79
01.0530-4 Pasewalk
12 chs, 383/410t

Stralsund Hbf		00.00		T	0 km
Wüstenfelde		09.04	95		
Miltzow		12.19	103		
Jeeser		15.21	108/120		
Mesekenhagen		17.21	125		
Greifswald	arr	21.30			31
	dep	00.00			
Greifswald Süd		02.55	86		
Gross Kiesow		08.51	110		
Züssow	arr	13.00			49
	dep	00.00			
Klein Bünzow		06.12	110		
Anklam	arr	12.10			
	dep	00.00			66
Ducherow		08.50	104		
Borckenfriede		12.10	120/96*		
Ferdinandshof		16.32	104		
Jatznick		20.50	106		
Sandförde		23.38	107		
Pasewalk	arr	28.08		2E	108 (67.5 miles)

01.0530 ex-works and driven unusually hard for this train and route.

21.40 Neubrandenburg (Malmö/Sassnitz)-Berlin Ostbahnhof *Berlinaren*
23.4.79
03.0085-5 Stralsund
7 chs, 282/290t

Neubrandenburg	00.00		32L	0 km
Burg Stargard	07.33	87		
Cammin	12.43	113		
Blankensee	15.01	127/105*		
Neustrelitz	23.23	115/102*		35
Strelitz Alt	-	111		
Düsterfelde	30.33	120		
Fürstenberg	34.18	120/107*		56

Drögen	37.23	112		
Dannenwalde	40.56	131		
Altlüdersdorf	43.20	128		
Gransee	45.58//51.43	sigs stand	77	
Buberow	56.23	80/ sigs 65*		
Guten Germendorf	58.03	100		
Löwenberg	62.15	sigs 30*		
Grüneberg	64.53	120		
Nassenheide	68.02	131		
Fichtengrund	69.46	128		
Sachsenhausen	-	120		
Oranienburg	72.26	sigs 2*	106	
Lehnitz	74.30	90		
Borgsdorf	76.48	99		
Birkenwerder	78.52	96/88*		
Hohen Neuendorf	80.31	105		
Bergfelde	82.51	65*		
Schönfliess	84.06	115 / sigs 40*		
Springfühl	98.51	120/ 105*		
Wühlheide	100.36	50*/105		
Rummelsburg	104.31	112		
Warschauerbrücke	106.15//113.53	sigs stand		
Berlin Ostbahnhof arr	117.24 (net 88 minutes)		43L	170 (106 miles)

03.0085 was driven hard from every slack in an attempt to regain time on a sharp schedule. It followed a parcels train from Gransee to Löwenberg and joined a queue of trains waiting a platform at Berlin Ostbhf. The net time gives an average start to stop speed of 72mph. This was my fastest DR run, with two maxima of 82mph (131kph).

07.25 Berlin Schöneweide-Leipzig, D563
28.4.79
03.2058-0 Lutherstadt Wittenberg
14 chs, 452/505t

				km
Berlin Schönefeld	00.00		½ L	0
Via Spiral	-	80 / pw 15*		
Genshagener Heide	16.58	89		
Birkengrund Süd	18.09	100		
Ludwigsfelde	19.21	105		
Thyrow	22.41	111		
Trebbin	25.02	110		
Woltersdorf	33.39	pw 30* /96		
Luckenwalde	36.09	90*/ 96		
Forst Zinna	39.58	pw 40* (long)		
Grünna Klein Zinna	44.22	65		
Jüterbog	47.51	89/94	60	
Niedergörsdorf	52.09	96/87 min		
Blönsdorf	56.03	95		
Klebitz	58.50	106		
Zahna	61.23	115		
Bülzig	63.15	108		
Zönigall	64.28	105		
Lutherstadt-Wittenberg	67.55	65*	92	
Pratau	70.53	90		
Bergwitz	74.50	99/88		
Radis	79.53	83 min		
Gräfenhainichen	82.43	104		
Burgheunitz	85.50	112		
Muldenstein	88.27	120		
Bitterfeld	91.47	96*	129	

Petersroda		97.15	sigs 30* /80
Delitzsch		104.00//109.45	sigs stand
Zschortau		116.10	70
Rachnitz		120.02	80
Neuwiederitzsch		123.36	90
Leipzig Hbf	arr	132.05	(111 mins net) 11L 163 (102 miles)

Two-cylinder coal burning 03.2058 was filthy and was driven hard with this very heavy load. The train was packed and would probably have arrived punctually but for the dead stand at Delitzsch and laboured recovery. This was the only daily steam hauled express between Berlin and Leipzig which finished in June when the electrification was switched on. The p-way slacks between Woltersdorf and Forst Zinna were in connection with electrification.

Appendix 3

Conclusions – The highs and lows of 200,000 miles behind steam locomotives in the UK

Introduction

I have reflected on a lifelong interest in train performance, especially the performance of the steam locomotive. Performance is all about consistent reliability in being able to meet the demands of the timetable. This prompted me to analyse my own records as I timed all my long distance runs and many shorter mainline or suburban runs behind steam in the period from 1957 - 1968, and a few steam specials in that era and since 1971. I am therefore reporting my own experience on the reliability and performance of British steam locomotives during this period, cataloguing the good and the bad – positive details of the high speed exploits I've experienced as well as the failures and acute loss of time for locomotive reasons on other journeys.

I was living in Woking whilst attending London University from 1957-60, and travelling daily to London for work in 1961, after which I became a WR Traffic Apprentice (1961-4), located variously on the WR in the Reading Division, South Wales and the West Country. As an enthusiast, I made many runs outside the demands of my job on all BR regions – I have details of some 4,676 runs, hauled by 1,934 individual locomotives, of which I calculate 782 were over 50 miles mainline (most much longer) and 3,894 were shorter distance, over 15 miles but less than 50, mainly Woking-Waterloo and return, or Paddington-Slough-Maidenhead-Reading-Oxford, or Cardiff-Newport/Pontypool Rd, or Cardiff-Bridgend-Swansea-Llanelly-Carmarthen. After 1964, my journeys were mainly during vacations or weekends covering main line journeys as steam was gradually disappearing.

Analysis

The analysis is based on the following distribution of runs:

Main line/Long distance:

WR	273
SR	144
LMR	132
ER	177
BR Std	56

Suburban/Short distance:

WR	711
SR	2,676
BR Std	507

(I have not travelled on suburban routes regularly behind LM or E locos to make an analysis meaningful)

Locomotives hauled behind in total (includes some haulage short distance not included in 'timed' runs):

WR	748
SR	431
LMR	306
ER	244
BR Std	205

For my analysis, which I now wish to elaborate, I searched all my records for evidence of failures — and I also extracted details of high speed exploits to counter the potential negative focus of this account. I have identified as 'failures' only locomotive causes resulting in either loss of time through shortage of steam (5 minutes or over for short distance, 10 minutes or over for longer distance – as analysed by BR for its punctuality statistics) or mechanical breakdown resulting in removal of the locomotive from the train or very severe loss of time from an obvious mechanical defect. I have not included against the locomotive time lost through infrastructure problems, poor operating or just lazy or unenterprising driving, when it was obvious that all was well with the loco.

My conclusions - long distance trains (over 50 miles)

My conclusions? Overall, 1.82 per cent of my runs had loco 'failures' meeting these criteria – 6.4 per cent of my longer distance runs and 0.87 per cent of the short distance or suburban runs. There are some very surprising conclusions.

London Midland Region – 13.3 per cent

By far my worst experiences were with LM locomotives, with Jubilees and Royal Scots being the main culprits. 35 per cent of my twenty Jubilee runs lost time, mainly through shortage of steam, and I had some shockers with Royal Scots (17.9 per cent of 28 runs) admittedly during the last two to three years of their existence. Some of the classics I remember include a Friday night relief London - Glasgow sleeper, a heavy thirteen coach train, with which 46150 *The Life Guardsman* struggled to Rugby with speed hovering in the mid-40s for most of the way, clearly in trouble for steam, only to fail and be removed at Rugby with a hot box of all things! Our replacement, a Rugby 'Black 5' (44862), fared little better with this heavy load, and things did not look up until a Britannia took over at Crewe. 46123 *Royal Irish Fusilier* on the Midland mainline struggled up from Leeds on a winter morning managing to lose nearly 40 minutes to St Pancras with a lot of the steam it was attempting to make being wasted in the fog of leaks around the front end.

One of the run-down Royal Scots transferred from the West Coast Main Line to the semi-fast Great Central services, 46143 *The South Staffordshire Regiment* [but shorn of its nameplates] at Woodford Halse with the six coach 5.15pm Nottingham-Marylebone, 8 June 1963. (*Author*)

45562 *Alberta* after a disastrous run from Leeds via the Diggle and Shap routes on a rail enthusiasts' special train, waiting at Carlisle to resume its equally poor run back at 3.50pm to Leeds via Hexham and Newcastle, 25 February 1967. (*Author*)

Several of my Jubilee debacles were on enthusiast specials when one would have expected that the engine would have been well prepared. 45562 *Alberta* on a special from Leeds to Carlisle out via Lancaster and the WCML, returning via Hexham and Newcastle, was in trouble for steam all the way, there and back; 45697 *Achilles* on the Settle and Carlisle, 45647 *Sturdee* on the Diggle route, did not distinguish themselves either. 45561 *Saskatchewan* on the Up *Waverley* from Nottingham managed to lose half an hour on the mile a minute schedule, again through shortage of steam, as well as suffering from a general rundown condition. The down trip to Nottingham that day was interesting also – although 45566 *Queensland* did not quite qualify as a 'failure' under these criteria, it managed to lose 6 minutes on an admittedly sharp schedule by just being weak on the banks. However, if it wouldn't go uphill, by heavens it had to go down, so we had many exhilarating swoops into the high 80s to compensate and recover some of the lost time. My only 'total' failure with a Jubilee was Corkerhill's 45673 *Keppel* on the relief *Thames-Clyde Express* (Glasgow St Enoch - St Pancras), which relied almost completely on the Black 5 pilot (45171) until it was reclaimed at Dumfries by the local shed foreman, and then expired between Annan and Carlisle with a collapsed brick arch. The experience, however, provided my first Clan run (72005 was awaiting us at Carlisle) and what an unexpected cracker that was!

My experiences with Stanier pacifics were much better – one failure with 46203 on the up Midday Scot (shortage of steam in Scotland - it recovered in England!) and 46237 had to be left in a loop near Southwaite after losing its firebars on an overnight Glasgow-Birmingham train (we were rescued by 46250). Otherwise, no problem – indeed several of the Princess Royal runs were very speedy affairs.

Southern Region – 6.9 per cent

The SR main culprits were the light pacifics (three mechanical failures with unrebuilt engines, three short of steam events with rebuilt engines, 9.1 per cent from 66 runs). 34009 *Lyme Regis* failed at Salisbury with injector problems in 1956 on a Summer Saturday train to Ilfracombe, to be replaced by an Eastleigh Arthur, 30449 *Sir Torre*, which made a splendid run to Exeter. 34063 *229 Squadron* on the six o'clock from Waterloo slipped to a standstill on the climb to Buckhorn Weston tunnel while I was stationmaster at Gillingham and I was called out to investigate the 'train lost in section' – it eventually slithered into Templecombe over an hour late, the fireman having been forced to walk in front of the loco, throwing sand under the wheels. The third was the failure of 34067 *Tangmere* before the return Golden Arrow Anniversary run in May 2004, after a scintillating effort on the outward run to Dover. The three short of steam runs were all with rebuilt pacifics during the last year of service, two with 34093 *Saunton,* and one with 34004 *Yeovil,* both locos that gained a poor reputation in their latter days. I never had an unrebuilt Bulleid short of steam, either Merchant Navy or light pacific, in any of my hundreds of short and long distance runs with these locos, although 35005 had a series of spectacular failures on a short distance run for almost every cause apart from shortage of steam! I only had one Merchant Navy failure in 59 long distance runs – rebuilt 35014 lost time through shortage of steam on the 10.30am Waterloo-Southampton (when a press man was on the footplate!). I had no failures with Maunsell 4-6-0s on long distance runs (I had very few runs with them anyway over 50 miles), except for a shocker with H15 30523 which ran from Salisbury to Waterloo on a summer Saturday relief from Sidmouth without exceeding 50mph – shortage of steam appeared to be the problem from the colour of the smoke which drifted into our compartment.

Eastern Region – 5.6 per cent

Most of my failures with Eastern Region or ex LNER engines took place on the Scottish Region! Unduly weighting the figures was a well-known and catastrophic railtour from Glasgow to Mallaig when the preserved *Glen Douglas* and two of the three J37 0-6-0s used became casualties. 60009 was replaced by a Black 5 at Perth after its firebars collapsed (a similar failure to 4079 on the famous 'Castle' swansong to Plymouth in 1964) and 60004 failed at Perth in the up direction when a hotbox on its tender burst into flames. A3 4472 lost time on a railtour through shortage of steam and V2 60919 failed to appear on another railtour from Waterloo having travelled down specially from Dundee for the occasion! Another V2's lubrication system disintegrated whilst descending Stoke Bank (at 88mph) and two A1s ran out of steam – 60145 on an up Leeds train and 60154 on the G&SW (in Scotland again). However, in 45 runs with double-chimneyed A3s I had no failures at all, although a dire run behind a filthy Darlington 60076 between Edinburgh and Glasgow (Scotland again!) was saved from being a failure only because the schedule was so slack.

Western Region – 3.3 per cent

And the Western – only 3.3 per cent of the 273 runs. Only one King failure in 51 runs (6024 *King Edward I* stalling on Shap short of steam on a railtour) and only two mechanical failures which were 4079 *Pendennis Castle* on the 9 May 1964 special when the firebars melted and 5037 *Monmouth Castle* removed at Cardiff on a winter up South Wales express because the steam pipe between tender and first coach burst and another Castle was substituted quickly as a replacement pipe was not to hand! To be quite honest, I don't think the latter should really be classed as a failure despite the engine change. In fact 5037 had performed very competently from Swansea (it was already covering a Hymek failure) and it was a pity that its replacement, 5096 *Bridgwater Castle,* was in poor condition and unable to recover the time lost in the exchange.

There were just three examples out of 144 Castle long distance runs when steaming was a problem – one of which was with 7034 *Ince Castle* on the North & West in the loco's last month of existence. In 1958 during my Old Oak Common vacation job, I was aware of locos booked for Up runs advised to us by the country depots and one Saturday I deliberately rode to Newport to pick up an evening Swansea-Paddington express for which 4097 *Kenilworth Castle* had been earmarked. Now 4097 was the latest double chimney convert and I talked to the Newport crew on the platform there whilst awaiting the train, expressing my interest in a good run behind one of the newly modified locos. In the event a highly polished single chimney Landore 4094 *Dynevor Castle* turned up instead of 4097, and the run rapidly deteriorated until we stood in the middle road at Swindon for a 'blow-up' and arrived over 50 minutes late at Paddington. The demoralised Ebbw Junction crew blamed the Landore running foreman for switching engines, retaining the double chimney engine for the Landore double-home turn on the next working and giving 4094, which was overdue for a boiler washout and coaled with ovoids, to the Newport men! The other Castle failure was 5066 *Sir Felix Pole* which lost 10 minutes on the Oxford Flyer (5.30pm Oxford-Paddington non stop, 63 miles booked in the even hour) after a fast start, but appeared winded after Goring as the fire had stood untended for too long on Oxford shed and was then badly clinkered.

BR Standard Locomotives (all Regions) - 8.9 per cent

The Britannias whilst mainly working on the LMR were the main culprits – 12.5% per cent from 32 runs – injector failure seemed a common cause which afflicted 70003 *John Bunyan* on a southbound Glasgow-Blackpool train and 70052 *Firth of Tay* on a Birmingham-Carlisle enthusiasts' special (ably rescued at Carnforth by 45018). 70035 lost time on an early morning Perth-Edinburgh service falling to walking pace on the 6-mile 1 in 75 bank to Glenfarg. Clans had a bad reputation, but my only experiences with them were positive, including recovering time from an earlier (Jubilee) failure. Failures with smaller Standard locomotives occurred only on my short distance runs.

Britannias transferred to Crewe and Kingmoor during their last couple of years frequently suffered mechanical failures such as defective injectors causing engine replacement. Here 70032 *Tennyson* manages a Friday relief train from Euston to Perth, which it worked from Crewe to Carlisle, 30 July 1965. (*Author*)

My conclusions – short distance trains (15-50 miles)

On the suburban front, the 'stars' were the Maunsell King Arthurs (577 runs) and Schools (323 runs), West Country/Battle of Britains (890 runs) and Halls (246), none of which incurred a failure of any type. Other types with very low failure rates (less than 0.3 per cent) were BR Standard 5s (412 runs), Merchant Navies (414 runs) and Castles (386 runs). The only class which really fell down badly on the suburban services were the Lord Nelsons – 24 instances of shortage of steam between Woking and Waterloo, most on the morning 6.04 Southampton Terminus-Waterloo (we used to joke in winter that we could have steam heating or arrive on time, but never both!). That was 6.3 per cent of the 379 commuter runs behind these locos.

Lord Nelsons on commuter services from Basingstoke and Woking frequently suffered from shortage of steam. Here 30865 *Sir John Hawkins* [named after the chief architect of the Elizabethan navy and the first British slave trader!] stands in the slow platform at Woking with the 11.53am Woking-Waterloo, a stopping service from Basingstoke, 1959. (*Author*)

Overall

Western locomotives had by far the fewest mechanical problems requiring engine change (the two mentioned earlier were hardly signs of poor maintenance) even though many of the runs were in 1961-4 when WR steam was being phased out, which must say something about the standard of maintenance at Swindon works and the local depots.

Thirteen of my 51 main line 'failures' were on railtours either in the last couple of years of regular steam, or since. I have timed 117 enthusiast steam specials in total, which means that 11.1 per cent of them suffered a locomotive change because of failure or lost more than 10 minutes due to shortage of steam. The regional breakdown of failures on these specials is: WR 7.1 per cent, BR Standards 10 per cent, ER 12 per cent, LMR 14.3 per cent and SR 16.7 per cent. That is an extraordinary contrast with the general reliability of steam during the last ten or so years of regular steam, despite the apparent run down at the end. I'll leave others to speculate why this was so and wonder if I was just unlucky (or whether in BR days I was conversely extremely fortunate!).

High Speed

I'll now turn to compare performance at the opposite end of the spectrum – and recount my highest speed recordings. I'll start by admitting that I timed then by sweep second watch and rail joint counting (in the days when one could) rather than by stopwatch milepost timings, so I can only be accurate to the nearest 2mph or so. I have been tempted to correct my speeds when I have been jointly timing with someone more expert or when the logs have been published, but I have retained my speeds recorded as I feel the importance is the comparisons and I need some consistency for that. Please therefore bear in mind that my speeds could be about 2mph too fast – the highest speed I recorded ever (with 7030 *Cranbrook Castle* on the special track testing trial of May 1962) which I recorded as 105mph, I modified to 103mph for the log submitted to, and published by, O.S.Nock, as the times I took for successive mileposts on that run only gave me one recording of the higher speed.

There is of course bias in my logs stemming from the frequency of my runs and the locations where high speed was the norm. The places which figure most prominently and not unexpectedly are the descent of Stoke bank (around Essendine) and the racing stretch (although nearly level) from Basingstoke to Woking, which was exploited by Southern drivers during the Indian Summer of steam in 1965-67. The Western descents of Ardley bank towards Blackthorn and Gerrards Cross bank at Denham on up Birmingham expresses also figure well.

I have depicted below all runs where I have recorded speeds of 90mph or over and all runs with 'class 4 or 5' locomotives with speeds in excess of 80mph. I have then listed the highest speeds I have recorded with other major classes, which do not meet those criteria.

7032 *Denbigh Castle* of Old Oak Common at Paddington at the head of the 9.15am to Worcester and Hereford, October 1963. There was an inspector on board and 7032 achieved 102mph on this trip descending Honeybourne Bank, and was later selected as the standby engine at Bristol for the 'Castle' special 1X48 of 9 May 1964. (*Author*)

Speeds in excess of 90mph:

105	7030 *Cranbrook Castle*	Blackthorn	Track Testing Special
103	7030 *Cranbrook Castle*	Denham	Track Testing Special
102	7032 *Denbigh Castle*	Honeybourne	9.15am Pdn - Worcs
98	7029 *Clun Castle*	Norton Fitzwarren	1964 Castle Special
98	4079 *Pendennis Castle*	Lavington	1964 Castle Special
97	35013 *Blue Funnel*	Fleet	2.34pm B'mouth – W'loo
96	5054 *Earl of Ducie*	Little Somerford	1964 Castle Special
96	6021 *King Richard II*	Denham	7.35pm W'hampton - Pdn
96	7030 *Cranbrook Castle*	Haddenham	Track Testing Special
95	34044 *Woollacombe*	Fleet	2.34pm B'mouth – W'loo
95	34060 *25 Squadron*	Winchfield	6.15pm Weymouth - W'loo
95	5084 *Reading Abbey*	Dauntsey	Down *Bristolian*
94	6008 *King James II*	Denham	Up W'ton - Pdn Special
94	7029 *Clun Castle*	Yatton	1964 Castle Special
94	46235 *City of Birmingham*	Calthwaite	3.48pm Crewe – Glasgow
94	60005 *Sir Charles Newton*	Essendine	Up Newcastle express
93	4472 *Flying Scotsman*	Essendine	Up Leeds - KX Special
93	60063 *Isinglass*	Essendine	Up *Heart of Midlothian*
93	60107 *Royal Lancer*	Essendine	Up *West Riding*
92	5001 *Llandovery Castle*	Taplow	5.30pm Oxford - Pdn
92	5043 *Earl of Mount Edgcumbe*	Dauntsey	7.30am Pdn – Paignton
92	5054 *Earl of Ducie*	Uffington	1964 Castle Special
92	5054 *Earl of Ducie*	Southall	1964 Castle Special
92	6021 *King Richard II*	Blackthorn	7.35pm W'hampton - Pdn
92	34086 *219 Squadron*	Porton	7.00pm W'loo - Exeter
92	35013 *Blue Funnel*	Surbiton	2.34pm B'mouth – W'loo
91	60019 *Bittern*	Raskelf	Edinburgh - York Special
91	60049 *Galtee More*	Essendine	Up Leeds express
91	60120 *Kittiwake*	Three Counties	6.12pm KX - Leeds
90	7030 *Cranbrook Castle*	Maidenhead	5.30pm Oxf-Pdn [Footplate]

90	6003 *King George IV*	Blackthorn	W'ton - Pdn exp
90	34004 *Yeovil*	Winchester	5.23pm (FO) W'loo - B'mth
90	34086 *219 Squadron*	Hurstbourne	7.00pm W'loo - Exeter
90	35003 *Royal Mail*	Fleet	Up Exeter - W'loo exp
90	35003 *Royal Mail*	Byfleet	Up Exeter - W'loo exp
90	35003 *Royal Mail*	Templecombe	7.00pm W'loo - Exeter
90	35007 *Aberdeen Commonwealth*	Farnborough	B'mouth - W'loo exp
90	35016 *Elders Fyffes*	Brookwood	Up *Bournemouth Belle*
90	35026 *Lamport & Holt Line*	Thirsk	N'castle - York Special
90	46203 *Princess Margaret Rose*	Beattock	Up *Midday Scot*
90	60014 *Silver Link*	Arlesey	Down SO *Elizabethan*
90	60032 *Gannet*	Arlesey	18.26 KX-Doncaster
90	60111 *Enterprise*	Connington	KX - N'castle exp

Of the forty-four runs above, eighteen were on the WR (fourteen Castles, four Kings), thirteen on the Southern (8 Merchant Navies and five light pacifics of which two were unrebuilt), eleven on the Eastern (five A4s, 5 A3s and one A1), and just two on the LMR (one Duchess and one Princess Royal). The Princess Royal had just spent thirty minutes for a 'blow-up' at Carluke and staggered over Beattock summit at walking pace and was then left to freewheel under light steam without any hindrance on the descent! It is also of note that the 93mph with 60107 was on the last day of steam into King's Cross in June 1963. Thirteen out of the forty-four runs were on enthusiast specials.

Speeds 80-90mph with secondary express and mixed traffic locomotives

I now turn to the interesting assortment of 'lesser breeds' exceeding 80mph or above:

89	6999 *Capel Dewi Hall*	Curry Rivel Jcn	1964 Castle Special
86	6965 *Thirlestaine Hall*	Lavington	12.05pm Pdn-Kingswear SO
84	7911 *Lady Margaret Hall*	Taplow	5.30 Oxf-Pdn [Footplate]
84	43106	Gretna Jcn	Leeds – Carlisle - Beattock Special
83	4930 *Hagley Hall*	Wellington	Paignton - Pdn SO relief
83	30923 *Bradfield*	West Weybridge	Commuter train
82	30777 *Sir Lamiel*	West Weybridge	Commuter train
82	44721	Coupar Angus	*The Grampian*
82	45018	Calthwaite	Spl after 70052 failure
82	73152	Glamis	*The St Mungo*
81	5974 *Wallsworth Hall*	Acton	Weymouth - Pdn exp
81	30765 *Sir Gareth*	West Weybridge	Commuter train
81	44896	Tebay	Glasgow - B'pool SO
81	61187	East Leake	GC Nott - M'bone
81	73087 *Maid of Astolat*	Hersham	Three coach train
80	30449 *Sir Torre*	Sherborne	W'loo - Ilfracombe SO
80	4708	Maidenhead	Friday relief ex S'don
80	7917 *North Aston Hall*	Taplow	Weymouth - Pdn exp
80	30919 *Harrow*	Esher	Commuter train

Of the nineteen runs, seven were WR (six Halls of which four were the later Hawksworth 'Modified' variety and one 47XX theoretically restricted to 60mph), four were LMR (three Black Fives and a 'Flying Pig'), five were SR (two Schools and three King Arthurs), two BR Standards (one Standard Five and one Caprotti Five) and a solitary ER B1.

Other highest class speeds recorded were:

88	60909 (V2)	Essendine	(Failed Peterborough)
86	46122 *Royal Ulster Rifleman*	Wendover	2.38pm M'bone - Nott
85	45566 *Queensland*	Flitwick	St P - Nott two hour exp
84	70003 *John Bunyan*	Tebay	Glasgow - B'pool SO
84	70012 *John of Gaunt*	Hartford	Crewe - B'pool
79	1019 *County of Merioneth*	West Drayton	Up Bristol - Pdn
79	61613 *Woodbastwick Hall*	Brentwood	Up Clacton - L'pool St

| 79 | 72008 *Clan Macleod* | Murthat | Perth - C'lisle [13 ch load] |
| 78 | 30861 *Lord Anson* | Shawford | 12.22pm SO W'loo - B'mouth |

The only significant classes of 'class 6' power or more behind which I had several runs and failed to exceed 75mph were the LMR rebuilt Patriots and the ER A2 varieties.

The Highlights

The highlight for me — apart from the very obvious special track testing train to Wolverhampton and back behind 7030 which exceeded 100mph at Blackthorn and Denham (continuing to Greenford!) and 96mph at Haddenham on the down run — was one of two footplate runs I had that figures on this list – again with *Cranbrook Castle* – on the following day, my 24th birthday, when I rode the Oxford Flyer (the 5.30pm Oxford-Paddington) and we ran to London in 56 minutes with speed in the high 80s all the way from Goring to Acton with a maximum of exactly 90 at Ruscombe Sidings just before Maidenhead. However, I'll admit roaring through Reading on the middle road in the high 80s, whistle screaming, while I watched smugly from the fireman's tip up seat, was a very special thrill!

What conclusions do I draw? Was I very biased in favour of the Western – after all I trained there? Does the WR figure well just because I had more long distance runs there (but of course more opportunities to come a cropper)? Or was I just lucky? A recent video about the Castles has a Swindon spokesman saying that the Castles were fine unless the pressure dropped – even a 20-25psi drop could cause performance to lose its sparkle and once below 180psi, real trouble brewed. However, I was mightily impressed during my footplate experience at the professionalism and conscientiousness of WR fireman and their apparent ability to keep the pressure on the mark. Even I, under expert tuition, successfully fired 7001 *Sir James Milne* on a Gloucester train west of Swindon and 4096 *Highclere Castle* between Paddington and Reading on a down Cheltenham express, so it can't have been that difficult. Perhaps this was the difference for the poor old 'Nelsons' on the Southern. All the other SR engines were so easy to fire that the expertise required for a long narrow firebox engine was a skill not so easily acquired. Perhaps a Western fireman, used to Kings and Castles, could have got the Nelsons above the humdrum performance that I always experienced. I'm sure that will get a few people going.

A colleague of the author, Alistair Wood, frequently bemoaned the performance of 'Clan' pacifics. In contrast 72008 *Clan Macloed* on the 8.25pm FO Perth – Euston managed a thirteen coach train admirably from Carstairs to Carlisle reaching 79mph on the descent of Beattock, 16 July 1965. (*Author*)